AQUINAS ON SCRIPTURE

Also available from T&T Clark:

Aquinas on Doctrine, edited by Thomas G. Weinandy, Daniel A. Keating and John P. Yocum

AQUINAS ON SCRIPTURE

An Introduction to his Biblical Commentaries

Edited by
Thomas G. Weinandy, OFM, Cap
Daniel A. Keating
and
John P. Yocum

T & T CLARK INTERNATIONAL
A Continuum imprint
LONDON • NEW YORK

T&T Clark International
A Continuum imprint

The Tower Building
11 York Road
London SE1 7NX, UK

15 East 26th Street
New York, NY 10010
USA

www.tandtclark.com

British Library Cataloguing-in-Publication Data
A catalogue record for this book is available from the British Library.

ISBN: HB: 0-567-08474-4
PB: 0-567-08484-1

Library of Congress Cataloguing-in-Publication Data

Aquinas on scripture: an introduction to his biblical commentaries / edited by Thomas G. Weinandy, Daniel A. Keating, John P. Yocum.
p. cm.
Includes bibliographical references and indexes.
ISBN 0-567-08474-4 (hard) – ISBN 0-567-08484-1 (pbk.)
1. Thomas, Aquinas, Saint, 1225?-1274. 2. Bible-Commentaries-History and criticism 3. Theology, Doctrinal-History-Middle Ages, 600-1500. I Weinandy, Thomas G. (Thomas Gerard) II. Keating, Daniel A. III. Yocum, John.

B765.T54A685 2005

220.6'092–dc22

2005041881

Typeset by Data Standards Ltd, Frome, Somerset, UK
Printed and bound in Great Britain by MPG Books Ltd, Cornwall

To the Mediaeval Commentators on Sacred Scripture

Ignorance of the Scriptures is ignorance of Christ.

St Jerome

CONTENTS

THE CONTRIBUTORS

Mark Edwards   Christ Church College, Oxford

Nicholas M. Healy   St John's University, New York

Jeremy Holmes   Marquette University, Milwaukee, Wisconsin

Daniel A. Keating   Sacred Heart Major Seminary, Detroit

Matthew Levering   Ave Marie University, Naples, Florida

Francesca Aran Murphy   University of Aberdeen, Scotland

John Saward   Greyfriars, Oxford and International Theological Institute, Gaming, Austria

Joseph P. Wawrykow   University of Notre Dame, Indiana

Thomas G. Weinandy   Greyfriars, Oxford and the United States Conference of Catholic Bishops, Washington, DC

John P. Yocum   Greyfriars, Oxford and Loyola School of Theology, Ateneo University, Manila

PREFACE

This volume is the direct offspring of *Aquinas on Doctrine: A Critical Introduction*. As the editors of that volume, we noted how frequently the contributors relied upon Aquinas' biblical commentaries as a foundation for the explication of doctrine in his systematic works. The significance of his biblical commentaries for any inquiry into his theology became more and more plain to us. Consequently, almost immediately after sending the manuscript for *Aquinas on Doctrine* off to our publisher, we conceived the idea of organizing and editing a second volume, to be devoted specifically to the biblical commentaries of Thomas Aquinas.

The biblical commentaries are in many respects the forgotten corpus of the Angelic Doctor. For some time now commentators have studied Aquinas primarily for his philosophical contributions, and when his theology comes up for examination, it is the *Summa Contra Gentiles* and especially the *Summa Theologiae* that are consulted. Thomas' vast output of biblical commentary is little known and even more rarely studied. The great irony in all this is that, though Aquinas never publicly taught either of the *Summae*, he never ceased commenting on the Sacred Scriptures. During his entire career he fulfilled the office of 'master of the sacred page' (*magister in sacra pagina*) through continuous commentary on many books of the Bible. Both his systematic works and his biblical commentaries reveal his prodigious knowledge of the whole of the Bible, and his mastery of the Patristic commentary available to him (displayed most fully in the *Catena Aurea*) demonstrates his commitment to interpret the Bible within the broad tradition of the Church. All this underlines the conclusion that Thomas Aquinas was deeply and profoundly a biblical theologian. Whether directly or indirectly, his theology is grounded in, and nourished by, Sacred Scripture.

There is, of course, nothing to be gained by pitting his various works against one another. The *Summae* are magisterial productions that represent Aquinas' own synthesis of the vast terrain of Christian doctrine, and they are rightly studied with great interest and intensity. But if we are to gain a rounded and thorough understanding of his theology, the biblical commentaries need to be brought into the discussion and studied once again.

There are at least two major obstacles that stand in the way of the reintroduction of Aquinas' biblical commentaries. First, critical editions for almost all of the individual commentaries are lacking, and only half of the commentaries have ever been translated into English (no doubt due in part to the lack of critical editions). Most of these translations are out of print and very difficult to obtain. Second, the commentaries admittedly make for difficult reading. Thomas follows a rather tedious method of scholastic commentary on the Bible that takes some wading through for the modern reader. These are not highly rhetorical expository homilies, meant to inspire, like the Tractates on John by St Augustine or the Homilies on Paul's Letters by John Chrysostom. Aquinas gives us straight-forward explanations of the biblical text designed for the mediaeval classroom. It takes a significant commitment to work through one of his commentaries – but the effort is repaid by the rich exegetical and theological material that Thomas mines from the text of Scripture.

The contributors to this volume were each given the challenging task of introducing readers to the individual commentaries, opening up for us Aquinas' approach to the scriptural text, highlighting key theological themes he draws from the biblical book, and relating the commentary in some fashion to his systematic works, especially the *Summa Theologiae*. Given the lack of critical editions to work from, and the sheer difficulty of summing up entire commentaries on books of the Bible, we are especially grateful for the significant labour undertaken by all the contributors. They have with clarity, insight and profound scholarship opened a path for a re-appropriation of Aquinas' biblical commentaries. We are also delighted by the wide variety of approaches taken by our contributors, which display and bring to bear their unique strengths, creative insights, and analytical, philosophical, and historical skills.

In the opening essay, Nicholas Healy introduces us to Aquinas as a biblical theologian in historical context, and argues that his theological approach to the Bible, grounded in the conviction that teachers and preachers must return ever anew to the Scriptures, provides a model of exegetical practice today. John Yocum then begins our trek through the individual commentaries with a study of Thomas' *Literal Exposition on Job*. He estimates that Aquinas' interpretation of Job compares favourably with much modern commentary, and that within the presuppositions of Christian faith, Aquinas presents a theologically compelling and unitive reading of Job. Joseph Wawrykow, in a study of Aquinas' commentary on the prophet Isaiah, opens up for us the varying features of this largely literal commentary, and through a comparison of how Aquinas treats Isaiah 6 and 11 in the *Expositio* on Isaiah and the *Summa Theologiae* respectively, displays the benefit of reading Aquinas' exegetical and systematic works together.

Turning to the New Testament, Jeremy Holmes convincingly locates and contextualizes Aquinas' Lectures on Matthew in the final period of his university career, and displays how Aquinas masterfully handles this Gospel as a revelation of both the humanity of Christ and a compendium of his teaching. Matthew Levering then ranges across the entire Commentary on John in order to display the variety of Aquinas' exegetical techniques and sources. He concludes that, for Thomas, Scripture is God's teaching through human words that enhances our insight into God's inexhaustibly rich teaching and contributes to the Church's ongoing proclamation of the divine mysteries. In an examination of the commentaries on 1 and 2 Corinthians, Daniel Keating shows how Thomas reads these paired epistles as a study of the sacraments and their ministers, and at the same time supplies an impressive pastoral theology for leaders in the Church.

In an essay that places Thomas firmly within his patristic heritage, Mark Edwards explores a range of topics that arise from the commentaries on Ephesians and Colossians. He concludes that, despite shortcomings in Aquinas' method and use of history, these commentaries show an impressive philosophical rigour, and display a humility and circumspection in exegesis worthy of emulation by the modern theologian. Francesca Murphy next considers the commentaries on Philippians, 1 and 2 Thessalonians, and Philemon together, illustrating how Thomas moves from a three-dimensional presentation of the Church, to a treatment of grace, and finally to a consideration of the theological virtues as the efflorescence of the Church. John Saward then takes up in the commentaries on the Pastoral Epistles the theme of the grace of Christ in his principal members. He suggests that Aquinas not only offers an extensive treatment of the pastoral ministry of the bishop in these commentaries, but that he also anticipates some of the chief themes that appear in the *Summa Theologiae*. In a final essay, Thomas Weinandy shows how Aquinas interprets the Letter to the Hebrews as a study of the supremacy of Christ in the Incarnation and in his priestly sacrifice, but at the same time as an account of how the Church subjectively appropriates the salvific work of Christ through faith.

The editors would like to express special thanks to Geoffrey Green of T & T Clark for his initial and immediate support for this volume coming to be, to Fiona Murphy of Continuum Press for her support and encouragement from the beginning, and finally to Rebecca Vaughan-Williams and Sarah Douglas, also of Continuum Press, for their amiable assistance in seeing the project to completion.

This volume, like the previous one, *Aquinas on Doctrine*, is something of a Greyfriars, Oxford project. The editors first began to work together while all three were at Greyfriars, and John Saward is at present a fellow of Greyfriars Hall. We offer this volume in the conviction that, in the words of the Second Vatican Council's Constitution on Divine Revelation, *Dei Verbum*, 'the study of the sacred page ... is the soul of sacred theology'. Together with Jerome we acknowledge that 'ignorance of the Scriptures is ignorance of Christ'. In keeping with the entire patristic heritage, and with the witness of the mediaeval commentators – among whom Thomas Aquinas was pre-eminent – we recognize that the Christian faithful must ever be about the business of 'searching the Scriptures' (Jn 5.39), for it is they that bear witness to Christ.

THOMAS G. WEINANDY, DANIEL A. KEATING, JOHN P. YOCUM
Feast of Venerable Bede, 2004

INTRODUCTION

Nicholas M. Healy

Thomas Aquinas' commentaries on Scripture have never been
generally well known to theologians. Even within Thomistic circles
they have not received the kind of attention accorded the 'major'
works, the *Summa Theologiae* and *Summa contra Gentiles*. To be
sure, there have always been experts who worked carefully through
the commentaries and at intervals published articles on Thomas'
exegetical theory and practice. But the great majority of Thomistic
theologians and philosophers, from his age almost to our own, spent
little or no time on the commentaries, preferring instead to focus on
his doctrinal works and their philosophical implications or under-
pinnings. The lack of interest is indicated by the commentaries'
relative unavailability. While almost all of Thomas' commentaries
on Aristotle's philosophical works have been translated into
English,[1] only about half the biblical commentaries have, and of
these, most are out of print. Likewise, the commentaries are among
the last works to be published as part of the definitive Leonine
edition. Almost all the philosophical commentaries have been
completed, some for many years, but to date the Leonine editors
have published only the volumes for Isaiah and Job, with Romans
expected shortly.

It is therefore not surprising that some perceive Thomas to be the
prime example of that form of traditional Catholic theological
inquiry which emphasizes philosophical reasoning, in contradistinc-
tion to the Scripture-based tradition of the Reformers and their
heirs. This perception is quite mistaken, however, and evidently so
to anyone who has actually read Thomas' commentaries and is
aware of their bearing upon his other work. Fortunately the
perception shows signs of change, as does the underlying lack of
interest in or awareness of Thomas' exegesis that helped produce it.
While it may be premature to predict long-term momentum, there

---

[1] Very few of the commentaries on Aristotle have been translated into French,
reflecting perhaps the historical differences between the British and the French
schools of Thomas studies, differences that may now be diminishing somewhat.

has been a definite increase in interest in Thomas' Scripture commentaries in the last couple of decades or so. Moreover, that interest is far broader and more ecumenical in intent than any hitherto. The commentaries have been quoted and discussed with increasing frequency by theologians who would not necessarily regard themselves as specialists in Thomas, by constructive as well as historical theologians, and by not a few who are from Christian traditions other than the Roman Catholic.[2]

A number of reasons could be adduced for the new interest in Thomas' exegesis. For a decade or more after Vatican II, Thomas' work was almost completely eclipsed within Roman Catholic theology. To many, he represented the beginning of a trajectory that had reached a dead-end in the dry and defensively anti-modern theology of neo-scholasticism and the church politics that supported it. To those who sought to move the Church into the twentieth century, whether through re-presenting doctrine and practices so as to bring them more up to date (*aggiornamento*) or through recovering more ancient, ecumenical and Scripture-attentive theological traditions (*ressourcement*), Thomas often seemed to be little or no help, even an obstacle to reform. More recently, a marked decline in the almost exclusive focus upon transcendental Thomism within constructive Roman Catholic theology, together with a decline in portrayals of Thomas' work as the systematic philosophico-theological alternative to any constructive response to the modern world, have made room for interest in Thomas the insightful, flexible and thoroughly scriptural *theologian*.[3] Subsequent to this shift has come the somewhat belated recognition that his commentaries are part and parcel of his theological work. They not only help us better understand more widely read texts like the *Summae*, but they may often have significant exegetical value in themselves. Some theologians, moreover, have argued that since the historical-critical method has failed to demonstrate its theological and pastoral usefulness, other approaches should be considered. Among these are the various forms of premodern exegesis, including

---

[2] See, e.g., Bruce Marshall's use of Thomas in his *Christology in Conflict: The Identity of a Saviour in Rahner and Barth* (Oxford: Blackwell, 1987); also Eugene F. Rogers, Jr, *Thomas Aquinas and Karl Barth: Sacred Doctrine and the Natural Knowledge of God* (Notre Dame: University of Notre Dame Press, 1995). Neither theologian is Roman Catholic.

[3] See J.A. DiNoia, 'American Catholic Theology at Century's End: Postconciliar, Postmodern, Post-Thomistic', *The Thomist* 54 (1990) pp. 499–518. DiNoia's article was written before the 'belated' interest in Thomas' scriptural commentaries had got really underway.

Thomas', some of which may be adaptable for use in a Church no longer quite so constricted by the norms of modernity.[4]

The purpose of this introduction is to prepare some of the ground for the detailed discussion of Thomas' commentaries in the chapters to follow. In the first section, I situate Thomas' exegesis within its historical and cultural context. In the second section, I address Thomas' more properly theological and doctrinal accounts of what Scripture is and how it is best read. Finally, I note very briefly some of the reasons why I think the commentaries of a premodern theologian like Thomas should be read today. It is worth remarking at the outset something that will be apparent to any attentive reader of books on Thomas, including this book, namely that there are multiple and often conflicting interpretations of his work. So, while the account in this chapter is not especially controversial, it is one that may not always be supported in every detail by the writers of the other chapters in this volume.[5]

Aquinas as biblical exegete

For the last couple of centuries or so, it has been possible, if not always and everywhere regarded as particularly admirable, for a theologian to work without spending any appreciable amount of time directly engaged with Scripture. A historical theologian, for example, may be devoted to texts other than Scripture, such as those of a particular theologian or Church controversy or those which show the development of a doctrine over time. Philosophical theologians may concern themselves with arguments and questions that make no explicit or even implicit reference to Scripture. Even systematic theologians may work largely without directly addressing exegetical questions. For example, some traditional Roman Catholic theologians base their work largely upon the texts of Vatican II and other conciliar documents. To be sure, these are somewhat exceptional cases, but they are well known. Indeed, there are theological reasons why such cases are not uncommon among Roman Catholics, for whom theology has in recent centuries (especially since Vatican I) often been thought of as charged with

---

[4] See Stephen E. Fowl (ed.), *The Theological Interpretation of Scripture: Classical and Contemporary Readings* (Oxford: Blackwell, 1997).

[5] Recently a number of books have discussed or illustrated the diversity of interpretations of Thomas. See Fergus Kerr, *After Thomas* (Oxford: Blackwell, 2002), and F. Kerr (ed.), *Contemplating Aquinas: On the Varieties of Interpretation* (London: SCM Press, 2003); also Paul van Geest, *et al.* (eds.), *Aquinas as Authority* (Louvain: Peeters, 2002).

the task of making sense of the teachings of the magisterium, rather than unpacking the riches of Scripture.[6]

For Thomas and his theologian colleagues in the Middle Ages, however, as for the premoderns more generally (including, of course, the Reformers), such cases were simply unknown. Theological inquiry was based upon and sustained by ongoing exegesis.[7]

Thomas was born in 1225 or 1226 and died in 1274, during a time when a renewed emphasis upon Scripture and the gospel, begun in the previous century, was producing abundant fruit. The renewal was vital for the Church, for it faced a pastoral and doctrinal crisis brought about by new and unorthodox religious groups, especially those variously called the Cathari or the Albigensiens, who arose in the early eleventh century and had become widespread in France and Germany by 1200. The new sects rejected traditional interpretations of Scripture and, with them, much Church doctrine and many customary practices. They read Scripture in Gnostic and dualistic ways, and advocated practices unusual for the time, such as usury, vegetarianism and lay celibacy. Initially, the Church found it difficult to respond effectively and constructively to this threat. Parish priests usually lacked the education and means to do anything, while the hierarchy could only condemn the sects, as they began to do as early as 1022 at a council in Orleans.

Within the monasteries lived the men and women who had the best intellectual and spiritual resources to mount a real response. But they and the culture more generally were inhibited by their belief that the best form of the Christian life (the *status perfectionis*, i.e., potentially the most completely realized way of being Christian while still on this earth) was constituted by a search for holiness through union with God, and that such a search required one to retreat from the world, rather than work within it for the salvation of the ordinary folk of Christendom.

Beginning around the early part of the twelfth century, a new and rather different kind of response to the crisis began in various quarters. One of these was specifically intended to counter the Cathari. In 1173, the wealthy layperson Valdensius sold all his possessions and began to wander about preaching the orthodox gospel and begging for his daily bread. He and his followers – the Waldenses – sought to live the life they read about in the New

---

[6] A (still) pertinent discussion of this topic can be found in Per Erik Persson, *Roman and Evangelical* (Philadelphia: Fortress, 1964).

[7] Thomas, of course, also wrote commentaries on philosophical works that are less directly engaged with Scripture. It is arguable, however, whether these bear upon his theology and thus, indirectly, upon his exegesis, and *vice versa*.

Testament. They sought 'to renounce the riches of the world, to read and study the Scriptures, and to preach the Gospel to the poor'.[8] Valdensius' work was complemented on the intellectual side by Durand of Osca, who wrote a treatise arguing against the Cathari's beliefs. However, because Valdensius and his followers were lay people, they could not receive authorization from the Church to preach, and since they insisted on doing so, they were soon subjected to persecution as an anti-clerical movement.

An ultimately far more successful movement began in the generation following Valdensius with the founding of the two orders of friars by St Francis (in 1209) and St Dominic (in 1215). Both the Franciscans and the Dominicans used much the same two ways of countering the new sects. That is, they sought to display the gospel by living in a way that directly reflected Scripture, and they taught their members how to formulate good arguments against heresies. Through their founders' efforts and because they were vowed religious, they were able to win the full support of the Pope. Yet because they represented a new way of being Christian, they found themselves subject to criticism from both monks and secular priests.

Thomas found himself frequently having to defend his own order, the Dominicans, in the course of his career. His argument was that the friars followed the way of life of the apostles, the *vita apostolica*, as it is described in the Gospels and the Acts of the Apostles. There we see that the apostles lived in evangelical poverty, without possessions of their own, holding everything in common and giving themselves to others. In this they followed Jesus Christ himself, who practised spiritual poverty throughout his ministry and, in the highest and most exemplary form, on the Cross, where he 'was deprived of every exterior good, even to the point of nakedness'.[9] In contrast to the Franciscans, however, the Dominicans believed that poverty is finally but an instrumental means to a greater end and so only a relative principle. Ultimately, the Christian life does not 'consist per se in exterior perfections, such as poverty, virginity and

---

[8] For a brief, sympathetic account of the Waldenses, upon which my own is largely dependent, see Euan Cameron, 'The Waldenses', in G.R. Evans (ed.), *The Medieval Theologians: An Introduction to Theology in the Medieval Period* (Oxford: Blackwell, 2001), pp. 269–86. The quotation is from p. 269.

[9] *Contra Retrahentes*, 15. Cited by Jean-Pierre Torrell, *Saint Thomas Aquinas:* vol. I, *The Person and His Work* (trans. Robert Royal; Washington, DC: Catholic University of America Press, 1996), p. 16.

suchlike, unless these things are instrumental to charity'.[10] 'The
perfection of the Christian life consists radically in charity',[11] and it
is charity, the work of the Holy Spirit in us, which unites us to
Christ as we become obedient to him in faith. So the absolute rule is
that we humbly and obediently follow the exemplary manner of life
of Christ and his first followers, as it is described in Scripture.[12]

Jesus and the apostles lived within and for the world, amongst
ordinary folk, preaching the gospel and teaching all who would hear
them. It therefore follows, as Thomas argued against the cloistered
monks, that the *vita apostolica* cannot consist of a life of mere
contemplation. Christ and the apostles showed us that contemplation is not sufficient of itself for what must be accomplished by the
Church in the present time. Pastoral exigencies – specifically the
need to preach the gospel, to train people to follow Christ and to
combat error – require the Church to consider the *status perfectionis*
as requiring action for others as well as contemplation, and never
one without the other if it is to be truly apostolic.[13] Certainly, in
heaven matters will be different, for there the blessed have only to
contemplate God, who is their eternal reward and always more than
all they could possibly need or want. But while we yet live on earth
and journey toward the next life it is best if our activity takes the
form of passing on to others the fruits of our contemplation through
preaching and teaching.[14] Growth in the spiritual life for the
Dominicans was thus a function of their work as preachers. They
grew closer to God through hard intellectual labour and by giving
the fruits of this labour and, indeed, by giving themselves, to
others.[15]

Accordingly, the friars read Scripture with a somewhat different
purpose than the monks did, and their understanding of 'contemplation' underwent some modification. The monks practised the
patristic forms of exegesis, which centred on the *lectio divina*, or
contemplative reading. By studying Scripture for long periods of
time, reading it prayerfully and piously, each monk sought to so
immerse himself in the text that he would be transformed by it and
move further on his path towards greater holiness. The Rule of St

---

[10] *In Matt.* 4.20 [373]. The number in brackets refers to the paragraph number in
the Marietti edition of Aquinas' commentaries. For Matthew: *Super Evangelium S.
Matthaei Lectura* (ed. Raphaelis Cai; Rome: Marietti, 5th edn, 1951); for John: *Super
Evangelium S. Loannis Lectura* (ed. Raphaelis Cai; Rome: Marietti, 5th edn, 1952).

[11] *ST*, II–II, 184, 1.

[12] *ST*, II–II, 188, 7; *In Matt.* 19.21 [1598].

[13] *ST*, II–II, 182, 1, ad 3; III, 40, 1, ad 2.

[14] See *ST*, II–II, 188, 6; *In Matt.* 19.21 [1594–98].

[15] Simon Tugwell (ed.), *Early Dominicans: Selected Writings* (New York: Paulist,
1982), p. 4.

Benedict, for example, required monks to read Scripture by themselves every day for two hours, three hours during Lent.[16] Those who directed others within the monasteries approached Scripture with the aim of helping those in their charge read more spiritually. Thus *lectio divina* was itself a kind of prayer or, alternatively, a form of contemplation worth many prayers.

This approach had been both informed and encouraged by the Neoplatonism prevailing from the early commentators such as Augustine and Jerome through to Gregory and Bernard.[17] The ontology of image and its underlying and possibly contrasting reality was applied to Scripture. The visible surface of the text, its 'literal' sense, was regarded as of secondary importance compared with its invisible depths, for it was in the latter that the true meaning of the text lay, through which one might ascend towards God. The monks thus tended to read through or around the literal meaning of the words in order to discern their more significant 'spiritual' meaning.

According to a well-established formula, there are three such 'spiritual senses'. The allegorical sense is the meaning brought to light when one links something in the Old Testament with something corresponding in the New or with the present life of the Church. People and events and things in one Testament are taken to be 'figures' of people, events and things in another, as Israel or the bride in the Song of Songs are figures of the Church. The tropological sense is the meaning of a text when its moral teaching, hidden under the literal, is brought to light. The anagogical sense is the meaning which pertains to the next life in heaven. Armed with these hermeneutic rules of thumb, the task of a spiritual advisor or a commentator was to help the monks pull back the 'veil' of the literal meaning of the text. As they progressed in the spiritual life, they would be able to discern the spiritual meanings more readily and deeply for themselves. The text, then, was an instrument of mystical ascent, to be used contemplatively by delving deep into its recesses to find hidden meanings couched in figures and allegories, and sometimes in number symbolism and fanciful etymological speculations.[18]

The friars did not exactly reject this tradition, but they did modify

---

[16] Beryl Smalley, *The Study of the Bible in the Middle Ages* (Notre Dame: University of Notre Dame Press, 1964), p. 29.

[17] I generalize, to be sure; my aim is only to note the contrast between Thomas' approach and that of earlier commentators. For a detailed account of the various forms of earlier exegesis, see Smalley, *The Study of the Bible in the Middle Ages*.

[18] For a rich discussion of the tradition of spiritual exegesis, see Henri de Lubac, *Medieval Exegesis*. vol. 1: *The Four Senses of Scripture* (trans. Mark Sebanc; Grand Rapids, MI/Edinburgh: Eerdmans/T&T Clark, 1998).

it significantly. One major change was to read Scripture with greater attention to its literal or historical sense than to its spiritual senses. Though the latter were by no means ignored, for Thomas especially it is the literal sense that is normative and the basis for all theological argumentation. There are a number of reasons for the change in emphasis. First, it was in part a reaction to the consequences of the more extreme forms of spiritual reading. The Cathari's beliefs and practices drew upon a radically spiritual reading that conflicted directly and emphatically with the literal sense, resulting in massive distortions of orthodox Christian doctrine. Similarly, the Cistercian Abbot, Joachim of Flora (d. 1204) worked out a mystical reinterpretation of the doctrine of the Trinity that, according to Beryl Smalley, represents 'a *reductio ad absurdum* of the spiritual exposition'.[19] According to his speculative exegesis, in about 1260 the Church would move from the time of the Son, associated with the New Testament and grace, to that of the Holy Spirit, associated with liberty and the church of the spirit. Joachim's followers were a source of great concern to the orthodox during the first half of Thomas' life. By insisting upon the priority and normativity of the historical and literal sense of Scripture, Thomas could rule out these and other spiritual interpretations that conflicted with the plain sense of the text accepted by the tradition and embodied in the Church's defined doctrines and customary practices.

A second reason for the shift towards the literal sense was a more general shift in the conception of reality that came to prevail within Europe. The newly recovered and widely read works of Aristotle no doubt contributed to this by fostering the acceptance of an alternative ontology to that of Neoplatonism.[20] Yet even among those who were less than fully convinced of the usefulness of Aristotle for Christian theology there was a demonstrably greater interest in the visible realities of the world around us. These could now be understood as good and true and beautiful in themselves, without having to look to that of which they were merely the image. Correspondingly, the 'surface' of the text of Scripture, its literal and

[19] Smalley, *The Study of the Bible in the Middle Ages*, p. 288.
[20] Torrell points out that the old idea of an Aristotelian camp (headed by Thomas) over against an Augustinian camp (headed by Bonaventure) is quite incorrect. Everyone, including 'Augustinians' like Bonaventure, read and made use of Aristotle, while Thomas and the more enthusiastically-Aristotelian theologians thought of themselves as working within the Augustinian tradition. Torrell, *Saint Thomas Aquinas*, vol. 1, p. 39.

historical meaning, was more readily accepted as the truthful witness to the revelation of the Word of God.[21]

However, for Thomas at least, as increasingly for many others, the more profound reason for the renewed privileging of the literal and historical sense of Scripture was because of what it actually described, namely the history of salvation. It is this history – identified with the gospel as such – which became the subject of preaching and teaching and the basis for the counter challenge to the new sects. For the friars, Scripture was about God's revelation of God in and through the history centred upon Jesus Christ. It was their most fundamental desire to follow Christ's manner of life and teaching in obedience, humility and poverty. So the exegetical task cannot be to penetrate beyond or beneath the history, but to stay with it in order better to understand him whom the text describes.[22]

Another significant modification of the older form of *lectio* came as a result of the new setting of Scripture study, the University. There Scripture was taught in lecture style by a community of masters (*universitas magistrorum*) to their students who, once their studies were completed, were expected to go out into the world as friars to preach and teach others. They probed the text of Scripture just as intently as the monks, but not for spiritual meanings lying below the literal sense that would enhance one's religious experience. Rather, the aim was to use reason and logic to raise difficulties and questions that, once resolved, would deepen understanding of the text. Dialectical inquiry – the formulation of objections and their solutions to issues arising within or prompted by the text – clarified Scripture's meaning and, it was believed, would result in better preaching of the gospel.

As a product of the schools, the commentaries of Thomas differ considerably from both the earlier patristic commentaries as well as those from the Reformation and the modern period. The limitations of his exegetical style – though not its content – must, I think, be admitted. Like many of his colleagues, Thomas uses technical and highly formal language and for the most part avoids extended metaphor. He makes careful distinctions, sometimes where none

[21] The exegesis of Maimonides (d. 1204), with which Thomas was very familiar, had already moved considerably in this direction in the previous century.

[22] It is worth noting that St Francis discouraged *lectio divina* in favour of prayerful meditation upon the Cross; see Smalley, *The Study of the Bible in the Middle Ages*, p. 283. Thomas himself developed a strong reverence for the crucifix in his prayer life, according to Torrell, *Saint Thomas Aquinas*, vol. 1, p. 287. For some excellent essays on the Christ-centredness of the early Dominicans, see Kent Emory, Jr and Joseph Wawrykow (eds.), *Christ Among the Medieval Dominicans: Representations of Christ in the Texts and Images of the Order of Preachers* (Notre Dame: University of Notre Dame Press, 1998).

seem to be particularly required. He engages in detailed grammatical and logical analyses, and organizes the text under headings and in sections in ways that do not always help to clarify the text's larger meaning. The analytic style can be off-putting for modern readers until they get used to it and begin to see within it the depth and insight of Thomas' exegesis.

In view of some misleading neo-scholastic and Thomistic interpretations of Thomas' intentions, and bearing in mind the sharp contrast between the mediaeval and the modern university, it is worth stressing the fact that Scripture was very much the basis and ongoing centre of Thomas' work as a university theologian. Thomas is likely to have begun to teach at Cologne sometime after 1248, working under Albert the Great.[23] At this first stage of his career he was *baccalarius biblicus*, a bachelor of Scripture. His task was to teach his students by 'reading' (*lectio*) through the Scriptures. At the bachelor level, he was to read quickly (*cursorie*) through the text, giving an exposition (*expositio*) of its literal meaning and resolving difficulties as they came up. It was not his role to raise larger questions about, say, a particular passage's bearing upon interpretations of other parts of Scripture or upon Church doctrine and practice; nor was he to address its spiritual meaning. That more detailed kind of commentary was reserved to the master alone.

Though there is no full agreement on the matter, it now seems likely that during his time at Cologne Thomas took his students through part or all of Isaiah. Some of the chapters of the resulting commentary survive in his own, barely decipherable handwriting.[24] If this dating is correct, the commentary constitutes his first theological work, for besides the rapid *expositio*, it contains groups of references in the margins to other passages of Scripture. These were named *collationes* by an early transcriber; their function seems to have been to help the reader preach on the text.[25] It is likely that

---

[23] Some believe Thomas began to teach as biblical bachelor only upon his arrival at Paris, e.g., M.-D. Chenu, *Toward Understanding Saint Thomas* (trans. A.-M. Landry and D. Hughes; Chicago: Regnery, 1964), p. 242. My dating follows James A. Weisheipl, *Friar Thomas D'Aquino: His Life, Thought and Works* (Washington, DC: Catholic University of America, 1983), p. 45 and Torrell, *Saint Thomas Aquinas*, vol. 1, p. 27. Either way, the training would take the same form.

[24] Again, this dating follows Weisheipl and Torrell. Others differ, including the Leonine editors of Isaiah, who put the commentary soon after 1252, during the first year of Thomas' teaching at Paris. Chenu places it towards the very end of Thomas' life (*Toward Understanding Saint Thomas*, p. 248), but Chenu was working prior to more recent discoveries and arguments. The starting point for discussion of the chronology of Thomas' commentaries is Mandonnet's, an outline of which can be found in Weisheipl, *Friar Thomas D'Aquino*, p. 118. The chronology of Thomas' commentaries, to repeat, is not fully established to everyone's agreement.

[25] See Torrell, *Saint Thomas Aquinas*, vol. 1, pp. 29–31.

the commentaries on Jeremiah and Lamentations (which also contain collations) also come from this period.

It is probable that upon his arrival at the University of Paris, Thomas had completed this part of his training and had begun the second stage, moving on to become *baccalarius sententiarum*, a bachelor of the 'Sentences'. This position required Thomas to lecture on Peter Lombard's four-book collection of authoritative opinions (*sententia*), drawn from the Fathers and covering a wide range of theological topics. The study of the Sentences was ratified as an essential part of theological training by the Fourth Lateran Council in 1215. By Thomas' time, commenting on them was something like writing an extended form of a modern Ph.D. dissertation. The bachelor was expected to do more than simply discuss the meaning of the excerpts and their coherence with Scripture. He was required to discuss and resolve the questions arising from his analysis, as well as introduce and resolve new questions of his own. Thereby the bachelor had the opportunity to develop a well-rounded understanding of the theology of the Fathers and its bearing upon contemporary issues. Thomas took full advantage of the opportunity, recasting the Lombard's work to some extent, and including many citations from Aristotle.

Having worked through the Sentences and produced his commentary, the *Scriptum super libros Sententiarum*,[26] in 1256 Thomas became a university master in the faculty of theology, acquiring the title of *magister in sacra pagina* (master of the sacred page) or what was becoming the more common title, *doctor sacrae scripturae*. As the titles indicate, his primary task was to teach Scripture, which he did throughout the remainder of his life, often as he wrote his more doctrinally-oriented works. As master, his *expositio* was considerably more detailed than the cursory *lectio* permitted the bachelor. All his commentaries have come down to us either as notes taken by a student – often Thomas' *socius*, Reginald of Piperno – as Thomas lectured, or else directly from Thomas. The lecture notes (*reportatio*) were sometimes corrected and expanded by Thomas, sometimes not. If a commentary is a *reportatio*, its Latin title is usually *Lectura*, as the commentary on Matthew, *Lectura super Matthaeum*. On the other hand, if the commentary was written or dictated by Thomas himself, it is called an *Expositio*.[27]

The job of a master, though based on *lectio* and *expositio*, drew upon the skills acquired in commenting on the Sentences. The

---

[26] There is no translation except of part of the last book, which is used to replace the uncompleted concluding part of the *Summa Theologiae*.

[27] See Weisheipl, *Friar Thomas D'Aquino*, p. 117. Sometimes either form may be called a *Postilla*.

position's requirements were delineated by Peter the Chanter (a master at Paris in the last quarter of the twelfth century) in words that accurately reflect Thomas' own view:

> Engaging with Scripture (*exercitium sacrae scripturae*) requires three elements: reading (*lectio*), disputation (*disputatio*) and preaching (*praedicatio*) ... Reading is, as it were, the foundation and basement for what follows, for through it the rest is achieved. Disputation is the wall in this building of study, for nothing is fully understood or faithfully preached, if it is not first chewed over by the tooth of disputation. Preaching, which is supported by both the former, is the roof, sheltering the faithful from the heat and wind of temptation. So we should preach after, not before, the reading of Scripture and the investigation of doubtful matters by disputation.[28]

According to the scholastics of the High Middle Ages, therefore, it is not enough to read Scripture alone, however piously, and then go ahead and preach on it. Without good training one can be led astray by misunderstandings over the literal sense, to say nothing of spiritual speculations. Proper training requires one to practise theological inquiry which, as Thomas states in the first question of the *Summa Theologiae*, is fundamentally a matter of argument over how best to interpret Scripture.[29] The pedagogical function of theological inquiry is to train readers of Scripture so that they read it more profoundly and with less error, in order that they may go forth into the world and preach the gospel. The best kind of training is that whereby students discuss Scripture under the authority and guidance of their master, using reason and dialectic. The master, and following him, the students, probe Scripture by careful analysis and by raising questions and arguing over their resolution.[30] In its scholastic form, then, *lectio* is a thoroughly communal and, as it were, active form of contemplation. It also constitutes a tradition of inquiry that stretches back in time, for both *lectio* and *disputatio* involve analysing and questioning earlier interpretations and judgments.

Both the form of Thomas' training and his job description as master of the sacred page indicate the vital relation between exegesis and doctrine in Thomas' theology. Exegesis is necessarily 'theological exegesis', always informed by doctrine, and what is now called systematic or doctrinal theology is necessarily authorized and

---

[28] Cited by Smalley, *The Study of the Bible in the Middle Ages*, p. 208. I have amended her translation somewhat.

[29] *ST*, I, 1, 8.

[30] *Disputatio* may on occasion be best done separately from *lectio*, and there arose a custom of devoting particular days each year to debate. See Chenu, *Toward Understanding Saint Thomas*, pp. 88–91.

informed by exegesis.[31] Those works, like the two *Summae*, which
seem more 'purely' doctrinal, or which have been read as such, are
therefore better thought of as a kind of second-level exegesis. And
all Thomas' commentaries bear significantly upon his more 'theological' works. In sum, as Jean-Pierre Torrell remarks: 'if we wish
. . . to get a slightly less one-sided idea of the whole theologian and
his method, it is imperative to read and use in a much deeper fashion
these biblical commentaries in parallel with the great systematic
works'.[32]

Aquinas' theological understanding of Scripture

Thus far I have addressed the historical and cultural background for
Thomas' approach to Scripture, working thence towards some of
the more directly theological reasons for the centrality of exegesis in
his work. These reasons now need to be discussed in more detail. I
will examine the question of what, more precisely, Scripture is, for
the answer has significant consequences for Thomas' exegesis, as it
does for his understanding of theological inquiry. But first it will be
helpful to examine a little further Thomas' idea of Christianity and
what makes it possible for Christians to follow Jesus Christ today.

For Thomas, Christianity is a way of life founded upon the assent
of believers to what they have heard of God's revelation. That
assent – faith – is made possible by the Holy Spirit and the
preaching of the Church.[33] Revelation is the necessary basis for
Christianity because Christians are oriented to a goal that is beyond
our natural capacities not only to attain, but even to know anything
about. Our final goal is perfect knowledge of the triune God as we
are brought to the Father in the Son through the Holy Spirit. This
perfect and participatory knowledge of God is possible only for the
blessed in heaven, for their minds are raised up so as to know God
as such by means of the *lumen gloriae*, the light of glory. That is the
highest and most complete form of revelation possible for us. But,
to repeat, since we come to know the triune God only through
God's action and cannot acquire such knowledge by our intellectual
activity alone, we need revelation to make known to us here and
now the form of our salvation and future happiness.[34] It is this
revelation which was given to a few chosen people on earth.
Through the Spirit's gift of a special intellectual light, the *lumen
propheticum*, the minds of the prophets, apostles and evangelists

---

[31] Chenu, *Toward Understanding Saint Thomas*, pp. 253–60.
[32] Torrell, *Saint Thomas Aquinas*, vol. 1, p. 55.
[33] *ST*, II–II, 4, 1.
[34] *ST*, I–II, 62, 1.

were temporarily raised up so as to receive knowledge beyond their ordinary powers to attain, and were enabled to make the proper judgment as to its content. Some may have received this revelation in the form of a special experience, such as a vision. Others may have been entirely unaware of what the Spirit was doing, for revelation need not be accompanied by any unusual experience.[35]

Revelation is thus a 'divine strengthening of the power of reason to interpret and judge knowledge' that happens to those chosen to receive the revelation.[36] Unlike some later theologians, Thomas believes revelation is an event in the mind rather than something public. Anything may be the visible vehicle for revelation (the burning bush, for example), but it is only when the mind is so illumined that it receives knowledge and understanding through that vehicle that revelation occurs. It follows from this that even the 'event' of Jesus Christ, the Incarnate Word, is not strictly speaking revelation as such. Christ was unique among men in that during his ministry he had all and more of the knowledge and judgment of a *comprehensor*, of one of the blessed in heaven who 'comprehend' God. His perfect knowledge was not due to revelation, however, for it was neither given to him nor was it temporary; it was his by reason of his personal union with the Word.[37] Because his knowledge is perfect, Christ is the foremost and perfect teacher.[38] He instructed his disciples, teaching them all that we need to know to attain eternal life.[39] Further, he 'showed us in his own person the way of truth, whereby we may attain to the bliss of eternal life',[40] for all his actions, especially upon the Cross, are 'our instruction'.[41] But, again, it was only in the new understanding and judgment of those who heard him in the power of the Holy Spirit that revelation occurred. The disciples had need of the prophetic light to raise up their minds so they could hear and understand what he taught them. This helps explain why not everyone became an apostle or a follower of Jesus, and why the disciples initially failed to understand so much.

Revelation is never given to someone for his own sake alone. The prophetic light is one of the 'graces freely given' (*gratia gratis data*),

---

[35] *ST*, II–II, 171; *ScG*, III, 154.
[36] Per Erik Persson, *Sacra Doctrina: Reason and Revelation in Aquinas* (Oxford: Blackwell, 1970), p. 24. My account of Thomas' understanding of revelation draws heavily upon Persson.
[37] *ST*, III, 15, 10.
[38] *ST*, III, 7, 7.
[39] *ST*, I–II, 108, 3.
[40] *ST*, III, prol.
[41] *ST*, III, 40, 1, ad 3.

all of which are intended for the good of the Church.[42] The gift of revelation required the prophets to preach to Israel what they learned by its means. Knowledge issues in speech; spoken witness to internal revelation makes possible the assent of the faithful to what they hear from without. So, likewise, Thomas writes of Christ instructing and gathering his disciples as an army is assembled by a king to be sent out to do battle against an enemy. In this case, the enemy is the devil and the weapon is the preaching of the gospel.[43] The apostolic church is to follow Christ likewise by preaching and teaching as he did, handing on (*traditio*) saving knowledge to the faithful.

The knowledge which the Church teaches is embodied authoritatively in Scripture. Scripture cannot be identified with revelation. It is the closest possible thing we have to revelation, since it is the apostolic witness to that revealed knowledge, brought about in the minds of the prophets and the apostles, of matters otherwise unknowable to us. But it is a human document. Although it is the authoritative expression of revealed knowledge, it is nothing more than an expression, not the revelation itself. Accordingly, Thomas takes issue with John Chrysostom who, interpreting John 10.1-13, which speaks of the door through which the sheep are to enter, says that it is Scripture which is the door. With Augustine, Thomas insists that it is Christ alone who is the door. It is revelation as such, the event of God's Word, which is the truth that leads us to God. Scripture is not that perfect, divine truth. But it is the sure and sufficient witness to that truth, and it is on that account true.[44]

There is, then, a distinct gap between Scripture and revelation. The salvific knowledge God intends us to receive is conveyed uniquely through the written witness of the human authors of Scripture. The human authors were instruments of God's communicative will. Since they were personal agents and sought to express in their way the revealed knowledge they alone received, their own intentions and their customary word usage (*modus loquendi*) bear upon the text and must be considered in its interpretation.[45] But the gap cannot be widened any further. There can be no going behind the text to reconstruct it in the form of a historical or systematic or spiritual re-presentation that is somehow more profound or true

---

[42] *ST*, I–II, 111, 5, ad 1; III, 7, 7.

[43] *In Matt.* 4.23 [383].

[44] *In Io.* 10.2 [1370–71]. Thomas' account of the hierarchical relation among revelation, Scripture and preaching is not dissimilar to Karl Barth's conception of the threefold Word of God. See his *Church Dogmatics: 1/1. The Doctrine of the Word of God* (Edinburgh: T&T Clark, 1975), pp. 88–120.

[45] *Quodl.* 7, 14, ad 5.

than the original. The fundamental reason why this is so is that, unlike any other writing, God is the primary author of Scripture.[46]

God conveys salvific knowledge through Scripture in two ways, one of which, the spiritual sense, is unique to Scripture. The meaning of ordinary writings is limited to their literal sense. But Thomas allows 'literal' a far broader scope than is usual today. The literal sense includes not only words used in their more or less customary sense, but metaphor and other poetic tropes, too. Thus a poem, even one by a 'difficult' poet like John Ashbery, can be interpreted only 'literally', in Thomas' sense of the word, since it is not authored by God. Scripture likewise conveys meaning through the literal sense when it describes the history of salvation in the books from Genesis to Revelation. When it tells of God as having a 'strong right arm' or as getting angry or by any such anthropomorphisms and metaphors, Scripture is still literal. Moreover, Thomas insists that we must interpret literally Isaiah's prediction that a virgin will give birth to a child, because the saying refers directly to Christ and is therefore intended in the historical sense.[47] Thus there is nothing at all to suggest that, by the word 'literal', Thomas might mean non-theological or 'natural' or merely historical in the modern, immanentist sense. The literal sense is that which the words of Scripture convey, namely the history of salvation centred upon Jesus Christ.

Scripture is unique, however, in that its divine author has the power to convey meaning not only by its words but by the events and persons described there, too. Discerning God's intended meaning in such things requires addressing the spiritual senses in their various forms. While Thomas is clearly far more interested in the literal interpretation of Scripture than were many earlier commentators, he is always willing to engage in spiritual interpretation, especially when it refers in some way to Christ. Yet, to repeat, the *sensus historicus vel litteralis* remains normative for any spiritual interpretation, and he insists that it alone is the basis and norm for any theological argument.[48] There can be no possibility of basing a theological proposal or spiritual interpretation upon anything other than the literal sense, for it is that sense which most authoritatively conveys God's intention. Indeed, Thomas notes that anything learned by means of the spiritual sense is always conveyed elsewhere by the literal. It follows that all spiritual interpretations and all theological proposals are in effect more or less successful explications of the literal-historical meaning of Scripture, the story of

---

[46] *ST*, I, 1, 10.
[47] *In Matt.* 1.23 [148].
[48] *ST*, I, 1, 10.

salvation centred on Jesus Christ. Exegesis of that story is thus a necessary part of all theological inquiry.[49]

Thomas' conception of the primacy of the literal sense does not require him to say that Scripture is 'literally' true in any modern sense of 'literal'. He does not assert the complete accuracy of Scripture's account of history, in the modern sense of the word, or of its description of things that would nowadays fall under the purview of the hard sciences. Thomas seems to have thought that most of it was accurate in that way. But like earlier exegetes, he was willing to reinterpret a passage when it seemed to assert something he knew could not be true on logical, historical or scientific grounds. His basic principle was: 'nothing false can ever underlie the literal sense of Scripture'.[50] So when Scripture appears to be claiming something clearly untrue, its divine author must intend a meaning other than the apparent, one that can be true. The interpreter's responsibility is to find that meaning. A good example of this is Thomas' discussion of Genesis 1.6.[51] He notes that the idea of a body of water surrounding the firmament does not seem at all likely in light of contemporary knowledge. Accordingly, he suggests that 'water' be taken to mean 'formless matter or any kind of transparent body'. That interpretation enables the divine and human authors of the passage to convey saving truth to the contemporary Church. Not incidentally, Thomas' move is not to appeal to a spiritual sense but to propose an alternative literal reading, one which takes 'water' as a kind of metaphor.[52] This is a reasonable move because the author of Scripture is God, who can intend a word in Scripture to mean more than one thing, even according to the literal sense.[53]

Scripture is the authoritative means by which revealed knowledge is handed on to the contemporary Church, which in turn hands it on to the faithful by teaching and preaching on Scripture. Both the content of that teaching – what is handed on – and the means – how it is handed on – are covered by the phrase *sacra doctrina*, sacred teaching. Unlike many of his contemporaries, Thomas prefers this phrase to the word 'theology', reserving the latter for more general knowledge of God, including that which is neither revealed nor sufficient for salvation, such as the *theologia* of the ancient philosophers. *Sacra doctrina* indicates the combination of human

---

[49] See also Rowan Williams, *On Christian Theology* (Oxford: Blackwell, 2000), pp. 44–59, esp. 47–8.

[50] *ST*, I, 1, 10, ad 3.

[51] *ST*, I, 68, 3.

[52] This may seem to anticipate Hegel, but more widespread *wissenschaftlich* sublation of theological language is ruled out for Thomas by his strong emphasis upon the primacy of the historical-literal form of saving knowledge.

[53] *ST*, I, 1, 10, ad 1.

and divine action that makes possible the faith of the Christian. *Doctrina* is *sacra* because it originates with God; it is knowledge primarily about God and only secondarily about other things as they are in relation to God; and it can be handed on by the Church to others only with the help of the Holy Spirit. *Sacra doctrina* is both that which is taught to the faithful as well as the action of teaching it.

Sacra doctrina is in some important respects identifiable with Scripture. *Sacra scriptura* is the written witness to the revelation made to the prophets and apostles and evangelists. As the teaching of the Church, *sacra doctrina* is likewise a form of witness, and is apostolic in origin and intent. Thomas often uses the two phrases as if they were almost interchangeable.[54] But *sacra doctrina* is not normative, or not in anything like the way Scripture is. The teaching of the Creeds is fundamental, not because it is a product of the Church but because the credal statements are drawn from Scripture. The teachings of the Fathers have authority, but only of a probable kind. While Thomas treats the 'holy doctors' with immense respect, he does not hesitate to correct their imperfections, 'loyally explaining' or 'reverently expounding' (*exponere reverenter*) their remarks so that they better conform to Scripture.[55] He insists that 'faith rests upon the revelation made to the apostles and prophets who wrote the canonical books and not on the revelations (if any such there are) made to other doctors'.[56] Thus Thomas does not anticipate the later Roman Catholic doctrine of two sources of revelation, Scripture and Church tradition. Though he admits an oral apostolic tradition, this has no authority with regard to doctrine, but applies only to specific practices.[57] Scripture alone is the basis of our faith, and of itself it gives us knowledge sufficient for our salvation, to which nothing new can be or need be added.[58]

In sum, the exegesis of Scripture can never be dispensed with. We cannot rely upon intermediary work, whether theological systems or conciliar documents or papal teachings. Such intermediaries are vital and constitute the ongoing *disputatio* that informs the Church's quest for more truthful preaching and witness. But for that quest to be successful, teachers and preachers must return ever anew to Scripture.

---

[54] For example in *ST*, I, 1, 7 and 8.
[55] See Chenu, *Toward Understanding Saint Thomas*, pp. 145–47.
[56] *ST*, I, 1, 8, ad 2.
[57] *ST*, III, 64, 2, ad 1.
[58] Persson, *Sacra Doctrina*, pp. 71–90.

Aquinas' biblical commentaries for today

Why read Thomas' commentaries today? The following chapters will offer many examples of Thomas' exegetical insights that cumulatively make a strong case for the benefits of spending time with his commentaries. Here I will conclude by suggesting that we can learn from Thomas' exegetical practice. While it would not be sensible to suggest that we should adopt all his scholastic mannerisms, there are some aspects of his approach to Scripture, not often found today, which may be well worth retrieving.

One of the more significant differences between contemporary exegesis and his is that Thomas does not seem to think that the exegete's task is to determine 'the' meaning of Scripture. To be sure, he *is* concerned to rule out false interpretations. But he does not seem to regard Scripture as if it were a kind of puzzle that sophisticated methods of interpretation can solve by rendering it into a normative re-presentation. Scripture is the focus of theological argument, but the goal of such argument is not, or not primarily, to achieve consensus upon a single meaning. Instead, it is to enrich our understanding of what Scripture is saying to us, or, to say the same thing in a different way, to hear what its divine author is saying to us here and now by its means. The purpose of *lectio* and *disputatio* is to see to it that the Church and its members live the Christian life more apostolically, in greater obedience to Jesus Christ. That purpose may be achieved without trying to fix the meaning of Scripture

Modern commentaries often refer to alternative interpretations as they seek to decide upon the (sole) correct reading. The general practice has been to limit discussion of alternatives to those that are the product of the correct methodology, and thus usually to a relatively small group of contemporaries. By contrast, Thomas engages in conversation with everyone he can possibly think of, irrespective of their methods or even their religious beliefs. A glance at his commentaries will find him referring to Aristotle and other philosophers and their commentators (including mediaeval Muslims), Church doctrines, papal definitions, ancient heresies, the exegesis of the Fathers, and contemporary proposals, together with a cloud of references to other parts of the Bible. All potential sources of truth are brought into the discussion in order that Scripture may be the more deeply probed and understood. Yet none of the non-biblical sources are permitted to govern the interpretation, which lies with the *sensus litteralis vel historicus* alone. Instead, it is they who are brought within Scripture's orbit and made to serve its divine author's communicative intention.

If something like Thomas' practice of *lectio*, with its concomitant *disputatio*, were understood to be the fundamental form of the Church's theological quest for truth, significant ecclesiological consequences would follow. The Church could not simply rest content with repeating its past *sacra doctrina* or with appealing to its authorities and traditions and councils. It would be required to probe the apostolic witness ever further, and bring all possible interlocutors into the *disputatio*. Controversy would be expected as a matter of course, and as something that can often be good and healthy, a sign of the Spirit working in the midst of the Church. It would be seen that if *disputatio* is too quickly cut off by Church authorities or by shrillness, partisanship or schism, the truthfulness of the Church's exegesis and its preaching is likely to decline. In short, Thomas' commentaries, like his theology more generally, display for us the clear-headed *lectio* and the charitable and ecumenical *disputatio* that he, I think rightly, believed was vital to the Church's future.

1

AQUINAS' LITERAL EXPOSITION ON JOB

John Yocum

Of all Thomas' biblical commentaries, the *Expositio super Iob ad litteram* has received the most attention and exerted the greatest influence.[1] In this remarkable work, Thomas adumbrates a theology of providence that aims to show the coherence of the Christian doctrine that God cares for all rational creatures individually, bringing them through this present life toward the life to come, an eternal life in which they will be justly punished or rewarded. He aims to show that this doctrine not only has the merit of internal coherence, but also that it is supported by 'probable reasons', available to those who observe the nature of beings and events in the world. That is to say, while the truth of the divine rule and care for all individual rational creatures is not something that can be demonstrated, that is, definitively proved, once one has grasped the doctrine as revealed in the New Testament, including the promise of resurrection to a future judgment, it increases the intelligibility of the world.

There has been a profusion of scholarly work on the *Expositio* over the last four decades or so, in large part because in 1965 a highly praised critical text of the *Expositio* appeared in the Leonine series, one of only two of Aquinas' biblical commentaries so far prepared.[2] This article will sketch the main outlines of Aquinas'

---

[1] For background to the *Expositio*, see the introduction to the Leonine text by A. Dondaine, Thomas Aquinas, *Expositio super Iob ad litteram: Opera Omnia* ed. Leon; (vol. 25; Rome: Cura et Studio Fratrum Praedicatorum, 1965). The text of the *Expositio* is vol. 26.

[2] English translation: *Thomas Aquinas, The Literal Exposition on Job: A Scriptural Commentary Concerning Providence* (trans. Anthony Damico, with interpretative essay and notes by Martin D. Yaffe, The American Academy of Religion, Classics in Religious Studies; Atlanta: Scholars Press, 1989). The most substantial treatment of the *Expositio* is that of Denis Chardonnens, *L'Homme sous le regard de la providence: Providence de Dieu et condition humaine selon l'Exposition littérale sur le livre de Job de Thomas d'Aquin* (Paris: Librairie Philosophique J. Vrin, 1997). Substantial shorter treatments, include: Susan Schreiner, *Where Shall Wisdom be Found? Calvin's Exegesis of Job from Medieval and Modern Perspectives* (Chicago/London: University of Chicago Press, 1994); Martin D. Yaffe, 'Interpretive Essay', in *Thomas Aquinas,*

reading of the book of Job, highlighting his method of exposition
and three crucial aspects of his interpretation. It will also argue that
this reading is cogent, superior in some notable respects to some of
the main alternatives, and, when the premises supplied by Christian
faith are accepted, provides a compelling account of human life
under just divine rule.

The *Expositio* dates, according to the best arguments, from
Thomas' time in Orvieto, a time of intense study in service to both
the Dominicans and to Pope Urban IV, from 1261–65.[3] This is also
the period when he wrote the third book of the *Summa contra
Gentiles* (*ScG*), which deals with the doctrine of divine providence.
As a *magister in sacra pagina*, one of Thomas' three central duties
was to lecture on the Scripture,[4] and the book of Job was a fitting
complement to the systematic doctrinal work he was concurrently
carrying out on the *ScG*. Whether the *ScG* treats providence at such
length because Thomas was working on the book of Job,[5] or
whether he chose the book of Job as his text for commentary
because he was working on the theme of providence in the *ScG* is
unclear.[6] The conjunction, in any case, points to the close
connection between Thomas' biblical commentaries and his systematic works.

Thomas' exposition follows what he takes to be a progression in
the book itself. Following a Prologue introducing the work and
setting out the theme of the book as a whole, he breaks the book
into four sections: the opening prose narrative; the debate between
Job and his friends, including the intervention of Elihu; God's
revelation to Job; and the narrative epilogue. These divisions within
the book are fairly obvious, and almost all commentators observe
them. This brief article will follow Thomas through his exposition,
noting significant themes and issues as they arise, and conclude with
comments toward assessing Thomas' work.

Prologue: Job's intention and Thomas'

According to Aquinas, 'The whole intention of [the book of Job]
turns on showing through plausible arguments (*per probabiles*

The Literal Exposition on Job, pp. 1–65. Other shorter studies will be noted in the
course of this essay.
   [3] Jean Pierre Torrell, *St Thomas Aquinas:* vol. I, *The Person and his Work* (trans.
Robert Royal; Washington: Catholic University of America Press, 1996), pp. 117–41.
   [4] See Torrell, *St Thomas Aquinas*, pp. 54–74.
   [5] Suggested by Torrell, *St Thomas Aquinas*, p. 115.
   [6] Suggested by Dondaine, 'Introduction', *Expositio super Iob ad litteram*, p. 5.

rationes) that human affairs are ruled by divine providence.'[7] When Thomas speaks of 'providence', he means the ordering of things to their end, the purpose for which they were created. In a work that precedes the *Expositio*, the *Quaestiones disputatae de ueritate*, Thomas distinguishes the divine art that produces things, the disposition that keeps them in harmony, and the providence that orders them to their end.[8] Underlying this distinction is a profound Christian metaphysics, synthesizing the causal theory of Aristotle and the Christian doctrine of *creatio ex nihilo*. This distinction is also apparent in the *Summa contra Gentiles*. At the beginning of Book III, which is devoted to divine providence, Thomas begins by recapitulating briefly what he has already said in the previous book, that as Creator, God is the source of all being, and endows creatures with being.[9] Each thing so produced has an end, a purpose which it achieves through its own action, directed to its end by the Creator who endowed it with the power and principles of its action.[10]

The human being, Thomas says, is a special case:

> Some beings so exist as God's products that, possessing understanding, they bear his likeness and reflect his image. Consequently, they are not only ruled, but are also rulers of themselves, inasmuch as their own actions are directed to a fitting end. If these beings submit to the divine rule in their own ruling, then by virtue of the divine rule they are admitted to the achievement of their ultimate end; but, if they proceed otherwise in their own ruling, they are rejected.[11]

So, Thomas' conception of divine providence in the affairs of those beings endowed with God's image is bound up with the notion that human actions have ordered consequences. Providence, as Thomas will argue in the *Expositio*, is concerned with a just order in the affairs of human beings, in which the consequences of human actions are not left to chance, nor governed by caprice, but by divine wisdom that includes appropriate rewards and punishments that culminate in final attainment or non-attainment of one's end.[12]

Thomas tells us that various philosophers have held divergent

---

[7] *On Job*, Prol., 55–57 (p. 68). I will make use in this chapter of the translation by Damico, indicating any points at which I have modified it. For ease of reference, citations to the *Expositio* will cite the chapter and verse commented on, the line numbers in the Leonine edition, and, in parentheses, the page number in the Damico translation.

[8] *De Ver.* 5, 1, ad 9. On the dating of this work to around 1256–59, see Torrell, *St Thomas Aquinas*, pp. 59ff.

[9] *ScG*, III, 1, 1.

[10] *ScG*, III, 1, 2.

[11] *ScG*, III, 1, 4. See also *On Job* 7.12, 272–81 (p. 151).

[12] See *ScG*, III, 140–41.

opinions on the matter of divine providence. 'Although the opinion of the majority of men was confirmed in the belief that natural things were not driven by chance but by providence because of the order which manifestly appears in them, doubt emerged concerning the actions of men.'[13] This doubt is deleterious, Aquinas says, because if belief in providence is taken away, 'no reverence or fear of God based on truth will remain among men', and that will lead to an apathy toward virtue and a proneness to vice.[14] Now, this is an interesting statement. One might parse this as meaning that Thomas is concerned to encourage virtue and discourage vice, based on reverence and fear of God; that is, if one can convince people to hold God in reverence, as the rewarder and punisher of human actions, then this places a kind of constraint on human behaviour, a means to a good end. But several things make this an inadequate estimate of Thomas' meaning.

First, Thomas sees reverence and fear of God as itself the end of the human being.[15] Elsewhere, he analyses reverence as a natural obligation to God.[16] So Thomas must mean that a defect in this virtue is contributory to defects in all other kinds of virtues, or the habits of right living, in general. Far from being a means to some other end – a support to civility or decency, for example – Thomas takes reverence toward God to be the proper end of the human being. The relation between this virtue[17] and other virtues is intrinsic, not external. Second, a few lines further on, Thomas substitutes for the term 'reverence', 'love ... for God';[18] so the kind of relation to God Thomas is interested in is based on love: 'he who clings to God with his mind orders himself toward God as a servant of love, not of fear'.[19] Finally, Thomas says that apart from a conviction that divine providence rules the affairs of human beings, 'no reverence or fear of God *based on truth*' will remain. The kind of reverence and fear that Thomas is interested in is love based on a conviction about the truth of the relation between God and human beings. Concern for the truth of the matter leads to one of the most startling statements in Thomas' whole corpus, that one ought not be a 'respecter of persons', even toward God.[20]

---

[13] *On Job*, Prol., 24–29 (p. 67).

[14] *On Job*, Prol., 41–46 (p. 68).

[15] See *ScG*, III, 116.

[16] *ScG*, III, 116.

[17] Chief among the virtues, Thomas says, is the intention of the proper end. *ScG*, III, 143, 5.

[18] *On Job*, Prol., 46–48 (p. 68). See *ScG*, 115–16, 119.

[19] *On Job* 1.8, 431–33 (p. 80). See also *On Job* 1.10, 18–22 (p. 82).

[20] *On Job* 13.7-8, 89–153 (pp. 215–16). See E.T. Oakes' review of *The Last Word* by T. Nagel, *Commonweal*, 125/2 (1998), pp. 22–24.

Thomas says that the chief difficulties with accepting that God governs human affairs providentially arise from the fact that 'no certain order appears in human events'.[21] For good things manifestly happen to bad people, just as clearly bad things happen to good people.[22] The first of these is not such a grave difficulty, Thomas says, because one can easily ascribe to divine mercy the fact that good things happen to bad people;[23] and mercy, in its pure form, he says elsewhere, is a uniquely divine attribute.[24] 'But that just men should be afflicted without cause seems to undermine totally the foundation of providence.'[25] In other words, while natural occurrences, such as the movement of the planets, follow orderly courses, human events do not seem to display an order in keeping with divine justice. Therefore the afflictions of one representative human being are posed, Aquinas says, as a kind of *quaestio* for debate, the participants being Job and his three friends.[26] The speeches of Job, Eliphaz, Bildad and Zophar constitute a kind of mediaeval *disputatio*, which is eventually 'determined', or judged, by God Himself.

For Thomas, Job is a real historical figure, though he need not be; the truth of the book could be conveyed, he says, through a parable, a kind of hypothetical situation set up as the platform for a debate. This, however, would contradict Scripture, Thomas avers, because Ezek. 14.14 names Job alongside Noah and Daniel, whom he takes to be clearly 'men in the nature of things'. In addition, Jas 5.1 points to Job as a model of patience in suffering.[27] Besides this, Thomas points to certain details in the narrative that suggest Job is a real person, such as the fact that he, his friends and his homeland are named.[28]

While Thomas says the story could be a parable and still convey its message, if one takes the story to be historical, as Thomas does, it at least sharpens the point that he understands it to be making. In the *Expositio*, Mary Sommers argues, it is significant that Aquinas argues, and sees Job as arguing, *per probabiles rationes*.[29] The

[21] *On Job*, Prol., 31–32 (p. 68).

[22] *On Job*, Prol., 33–35 (p. 68).

[23] *On Job*, Prol., 62–66 (p. 68).

[24] See Yves Congar, 'Mercy, God's Greatest Attribute' in *The Revelation of God* (New York: Herder & Herder, 1969).

[25] *On Job*, Prol., 66–68 (p. 68).

[26] *On Job*, Prol., 68–71 (p. 68).

[27] *On Job*, Prol., 72–90 (pp. 68–69).

[28] *On Job* 1.1; 13–16 (p. 71).

[29] Mary C. Sommers, 'Manifestatio: The Historical Presencing of Being in Aquinas' *Expositio super Iob*', in *Hermeneutics and the Tradition*, Proceedings of the American Catholic Philosophical Association, 62 (1988), pp. 147–56 (149).

discussion proceeds by testing hypotheses about the nature of providence for their adequacy in explaining the experience of Job. Job's story is the evidence upon which any conclusion must be based, and that evidence is historical in nature.[30] Sommers shows that for Aquinas, if doubts about divine providence are rooted in observation of the world, then a convincing response to such doubts must also help to make situations like Job's more intelligible.

Finally, Thomas tells his readers at the end of the Prologue that his intention is to comment upon the literal text because 'Blessed Pope Gregory has already disclosed to us its mysteries so subtly and clearly that there seems no need to add anything further to them.'[31] When Thomas speaks of the literal sense, he means something different than do modern exegetes, who usually use the term to refer to the conscious intention of the human author. For Thomas the meaning of the literal text may go beyond what the human author understood. In addition to this, while human authors use words to signify things, God, the Creator of all things, may use those things signified by the words of the text to signify other things.[32] Literal exposition is distinguished from spiritual exposition, in that literal exposition confines itself to working from the letter of the given text, while spiritual interpretation searches out not only the things signified by the words, but the further things that those things may signify; so for example, Job's sufferings may signify those of Christ and the Church. Thomas defines what he means by the literal text in a comment on Job. 1.6: 'The literal sense is that which is intended by the words, whether they are used properly or figuratively.'[33] Therefore, the literal sense includes metaphors and other poetic devices.[34] This is important for Thomas' interpretation of Job, because a good deal of his effort is directed at unpacking the poetic figures Job uses to describe his condition or to make his argumentative points.

Furthermore, the literal meaning of the Scripture for Thomas – the meaning intended by the divine author – is the meaning that

---

[30] Sommers, 'Manifestatio', p. 150.

[31] On Job, Prol., 96–102 (p. 69).

[32] Compare the working definition of 'the literal sense' in modern biblical scholarship that Raymond Brown gives: 'The sense which the human author directly intended and which the written words conveyed.' Raymond Brown, 'Hermeneutics', in The New Jerome Biblical Commentary, eds. Raymond Brown, Joseph A. Fitzmyer, Roland E. Murphy (Englewood Cliffs: Prentice Hall, 1990), p. 1148.

[33] On Job 1.6; 232–34 (p. 76). See also ST, I, 1, 10, ad 3.

[34] This differs from the understanding of some ancient authors. For example, Origen used the term 'literal' to refer to the sense pertaining to historical events and things, while metaphor and parable were part of the allegorical sense. See Henri Crouzel, Origen (trans. A.S. Worrall; Edinburgh: T&T Clark, 1989), ch. 4.

emerges from reading the Bible as a whole, the work of a single divine author. Among modern options this is probably closest to, but still distinct from, what modern Catholic exegetes sometimes call the *sensus plenior*.[35] In this, Thomas reads the Bible not only as his mediaeval contemporaries did, but as the Christian tradition since at least the close of the second century had done: with a strong commitment to a closed canon and a conviction that both Testaments were written under the inspiration of the same Spirit.[36]

Yet, Thomas does not approach the book of Job primarily as a mine for figures of realities found in the New Testament. In numerous places, where Gregory the Great sees Job's sufferings as a foreshadowing of the sufferings of Christ and the Church,[37] Thomas' exposition does not refer to Job as a type of Christ.[38] Even in the chapters on behemoth and leviathan, which he reads allegorically, he takes the figural meaning to be indicated within the letter of the text, and thus his exposition of them as such remains, in Thomas' mind, on the literal level. This does not mean that Thomas rejects the Gregorian interpretation of other parts of the book. If we take his statement in the Prologue seriously, he accepts Gregory's mystical reading as both valid and seemingly unsurpassable. It simply means that Thomas aims to till a field of exposition in which there is work yet to be done. Where Gregory had richly nourished the contemplative *lectio divina* of the monk, Thomas intends to meet the exigencies of the theological schools founded to equip friars to preach.[39]

[35] See Brown, 'Hermeneutics', p. 1157. For a concise contrast between the *sensus plenior* principle and that of more traditional 'spiritual interpretation', see Henri de Lubac, *The Sources of Revelation* (New York: Herder, 1968), pp. 150–53. This is a translation of *L'Écriture dans la tradition* (Paris: Aubier, 1967), in which de Lubac gives a summary of the main themes of his comprehensive four-volume work, *Exégèse Médiévale: Les quatre sens de l'Écriture*, Theologie 41, 42, 59 (Paris: Aubier, 1959–64). On Thomas' use of the spiritual interpretation, see *Exégèse Médiévale* 4/2, 2, pp. 285–302.

[36] See the citations in Luke Timothy Johnson and William S. Kurz, *The Future of Catholic Biblical Scholarship: A Constructive Conversation* (Grand Rapids: Eerdmans, 2002), p. 49 n. 23.

[37] In his preface to the *Moralia*, Gregory points to one of the keys to his interpretation of Job. It is fitting that Job 'should signify by his words the One whom he proclaimed by his voice and by all that he endured should show forth what were to be the Lord's sufferings and should foretell the mysteries of his passion as he prophesied not only by speaking but also with his sufferings'. *Moralia in Job*, Pref., 14.

[38] For example, compare the comments on 1.12; 9.23-24; 19.15; Gregory reads all of these christologically, while Thomas' comments do not make reference to Christ's sufferings. On Gregory's Christological interpretation, see de Lubac, *Medieval Exegesis*, vol. I, 187–98; II/1, 537–48, 586–99; II/2, 53–98; see also Schreiner, *Where Shall Wisdom be Found?*, pp. 22–54.

[39] See Chardonnens, *L'Homme sous le regard de la providence*, pp. 22–26, 283–85.

As a *magister in sacra pagina*, Thomas' task was to offer
theological teaching, built upon the literal sense, the only sense
suited to and acceptable in theological argument.[40] He brought to
this all the tools of the mediaeval university: grammar, rhetoric,
dialectic, and natural science.[41] It was Thomas' task to interpret the
specific text under examination within an understanding of the truth
that derives from reflection on the Bible as a whole, which then
informs further reading of the Bible. There is thus a reciprocal
relationship between the individual text commented upon, the Bible
as a whole, and the dogmatic theology that derives from such
reflection.[42] To read the book of Job in light of the fuller teaching
on the resurrection of the body, for example, is not illegitimate, but
rather required by the demands of the theological exegesis that was
the goal of the *magister in sacra pagina's* work. This could suggest
an arbitrary approach to the text that Thomas has claimed he will
interpret according to the letter; but this impression would be
imbalanced. Thomas finds indications of what further doctrines –
such as the resurrection of the body – are germane to the book of
Job, within the book of Job itself. This is evident in the fact that in
commenting verse by verse upon the text, Thomas cites other texts
within Job 410 times, while citing other biblical texts somewhat
sparingly, when they are suggested by something within the text.[43]

The foundation of the debate: the history of a just man afflicted

Thomas sees the prose narrative in the opening two chapters of Job
as 'the premised foundation of the whole debate',[44] which follows.
The heavenly scene of this narrative, Thomas says, is a figural
representation of the truth that God takes care of human affairs and
orders them.[45] The figural nature of the scene is apparent in the fact
that it speaks of Satan coming and going, angels walking and
standing, and other impossibilities.[46] Most importantly, he warns,
one ought not to think that God was induced by Satan to permit
Job to be afflicted, rather, 'he ordained it in his eternal disposition to

---

[40] Torrell (*St. Thomas Aquinas*, p. 58) points out that this conviction is one which
characterizes Thomas' approach throughout his works, citing *Quodlib.* VII, 6, 1–2;
ST, I, 1, 10; *In Gal.* ch. 4, lect. 7.

[41] See the introduction to this volume.

[42] Chardonnens, *L'Homme sous le regard de la providence*, p. 283.

[43] See Christopher T. Baglow, *Modus et Forma: A New Approach to the Exegesis of
St. Thomas Aquinas with an application to the Lectura super Epistolam ad Ephesios*,
Analecta Biblica 149 (Rome: Editrice Pontifico Istituto Biblico, 2002), pp. 49–50; and
Damico, *Thomas Aquinas, The Literal Exposition on Job*, appendix.

[44] *On Job* 1.1, 1–6 (p. 71).

[45] *On Job* 1.6, 216–26 (p. 76).

[46] *On Job* 1.6-12 *passim*, 216–585 (pp. 76–83).

manifest Job's virtue'.[47] Thomas finds three things in this narrative that are crucial for what follows in the exposition. First, it establishes Job's condition and character. Job was a prosperous and a virtuous man, free from sin, and these two qualifications are connected. The description of Job's prosperity, Thomas says, shows us the sharpness of his afflictions by contrast. It shows something further as well: 'according to God's first intention, not only spiritual, but also temporal goods are bestowed on just men ... even in the beginning man was instituted in such a way that he would not have been subject to any disturbance if he had persisted in his innocence'.[48] So, Thomas' interpretation, drawing implicitly on the opening chapters of Genesis, sets the whole debate that is to follow on the question of the sufferings of the righteous in the context of a history in which not only moral evil, but temporal misfortune arises from the loss of human innocence.[49] Even after the entry of evil into the world, however, there is a distinction between the sufferings of the virtuous and the wicked. God visits retribution upon the wicked, at least in another life,[50] and here perhaps remedially,[51] but evils that come upon good human beings are attributable to God's providence, 'not from the principal intention', but rather accidentally (*per accidens*).[52] God turns this affliction to good purpose, by using it to make the virtue of just men conspicuous to others, in order to judge them, leading some to correction.[53]

Second, Aquinas establishes the mediating activity in God's providence of the incorporeal intellectual beings that the Bible calls angels or demons. While the dramatic events and dialogue of the heavenly court are figurative, the underlying truth is that divine providence works through higher beings to govern lower ones, and uses incorporeal intellectual beings in his government of human beings.[54] The good spirits, called angels in the Bible, who have maintained their purity, move human beings to good actions, while the demons, who are evil because they have corrupted their good

[47] *On Job* 1.12, 580–85 (p. 83).

[48] *On Job* 1.1-3, 47–53 (p. 72).

[49] Thomas cites or alludes to Genesis 1–3 seventeen times in the commentary, and also cites the murder of Abel in Gen. 4.10.

[50] *On Job* 14.6, 57–61 (p. 225).

[51] *On Job* 9.11, 311–15 (p. 172); *On Job* 9.16, 411–21 (p. 174).

[52] *On Job* 1.6, 312–14 (p. 78).

[53] *On Job* 1.12a, 458–79 (p. 81).

[54] *On Job* 1.6, 235–41 (p. 76). For a systematic account of Thomas' understanding of the order of the universe, which, however, makes almost no use of the *Expositio*, see John Wright, *The Order of the Universe in the Theology of St. Thomas Aquinas*, Analecta Gregoriana 39 (Rome: Gregorian University Press, 1957).

nature, move human beings to evil actions.[55] The former act according to the divine will, but the latter resist the divine will.[56] Thus, Satan performs acts that God permits him to perform, but his intention is to lead Job to blasphemy, while God's intention is to use Job's affliction to make a show of his virtue.[57] God permits the actions of demons, but does not endorse them, and uses them to bring about good. Thomas is also insistent, however, that an evil human being participates in his or her own corruption by abandoning the spiritual goods which are the end of one possessing a rational nature, in favour of the earthly goods, which correspond to human fleshly nature.[58] Aquinas, then, holds together several things in his exposition of the opening drama: the eternal disposition of all things by God; the accomplishment of affliction and evil by intelligent beings with divine permission, but not by divine intention; the active co-operation with evil by unjust human beings, and its resistance by the just, so that free human agency is maintained; the turning of affliction and evil intention to a good purpose.

Third, having alluded to the distinction between spiritual goods and earthly goods, fleshly and rational nature, as the affliction of Job progresses, Aquinas further elaborates a scheme of what constitutes human good. In the story, Job remains steadfast after the loss of his property and children, and this prompts Satan to charge that Job has remained faithful only because such goods are outside his own person. When God grants permission to Satan to afflict Job's body, Thomas takes the occasion to comment on the various goods proper to human life and their relation to one another:

> Man's good is threefold, namely of the body, of the soul, and of external things. [These] are ordered to one another in such a way that the body is for the sake of the soul whereas external things are for the sake of the body and the soul. Therefore, just as it is wrong if someone intentionally subordinates the goods of the soul to the advantage of external goods, so it is wrong if someone intentionally subordinates the goods of the soul to the health of the body. And indeed, that Job abounded in the practice of the virtues, which are the goods of the soul, could be sensibly manifest to all.[59]

[55] On Job 1.6, 241–61 (pp. 76–77).
[56] On Job 1.6, 286–300 (pp. 77–78).
[57] On Job 1.12, 596–611 (p. 86).
[58] On Job 1.6, 380–90 (p. 79).
[59] On Job 2.1, 1–10 (p. 91). See also ScG, III, 28–32, where Aquinas discusses what makes for human happiness.

The external goods of the human being are those outside his own body, whether material, like Job's wealth, or social, like his children. The internal goods of the human being are twofold: those goods related to the body, fundamentally bodily health; and those that pertain to the soul, the virtues.

Eleonore Stump has pointed out that Thomas does not deal in this work with 'the problem of evil' *per se*, that is, the problem of reconciling the existence of evil in the world with the existence of a good, omnipotent, omniscient God, though he does raise this issue in the *Summa Theologiae*.[60] Almost all modern readers, however, or at any rate most of them, think that the primary intention of the book of Job is to address the problem of evil. That easily leads to some misreadings of Thomas' *Expositio* because this book is not intended to address that issue comprehensively. Nevertheless, she argues, Thomas has some things to say here that may inform discussion of that question, at least by offering a radically different set of assumptions than those common to the modern debate. Chief among these is that the purpose of human life is union with God, that this present life is marked by disorder consequent upon the sin described in Genesis 3, that suffering in this life is turned by God to a good end, and that the fulfilment of human life is to be found in another life, in which human beings will attain the end for which they were created.[61] This last point, which is crucial to the whole account, emerges in the debate among Job and his three friends.

The Disputatio *among Job and his friends: anthropology, teleology, eschatology*

Job's friends, as is well known, argue that if he has experienced the kind of suffering which he has experienced, then this must be recompense for sin. If he will repent, he will be restored. If he does not repent, then this is final proof of his sinfulness. Job denies any consciousness of the kind of sin that would account for the level of punishment that he has experienced. He says, poetically, that he wishes to see his sins weighed against his punishments (6.1). Thomas is careful to say that Job is not, strictly speaking, morally unblemished. 'Because of the frailty of the human condition, no man, however just he may appear, is immune from sin. Nevertheless, in just men sins are not grave and mortal, but light and venial, and they come about from negligence and error.'[62] The

---

[60] Eleonore Stump, 'Aquinas on the Sufferings of Job', in Stump (ed.), *Reasoned Faith* (Ithaca and London: Cornell University Press, 1993), pp. 328–57 (p. 333).

[61] Stump, 'Aquinas on the Sufferings of Job', pp. 343–45.

[62] *On Job* 6.1ff.; 13–18 (p. 137–38). On mortal and venial sins, see *ScG*, III, 139.

point is that Job's sins have not merited what he took to be a reasonable recompense. The case of the friends amounts to saying there is a visible cause and effect at work: Job has sinned because he has suffered adversity, and indeed, he must have sinned greatly because he has suffered greatly.

While the exposition of the speeches is detailed and interesting, I will pick out three elements in Thomas' interpretation of the debate that are noteworthy. First, Thomas holds a rich anthropology that builds on that of Aristotle, taking full account of the realities of the bodily and social nature of human beings, as well as the distinctive intellectual human powers that enable a life of *contemplatio*, which is the true end of the human being. Second, Thomas extends teleology into eschatology, finding in Job's speeches a confession of the resurrection to come, when human beings will be rewarded and punished according to the justice of their lives in this age, and the virtuous will be freed from the corruption and limitations that mark this age, so as to reach their divinely ordained end. Third, this eschatology is knowable only by revelation, a revelation given finally in the New Testament, and vouchsafed to Job by a special prophetic insight; nevertheless, this revelation does not nullify, but completes what is available to human reason, so that the evidence of the world of sense and history is rendered more, not less intelligible by it.

In interpreting Job's laments, Thomas gives the outlines of a subtle anthropology, which is able to account for Job's plaintive cries without recourse to an allegorical interpretation, while yet maintaining Job's innocence and patience intact.[63] Job's laments are expressions that arise spontaneously from his bodily, animal nature.

> Now someone could say: You do indeed have cause for pain, but you ought not to burst forth into words of pain over it. Against this objection Job responds on the basis of reactions which are found in other animals. For man is like other animals in his sensitive nature; hence, reactions which are found in the sensitive nature are present in man naturally, just as they are in other animals. But what is natural cannot be totally

---

[63] For a résumé of Thomas' anthropology in the *Expositio*, see M.F. Manzanedo, 'La antropologia filosófica en el comentario tomista al libro de Job', *Angelicum*, 62 (1985), pp. 419–71 and 'La antropologia teológia en el comentario tomista al libro de Job', *Angelicum*, 64 (1987), pp. 301–31. While fairly exhaustive, the articles are arranged topically, with little analysis, and the distinction between 'theological' (pertaining exclusively to a human being's relationship to God) and 'philosophical' (covering everything else) is not apt.

suppressed ... it appears natural for animals to express internal afflictions with the voice.[64]

Because of the sensitive nature of the human being, the kind of suffering Job has experienced leads inevitably to sensual pain and emotional sadness.[65] But Job's patience is precisely his determination not to be overwhelmed by it: 'Now the condition of impatience exists when someone's reason is so reduced by sadness that it contradicts divine judgments. But if someone should suffer sadness according to his sensual side but his reason should conform to the divine will, there is no defect of impatience.'[66] At this point Thomas explicitly identifies Job's position as that of the Peripatetics, in contrast to the Stoics, 'that a wise man is indeed saddened, but through reason he strives not to be led into an unsuitable condition'.[67] While the comparisons to the Stoics and Peripatetics may strike one as fanciful, in fact, close examination of Job's reasoning makes the comparisons apt. Aquinas is obviously not saying that Job explicitly thought in these categories, but he makes a strong case that Job's view supports that of the Peripatetics, that the animal nature of the human being precludes an elimination of sadness. What Thomas means by 'sadness' is bodily, social and emotional discomfort. Christian patience has a different character, and Aquinas is clearly saying that Job displayed that kind of patience in the face of bodily affliction.

Thomas is sympathetic to Job's plight, in part, because he holds that pain impedes one's reason, and thus Job's condition makes for a struggle. 'For where there is vehement pain in the senses, it is necessary that the attention of the soul be distracted or impeded from the consideration of intellectual matters.'[68] This potential disharmony, which Aquinas calls distraction, itself results from the sinful state of human beings in the time after the first sin, resulting in a kind of battle within the human being.[69] So, Aquinas does not

[64] *On Job* 6.5, 63–70, 76–77 (pp. 138–39). Interestingly, Aquinas makes a similar point about the advantage of vocal prayer as especially fitted to man's bodily nature in *ST*, II–II, 83, 12.

[65] *On Job* 6.5, 81–94 (p. 139). See also Schreiner, *Where Shall Wisdom be Found?*, pp. 78–79 on the difference in attitude toward suffering between Gregory and Thomas. Schreiner's contrast may be too sharply drawn, since Aquinas does admit the variety of purposes of suffering that Gregory posits (*On Job* 7.21, 527–37 (p. 156)). As with his positive evaluation of Gregory's work in the Prologue, it is best not to take too lightly Aquinas' approbations. On the estimation of Gregory, see de Lubac, *Exégèse Médiévale* 4/2, 2, pp. 285–302.

[66] *On Job* 6.10, 128–33 (p. 140).

[67] *On Job* 6.12, 163–68 (p. 140).

[68] *On Job* 16.7, 70–72 (p. 245).

[69] *On Job* 7.10, 474–80 (p. 155). See also *ST*, I, 94, 1.

deny or minimize the suffering of Job. For Aquinas, it really is the case that someone in Job's condition, who has lost his property, his children, his health, and now his reputation and the consolation of friends, has good grounds for wishing to die, and even a certain case for cursing the day of his birth – unless there is held out to him the prospect of a better hope in which all this will be turned to good.[70]

So Job undertakes to argue with his friends, asserting his innocence and pointing to the faultiness of their own reasoning, especially in claiming that he was receiving a just punishment for a sin that, on the evidence of the life Job describes in chapter 29, must have been invisible. In the course of commenting on this debate, Thomas makes one of the most startling comments in the whole of his corpus. Recall that the premise of Thomas' interpretation is to take seriously what God has said in the heavenly scene at the outset: Job fears God. Job's friends had, then, unjustly accused him, and indeed with mounting vehemence, in the course of their debate with him. Drawing on the Old Testament prohibition of being a 'respecter of persons', Thomas comments on 13.8 thus:

> It is respect of persons if someone contemns another's apparent justice or denies it because of the greatness of the other disputant although he does not know his justice. If Job's friends judged him to be iniquitous, then, although they saw manifest justice in him, and they did so solely out of consideration for divine greatness, although they could not understand according to their own dogmas how Job might justly be punished by God, in their own judgment, by which they condemned Job, they seemed as it were to be respecting the person of God.[71]

In other words, to betray their own best judgment, in the apparently pious cause of defending God's righteousness, is injustice. Thomas goes on to note with Job that God does not need their help.[72]

---

[70] 'Although being and living, considered in itself, is desirable, yet being and living in misery in a situation of this kind is to be renounced, although sometimes being in misery may be sustained willingly for the sake of some end.' *On Job* 3.3, 81–85 (p. 101). Timothy Jackson disputes the claim that Job must be sustained by the hope of a remedy, let alone immortality: 'Because the possibility of all persons loving and being loved is such an overwhelming good ... it could outweigh even in the minds of the afflicted the tragic losses they experience in reality.' 'Must Job Live Forever? A Reply to Aquinas on Providence', *The Thomist*, 62 (1998), pp. 1–39 (34). One must choose which of these estimations of Job's situation seems more realistic. Furthermore, Jackson wants to identify with the Armininan tradition (p. 18), while questioning the certitude of God's triumph over evil (pp. 19–20). But Arminius confesses what Jackson does not: the final triumph of God, and the creatures He redeems, over sin, death, mourning, pain, and weeping. Such promises occur so often and so unqualifiedly in the New Testament, that Jackson's counter-proposals are simply staggering in their audacity.

[71] *On Job* 13.8, 94–103 (p. 215).

[72] *On Job* 13.9, 121–24 (p. 215).

Moreover, 'since God is truth, but every lie is contrary to the truth, whoever uses a lie to show God's magnificence by this very fact acts against God'.[73] Sophistry, even when cleverly employed to defend God's honour, is not just bad philosophy, but an offence to God. For Aquinas, philosophical and theological truth complement and never contradict one another.[74] What is revealed renders what is observable more intelligible.

A better hope is just what Thomas has Job confess, as he slowly builds his case.[75] He assails the easy correlation his friends affirm between righteousness and prosperity, sinfulness and suffering in this life.[76] If the friends want to affirm that divine government corresponds to anything human beings can call just, then they have to abandon their straightforward moral calculus. But further, Job shows that there is something in the human being that is orientated toward another life. Using something like an anthropological argument, Job asserts that human desires are future-orientated, and infers that this points in some shadowy way to something more than one can attain in this present life.[77] He also takes note of the assertion within the Jewish tradition of God's care for human beings, and argues that this is unreasonable and difficult to ascertain, if it extends only to this present life.[78]

Job's convictions, however, do not arise simply from observation, but from faith in a special prophetic revelation. The crux of Job's claim is that divine justice and providence will be apparent in a future life, where he hopes for vindication. Despite the fact that he can expect no help from other human beings (and his friends seem to be proof of that), nor can he help himself, [79] Job asserts that God will help him, and indeed vindicate him. 'For I know that my Redeemer lives, and on the last day I will rise from the earth. And I will be surrounded by my own hide again and in my flesh I shall see God. Whom I myself am going to see and my eyes are going to behold, and no one else' (Job 19.25-27). This passage is not without its interpretative difficulties, both in understanding the meaning of the underlying Hebrew term *goel*, which the Vulgate here translates

[73] *On Job* 13.9, 1131–35 (p. 215–16).

[74] Yaffe, 'Interpretive Essay', pp. 1–11. The well-known Thomistic principle is found in *ST*, I, 1, 8, ad 2; I, 60, 1, ad 3.

[75] Job has held to the hope of eternal life all along, but only reveals this in the course of the debate, as he attacks the arguments of his friends. See *On Job* 3.13, 349–51 (p. 106).

[76] See *On Job* 6.1ff; 1ff. (pp. 137ff.); *On Job* 9.1ff.; 1ff. (pp. 165ff.); *On Job* 13.1ff., 1ff. (pp. 213ff.).

[77] *On Job* 14.18ff.; 247–335. See Chardonnens, *L'Homme sous le regard de la providence*, pp. 81–85.

[78] *On Job* 14.5-6, 1–10 (p. 224).

[79] *On Job* 6.10-11, 169–240 (pp. 141–42).

redemptor, and in determining whom Job is calling upon.[80] The
Jewish exegete Robert Gordis takes the view that in the midst of his
bitterness, Job 'rises to a vision of faith in the God of justice, whom
he sees vividly before him, acting as his kinsman and Redeemer, the
avenger of the wrongs he has suffered'.[81]

Yet, Gordis also notes that in interpretation of 19.25-27,
'Virtually the only point of consensus among moderns, as against
older exegetes, is that the passage does *not* refer to resurrection after
death, in view of Job's clear-cut rejection of the doctrine in 14.7-
23.'[82] By contrast, 'the older Jewish and Christian exegetes saw in
19.25 and the following an affirmation of faith in bodily resurrection'[83] because they, like Thomas, read Job's lament in 14.7ff. in a
radically different way than modern exegetes. First, Thomas, like
many older Jewish exegetes, following one of two possible readings
in the Masoretic tradition,[84] reads a confession of faith in 13.15:
'Even if he kills me, I will hope in him, but I will still charge my own
ways in his sight.'[85] Modern exegetes generally follow a reading that
gives the translation, 'He will slay me; I have no hope' (Revised
Standard Version). What follows in Thomas' interpretation of
chapter 14 is a discussion of the frailty of the human being, and
particularly a demonstration of the reasonableness of the suppos-
ition of the human being's eternity, based on the great esteem and
care God shows to him.[86] Having now for the first time disclosed his
conviction about another life, Thomas says, Job in 14.7ff. speaks
poetically about the condition of the human being in this life,
considered in itself.[87] So, Thomas' reading of these crucial texts,
while not popular among modern commentators, is at least not
tendentious, and parallels traditional Jewish and Christian readings.

In commenting on 19.25-27, Thomas gives a fully-fledged

---

[80] For discussion of the complexities of translating the term, see Edwin M. Good, *In
Turns of Tempest: A Reading of Job* (Stanford: Stanford University Press, 1990), pp.
257–58.

[81] Robert Gordis, *The Book of Job: Commentary, new translation, and special
studies* (New York: Jewish Theological Seminary of America, 1978), p. 528. Gordis
also offers supporting arguments for the identification of the vindicator with God (pp.
205–6); for this identification, see also E. Dhorme, *A Commentary on The Book of Job*
(London: Thomas Nelson and Sons, 1967), pp. 283–84; Robert Gordis, *The Book of
God and Man: A Study of Job* (Chicago/London: University of Chicago Press, 1965),
pp. 223–24. For a survey of the history of exegesis of Job 19.25-27, see J. Speer, 'Zur
Exeges von Hiob 19.25-27', in *Zeitschrift für die alttestamentliche Wissenschaft* 25
(1905), pp. 47–140.

[82] Gordis, *The Book of Job*, p. 528.

[83] Gordis, *The Book of Job*, p. 204.

[84] See Gordis, *The Book of Job*, p. 144.

[85] *On Job* 13.15, 217–32 (p. 218).

[86] *On Job* 14.5-6, 1–10 (p. 224).

[87] *On Job* 14.6, 7, 57–61, 62–67 (p. 225).

Christian interpretation, digressing three times to bring in seven scriptural quotations, six from the New Testament. At this point, the teleology that Thomas has earlier adumbrated, that is, that the end of the human being is union with God, becomes an eschatology: the Redeemer is Christ and this end will come with the resurrection of the dead at the last day.[88] In his confession, Job speaks 'in the spirit of faith'.[89] What he affirms here coheres with and completes what he had argued for on the basis of the realities of human life and the implications of affirming that God is just.[90]

God's speech to Job and the narrative epilogue

When the debate has run its course, and Elihu has intervened, objecting to Job's friends, as well as Job, God then appears and speaks. Thomas interprets this as the recounting of a revelation given to Job. God acts here as the determiner, or judge, of a mediaeval disputation, since human wisdom is not sufficient to comprehend the truth of divine providence.[91] His speech accomplishes several things. First, he rebukes the friends of Job for the injustice of their charges against a righteous man. Second, he demonstrates to Job the paucity of his knowledge and power.[92] For Aquinas, the point of the long speeches about the wonders of creation is to show that Job fails to understand fully even God's effects in the realm of nature, let alone the nature of God Himself.[93] That something of God's reality may be inferred from his effects in creation is the foundation of Aquinas' theory of analogical language in theological discourse. This theory holds that while human language about God is not univocal, neither is it equivocal. Rather, because there is a relation between the Creator and his creatures, one can use human language to speak meaningfully about God, while that language is never adequate to its object. Aquinas never affirms this theory explicitly in the *Expositio*, but it is crucial to the *Summa contra Gentiles*, Book III, and it clearly underlies his interpretation of the divine speeches.[94] Thus, if Job cannot

---

[88] *On Job* 19.25-27, 245–337 (pp. 269–70).

[89] *On Job* 19.23, 259–60 (p. 269).

[90] Susan Schreiner says: 'Although the doctrine of immortality was, at one level, the subject of the debate between Job and his friends ... the perception of order was really at the heart of the controversy' (*Where Shall Wisdom be Found?*, p. 74). For Job of course, according to Thomas, it is only in light of immortality that such an order in history is plausible.

[91] *On Job* 38.1, 5–8 (p. 415).

[92] *On Job* 40.1, 6–16 (p. 443).

[93] *On Job* 38.1-2, 74–81 (p. 417).

[94] See Chardonnens, *L'Homme sous le regard de la providence*, pp. 237–51.

understand even the full reality of God's effects in creation, how can he hope to dispute with God? Now, Job, Thomas tells us, only wanted to dispute with God as a pupil, not an adversary. Nevertheless, while revelation may make the world more intelligible, and thus underline how we may properly call God just without resort to equivocation or sophistry, the true quality of his justice will always remain beyond our grasp.

The speech about Leviathan and Behemoth, Thomas tells us, is a figural representation of the power of the devil.[95] On a strictly literary level, this is less forced than one might think. Thomas notes that there are analogies explicitly mentioned in the text: the Behemoth is 'the beginning of God's ways' and Leviathan is 'king over all the sons of pride'. This suggests to him, not unreasonably, that these animals are meant to represent something.[96] In addition, Thomas points out, the whole book began with a heavenly accuser unleashed to afflict Job.[97] The literal depiction of the two great beasts of land and sea is intended to evoke awe in the woebegone Job, to convince him that he is in need of help against forces greater than himself, and to move him to take more care to temper his speech while faced with an enemy whose goal is to provoke blasphemy.[98] Third, God's speech leads Job to repentance. The text does not specify what he repents of, simply that he repents, and so this verse occasions a great deal of controversy among commentators. Thomas finds two elements. First, he repents of having spoken lightly, though not, according to Thomas, out of haughtiness or untruth[99] and so gave an occasion for scandal by calling God to a debate with him (13.3) and putting his justice first.[100] In other words, these smaller faults militate against the purpose of God, to manifest virtue in Job, and they cause scandal among his friends.[101]

---

[95] *On Job* 40.10, 221–24 (p. 448).

[96] *On Job* 40.10, 258–81 (pp. 448–49).

[97] *On Job* 40.10, 269–72 (p. 449).

[98] *On Job* 40.27, 655–64 (p. 457).

[99] On levity see *ST*, II–I, 122, 3; II–II, 68, 4; 73, 3. Aquinas' text translates 39.34 (MT, 40.4): *qui leviter locutus sum respondere quid possum* (What can I respond, who have spoken lightly?'). The RSV, following the MT (ën qallötî), translates the subordinate clause, 'Behold, I am of small account'. In the MT, Job makes a statement about his humble condition, while in the Vg. (both the Sixto-Clementine and the version Thomas used), Job confesses to a light manner of speaking. Nevertheless, in the following verse in all versions, Job rues his speech. Thomas is led to find precisely two types of regretted speech by the reference to having spoken twice, but this is probably a Hebrew parallelism of intensification, meaning several times. (See Gordis, *The Book of Job*, p. 466.)

[100] *On Job* 39.33-35, 343–61 (p. 441).

[101] *On Job* 38.1, 9–13 (p. 415).

Second, he repents, not of pride in action, but 'some inward proud thought', which God could see, even if his friends could not.[102]

In all of this, Thomas strikes a balance between his earlier affirmations of Job's justice and his moral imperfection. First, righteous Job is not held to be faultless. Even if he is not guilty of a grave sin, indeed is a model of virtue, he remains a man touched by sin. This is evident in his repentance in dust and ashes and his recognition of his need for God in the face of the threat of the adversary. Second, however, Thomas does not simply level all moral imperfection.[103] The righteous Job will go on to pray for his friends, and God will reward them because of his prayer. The friends had accused him unjustly. Human affairs are indeed ruled by a justice that human beings cannot fully comprehend, but that in the fullness of time will be manifest, and will be manifest as justice in a way that human beings can see and comprehend as such.

God restores Job's property and gives him children again, and Thomas takes pains to show that He does so wisely and in superabundance.[104] But doesn't that upset the whole eschatological scheme, and worse, doesn't it subvert the idea that reward and punishment don't appear in this life?[105] Thomas explains this in two ways. First, he cites Mt. 6.33, 'seek first the kingdom and all else will be added to you'. Second, he says that this is in keeping with the old covenant, 'in which temporal goods were promised so that in this way, through the prosperity which Job had recovered, an example might be given to others so that they might turn back to God'.[106] Without the divine rebuke of Job's friends, the situation might even lend itself to their interpretation, that God had punished Job, and now restores him because he had repented. So, for Aquinas, divine revelation is again crucial to interpreting human affairs properly.

---

[102] Yaffe maintains that Job, for Thomas, is 'perfectly wise, but not perfectly just'; 'Providence in Medieval Aristotelianism: Moses Maimonides and Thomas Aquinas on the Book of Job', *Hebrew Studies*, 20–21 (1979–80), pp. 62–74 (73–74). To posit full wisdom apart from full justice, however, is not in keeping with Thomas' correlation of theoretical and practical reason. Furthermore, Aquinas does not think Job was perfectly just, strictly speaking (*On Job* 6.1ff., 13–18 (pp. 137–38)). For an account of the complex connections between intellect, will and moral action in Aquinas, see Eleonore Stump, 'Aquinas' Account of Freedom: Intellect and Will', *The Monist*, 80 (1997), pp. 576–97.

[103] On the importance of this for Thomas, see *ScG*, III, 141–142.

[104] *On Job* 42.11-16, 119–205 (pp. 472–74).

[105] See Schreiner, *Where Shall Wisdom be Found?*, p. 90.

[106] *On Job* 42.101ff, 103–12 (p. 472)..

Assessing Thomas' interpretation

In assessing Aquinas' reading of Job, it is important first of all not to assume that there is some ground of assured modern scholarship on which one may stand in order to deliver a judgment. As Brevard Childs describes the contemporary state of discussion on Job: 'A review of the problems arising from the exegesis of the Book of Job confirms the impression that Old Testament scholarship has reached an impasse.'[107] Since no modern scholar seems to have won over the guild as a whole, or even a large part of it, even on the main issues, one cannot posit as a standard a 'modern interpretation' that results from progress in historical or philological studies since Aquinas' time.[108]

The ancient world, both Jewish and Christian, was not unaware of the difficulties of interpretation the book of Job posed.[109] Nonetheless, unlike some other of the Wisdom literature, such as Ecclesiastes, which was challenged as late as the Council at Jamnia, the canonical status of Job was never a matter of controversy.[110] Gordis explains this as the result of smoothing over the 'heretical' aspects of the book, since 'only the Job of the prose tale impinged upon the consciousness of ancient readers'.[111] In particular, Gordis claims that the later fortunes of Job depended upon finding in the book an affirmation, rather than a denial of the doctrine of the resurrection. This doctrine, Gordis claims, had gained the ascendancy by the late Second Temple period. In the early Second Temple era, when Gordis believes Job to have been written, the doctrine of resurrection had not yet penetrated Judaism.[112] Gordis, then, assumes that Job denied the resurrection and that later exegetes had to cover this heretical stance in order to save the book's canonicity.

Another way of viewing this process, however, would conclude that the ancient process of canonization involved, not a 'smoothing over' of 'heresies', but a theological reception and appropriation of Job, in which the text was harmonized with other texts within a larger theological synthesis – much like the process of theological exegesis that Thomas undertook as a *magister in sacra pagina*. In fact, the emphasis on Job's righteousness agrees with what we find

---

[107] See Brevard Childs, *Introduction to the Old Testament as Scripture* (Philadelphia: Fortress Press, 1979), p. 533; E. Dhorme, *A Commentary on The Book of Job* (London: Nelson, 1967), p. 533.

[108] Childs sketches the main disagreements on pp. 528–33.

[109] Childs, *Introduction to the Old Testament as Scripture*, p. 528.

[110] Gordis, *The Book of God and Man*, pp. 219–24.

[111] Gordis, *The Book of God and Man*, p. 222.

[112] Gordis, *The Book of God and Man*, pp. 217, 223–24.

in other canonical texts. The prose tale, which lauds Job's fear of God, seems to have 'impinged upon the consciousness' of the author or redactor of Ezek. 14.14, in which Job is ranged alongside Noah and Daniel as a model of righteousness. Jas 5.11 makes Job a model of patience in suffering as one awaits 'the coming of the Lord'. The Letter of James, like Aquinas, interprets Job's patience not only in light of a future resurrection, as the ancient Hebrew commentators did, but in light of the Christian expectation of the second coming of Christ. The reference to a resurrection, as Gordis acknowledges, is based on a reading of Job 19.25-27 that is rejected by modern exegetes, who assume that Job denies a doctrine of resurrection in Job 14.7ff. Thomas offers an alternative view of Job 14.7ff. that allows him to uphold the doctrine of the resurrection.

Thomas shares with other traditional exegetes a commitment to make sense of the text as a unified work. He avoids the 'atomization' of the text that Robert Alter deplores in historical-critical exegesis.[113] The atomization of the text arises in part from a shift in the locus of interest, away from the message the text bears within a tradition of faith and a shared way of life, and toward historical reconstruction of the circumstances and process of the text's production.[114] The results of this attempted reconstruction are particularly dubious in the case of the book of Job, about which so little consensus has emerged. Thomas' interpretation struggles with the text as it is, and employs a subtle anthropology and a profound metaphysics of God as the author, dispenser and end of all things,[115] in order to explain how the narrative prologue and epilogue and the speeches might be fitted into an overarching interpretation. It might seem that Aquinas falls into the other camp that Alter criticizes, those who pursue 'questions about the biblical view of man, the biblical notion of the soul, the biblical vision of eschatology', while neglecting character, motive and narrative design.[116] Thomas, however, gives close attention to these questions in the course of his exegesis. Furthermore, Alter recognizes that Job is 'philosophic' in character.[117]

Thomas, then, reads Job in a traditional manner. That is not the same thing as reading it in simply a conventional manner. If Thomas were bound by convention, his commentary would be much more in the shape of Gregory the Great's *Moralia*. Aquinas reads Job in a traditional manner, in that he reads from within a tradition,

---

[113] Robert Alter, *The Art of Biblical Narrative* (New York: Basic Books, 1981).

[114] Johnson, *The Future of Catholic Biblical Scholarship*, pp. 10–29.

[115] See Chardonnens, *L'Homme sous le regard de la providence*, pp. 53–117.

[116] Chardonnens, *L'Homme sous le regard de la providence*, p. 17.

[117] Chardonnens, *L'Homme sous le regard de la providence*, p. 33.

engaging in an ongoing, living appropriation of the text within a community in which the text functions canonically. In so doing he employs the philosophical tools and insights available to him, in order, from the text, to render life more intelligible. No one who appreciates Thomas' approach would deny that his exegesis might be surpassed by use of better historical and philological tools;[118] but his work itself is an ongoing reference point for Christian exegesis of the Hebrew Bible. The profound influence of the *Expositio super Iob ad litteram* testifies to the contribution Aquinas has made to ongoing theological engagement with this challenging text.

---

[118] Alter suggests a path between atomization and failure to recognize, not naïve, but artful and self-conscious redaction (pp. 19–20).

2

AQUINAS ON ISAIAH

Joseph Wawrykow

In this chapter, I examine the approach by Aquinas to the prophet Isaiah in two writings: the *Expositio super Isaiam ad litteram*, and, the *Summa Theologiae*.[1] The opening pages are given over to a review of the salient features of the *Expositio*; among other things I will point out, here drawing on the work of Torrell and Bouthillier and others, why the *Expositio* is of special value in recovering the spirituality and practical concerns of Aquinas. After some remarks about the *Summa* as a work of systematic theology, I will compare the *Expositio* and the *ST* in their respective presentations of common material from the book of Isaiah. Through this comparison, the significance of Isaiah for Aquinas should become the more apparent; the exercise will also underscore the varying purposes and ambitions of different writings in the Thomistic corpus.

---

[1] *Sancti Thomae de Aquino Opera Omnia* iussu Leonis XIII P.M. edita. Tomus XXVIII. *Expositio super Isaiam ad litteram*, cura et studio Fratrum Praedicatorum (Rome: Editori di San Tommaso, 1974). For the sake of convenience, in the following chapter, I will refer to this edition as the 'Leonine edition'. Part of the exposition of ch. 11, which will be discussed in the final part of this chapter, has been translated: see Thomas Aquinas, *The Gifts of the Spirit: Selected Spiritual Writings* (Hyde Park, NY: New City Press, 1995), pp. 87–91. The designation of this writing on Isaiah as an 'expositio' that is '*ad litteram*' shows the influence of Jacobino d'Asti; these words are found in the colophon to his copying in a clear hand of Aquinas' original. In his review of the Leonine edition, which is largely laudatory, Weisheipl has questioned the advisability of the title assigned by the Leonine editors, preferring 'postil' or 'gloss' for 'exposition'; 'Saint Thomas Aquinas: Opera Omnia XXVIII. *Expositio super Isaiam ad litteram*', *The Thomist*, 43 (1979), pp. 336–37. As will become clearer below in the text, the designation of the gloss as *ad litteram* (as if exclusively so) is not entirely accurate. For the *Summa*, I have employed the Ottawa edition, *S. Thomae de Aquino Ordinis Praedicatorum Summa Theologiae*, cura et studio Instituti Studiorum Medievalium Ottaviensis, in five volumes (Ottawa: Garden City Press, 1941), and consulted the English translation of the English Dominicans: *Summa Theologica*. Complete English Edition in Five Volumes, translated by Fathers of the English Dominican Province (Westminster, MD: Christian Classics, 1981).

Scholars have been uncertain about the precise dating and circumstances of the *Expositio*.[2] Earlier scholars had speculated that it is a magisterial work, the fruit of Thomas' labours as a regent master of theology, responsible for lecturing on Scripture.[3] In this view, the *Expositio* would have emerged from his classroom lectures, whether in his first (1256–59) or second (1268–72) Parisian regency. However, more recently a consensus has formed that the *Expositio* is to be dated to Aquinas' student days. The training of the bachelor in theology was designed to prepare him for his magisterial duties, of lecturing (on Scripture), disputing (on important theological topics) and preaching. Hence, as a bachelor, the budding theologian would offer his own set of lectures on a book of the Bible, to become versed in, and so prepare for, this aspect of his future responsibilities. There is, however, a difference between the biblical lectures of the bachelor, and of the master. The latter were to be detailed exposition of the biblical text, not only drawing out the meaning of the text but also engaging the various problems and questions that emerge from that text, as identified by the mediating exegetical and scholarly traditions. The lectures of the bachelor, on the other hand, are commonly deemed 'cursory'. They more typically 'run over' quickly the biblical text, noting its principles of organization and pausing only to gloss obscure or especially significant terms. The goal of the bachelor is not to plumb to its full extent the riches of the biblical text, or to relate a given text to others that address cognate issues, but to offer his hearers (other bachelors, for example) a greater familiarity with the text. While this commentary on Isaiah is to be dated to his student days, it is not, however, entirely 'cursory'. It is quite lengthy, covering some 256 pages in the Leonine edition. And, while Thomas can move briskly at times, especially as the commentary gets into the later chapters, the commentary on the first eleven chapters of Isaiah is exceptionally detailed. Here at least the exegesis can be subtle and rich and well developed, more typical of the magisterial exposition.

While there is now a consensus that the *Expositio* is an early work – indeed, it has been designated the first of Aquinas' major

[2] For the most thorough orientation to the *Expositio*, see the Preface of the Leonine edition, pp. 3*ff. More succinct is J-P. Torrell, *Saint Thomas Aquinas*; vol. 1, *The Person and His Work* (Washington, DC: Catholic University of America Press, 1996), pp. 27–35. For a good overview of the commentary, which places it in the history of interpretation, see B.S. Childs, *The Struggle to Understand Isaiah as Christian Scripture* (Grand Rapids, MI: Eerdmans, 2004), ch. 11.

[3] By the turn of the thirteenth century, the tasks of the scholastic theologian could be summarized in terms of *lectio, disputatio, praedicatio*. At the University of Paris in the Theology faculty, lecturing was exclusively on Scripture. For a more complete account, see Torrell, *Saint Thomas Aquinas*, ch. 4.

theological writings[4] – there is still some disagreement about dating and locale of composition. The Leonine editors had dated it to 1252–56, when Thomas was in Paris doing his advanced work as a bachelor of theology.[5] In his review of the Leonine edition,[6] Weisheipl has argued for an earlier dating, putting the commentary prior to the summer of 1252, while Thomas was still studying in Cologne under the direction of Albert the Great. When he was sent by his Order to Paris, it was to lecture on the *Sentences* of Peter Lombard – another important part of the training of the novice scholastic – not to serve as a biblical bachelor. Arguably, he would have already lectured on Scripture – on Isaiah, as well as cursorily on Lamentations and Jeremiah – in Cologne, and so already have received that part of his training. Weisheipl's earlier dating has received considerable affirmation, including from Torrell.[7]

Expositio super Isaiam ad litteram

Prooemium

Although it was incumbent on bachelor and master alike to lecture on Scripture, in both cases the choice of the particular biblical book on which to lecture was a matter of personal discretion. That the young Aquinas chose Isaiah tells us much – about his courage and ambition, in tackling a text comprised of sixty-six chapters; and about his sense of the intrinsic importance of Isaiah, a work heavily quoted in the New Testament[8] and which for Aquinas describes well the crucial elements of the faith. Thomas' *Prooemium* to the *Expositio* is worthy of our notice, for it sets the tone for the lectures that follow. In this introduction, Aquinas covers three principal topics: the author of the work, the mode of proceeding and the material included in Isaiah.[9] The author of the work, as of all of scripture, is the Holy Spirit, who works through human

[4] See the Preface to the Leonine edition, p. 20*.

[5] See the Preface to the Leonine edition, p. 20*.

[6] Weisheipl, 'Saint Thomas Aquinas', p. 336.

[7] Torrell, *Saint Thomas Aquinas*, p. 28.

[8] See Childs, *The Struggle to Understand Isaiah*, in the chapter on 'The Early Reception of the Hebrew Bible', p. 5.

[9] On medieval prologues to scriptural *auctores*, see A.J. Minnis, *Medieval Theory of Authorship* (Philadelphia: University of Pennsylvania Press, 1988), ch. 2. It was customary to organize the prologue to a scriptural commentary by the use of a saying or passage from Scripture. In the case of Aquinas' *Expositio* of Isaiah, a passage from Habakkuk 2 serves that role, providing the structure to the review of the author, mode, and matter of this book of the Bible. Isaiah 6.1, which will be discussed later in this chapter, will play that role in the prologue to Thomas' later commentary on the Gospel of John.

authors as through an instrument (*organum*). While the dignity and importance of the teaching is established by its divine authorship, the role of the human author is not inconsiderable. It pertains to the office of the minister of the Spirit to receive the vision of saving truth, and to pass this truth on to those who will encounter this writing.

In the next part of the *Prooemium*, Aquinas reflects more closely on the work of Isaiah, the human author, in conveying saving truth. As he will discuss in greater detail in the first lecture on chapter 1, it belongs to the prophet to speak of distant things, which have been revealed to him by God. Such things seen from afar have to do with God as the end of human beings and the way to that end, and the need to pursue that end and avoid what takes the human journeyer away from God and the attainment of God. This is the case in Isaiah as well. But, as Aquinas puts it in the *Prooemium*, the visions received by Isaiah by divine agency are so clearly described by him – and in terms appropriate to humans who know by the senses and so appreciate truth put in material terms – and so plainly explained by the prophet that the words of Isaiah seem to be more about what has happened than a foretelling about the future (here, Thomas is echoing the judgment of Jerome). Indeed, in his clarity of expression and explanation, this prophet excels the others, to the point, in fact, that this work seems 'more gospel than prophecy' (again echoing a judgment of Jerome). Isaiah, then, is an eminently useful work, well suited to accomplishing the goals that God has in revealing through Isaiah.

In discussing in detail the utility of this teaching (in concluding the analysis of the mode of proceeding in Isaiah), Aquinas refers to three ends (*finis*) found in human existence. Operative here is Aquinas' sense that life is a journey. The end of this journey comes only in the next life, when the successful journeyer enters into the presence of God and comes to share, by divine gift, in the life that is proper to God. The way to this end is in the present life. To come to God as end, one must believe and love correctly; the journey is a journey of the affections, and only those whose affections are correctly formed will attain to God as end. Also operative here is Thomas' sense of the history of the race, seen in terms of God's plan for salvation. While in other writings the enumeration of the stages of human history can be more elaborate, in the *Prooemium* Aquinas is content to speak of people under the Law, after the Law, and in the immediate presence of God (in the next life).[10] Thus, to return to the language of a

---

[10] A more thorough rendering of human history in soteriological terms would include the state prior to the giving of the Law.

threefold end (*finis triplex*) of humans: the three ends are that of the Law, of precept, and of life. To be more precise, Christ is the end of the Law. The Law was given to prepare people for the Christ who would save; and as Romans 10 states, believing in the Christ who brings the Law to its term puts the individual into correct relationship – one of justice or righteousness – with God. The end of the precept, in turn, is charity, as 1 Timothy 1 states. And so to move to God as end through Christ (the Christ foretold and described in Isaiah as part of the revelation of saving truth), one's faith must be shaped and informed by charity. The end of life is death; and so, as Matthew 21 says, the one who perseveres in formed faith until the end of earthly existence, by remaining faithful to God in Christ, will attain to eternal life, that is, enter into the presence of God.

In the final part of his *Prooemium*, Aquinas reinforces this assessment of the exalted status of Isaiah, by identifying in striking fashion the matter of this book. It has as its principal subject matter the '*apparitio filii Dei*', the manifestation or appearance of the Son of God. This *apparitio* is itself threefold; and again, in explicating the threefold apparition with which Isaiah is concerned, Aquinas is working from a notion of life as journey, set in the larger context of God's saving plan. The first manifestation is the incarnation, when the fully divine second person of God, without loss to himself, took up human nature and came to express that nature as well. Through this act, the kindness and love of God our Saviour towards people have been manifested (Titus 3). The second is the proclamation of the truth manifested in Christ, in the Christian faith that is to be believed by the world, which makes patent to all humans the grace of the saviour who teaches us (Titus 2). And the third has to do with the end of human existence in the next life, when those who have successfully journeyed in this life will come into God's presence, and will see God as he is, and be made like to God in Christ (1 John 3), that is, when those who have been joined to Christ in this life by faith and charity will enter, by adoption, into the inheritance that naturally belongs to the second divine person.

In line with the reading of Isaiah found in the New Testament, there can be a profound Christic cast to Isaiah, although there is nonetheless some distance between Isaiah and the New Testament (and Thomas). In Isaiah, this is a presentation of saving truth in the form of prophecy, of what lies in the distance, of what is to come in terms of fulfilment and at the end of time; in the New Testament and in Aquinas, Isaiah has found its fulfilment in the Christ event, in the Christ who has come and who fulfils the prophecies and who completes the revelation of God and of humans in relation to

God.[11] At any rate, it is because of Isaiah's attention to the threefold *apparitio*, Thomas adds, that the Church employs this prophet liturgically during Advent.[12]

Lectures on the Text of Isaiah

In the ensuing lectures on Isaiah, there is much that will be familiar to students of Thomas' exegesis.[13] In the first place, Aquinas displays a great concern for organization, for how Isaiah has structured this work. As he states in the second lecture on chapter 1, Isaiah would seem to be divided into two principal parts, the first running through chapter 39, and the second covering chapters 40–66; we have here, in other words, a mediaeval anticipation of the modern positing of a first and deutero-Isaiah. The second main part of Isaiah is especially concerned with the divine consolation of the just, by the promise of the resurrection and the final and decisive vindication of those who are faithful to God. The first main part (chapters 1–39) is more concerned with sin, with the identification of ways in which the people have fallen from correct order to God, and with the threat of divine punishment for sin. As he proceeds through the chapters of both main parts, Aquinas will similarly be concerned to limn the structure of Isaiah, the sub-grouping of chapters, in finer detail. The assumption here is that, as stressed in the *Prooemium*, Isaiah is indeed a skilled writer, who knows how to present the material provided him by the divine author in the most effective and efficient way.

In his glossing of individual verses or words in the text of Isaiah, Aquinas is principally concerned with the meaning and intent of the words, the literal sense; the title ascribed to this exposition by the Leonine editors, *ad litteram*, is in this sense warranted. Thus, he knows the words of Isaiah to be addressed to Israel, making clear, theologically, what is happening to the people at different points in its history, and offering encouragement or threat, as circumstances warrant, to his contemporaries. There is, at the same time, a

---

[11] In the text, I am extending to Thomas, and his reading of Isaiah, what Childs, 'The Early Reception of the Hebrew Bible', p. 6, says of the reception of Isaiah in the New Testament.

[12] Thomas repeats the point in one of his inaugural lectures, given on the occasion of his elevation to a chair in Theology. The text is translated in Ralph McInerny, *Thomas Aquinas: Selected Writings* (London: Penguin, 1998); for the observation of the Church's liturgical use of Isaiah at Advent, see p. 10.

[13] For a succinct introduction to Thomas' exegetical work, see T. Prügl, 'Thomas Aquinas as Interpreter of Scripture', in R. Van Nieuwenhove and J. Wawrykow (eds.), *The Theology of Thomas Aquinas* (Notre Dame: University of Notre Dame Press, 2005), pp. 386–415.

Christological dimension to Isaiah, as is already clear from the *Prooemium*, and Aquinas will endeavour to show how specific passages are about the Christ who was to come. Here, the prophetic sense – Isaiah foretelling what will be fulfilled in Jesus – is the literal sense. Thus, to take the obvious example, in his lecture on Isaiah 7.14, Aquinas insists, with the New Testament and the tradition, that this is about Jesus and his birth of a Virgin. He knows that there are counter-interpretations, that would make the verse about someone else (closer in time and circumstance to Isaiah himself), and knows that the word 'virgin' is itself open to challenge. But, such counter-interpretations are not convincing; more is at stake here than, say, the son of the prophet, as the context of 7.14 itself makes evident. It can only be about the Christ who brings salvation to the world, who alone fulfils the prophetic promise. Yet, at the same time, Aquinas is careful not to impose a Christological interpretation on every passage in Isaiah; he is practising exegesis, not eisegesis. Here a noteworthy example comes in the course of the lecture on 8.4. Again, as in 7.14 it is a matter of a 'sign' that has to do with a boy. But, despite the efforts of 'some' to read this Christologically, Aquinas insists that in this case, the boy in question is the child of the prophet. Hence, he concludes, the verse is not literally (*ad litteram*) about Jesus, although what is said of this boy as sign can be taken as a *figura* of the Christ who was to come. As the Leonine editors observe,[14] Aquinas' moderation could be disconcerting, and the fourteenth-century Nicholas of Lyra on the basis of this reading of 8.4 wondered whether the exposition was in fact by Thomas Aquinas.

In explicating Isaiah *ad litteram*, Thomas makes considerable use of other Scripture; Scripture is read in light of, and clarified by, Scripture. Extra-scriptural authorities, on the other hand, play little role, at least explicitly. There are only a handful of references to Aristotle, and explicit mention of such important Christian authors as Augustine, Pseudo-Dionysius and Bernard is kept to a minimum. And, as the Leonine editors make clear,[15] Thomas would seem not to be using such authorities at first hand. Rather, he was heavily dependent on two sources in working up these bachelor lectures: the *Glossa ordinaria*, and, the postils on Isaiah of his fellow Dominican, Hugh of Saint-Cher. This holds even for the Jerome that is occasionally cited in the course of a lecture; the echoes of Jerome noted above in dealing with the *Prooemium* should thus not mislead.

[14] Leonine edition, p. 3*.
[15] Leonine edition, p. 52*.

The Collations

The bulk of the *Expositio* is given over to literal commentary. Yet, the work also contains more spiritual matter, important for the discernment of the spirituality of Thomas Aquinas. There is extant an autograph of part of the commentary, running from chapter 34 to the beginning of chapter 50. In the margins of the autograph are some jottings in Aquinas' own hand; these are called '*collationes*' by Jacobino d'Asti, who in the late thirteenth century prepared a legible copy of the entire work. Each *collatio* is made up of a number of members (three, four, or more), each member being a phrase or sentence by Thomas followed by an apt biblical citation. A word or phrase in the text of Isaiah has elicited each collation; the word or phrase evokes for Thomas a series of associations, which have to do with the spiritual import and application of the word or phrase from Isaiah. In the biblical citations of the collation, the same word will appear; thus, what we meet in the collations is word association in the service of spirituality, by which Aquinas moves from the letter to the spiritual, as occasioned by the text of Isaiah. In preparing a clear copy of the *Expositio*, Jacobino moved these *collationes* into the body of the text. He numbered each member in a collation (first, second, third, etc) and introduced each grouping by a set formula: *nota* or *notandum* 'upon this word of Isaiah ...'. Thus, they are readily apparent to readers of the commentary, once their existence and function are highlighted. In the portion of the commentary that exists in autograph, there are twenty-four collations; in the *Expositio* as a whole, there is a total of one hundred and twenty-seven.

The *collationes* have received a fair amount of scholarly attention, and it is not too much to say that they are the most carefully studied portion of the *Expositio*. An article by Gils set the tone for subsequent work:[16] Gils identified the marginal writing as that of Aquinas, noted the importance of these 'assemblies' of sayings for the study of the spirituality of Aquinas, and insisted that the *collationes* were an integral part of the *Expositio*. The Leonine editors made good use of Gils' findings in their own Preface, endorsing his principal claims.[17] More recently, Torrell and Bouthillier have been instrumental in showing the value of these *collationes* for our knowledge of the spirituality of Thomas Aquinas.

---

[16] P.-M. Gils, 'Les *Collationes* marginales dans l'autographe du commentaire de S. Thomas sur Isaie', *Revue des Sciences Philosophiques et Théologiques* 42 (1958), 253–64.

[17] Leonine Edition, pp. 16*ff.

As Torrell puts it,[18] every important theme in Christian spirituality figures in these *collationes* – God as beginning and end of human existence; the life and activity of the triune God as model and goal of human activity; the road to God through Christ and his work, and discipleship to Christ; the value of prayer and proper affection for growing through Christ into God. Thus, in an article that they jointly authored, Torrell and Bouthillier review the twenty-four *collationes* found in the autograph portion of the *Expositio*, providing illuminating commentary on each of these by reference to pertinent passages in other works by Aquinas. In subsequent articles, Bouthillier has focused on the Christology of the *collationes*. Thus, in 'Le Christ en son mystère dans les collationes du *super Isaiam* de saint Thomas d'Aquin',[19] she identifies the twenty-seven collations (taken from the entire commentary) that have to do principally with Christ, and then focuses on one in which Christological titles are at the fore, in the process making clear the Christocentricity of the spirituality of Thomas Aquinas. In '*Splendor gloriae Patris*: Deux collations du *Super Isaiam*',[20] she focuses on the teaching of the *collationes* on the relations between the first and second divine persons, as the basis of Christ's work in the world; as with the Fathers, in Aquinas, trinitarian discourse goes hand-in-hand with Christology.

The collations are indeed significant, suggesting how for Aquinas spiritual practice is rooted in doctrine, and how doctrine must needs issue in correct practice. Two examples, both taken from the lecture on chapter 61, will help to show what is involved in these spiritual associations, as well as to confirm what has been said of Aquinas' spirituality. At the beginning of the chapter, the prophet states that the spirit of the Lord has been given to him, for Yahweh has anointed (*unxerit*) him. In his literal comment on the verse, Aquinas acknowledges that this can be taken as about Christ, on the basis of the resemblance in verbal formulation between this verse and that in chapter 11 (which for Thomas is to be read Christologically), about the spirit of the Lord being upon 'him'.[21] However, in the literal comment the first interpretation that Aquinas offers takes the saying

---

[18] See his article (in collaboration with D. Bouthillier), 'Quand saint Thomas méditait sur le prophète Isaie', reprinted in his *Recherches Thomasiennes* (Paris: J. Vrin, 2000), p. 246.

[19] In *Ordo Sapientiae et Amoris: Image et Message de Saint Thomas d'Aquin*, ed. Carlos-Josaphat Pinto de Oliveira (Fribourg: Éditions Universitaires, 1993), pp. 37–64.

[20] In *Christ Among the Medieval Dominicans* (eds.) K. Emery, Jr and J. Wawrykow, (Notre Dame: University of Notre Dame Press, 1998), pp. 139–56.

[21] Below I will discuss the approach to chap. 11 in the *Expositio* and in the *ST*.

as about the prophet himself: the prophet has been called by God to this work, designated through this anointing for this work.

In the two collations on this verse that are offered in quick succession, the focus by contrast is kept resolutely and exclusively on Christ. The first collation discusses Christ as anointed by the Father; the second turns to how devout servants of Christ can themselves be said to be anointed by Christ. Thus, in the first collation as occasioned by the word in Isaiah, 'he anointed me', we should note that God the Father anoints Christ with the oil of priestly dignity, just as a priest is anointed so that he might offer sacrifice; with the oil of kingly power, just as a king is anointed to rule; with the oil of great fortitude, just as a fighter who is to do combat; and, with the oil of great joy, as is the case of those who are free and generous in their compassion. In each case the association of a specific member in the collation with the occasioning text of Isaiah is confirmed by a biblical saying that employs the word 'anointed'; in this particular set, Aquinas cites in turn Ecclesiasticus 45, 2 Samuel 12 and then chapter 1, finally a combination of two Psalms. In the immediately adjacent collation, Aquinas notes the ways that Christ in turn anoints his devout servant: with tears of compunction (see Mt. 6); with the anointing of devotion (Lk. 7); with the oil of pure intention (Ecclus 9); and with the oil of praise and thanksgiving (Gen. 28). It is not exactly clear how Aquinas put together these collations in the precise form that they here take. It may be that he employed a concordance to provide biblical texts that secure the associations of the members of the collation to each other and to the occasioning text.[22] But Aquinas was famous for his prodigious memory, for his ability to recall pertinent passages as he went about the composition of his works;[23] and so here the text of Isaiah may be calling to his mind relevant texts that he has absorbed through his personal reading and that can appropriately be strung together for spiritual use.

To a modern reader, a collation can be quite taxing. The associations may in fact seem forced, with specific confirming biblical texts seemingly ripped out of context; and, to come at the matter from another angle, the collation is the more readily accessible the more complete one's biblical learning. As presented in the *Expositio*, a collation does take considerable work on the part of the reader, in order to derive the full benefit. The presentation is

---

[22] On the high mediaeval development of scholarly tools to facilitate the speedy locating of specific texts, see M.A. Rouse and R.H. Rouse, *Authentic Witnesses: Approaches to Medieval Texts and Manuscripts* (Notre Dame: University of Notre Dame Press, 1991), chs 6–7.

[23] See M. Carruthers, *The Book of Memory* (New York: Cambridge University Press, 1990).

more or less in point form, and the reader, lacking Aquinas' oral performance, will have to fill in the gaps to grasp the logic of the collation. Yet, as is likely apparent from the two examples here given, there is a logic to grasp, and the collations conform nicely to Aquinas' principal insights about the Christian faith and its possibilities, as expressed more plainly elsewhere. In the talk of the Father anointing Christ, the collation is underscoring the importance of Christ's humanity, through which the Word works human salvation. It is precisely as human that the Word incarnate does the Father's work, and makes possible the attainment of salvation, of realizing the end set for people by God. Christ does this not only as prophet, but as priest and king, and in the other ways mentioned in this collation. And, as the second collation suggests, those who will reach God will do so through Christ, by adopting the correct attitude towards God in Christ as limned in the members of this collation.

The Summa Theologiae

A Work of Systematic Theology

The other work to be considered in this chapter, the *Summa Theologiae*, is a rather different sort of writing, and it is highly unlikely that anyone would ever confuse the *ST* with the *Expositio*. For one thing, there is no equivalent in the *ST* of the *collationes* that mark the *Expositio*. In his master work, on which he worked towards the end of his career (1266–73), he does not engage in word associations in an effort to plumb the spiritual dimensions of any given text that might be employed in the *ST*. Rather, he leaves that to his exegesis[24] and to his express homilies, of which the Lenten conferences on the Creed, which he delivered in Naples near the end of his life, provide numerous examples.[25] Nor is Aquinas tied to a given or single text in the *ST*. The *Expositio* is, as should be obvious, thoroughly dependent on the text of Isaiah, which throughout occasions the literal exegesis as well as the spiritual forays that are the collations. The text of Isaiah accounts for the order in which Aquinas proceeds in the *Expositio*; the *Expositio* is Thomas' engagement with that particular writing. The *ST*, on the other hand, is not an exegetical piece, at least not in that sense.

Rather, the *ST* is a work in systematic theology, and in

---

[24] In addition to Isaiah, there are collations in his cursory commentary on Jeremiah.

[25] See *The Sermon-Conferences of St. Thomas Aquinas on the Apostles' Creed*, translated from the Leonine Edition, edited and introduced by N. Ayo (Notre Dame: University of Notre Dame Press, 1988).

constructing this work Aquinas has observed other criteria. Here, the brief Prologue to the entire *Summa*, as well as the very first question of the *Summa*, on sacred doctrine (*ST*, I, 1), must be given their due. In the Prologue, Aquinas states that he has composed this work for the benefit of newcomers, to facilitate their grasp of, and reflection on, the truths of the Christian religion.[26] He expresses dissatisfaction with what is currently available for this purpose; such works can be repetitive or confusing, and so counter-productive. Hence, in the *Summa* Aquinas proposes to present the truths of the faith according to the order of the discipline (*ordo disciplinae*), that is, in a manner that will, in a streamlined and effective fashion, make more manifest the deeper structures of the faith and the connections between different parts of Christian revelation.

The point is pursued in the *Summa*'s first question, about sacred doctrine. Doctrine or teaching is here taken in a double sense: what is taught, and the act of teaching. With regard to the former, sacred doctrine has to do with saving truth. Sacred doctrine is the body of truths necessary for salvation. With regard to the latter, the focus is kept resolutely on God. God is the principal teacher of this doctrine; it is God who reveals the truths necessary for salvation. In the question's first article, Aquinas addresses the necessity of this teaching. He observes that there are two kinds of truth in sacred doctrine. Both are revealed. One sort can in principle be demonstrated by reason; such truths as the existence of God are elsewhere designated by Aquinas 'preambles of faith'. While they are accessible to rational demonstration, it was still prudent for God to have revealed them as part of sacred doctrine, for such truths are attained only after a long time and with considerable effort, and even then with an admixture of error. The other kind of truth that falls under sacred doctrine is revealed by God, and cannot be argued to by reason; such truths, designated by Thomas the 'articles of faith', must be held by faith. But, although they cannot be demonstrated, as revealed by God and held by faith they can be reflected on, and their meaning pursued, and the connection among the articles more fully displayed through argument. They can also be defended from attack, for although they are above reason, they are not counter to reason, and so any argument that suggests that they are can be refuted (*ST*, I, 1, 8).

In introducing the articles of faith in *ST*, I, 1,1, Aquinas gives the

---

[26] There has been considerable dispute about the identity of the *incipientes*. I tend to think that this refers to those who are at an early stage of their theological training. See, however, the intriguing suggestion in L. Boyle, 'The Setting of the *Summa Theologiae* of St. Thomas', Etienne Gilson Lecture (Toronto: Pontifical Institute of Mediaeval Studies, 1982), that Aquinas' target audience is comprised of fellow Dominicans who are charged with pastoral responsibilities.

example of the transcendent end of human beings, which is God. God in love has freely established God as the end of human existence, and only in God will one find fulfilment. Apart from revelation, one would have no inkling of this transcendent end, nor for that matter, one might add, of the way to that end (through Christ). Not incidentally, Aquinas secures his point in the first article about the need for sacred doctrine when it comes to the articles of faith by quoting a verse from Isaiah (64.4: 'The eye hath not seen, O God, besides Thee, what things Thou has prepared for them that wait for Thee'), a verse that, as Thomas' first readers likely would have recognized, is quoted by Paul in 1 Corinthians (2.9) in conjunction with his discussion of Christ as crucified wisdom.[27]

Throughout the *Summa*'s first question Aquinas insists on that which provides the principal subject matter, and unity, of this doctrine (and by extension, the subject matter and unity of the theology that pertains to sacred doctrine; I, 1 ad 2). Sacred doctrine does not cover all truth or every kind of truth; nor is it about 'God and creatures', as if each member of that pairing were of equal status. Rather, sacred doctrine is principally about God, and only secondarily about creatures (I, 1, 3 ad 1; 7); it treats of creatures as they stand in relation to God as to their beginning or source and as to their end. Otherwise put, sacred doctrine and its theology will be shaped by a view of reality that has the motif of *exitus* and *reditus* at its heart – an account of the God who 'goes out' in bringing things into being and establishing God as the end of rational creatures; an account of rational creatures who having proceeded from their Creator return to their Source through their correct affection and behaviour, as made possible by God in Christ.

In constructing his theology according to the *ordo disciplinae* (Prologue), Aquinas will strive to observe this *exitus* and *reditus*, with the aim of showing the logic of God and of God's dealings, as Creator and Saviour, with created reality, and of the action of rational creatures in response to God, through Christ. Hence, in the *Summa*'s First Part, Aquinas looks at God *in se*, as Creator, and as the one who governs all things providentially. In the Second and the Third Parts of the *ST*, the focus shifts to the movement of the rational creature to God as end. The Second Part is itself divided into two parts. In the First Part of the Second Part, he reviews the end of human existence (in God, as freely established by God);

---

[27] The discussion of the articles of faith is resumed in detail at *ST*, II–II, 1, in terms of the object of faith. The principal division of the articles, summarized in the creed, is that half have to do with the divinity, the other half with the humanity of Christ, through which God works human salvation.

human acts and passions; and then the principles of human acts, both intrinsic (i.e., the habits, both good [virtues] and bad [vices]), and extrinsic. God is the extrinsic principle of human acts, instructing by law (in its various senses) and moving by grace. In the Second Part of the Second Part, Aquinas turns, in his account of the movement of the rational creature to God as end, to the specific – to the specific virtues, theological and cardinal, and their adjacent gifts (and opposing vices) that are involved in the successful journey to God. And, finally, in the Third Part, he completes the account of the movement to God as end, by displaying in great detail the Christological dimension of this movement to God. It is Christ, inasmuch as he is human, who is the way to God as end; one moves by the virtues and correct action through Christ to God.[28]

Although the focus in the *Summa*'s first question is kept on God as teacher, on the God who reveals the truths necessary for salvation, Aquinas does offer some comments about how humans can enter into the teaching process that is sacred doctrine. Crucial in this regard is I, 1, 8 ad 2, which identifies three levels of human contribution to sacred doctrine, and indicates the kind of authority enjoyed by those at each level. At the apex stand the human authors of Scripture. It is to them that saving truth has been revealed, and accordingly their authority is certain and intrinsic. It is intrinsic, proper, to sacred doctrine, because they pass on the truths needed for salvation that stand at the heart of sacred doctrine. It is certain because they share in the authority of God, who has revealed to them these truths. As Aquinas observes in the next article (9 ad 2), God has revealed the truths needed for salvation in such a way that the human authors of Scripture cannot be mistaken. In I, 1, 8 ad 2, Aquinas also mentions the Doctors of the Church, people such as Augustine and Cyril of Alexandria. Their authority too is intrinsic to sacred doctrine; in their activity, they have been preoccupied with the word of God, endeavouring to interpret it correctly and to pass on this truth to those in their care. Such have been recognized as faithful and worthy interpreters of Scripture. But their authority is less than that of the human authors of Scripture. No revelation has been made to them, and they can in fact make mistakes of interpretation. Hence, while intrinsic, their authority in sacred doctrine (and by extension, in the theology that pertains to sacred doctrine) is only probable. Finally, Thomas mentions philosophy; the philosophers too can have an authority in sacred doctrine.

---

[28] For a basic outline of the *ST*, see J. Weisheipl, *Friar Thomas d'Aquino* (Washington, DC: Catholic University of America Press, 1983), pp. 220–21; for the outline in somewhat greater detail, see the Author's Preface to my *Westminster Handbook to Thomas Aquinas* (Louisville: Westminster John Knox Press, 2005).

Theirs will, of course, be only probable; no revelation is made to them, and they can make mistakes (as the question's first article has reminded us). And their authority, when it comes to sacred doctrine, will only be extrinsic. The philosophers are not concerned with sacred doctrine, or with passing on God's saving truth; they have other interests. But, what they have written can be put to Christian use. In other words, they can be brought into the project of sacred doctrine, by those who are concerned with the faithful and fruitful interpretation of God's word, and who will thus use every resource at their disposal, including philosophy, to discharge their duties.

We need to keep in mind all of this – the construction of the work according to the *ordo disciplinae*; God, and creatures in relation to God as to their beginning and end, as the subject matter of this teaching; the usefulness of different sorts of authorities in the theological pursuit of an understanding of what God has revealed – when we ask about the place of Isaiah in Thomas' *Summa*. When it comes to the presentation of the truths of sacred doctrine, Isaiah enjoys the highest authority; God has revealed saving truth to Isaiah and has done so in such a way that Isaiah could not be mistaken. Thus, in his theology, Aquinas will call upon Isaiah in his own presentation of saving truth, confident of the value, and certainty, of Isaiah's teaching. Yet, Isaiah shares this status with others, with the other authors of Scripture, to whom revelation of saving truth has also been made. Hence, in the *ST* the use of Isaiah will not be exclusive; in presenting in his own theology God's saving truth and investigating its meaning and how the different articles of faith cohere, Aquinas will draw on the full range of Scripture, not simply Isaiah, and will complement what he finds in Isaiah with what he finds proclaimed elsewhere in Scripture. When it comes to God's revelation, other books of the Bible are of equal stature.

And in teaching the faith in the *ST*, Aquinas will not be constrained to follow the biblical ordering. Scripture is, of course, essential to the Thomistic theological project; it is in Scripture that God has revealed the truths necessary for salvation, the truths that require the full and sustained attention of the theologian. But, in constructing this theological writing, the requirements of the discipline, not replicating in form or style or ordering any book of the Bible, are to the fore. Thomas the systematician will have in this connection a keen sense of the structure of the faith, of where discrete areas of theological discourse should go, in order to re-present the scriptural revelation in a more disciplined and method-ical and illuminating way; hence, the structure of the *ST* in its different Parts, with their proper theological topics, as outlined above. What this means is that the truths proclaimed in Isaiah will be redistributed by Thomas across the whole breadth of the *ST*.

What is found in a given chapter in the book of Isaiah, and which would thus have received close attention in the corresponding lecture in the *Expositio*, will be strewn across different questions and different Parts of the *ST*, according to the logic of the discipline. It will be the same set of truths that will be presented, but now in a more discursive, methodical way.

Actually, there is more. Each Part of the *ST* is made up of questions. Questions can be grouped together according to important themes; hence, readers of the *Summa* will speak of 'treatises', made up of related questions. Each question, in turn, is composed of articles, which look at specific aspects of the topic covered by the question. The scholastic article is a complex division, showing the value of dialectic and rooted, remotely at least, in the disputes in which scholastics routinely engaged. In an article, there are four parts, each with their distinctive function. The article opens with objections, arguments that seek to complicate the position that eventually will be staked out by the scholastic on the aspect of the theological topic covered by the article. Next comes the *sed contra*, which indicates a certain plausibility, after the counter-indications of the objections, of the position that the scholastic will soon advance on the point at issue. Next comes the corpus of the article, and finally the responses to the opening objections. In the corpus, Aquinas will state his own position on the matter raised in the article. In the responses to the objections, he will continue to present his own position, but now with an eye to the considerations raised by the objections. The opening objections are not trivial, as if they consisted simply of straw-arguments that can easily be disposed. Rather, they bring to the table ideas that are important; they do not settle the issue, but Thomas will need to account for them, and show what is true in them, and so to be brought into accord with the position outlined in the corpus of the article.

An article is not a transcript of an actual debate, as if reporting what some have said (against what Thomas will hold) and then what Thomas himself holds. Thomas is the author of the entire article in each of its parts, and he includes each part of the article in order the more effectively to present his teaching. Quotation and paraphrase of authoritative sources will be found in each part of the scholastic article; and so the uses of any authoritative text, including the book of Isaiah, will be many and varied, corresponding to the different points in the article in which the authoritative source appears. Isaiah can be quoted to show the plausibility of what Thomas himself holds (*sed contra*), or to indicate the starting point and context of Aquinas' ruminations on the matter at hand (as in the corpus, or response to objections); Isaiah can also be used to complicate matters, as when cited in the objections with which the article begins.[29]

Isaiah 6

The distinctiveness in approach will be more readily grasped by reviewing the ways in which the *Expositio* and the *ST* deal with specific passages in the book of Isaiah: chapter 6 and chapter 11. In chapter 6, Isaiah recounts his vision of the Lord sitting upon a throne, attended by Seraphim, who ceaselessly proclaim God's praise ('Holy, Holy, Holy ...'). After asserting his own impurity, as well as that of the people, Isaiah is cleansed by a Seraph, who has descended to him. Isaiah then volunteers to serve as the messenger of God, who speaks the word of judgment on the people. They will listen, but not understand; they will look, but will not know. Their punishment will be utter. The sinful people will be hardened in their sin, left to the full consequence of their defection from God.

Aquinas' exposition of chapter 6 is finely detailed and thorough, revealing his keen concern for organization and structure. He opens by observing that the point of the chapter is the announcement of the final penalty of hardening in sin, and then states that the chapter falls into three main parts. The first (vv. 1–4) describes the Author of the judgment, God as judge; the second is concerned with Isaiah, the minister who will proclaim the judge's sentence (vv. 5–8); the third has to do with the sentence itself. As he proceeds in his verse-by-verse commentary, Aquinas will further divide each of these main parts, to show how carefully Isaiah has composed the entire chapter. Hence, the first part, on the Author of the judgment, itself falls into two parts: on the time of the vision that Isaiah received (i.e., in the year that the named king died); and about the vision itself. As is appropriate, Aquinas will devote much more attention to the latter. As he observes, the account of the vision itself can be divided into two segments: in the first, the seat of the judge is described; in the second is described the ministers who attend the judge, that is, the Seraphim. There is some debate, Aquinas informs us, whether Isaiah's vision was 'imaginary' or intellectual. If the former, what he reports (i.e., the vision of God sitting upon the throne, attended by the Seraphim) was in fact impressed upon him in the figures that he recounts. If the latter, he was presented by God with supernatural

---

[29] On the importance of viewing the *ST* in its literary relations to the various texts that it employs, see M.D. Jordan, 'The Alleged Aristotelianism of Thomas Aquinas', Etienne Gilson Lecture (Toronto: Pontifical Institute of Mediaeval Studies, 1992), and 'The Competition of Authoritative Languages and Aquinas's Theological Rhetoric', *Medieval Philosophy and Theology*, 4 (1994), pp. 71–90.

truth which he then rephrased in terms of figures accessible to his
readers. Whatever the case here – and Aquinas does *not* pursue the
issue further – when it comes to the vision itself, two things are
important: the figure that is employed, whether seen by the prophet
or composed by him; and, the meaning (*significatio*) of the figure.
And, he adds, the figurative expression which signifies will be
rendering a literal meaning, the supernatural truth that God wills to
convey through the prophet; in teasing out figurative meaning, and
locating that meaning at the literal level, Aquinas here anticipates
what he will note in the much later *ST* (see I, 1, 9–10, where he
repeats the point of the *Expositio*, that the meaning conveyed by
figures and metaphor is in fact literal).

As for the figure here presented, Aquinas then devotes a number
of lines to the Temple built by Solomon, in terms of which Isaiah's
vision of God and the Seraphim is portrayed. As for the meaning
(*significatio*) that is conveyed through the figure, Aquinas' discussion is quite lengthy. For there have been a variety of opinions,
which he notes, on the exact signification of this vision. One is that
the sitting on the throne foretells the oppression of a future
captivity, when the enemy will take over the Temple. Jerome has
offered a different interpretation, which is better, that through the
throne is signified the majesty of the Son of God, on account of
whom John 12 says: 'Isaiah spoke thus, because he saw his glory and
spoke about him [Christ].' Dionysius offers yet another explication,
which also is, Thomas says, better. Through the throne is signified
the eminence of the divine nature, which is said to be exalted
because of God's nobility, and elevated because it is higher than all
others, whom it exceeds infinitely.

After a brief 'scholastic' interlude (to be described below),
Aquinas returns to his presentation of the structure of the first
main part of the chapter (vv. 1–4), by looking at the other aspect of
the vision itself, the account of the Seraphim who attend the Lord
sitting on His throne. Aquinas offers some comments on the word
'seraph', and on the significance of the *six* wings of a seraph, noting
that various interpreters have discovered different sorts of meaning
in that number. Aquinas also comments at some length on the
praise that issues from the Seraphim. It shows their devotion to
God; it also shows their concord, for all pray the same. And, in the
'Holy, Holy, Holy', we meet in Isaiah the proclamation of the
Trinity of persons, who are at the same time one in their divine
majesty.

More than half of the exposition of chapter 6 is given over to this
first main part of the chapter. Although less space is given to the
remaining two main parts, Aquinas' exegesis nonetheless continues
to show his preoccupation with structure and detail. The second

main part of the chapter is on the one who will speak God's judgment to the people (vv. 5–8). This part on Isaiah himself is itself divided into three segments. In the first, we learn of Isaiah's humility: he recognizes his impurity, and confesses his sin. Next, we learn of his cleansing by the Seraph who flew to him and placed the burning coal on his mouth. And finally, we are told of his authority. It is God who will send him, and he will speak the sentence of judgment on God's behalf. God will be using him as an instrument, just as God employs angels to do God's will in the world.

The final main part of the chapter addresses the judgment itself, the point of the entire chapter. There are two segments to verses 9–13. One has to do with the hardening – God does not make the people hardened in their sin or oblivious to the call to repentance. God permits the people to suffer the consequences of their sin, by not giving grace to those who are unworthy. The other segment has to do with the duration of the penalty, describing at length Isaiah's question to the Lord and the Lord's dire response.

In working his way through Isaiah 6, Scripture plays an important role for Aquinas. Aquinas interprets this Scripture by bringing other Scripture to bear. Hence, to give but three examples: (1) he will shed light on the time of the vision by referring to other scriptural passages that deal with that king; (2) he cites pertinent Scripture to describe the Temple alluded to by Isaiah in stating his vision; and, (3) he will bring in such passages as Romans 11, to underscore the hardening of the people that is threatened towards the end of the chapter. As will already be apparent, Aquinas will also draw on post-biblical sources in this exegesis. On more than one occasion, he invokes Jerome and Gregory the Great and especially Pseudo-Dionysius, to clarify what is at stake in a given verse, at the same time making clear that important interpreters have not always agreed exactly on what is being conveyed through Isaiah.

For the most part, Aquinas offers in a straightforward way his exegesis of Isaiah. He cites a verse in the chapter, and explicates it, drawing on other Scripture and post-biblical authority, noting whether there are different possible readings of the verse, all the while reminding the reader where in the flow of the chapter we are. However, at two points in the exposition of Isaiah 6, the presentation takes on a different cast, as Aquinas introduces, in abbreviated form, what looks much like a scholastic article. The first comes in the course of the treatment in the first main part of the chapter of the vision enjoyed by Isaiah: 'I saw the Lord.' But, against this can be objected what is written in Exodus 33, 'no man shall see Me and live', and again in 1 John 4, 'no one ever saw God'. And so, goes this objection, neither did Isaiah. In responding to this objection, Aquinas gives a brisk review of his teaching on the

knowledge of God. Only one who can perfectly comprehend God –
grasp the essence of God, and totally – can be said to know God;
and that pertains to God alone. As for humans, they can know the
essence of God only if they are provided with a light that transforms
or elevates their natural capacities; here, Aquinas refers to the light
of glory, which is given to the blessed, that is, to those who have
completed their earthly journey and entered into the immediate
presence of God. He also refers to those who enjoy rapture, those,
that is, who in the present life are granted, in a transitory fashion, a
special light that permits the seeing of God in his essence. Aquinas
does not here give any examples, but in this regard he would be
thinking of Paul, when raised to the third heaven, and perhaps of
Moses. And, finally, he mentions another kind of knowledge of God
in this life, one in which he is not seen directly, but through figures.
In this connection, he refers to those who have received the light of
faith, which makes possible affirming truths about God; the light of
prophecy; and the light of reason, employed by the philosophers to
come to know some things about God, although they do not
penetrate to the divine essence itself. In each case, there is
knowledge, but of a sort that is indirect and so less than that of
the blessed or the rapt.

This quick survey of kinds of knowledge of God leads immediately, however, to another, related question; the 'scholastic' investigation, dealing with a problem that emerges from Isaiah's account,
continues and indeed takes on a fuller form. When the prophet sees
through the light of prophecy, does the prophet receive the vision
directly from God, or from God through the mediation of angels?
Isaiah's words would seem to indicate the former; he says, 'I saw the
Lord', not 'I saw an angel'. Moreover, in Exodus 33, it is said of
Moses that the Lord spoke to him face to face. And, finally, Isaiah
and Moses are said to have seen God in the *speculum aeternitatis*,
and that means to see God. As presented in the *Expositio*, the
preceding considerations stand as the objections of a scholastic
article. What follows is the equivalent of a scholastic article's
corpus, and then the response to these objections. In the corpus, the
authority of Dionysius in the fourth chapter of the *Celestial
Hierarchy* is pre-eminent: revelation to people from God is always,
without exception, through the mediation of angels. This holds even
of Moses, who received the Law through the angels. Hence, the
prophet received his vision through angels.

What then of the objections that opened this part of the
Expositio? To the first objection, it must be said (*ad primum ergo
dicendum*) that it is necessary to distinguish between the end of the
vision, and the principle of the vision. With regard to the end, the
angel who reveals intends to lead the recipient of the revelation to

the *cognitio Dei*, and not to knowledge of the angel; and thus the angel forms a vision of God, such that through what is seen by a figure, something comes to be known about God. And, as for the principle or source of the vision, the entire power of the angel to manifest something comes from God as its author; and so it is God who reveals through angels. To the second objection must be said (*ad secundum dicendum*) that Exodus 33, about Moses' face-to-face encounter with the Lord, has to do with the highest form of knowing possible to humans, offered by God to a select few as a gift, and so as a foretaste in this life of the beatific vision. And in this, Moses excelled the other prophets, enjoying by God's grace this special elevation. Finally, to the third objection it is to be said (*ad tertium dicendum*) that God Himself is not the *speculum aeternitatis*, to which the objection refers; that *speculum* is a species that is infused in the prophet in order to come to grasp some supernatural truth.

The other scholastic interlude comes in the treatment of the second main part of the chapter, on Isaiah himself. He is said to have been purified by a 'Seraph' who flew to him and applied the burning coal. Is this really what a 'Seraph' would do? As Pseudo-Dionysius has observed, there are different orders of angels, with Seraphim at the pinnacle. While all angels of whatever kind are at God's service and are involved in the working out of God's providential rule, there is, as Dionysius notes, an inviolable rule. Higher orders of angels, such as the Seraphim, do not come into direct contact with humans; only the lower orders do. Why then does Isaiah speak of the 'Seraph'? Dionysius, however, has also provided the solution to this problem. It was not in fact a 'Seraph' who flew to Isaiah. Rather, an angel of lower order did this work, but did so at the behest of the Seraphim, who in turn were acting on behalf of God. Since the cleansing was done at the urging of the Seraphim, Isaiah could thus say that it was a 'Seraph' who performed this work.[30]

Isaiah 6 is extraordinarily rich, and a number of significant theological themes emerge from Isaiah's presentation of his vision: God's providential rule over history, and concern for the people and for right ordering of humans to God; God's use of diverse ministers (angelic, human) in order to accomplish God's will; the responsibility for evil; the human knowledge of God, as in this case, through prophetic vision. All of these are noted and treated by Thomas in the course of his *Expositio* of chapter 6. But, in every case, it is the

---

[30] For a discussion of this reading of Isa. 6.6, which Aquinas repeats throughout his entire corpus, see W.J. Hankey, 'Aquinas, Pseudo-Denys, Proclus and Isaiah VI.6', *Archives d'histoire doctrinale et littéraire du moyen âge*, 64 (1997), pp. 59–93.

biblical ordering that drives and occasions the discussion; and
Aquinas will say only what needs to be said on each of these topics
to explicate the verse in question. Indeed, nowhere in the *Expositio*
of chapter 6 does he stand away from the biblical text and reflect on,
separately, what are the important theological topics raised by
Isaiah 6. He might have done so at the beginning of the chapter, as a
way of orienting the reading, or at the end of the chapter, as a way
of tying up what has come up in the verse-by-verse analysis. But he
does not. Nor does he offer in the *Expositio* a thorough examination
of any of these topics in the depth and nuance that each would
require. That work is left to a systematic writing such as the *Summa*.

Isaiah 6 is cited fourteen times in the *Summa*.[31] Isaiah 6.1 is cited
six times: I, 3, 1 obj. 4 (is God a body?); I, 12, 3 obj. 3 (can the
essence of God be seen with the bodily eye?); III, 5, 1 obj. 3 (ought
the Son of God have assumed a true body?); II–II, 171, 3 *sc* and
corpus (is prophecy only about future contingencies?); II–II, 174, 3
(can the degrees of prophecy be distinguished according to the
imaginary vision?); and I–II, 102, 4 ad 6 (cited in conjunction with v.
3, whether sufficient reason can be assigned for the ceremonies
pertaining to holy things?). Isaiah 6.2 is cited at I, 108, 5 *sc* (are the
orders of angels properly named?). Isaiah 6.3 is quoted three times:
I, 107, 4 obj. 2 (does local distance influence angelic speech?); I, 108,
3 *sc* (are there many angels in one order?); and II–II, 171, 3 (in
conjunction with v.1, is prophecy only about future contingencies?).
Isaiah 6.6-7 are cited at I, 112, 2 obj. 2 (are all angels sent in
ministry?), while 6.8 is cited at II–II, 185, 1 obj. 4 (is it lawful to
desire the office of bishop?). Isaiah 6.10 is cited twice: I–II, 79, 3 *sc*
(is God the cause of spiritual blindness and hardness of heart?), and
II–II, 15, 1 obj. 2 (is blindness of mind a sin?).

Put another way, Isaiah 6 appears in a number of treatises in the
ST: in the *Prima Pars*, in the treatise on God, and the account of the
angels and their role in divine government (I, 3, obj. 4 and I, 12, 3
obj. 3; and I, 108, 5 *sc*; I, 107, 4 obj. 2; I, 108, 3 *sc*; and I, 112, 2 obj.
2, respectively). In the *Prima Secundae*, Isaiah 6 appears in the
discussion of sin and its causes (I–II, 79, 3 *s.c.*), and as part of the
treatise on Law; in this case, the analysis of the Old Law, in itself
and in relation to its fulfilment in Jesus (I–II, 102, 4 ad 6). In the
Secunda Secundae, Isaiah is cited near the end of the treatise on faith
(II–II, 15, 1 obj. 2); a number of times in the treatise on the

---

[31] Information about authorities cited in the *ST* (and the *Summa contra Gentiles*)
can be found in *Sancti Thomae Aquinatis Doctoris Angelici Opera Omnia* iussu edita
Leonis XIII P.M. Tomus Decimus Sextus. Indices (Rome: Sta. Sabina, 1948). Also
useful is the following website, which surveys biblical citations in the *ST*, providing
links to the articles themselves in English translation: www.globalserve.net/~bumble-
bee/ecclesia/summa/.

gratuitous graces, among which prophecy holds the leading role (II–II, 171, 3 [bis]; II–II, 174, 3); and, in the course of the treatise that brings the *Secunda Secundae* to an end, on acts that pertain to some, not all, in the church (II–II, 185, 1 obj. 4). Finally, Isaiah 6 is used in the *Tertia Pars*, relatively early in the treatise on Christ, to underscore the reality of the Incarnation (III, 5, 1 obj. 3).

In the main, Aquinas employs Isaiah 6 to further the investigation of two important themes that surface throughout the *Summa*. One is human knowledge of God. That is an important concern for Aquinas from the first pages of the *ST*, as will be evident from the discussion earlier in this chapter of *ST*, I, 1, on sacred doctrine. Aquinas offers his fullest treatment of human knowledge of God shortly thereafter, as part of his treatise on God. In *ST*, I, 12, he reviews the human knowledge of God, devoting most of these articles to the conditions of the beatific vision in the next life, although concluding the question by noting the knowledge possible in this life, by reason, by faith, by prophecy. In this life, with the exception of Christ who enjoyed the beatific vision from the moment of his conception, and those (for example, Paul) to whom a momentary foretaste of vision has been given, it is impossible to have a quidditative knowledge of God, of God's essence. In this life, however, it is possible to know what God is not, and through the grace that provides for faith, or for prophecy, to attain in an imperfect and indirect manner a supernatural knowing of God. Elsewhere in the *ST*, Aquinas will develop this teaching. Hence, at the opening of the *Secunda Secundae* (QQ.1–16), he subjects faith to close scrutiny; in II–II, 171–75, he does the same for the transitory gift that is prophecy, and for rapture. Finally, in the *Tertia Pars*, in the course of the examination of Christ and his perfections, Aquinas returns to the question of the human knowledge of God, as in III, 7, 3, 8; and III, 9–12.

A review of the use of Isaiah 6 in such questions suggests that Isaiah's contribution is relatively modest. Isaiah does not provide the heart of the teaching about what we can, and cannot, know about God. Rather, Isaiah is cited to help to clarify the teaching that has been established on other bases and with more obvious dependence on other sources. Thus, in the treatise on prophecy, Isaiah is employed to make clear that while prophecy can deal with the future, it also has to do with God's truth in general, including the revelation of God as triune (II–II, 171, 3); and to help in the investigation of the topic only broached in the *Expositio*, of the hierarchy of 'imaginary' visions that are reported in Scripture (II–II, 174, 3). So too Isaiah 6.1 is quoted in the principal examination of the human knowledge of God; that Isaiah is said to have seen the Lord sitting on a throne would seem to run against the idea that

God is immaterial and so not to be seen by the bodily eye (I, 12, 3 obj. 3).

The role of Isaiah 6 in the presentation of a second principal theme – God's providential rule – is perhaps more significant. Again, Aquinas visits that theme throughout the *ST*. The tone is set in I, 22–23, on providence and predestination. Providence is God's plan for all creatures, by which God orders each creature to its appropriate end, in order to proclaim the divine goodness outside of God, in accordance with the wisdom of God. Secondarily, providence involves the execution of the plan; the execution is called 'divine government'. In achieving the plan, God employs secondary causes, respecting their proper causality. What God causes through secondary causes that are necessary, will be certain (as caused by God) and necessary, as caused by God through such a necessary cause. What is caused by God through a secondary cause that is contingent, will be certain and contingent (I, 22, 4). This assertion, reflecting Aquinas' well-honed sense of God as transcendent cause and repeated in terms of predestination in the following question (I, 23, 6), puts the discussion of the movement of the rational creature to God as end, in the *Secunda Pars*, through the rational creatures' acts, in its appropriate context. God orders the rational creature to its end, and moves the creature to the end through its acts. Predestination is the part of providence that deals with the ordering of some rational creatures to the special end that is God, God's own life. God elects some, in love, to come to eternal life, to come to share by God's gift in what is natural to God. And, predestination too involves the execution of this plan, which occurs through grace.

Aquinas continues his investigation of this theme of God's rule elsewhere in the *ST*. He examines at the end of the *Prima Pars* divine government (I, 103ff.), which is the implementation of God's providential plan. Here, the angels figure prominently, for God works out God's plan through these instruments of His power and wisdom. And, at the end of the *Prima Secundae* (I–II, 109–14), he turns to grace, which executes God's predestination of some to salvation. As he makes clear in that treatise (I–II, 111, 1), grace can be divided into two principal sorts: sanctifying grace (*gratia gratum faciens*), involved in the sanctifying of its recipient, and the gratuitous graces (*gratia gratis datae*), which are given so that someone might participate in the sanctification of another. The bulk of the treatise on grace is devoted to sanctifying grace.[32] As for the gratuitous graces, Aquinas subjects them – and in particular, that of

---

[32] Also pertinent here are the theological virtues (faith, hope, charity), which are infused with habitual grace and flow from it. See II–II, 1–46, which build on the general teaching on the theological virtues announced in I–II, 62.

prophecy – to close scrutiny in II–II, 171ff. Finally, the Christology of the *Tertia Pars* brings the presentation to term, reminding us that predestination is 'in Christ' and that the grace and virtues that are needed for the successful journey to God come through Christ and his work.

The contribution of Isaiah 6 to the working out of this second general theme comes at two particular points. First, what Isaiah proclaims about the heavenly court, its unending praise of the Lord, and work for God (as in the cleansing of Isaiah), makes its way into the account of divine government at the end of the *Prima Pars*. Isaiah 6 is cited four times in that treatise, to lend flavour and nuance to the account of what the different ranks of angels do in the service of God. And, secondly, Isaiah 6 has a certain prominence in the account of the gratuitous grace that is prophecy (II–II, 171ff.) That, of course, is hardly surprising. Isaiah is a major prophet, and the purpose of the treatise on prophecy is to make more understandable the biblical accounts of prophecy. In treating prophecy, Aquinas would seem to have two goals. The first has been noted in examining the topic of the human knowledge of God. He wants to make clearer what the prophets know, and how they know what they know. Yet, Aquinas also thinks of the prophets in terms of instrumental causality. It is through them that God furthers his will, by revealing the truths that are necessary for salvation and that must be believed in order to attain to eternal life. Hence, the citations of Isaiah in II–II, 171ff. (noted above) will also contribute to the unfolding of this second important theme.

Isaiah 11

What holds for chapter 6, holds for the *Expositio* of Isaiah 11. Aquinas goes to great lengths to unveil the order and structure of the chapter; employs Scripture to clarify Scripture; and calls upon post-biblical authority in reviewing the teaching of the chapter. (Jerome is evoked throughout; Gregory the Great is called upon to clarify the gifts of the Holy Spirit.) There is, as well, a 'scholastic' tone to part of the exposition: Aquinas offers what amounts to five brisk articles in the presentation of Isaiah's account of the gifts, here following closely what he found in the *Commentary on the Sentences* of his teacher, Albert the Great.[33]

[33] See in this connection R. Guindon, 'L'Expositio in Isaiam est-elle une oeuvre de Thomas d'Aquin 'bachelier biblique'?', *Recherches de Théologie Ancienne et Médiévale*, 21 (1954), pp. 312–21. As Guindon notes, in other works – in the *ST*, e.g., but also his own *Commentary on the Sentences* – Aquinas abandons Albert's order, in favour of another, in teaching the gifts. On this basis, Guindon answers the question posed in the title of his article affirmatively. Guindon wrote at a time when

There are a few differences, however, between the exposition of chapter 11 and that of chapter 6. For one thing, we meet in quick succession two *collationes* in the account of chapter 11 (the exposition of chapter 6 lacks a collation). In conjunction with Isaiah 11.1, Aquinas offers reflections on the Virgin Mary as *virga* (staff), and on Christ as *flos* (flower). More tellingly, there is an edge to this exposition that is lacking in that of chapter 6. Three main readings, Aquinas notes, have been offered of the chapter. Some read it as of specific, historical kings of Israel; others (the Jews) of the Messiah yet to come. The former interpretation, he insists very early in this exposition, is *extorta*, the latter, *stulta . . . et fabulosa*. Rather, as recognized by Jerome and other Christian saints, this chapter is about Jesus Christ and the reign of God that he inaugurates in his first coming and will bring to fruition in the second. The words of Israel in their full extent can apply only to him. In the succeeding exposition, Aquinas keeps the focus on the Christology of Isaiah 11, while taking swipes at these divergent, faulty interpretations.

According to Aquinas, chapter 11 is divided into two main parts. From verse 11 on, the restoration of God's people is depicted, looking in turn at their liberation, the condition of those liberated, and their preparation for liberation. In the first main part (vv. 1–10), the *restaurator* himself is portrayed, as to his nativity, his sanctity, and his dignity. For present purposes, it is what Aquinas does with v. 2, which addresses the sanctity of Jesus, that is of primary interest. He opens by noting the perfection in grace of Jesus. This includes the fullness of habitual grace and the full range of the seven gifts of the Holy Spirit (wisdom, knowledge, understanding, counsel, fortitude, piety, and fear) as found in the Latin of Isaiah at Thomas' disposal. He then engages in a more precise examination of the gifts, here following the order of Albert. First, he compares the gifts with the virtues and beatitudes. As are virtues, so gifts are habits; these habits are given by God to perfect the virtues, to make their possessor more amenable to the promptings of the Spirit. Beatitudes are the acts that proceed from the virtue perfected by the gift. Next, Aquinas reflects on the number of the gifts (seven), relating them to the active and contemplative lives. He then notes their order, and how certain gifts have to do with the

---

scholars still tended to date the *Expositio* on Isaiah as a magisterial work. The part of the *Expositio* of chapter 11 that includes these five articles is found in the translation by M. Rzeczkowski, mentioned in the first note above.

perfecting of the intellect, others with acting. In the fourth consideration, Thomas returns to the gifts as possessed by Christ, repeating his opening claim that Christ had these gifts to their fullest. Aquinas concludes this series of scholastic meditations by observing that the gifts are given to humans by the entire Trinity, although by appropriation they are ascribed to the Holy Spirit, who is the Gift.

Two points need to be stressed. First, while the *Summa*'s discussion of the gifts will follow a different ordering, and considerable detail and nuance will be added, the teaching of the *Expositio* about the gifts, materially speaking, is retained in the *ST*. In particular, the gifts are habits which perfect the virtues, although in the *ST*, Thomas will spell out more completely how the gifts perfect the intellect and will, and will go into much greater detail about how specific gifts perfect specific virtues, whether the theological virtues, or the cardinal virtues (prudence, justice, temperance, fortitude). Secondly, in the *Expositio*, there is a decidedly Christological cast to the rendering of Isaiah on the gifts. The gifts are gifts that Jesus possessed and possessed most perfectly. And, it is through Jesus that the gifts are passed on to others: it is to those who belong to Christ as to their Head that the gifts of the Holy Spirit are given, at Christ's behest.

Isaiah 11 is cited some thirty times in the *ST*. A few of the citations are found in the description of the life of Christ in the *Tertia Pars*: hence Isaiah 11.1 is cited in III, 35, 7 obj. 2, in the course of the discussion of why it was fitting for Christ to be born in Bethlehem; and Isaiah 11.10 ('his sepulchre will be glorious') is cited at III, 51, 2 *sc*, which treats of Christ's burial (was it fitting?). But, the overwhelming majority of the references to Isaiah 11 come in the *ST*'s treatment of the gifts of the Holy Spirit. That treatment is spread over three Parts of the *ST*. The most detailed treatment of the gifts en masse comes in I–II, 68. Individual gifts are then examined in the *Secunda Secundae*, in conjunction with the virtues that they perfect. Hence, Aquinas looks at the gifts of understanding and knowledge (II–II, 8–9) in connection with faith; the gift of fear, in relation to hope (II–II, 19); the gift of wisdom, as tied to charity (II–II, 45); and the gifts of counsel (II–II, 52), of piety (II–II, 121), and of fortitude (II–II, 139), that perfect the virtues of prudence, justice, and fortitude, respectively. Finally, Aquinas returns to the gifts in the *Tertia Pars*, now in connection with Christ. Christ had the fullness of habitual grace; he also had the gifts of the Holy Spirit to their fullest and as they exist in the blessed in heaven (III, 7, 5–6). Aquinas' preference, when it comes to Isaiah 11, is for verses 2 and 3; these are the verses cited repeatedly (over twenty-five times) in the account of the gifts as they reappear in these different Parts of the *ST*.[34]

The debt of the *ST* to Isaiah 11 is in fact profound. It is not too much to say that the principal treatment in the *ST* of the gifts, in I–II, 68, is itself an extended commentary on the teaching of the gifts in Isaiah 11. Isaiah 11 provides the heart of the teaching about the gifts in that question, and Aquinas returns over and over to Isaiah 11.2-3 in I–II, 68. If the use of Isaiah were removed, relatively little of substance would be left in I–II, 68. The absorption of Isaiah 11 in the *ST* is relatively straightforward and easy; and, comparatively speaking, Isaiah 11.2-3 have an importance to the *ST* on an important topic of the faith that outstrips that of Isaiah 6.

There is one aspect of the reception of Isaiah 11 in the *ST* that calls, however, for comment. For pedagogical reasons (recall the discussion earlier in this chapter of the *ordo disciplinae*), Aquinas distributes the examination of the gifts over the *Secunda* and *Tertia Pars*. In the *Secunda Pars*, he looks at the gifts in themselves, and without regard to their actualization in history (that is, as found in Christ first and then given to others through Christ). In the *Tertia Pars*, he turns to that aspect of the gifts, of their connection to Christ. As is well known, some readers of the *ST* have at times questioned the importance of Christ for Thomas Aquinas. Explicit Christological references in the *Prima* and *Secunda Pars* are kept to a minimum (and this is in the main true of I–II, 68 as well). Does this not mean that Aquinas can work out his most important ideas

---

[34] Hence, Isaiah 11.2 is cited at *ST*, I, 1, 6 obj. 2 (is sacred doctrine the same as wisdom?); I–II, 68, 1 obj. 1 (do the gifts differ from the virtues?); I–II, 68, 3 obj. 1 (are the gifts of the Holy Spirit habits?); I–II, 68, 4 s.c. (on the number of the gifts); I–II, 68, 7 obj. 1 (on their relations to each other); II–II, 4, 6 obj. 1 (is faith one virtue?); II–II, 8, 1 s.c. (is understanding a gift of the Holy Spirit?); II–II, 8, 6 s.c. (is the gift of understanding distinct from other gifts?); II–II, 9, 1 s.c. (is knowledge a gift?); II–II, 45, 1 s.c. (is wisdom to be reckoned among the gifts of the Holy Spirit?); II–II, 52, 1 s.c. (is counsel to be reckoned among the gifts of the Holy Spirit?); II–II, 121, 1 s.c. (is piety a gift?); II–II, 121, 2 obj. 2 (does the second Beatitude, 'Blessed are the meek', correspond to the gift of piety?); II–II, 139, 1 s.c. (is fortitude a gift?); III, 7, 1 s.c. (was there habitual grace in the soul of Christ?); III, 11, 1 s.c. (did Christ know all things by imprinted or infused knowledge?). Isaiah 11.3 is cited at I–II, 68, 1 (on the gifts as differing from the virtues); I–II, 68, 3 obj. 1 (are the gifts habits?); I–II, 68, 4 s.c. (on the number of the gifts); I–II, 68, 7 obj. 1 (on the relation of the gifts to each other); II–II, 8, 6 s.c. (is the gift of understanding a distinct gift?); II–II, 9, 1 s.c. (is knowledge a gift?); II–II, 19, 9 s.c. (is fear a gift of the Holy Spirit?); II–II, 67, 2 obj. 2 (is it lawful for a judge to pronounce judgment against the truth that he knows, on account of evidence to the contrary?); III, 7, 6 s.c. (was there habitual grace in the Christ's soul?); and III, 11, 1 s.c. (about Christ's infused knowledge). A few of the citations come in articles that are not principally concerned with the gifts. However, when Isaiah 11.2 is noted in I, 1, 6 obj. 1, it is to allow Aquinas to differentiate the wisdom that pertains to sacred doctrine from the wisdom that is the gift. And, when it is quoted in III, 11, 1 s.c., it is to underscore that Christ had the fullness of knowledge and understanding.

about God and about humans without needing to take Christ into consideration, and so leave Christ to the end of his systematic writing, to wrap things up? This is a misperception, of course, one that fails to take into consideration the difference between the proclamation of the faith (and the acceptance and living out of the crucial claims of the faith by the believer) and the requirements of a discipline that reflects on that faith and seeks to present anew that faith in a way that highlights its deeper structures. Or, put another way, Christ is not an afterthought for Thomas Aquinas. And yet, it is understandable that the order of procedure in the *ST* might nurture such doubts. In the *ST*, Aquinas has separated, for pedagogical reasons, what Isaiah 11, and in turn the *Expositio* of chapter 11, has kept together: Christ and the gifts of the Holy Spirit stand in intimate relation. Thus, in conclusion, by reflecting on the approach to Isaiah 11 in the *Expositio* and the *ST*, we can gain a better sense of the value of reading not only the systematic writings but the biblical commentaries as well.

3

AQUINAS' *LECTURA IN MATTHAEUM*

Jeremy Holmes

The years 1268–72 were a productive time for Thomas Aquinas. During that period, his second regency as a master in Paris, he wrote the longest part of the *Summa Theologiae*, the *Seçunda Pars*; he gave lectures on the Gospel of John, acknowledged by all to be a masterpiece; he wrote a number of disputed questions, including the *De Malo*; he wrote his commentaries on the books of Aristotle; from this period we also have a number of quodlibetal questions, and various minor works addressed to individuals.[1] Many theologians would be content to have produced an immortal work such as the *Secunda Pars* alone in four years, or the lectures on John.

Somewhere in all this activity, Thomas also gave his lectures on Matthew. So imposing is the literary output of Thomas' second stay at Paris that some scholars have thought he could not have given the lectures on Matthew during those years. It seems like too much.

I will take up this difficulty in the spirit of a scholastic *articulus*, in which a problem is posed, not because there is doubt about the answer ('Whether God Exists'), but because the exercise of answering the question opens the way to new insight. I will quickly review the evidence which places the lectures on Matthew beyond doubt in the years 1268–72. Then I will look at each of the three main elements of the *Lectura in Matthaeum*: the division of the text (*divisio textus*), the line-by-line comments, and the inserted *quaestiones* on various topics. But before anything else, it will be necessary to look at the manuscript witnesses for the *Lectura*. Whether we have reliable access to Thomas' lectures is a question which casts a shadow over all further inquiries.

---

[1] Jean-Pierre Torrell, *Saint Thomas Aquinas*, vol. I, *The Person and His Work* (trans. Robert Royal; Washington, DC: The Catholic University of America Press, 1996), pp. 197–223.

Manuscripts

Our access to Thomas' actual comments on the Gospel of Matthew
is much more limited than might be implied by a casual reference to
'Thomas' commentary on Matthew'. Thomas himself never wrote
out his lectures for publication. The term *lectura* denotes commentary delivered orally rather than committed directly to writing; a
commentary written by Thomas himself would be called an
expositio. The *lectura* come down to us through *reportationes*, that
is, notes taken down by persons in the audience and later filled out
from memory or other sources to look more like the actual
transcript of a lecture. Thomas never looked over the resulting
document to check its faithfulness to his intention.

Two individuals took down *reportationes*, namely Peter d'Andria
(who was responsible for preserving others of Thomas' works as
well) and one Leodegar of Besançon, a secular professor at the
university.[2] Neither *reportatio* is complete. Peter seems to have
written down the comments on chapters 1–12 of Matthew, while
Leodegar recorded the lectures from 6.9 through to the end of the
Gospel.[3] The result is unusual: from 6.9 through the end of chapter
12 we have two divergent yet equally authentic texts of the *Lectura
in Matthaeum*.[4]

Only four manuscripts survive of the lectures on Matthew.[5] In
three of these manuscripts, Leodegar's report of 6.9 through the end
of the Gospel has been completed by borrowing the earlier chapters
from Peter's transcript. Unfortunately, all three of these manuscripts have lacunae from 5.11–6.8 and from 6.14-19. When in 1517
Bartholomew of Spina brought out the first printed edition of the
lectures on Matthew, he based his text on a manuscript of this
hybrid type, but filled in the gaps in his manuscript source with
borrowed material from a commentary by Peter of Scala, a
Dominican of the thirteenth century.[6] Bartholomew's printed text

---

[2] We don't know much about Leodegar, but for more about Peter d'Andria, see A.
Dondaine, *Secrétaires de saint Thomas* (Rome: S. Tommaso, 1956), pp. 198–200.

[3] These complicated inter-relationships were only clarified by the discovery of the
Basel manuscript and its subsequent analysis by H.-V. Shooner, in 'La *Lectura in
Matthaeum* de S. Thomas (Deux fragments inédits et la *Reportatio* de Pierre
d'Andria)', *Angelicum*, 33 (1956), pp. 121–42.

[4] Louis-Jacques Bataillon offers a very helpful overview of the issues surrounding
the manuscripts of Thomas' many works in 'La Diffusione Manoscritta e Stampata
dei Commenti Biblici de San Tommaso d'Aquino', *Angelicum*, 71 (1994), pp. 579–90.
Regarding the *Lectura in Matthaeum*, see especially pp. 587–88.

[5] Compare this with 28 surviving manuscripts of the lectures on John, and 60 of the
commentary on Job!

[6] This 'fraud' was first exposed by Roger Guindon, 'La *Lectura super Matthaeum
incompleta* de saint Thomas', *Revue de l'Université d'Ottawa*, 25 (1955), pp. 213–19.

became the basis of later printed versions, with the result that even today the Marietti text of the *Lectura in Matthaeum* is spurious from paragraph numbers 444–582 and from 603–610.

The fourth manuscript was only discovered in 1955, at the university library in Basel. It had been marked as 'anonymous' and had lain unrecognized probably since the end of the thirteenth century, because the text begins at Mt. 1.22. It appears to be the *reportatio* of Peter d'Andria. This manuscript not only gives us Peter's divergent report of the lectures on 6.9 through the end of 12, but also fills in the lacunae in the previously known manuscripts. Unfortunately, the Basel manuscript has yet to be published as a whole: H.-V. Schooner, published the comments on 5.13-16, and J.-P. Renard made available the comments on 5.20-48.[7]

It appears then that the effort to record Thomas' lectures was not an organized one, and the resulting record was imperfectly transmitted. We will return to the question of whether one should put full weight on a *reportatio* as representing Thomas' thought.

Dating

Because of certain references to Paris and to French dialects (notably absent from the Basel manuscript), scholars have long thought that Thomas must have written the *Lectura in Matthaeum* during one of his stays as a regent-master at the University of Paris.[8] As was mentioned above, the lectures were initially dated to the first regency (1256–59), because Thomas wrote so much during his second stay that it seemed impossible to squeeze another work the size of the *Lectura in Matthaeum* into the same period. However, our ability to measure Thomas' literary output during a given

---

[7] Shooner, 'La *Lectura in Matthaeum* de S. Thomas'; J.P. Renard, '*La Lectura super Matthaeum* V, 20–28 de Thomas d'Aquin (Edition d'après le ms. Bâle, Univ. Bibl. B.V. 12)', *Recherches de théologie ancienne et médiévale*, 50 (1983), pp. 145–90. The lectures on Mt. 6.5-15 have been published in translation as 'From the Lectures on St. Matthew', in Simon Tugwell (ed.), *Albert & Thomas: Selected Writings* (The Classics of Western Spirituality; New York: Paulist Press, 1988), pp. 445–75. Otherwise, no translation of any part of the *Lectura super Matthaeum* has been published. While the Leonine commission is working on a critical edition of the *Lectura super Matthaeum*, no such tool for research is yet available. Aside from the texts published by Schooner and Renard, I have used the Marietti edition for my research. In citations, I will follow the custom of giving chapter and verse of the text commented upon, and then the Marietti paragraph number in brackets. For Matthew: *Super Evangelium S. Matthaei Lectura* (ed) Raphaelis Cai (Rome: Marietti, 5th edn, 1951); for John: *Super Evangelium S. Ioannis Lectura* (ed) Raphaelis Cai (Rome: Marietti, 5th edn, 1952).

[8] The references to Paris and to French dialects are found in the Marietti edition at n. 743 and n. 2296.

period is not as exact as one might think; a more positive answer to this difficulty will emerge in the course of this essay.[9]

It is highly unlikely that the lectures were given during Thomas' first regency at Paris. Thomas did not know about Aristotle's *Politics* before the year 1260, yet he makes reference to the *Politics* in the lectures on Matthew.[10] Similarly, Thomas first saw the *Libellus de fide Trinitatis*, spuriously attributed to Cyril of Alexandria, in the year 1263; but he seems to know of this work in the lectures on Matthew.[11] Thomas uses sources in the *Lectura in Matthaeum* such as the *Collectio casinensis* which otherwise first appear in his works in the *Catena Aurea*, written in 1263.[12] These converging facts make it nearly certain that Thomas gave his lectures on Matthew some time after his first regency at Paris.

Two further arguments push the date most probably into the second Paris regency (1268–72). A case can be made that Peter d'Andria revised his notes from the lectures on Matthew after the year 1273, and it does not seem likely that he would have waited many years after the lectures were given to revise his notes for publication. Finally, Thomas echoes several arguments which had arisen in a dispute with Gerard of Abbeville in 1270 over the state of perfection; in particular, in his commentary on Mt. 19.21 [1594] he echoes a phrase which Gerard had brought into the discussion from a text by Chrysostom, according to which a bishop is in a higher state of perfection than any monk, 'be it Elijah himself'.[13]

---

[9] See P. Glorieux's critique of Mandonnet's method in 'Essai sur les commentaires scripturaires de saint Thomas et leur chronologie', *Recherches de théologie ancienne et médiévale*, 17 (1950), pp. 237–66, esp. pp. 261–64.

[10] I.T. Eschmann, 'The Quotations of Aristotle's *Politics* in St. Thomas' *Lectura super Matthaeum*', *Medieval Studies*, 18 (1956), pp. 232–40.

[11] Michael Arges, 'New Evidence Concerning the Date of Thomas Aquinas' *Lectura* on Matthew', *Medieval Studies*, 49 (1987), p. 520.

[12] Arges, 'New Evidence', p. 519.

[13] Torrell, *Saint Thomas Aquinas*, pp. 55–56. Arges ('New Evidence', pp. 517–23) argues for an earlier date *between* the Paris regencies. In the lectures on the Gospel of John, Thomas opines that the dove descending at the Lord's Baptism was a real dove, following a quotation from Augustine in his *Catena* on John; in the *Scriptum super Sententiis* and the *Lectura super Matthaeum*, he says it was not a real dove. This suggests that Thomas' opinion was changed by the Augustine quotation in the *Catena* on John, which he composed in 1263. Similarly, Thomas attributes the *De ecclesiasticis dogmatibus* to Augustine in his earlier works and in the *Lectura super Matthaeum* (although this attribution is absent from the Basel manuscript), while in his later works he avoids this error, first correctly mentioning Gennadius as the author in the *Catena* on Matthew, composed in 1263. These are solid arguments, but do not outweigh the evidence given above for a date during the second regency at Paris. The first argument depends on the working premises that a) Thomas cannot have changed his mind more than once, and b) he kept careful track of the Spirit/dove issue rather than following the patristic source he happened to have in front of him at the time. The second argument is stronger, but is called into doubt by a) the

The date of the lectures' production is foundational for understanding Thomas' accomplishment. He commented on the Gospel of Matthew toward the end of his life, after he had composed the *Catena Aurea* on Matthew (1263), and during the same general period as he was researching and writing the later parts of the *Summa Theologiae*; he probably began his lectures at some point during the composition of the *Secunda Pars* and completed them some time before the writing of the *Tertia Pars*.[14] Hence the Aquinas who undertook to comment on Matthew's Gospel was Aquinas at the height of his powers, with the entire patristic tradition at his fingertips and a complete command of scholastic theology. This fact will be the key to the production of the *Lectura in Matthaeum*.

Division of the Text

We are now in a position to look at the lectures themselves. As in all of his commentaries, Thomas begins his division of the text by stating the central intention or proposition of the work.[15] The first line of his comment on Mt. 1.1 states that, 'Among the evangelists, Matthew is especially concerned with the humanity of Christ.'[16] Jean-Pierre Torrell has connected this central concern with Thomas' choice of books on which to comment:

> To all appearances, Thomas took the books of the New Testament in their canonical order. In passing directly from Matthew to John, he must have thought that Matthew took the place of the other two Synoptics, while John had something special to say. Furthermore, he is clear enough on the subject in his *Prologue* [to the commentary on John]: 'The other evangelists deal principally with the mysteries of Christ's humanity; in his Gospel, John puts first and in a special way Christ's divinity.'[17]

This is a valuable insight, but perhaps more can be said. In his inaugural lecture as a master at Paris in 1256, Thomas gave a *divisio textus* for all of Scripture. For the Gospels, he offered two views about their individual themes: according to the first view, John

---

disagreement among the manuscripts and b) the difficulty involved in arguing from single words or phrases in a *reportatio*, which may or may not represent Thomas' own words and knowledge.

[14] Torrell, *Saint Thomas Aquinas*, pp. 146–47.

[15] This is a description of the division as Thomas presents it. For more detail on how Thomas may have arrived at the division of the text, see Margherita Maria Ross, 'La "divisio textus" nei commenti scritturistici di S. Tommaso d'Aquino: Un procedimento solo esegetico?', *Angelicum*, 71 (1994), pp. 537–48, esp. pp. 540–44.

[16] *In Matt.* 1.1 [11]. Unless otherwise noted, all translations are my own.

[17] Torrell, *Saint Thomas Aquinas*, pp. 199–200.

emphasizes the divinity of Christ, while the other three each take up
one of the three dignities attendant upon His humanity, namely the
offices of king (Matthew), prophet (Mark), and priest (Luke);
according to the second view, Matthew deals principally with the
mystery of the Incarnation, Luke with the mystery of the passion,
Mark with the victory of the resurrection, and John with Christ's
divinity.[18] In the *Lectura super Matthaeum*, Thomas offers a
division of the Gospels which takes up aspects of both theories.
Commenting on the opening lines of Matthew, he notes that the
four evangelists have divided amongst themselves the various errors
concerning Christ. John and Mark devote the first lines of their
Gospels to destroying the errors which concern Christ's divinity,
while Matthew and Luke take aim at the errors which concern His
humanity.[19] Further on, commenting on the genealogy in Matthew,
Thomas notes that Luke's genealogy of Christ is different, and gives
the reason: while Luke focuses on Christ's dignity as a priest,
Matthew focuses on the humanity of Christ.[20]

Of the three Synoptic Gospels, Matthew is the one which focuses
on the humanity as such of Christ in the Incarnation. This suggests
that Thomas did not see the Synoptic Gospels as interchangeable.
He did not pass over Mark and Luke because they do not have
anything distinctive to say: rather, he chose Matthew because
Matthew *does* have something distinctive to say. Of the four
Gospels, Thomas – ever the systematic thinker – chose to comment
on the one which specially focuses on the humanity of Christ in the
Incarnation, and on the one which focuses specially on the divinity
of Christ.

Thomas carefully follows this special focus of Matthew throughout his division of the text. The Gospel falls into three main parts,
closely resembling the division Thomas will later give to his 'life of
Christ' in the *Tertia Pars* (QQ. 27–59): chapters 1–2 of Matthew
treat of the entrance of Christ's humanity into the world; chapters
3–20 treat of the advance of Christ's humanity in this world – which,
Thomas notes, is more or less synonymous with the advance of
Christ's teaching; chapters 21–28 deal with the departure of Christ's
humanity from this world.

Within the first division, chapter one describes the generation of
Christ, both through the genealogy and the birth, while the story of
the magi in chapter two is a 'manifestation' of Christ's generation.

---

[18] *De Commendatione et partitione sacrae Scripturae*, in *Opuscula theologica*, vol. 1
(Rome: Marietti, 1954), n. 1208.
[19] *In Matt.* 1.1 [21].
[20] *In Matt.* 1.2-3 [24–27].

This differs slightly from the *Summa*, in which the first division also includes the Baptism of the Lord.[21]

The central and longest division, the 'advance' of Christ's humanity, is arranged entirely around the teaching of Christ. The Baptism of the Lord and the Temptation in the Wilderness (chapters 3–4) are labelled as preparation for the teaching. 'The teaching itself' is identified as the Sermon on the Mount (chapters 5–7), which is followed by miraculous confirmation of the teaching (chapters 8–9), instruction of those who will pass on the teaching (chapter 10), and confounding of its adversaries (chapters 11–12). Chapters 13–14 present the power of the teaching, first in words and then in deeds. The end to which Christ's teaching leads, namely future glory, forms the subject of chapters 15–20: it is made brilliantly manifest in the transfiguration (chapter 17) and then explained in words in the following chapters.

The last part of the Gospel, the departure of Christ's humanity from the world, also takes in elements which Thomas will call Christ's 'exaltation after this life' in the *Tertia Pars*.[22] Chapters 21–23 deal with the way in which Christ provoked His opponents, thus leading to His death, while chapters 24–25 have Christ strengthening His disciples for the coming ordeal. Chapters 26–27 cover the passion of Christ, while chapter 28 treats of the resurrection.

The Beatitudes

Clearly, the Sermon on the Mount carries tremendous weight in this outline of Matthew's Gospel. It is the driving element in the longest part of the Gospel, so much so that it displaces all the discourses afterwards through chapter 20 into supporting roles. Thomas narrows his focus even more when he argues that 'just as Moses first set down the commandments, and afterwards said many things which were all referred back to the commandments he had set down, so Christ in His teaching sets out these beatitudes, to which all the other things are referred back'.[23] As the Ten Commandments contain the essence of the moral precepts of the Mosaic Law, the

---

[21] The divisions of Thomas' 'life of Christ' treatise are spelled out at *ST*, III, 27, 1, in the introduction.

[22] *ST*, III, 53, 1.

[23] *In Matt.* 5.3 [411].

beatitudes are the touchstone of Christ's teaching in the Sermon on the Mount.[24]

The Beatitudes are the natural centre of gravity of Thomas' *divisio textus*. He begins his lecture on a note of humility: 'Now, one should note that many things are set down here about the beatitudes; but never could anyone speak so subtly about the Lord's words that he could attain to the Lord's [full] purpose.'[25] This admonition is matched by another comment at Mt. 25.1, 'when Jesus had completed all these words': 'And he speaks thus because he alone is able to complete [his words]. We can begin, but we cannot bring it to completion, in accord with Sir. 43.29, "We say many things, and we fall short".'[26] Because Thomas takes 'all these words' as referring to all the words Jesus had spoken since the beginning of His ministry, these two warnings to the exegete form bookends around our Lord's teaching.

Then, before proceeding to his usual word-by-word commentary, he offers a discourse on the Beatitudes in which he divides and orders the Beatitudes according to which mistaken idea of happiness they correct. First, the Lord unconditionally condemns the position that happiness is found in an abundance of material goods or in living as one wishes. Next, he partially condemns the idea that happiness is found in the virtues of the active life – but only partially, in so far as some think that these virtuous acts themselves are happiness rather than being ordered to something further. Lastly, he more or less condones the theory that happiness is found in contemplation, but adds the minor corrective that the contemplation which gives true happiness is not found in this life, but in the next. Thomas' detailed outline looks like this:[27]

Happiness is thought to be:
— Abundance of material goods
  • Blessed are the poor (v. 3)
— Living as one will, according to three appetites:
  • Irascible: but 'Blessed are the meek' (v. 4)
  • Concupiscible: but 'Blessed are they who mourn' (v. 5)

[24] Servais Pinckaers has pointed out the contemporary relevance of this emphasis in Aquinas' teaching in 'The Use of Scripture and the Renewal of Moral Theology: The *Catechism* and *Veritatis Splendor*', *The Thomist*, 59 (1995), pp. 1–20. See especially pp. 7–8: 'A major innovation in the *Catechism* and in the encyclical is that the New Law and the Sermon on the Mount have been reintroduced into the domain of Christian moral teaching. As the Decalogue stood to the Old Law, so the Sermon on the Mount stands to the New, as its specific text. This is a return to the tradition of the Fathers which led to Saint Thomas.'
[25] *In Matt.* 5.3 [404].
[26] *In Matt.* 25.1 [2118].
[27] *In Matt.* 5.3 [404–13].

- The will, which seeks two things:
  - To be free from higher law: but 'Blessed are they who hunger and thirst after justice' (v. 6)
  - To bind others as subjects: but 'Blessed are the merciful' (v. 7)
— The active virtues, which are two kinds:
  - Those ordered to oneself, such as temperance: 'Blessed are the clean of heart', but because of an ordering to something further: 'for they shall see God' (v. 8)
  - Those ordered towards others, for the sake of peace: 'Blessed are the peacemakers', but because of an ordering to something further: 'for they shall be called sons of God' (v. 9)
— The contemplative virtues: the minor error in this theory is corrected by our Lord's use of the future tense, 'they SHALL see'
  - Substantially required is that the act be of the highest intelligible, hence 'they shall see GOD'
  - Formally required is the delight and love of this act, hence 'they shall be called sons of God', which pertains to the union of love

'These things having been prefaced', Thomas concludes, 'let us proceed to the text.' He goes on to comment at much greater length on the Beatitudes, proceeding not just line by line but word by word. Along the way, as usual, he offers a division of the text as he comes to each part. Interestingly, the division he offers in his detailed commentary is quite different from the division he gave immediately before, in his discourse! This time he bases his division on the several effects of virtue:[28]

Virtue does three things:
— It removes one from evil
  - From lust, hence 'Blessed are the poor'
  - From cruelty or disturbance, hence 'Blessed are the meek'
  - From harmful pleasure, hence 'Blessed are they who mourn'
— It works and makes one to work for what is good:
  - The good of justice, hence 'Blessed are they who hunger and thirst after justice'
  - The good of mercy, hence 'Blessed are the merciful'
— It disposes one to what is best:
  - The vision of God, hence 'Blessed are the clean of heart'
  - The love of neighbour, hence 'Blessed are the peacemakers'

While following Thomas' *divisio textus* for the whole Gospel brings out his conception of Matthew's special purpose in writing, the phenomenon of divergent divisions of the text offered in quick succession raises questions as to whether Thomas believes a single

[28] *In Matt.* 5.3-12 [414–46]

'original' meaning can be discovered. Perhaps this was the import of his opening observation: 'Never could anyone speak so subtly about the Lord's words that he could attain to the Lord's [full] purpose.'[29]

Within a few years of delivering the *Lectura*, Thomas will devote an article of the *Tertia Pars* to the order of the Beatitudes. There he will offer yet a third division of the text, although it appears to be an improved version of the original division above rather than something completely different:[30]

> Happiness is thought to be:
> — In a voluptuous life, in two ways:
>   • In the abundance of riches: but 'Blessed are the poor'
>   • In pursuit of one's passions:
>   • The irascible: but 'Blessed are the meek'
>   • The concupiscible: but 'Blessed are they who mourn'
> — In the life of the active virtues, consisting principally in what we do towards others, either
>   • What is due in justice: 'Blessed are they who hunger and thirst after justice'
> or
>   • Spontaneous generosity: 'Blessed are the merciful'
> — In the life of the contemplative virtues; these beatitudes concern not actions, but effects of the active life which dispose us towards the rewards of contemplation:
>   • As regards ourselves: 'Blessed are the clean of heart'
>   • As regards others: 'Blessed are the peacemakers'

According to this division, our Lord condemns the notion that happiness is found in a voluptuous life. He condones the notion that the active virtues lead to happiness, but commands that His disciples pursue active virtues perfected by the gifts of the Spirit, leading to a much more intense pursuit of justice and mercy than is possible by simple human virtues. He also condones the notion that happiness is found in contemplation, but He does not set down commands in this part, since contemplation is itself the reward; instead, He sets down certain effects of the active life and shows what good they lead to.

This last division improves on the first in several ways. First, 'abundance of material riches' and 'living as one will' are collapsed into a single heading, 'a voluptuous life', yielding an overall division

---

[29] See John F. Boyle, 'Authorial Intention and the *Divisio textus*', in *Reading John with St. Thomas Aquinas*, eds. Michael Dauphinais and Matthew Levering (Washington, DC: The Catholic University of America Press, 2005), pp. 3–8 for similar reflections based on statements in the *De Potentia*.

[30] *ST*, I-II, 69, 3.

of the Beatitudes into three sections rather than four. Divisions into two or three are usually cleaner, and in this case the heading 'a voluptuous life' is more convincing. Second, the fourth and fifth Beatitudes are treated in the *Lectura* as opposing the tendency of the will to pursue its own way, but in the *Summa Theologiae* they settle more convincingly under the heading of our Lord's approval of the active virtues. Lastly, the *Lectura* attempts to find an element of correction in the seventh and eighth Beatitudes by emphasizing the future tense of our Lord's words; the *Summa Theologiae* abandons this forced effort and instead gives the final Beatitudes the position of culminating the previous six. These advances, together with the similarities between the two attempts, suggest that the first division given in the *Lectura* was a draft, so to speak, of Thomas' future article in the *Summa*.[31]

Divisio Textus *and the meaning of the Gospel*

The *divisio textus* is clearly an important feature of Thomas' effort to penetrate the meaning of the Gospel. However, one feature of the *Lectura* which might call into question the *divisio*'s central role is Thomas' failure to pursue it to its furthest implications. He does not give his outline of the Gospel all at once, at the beginning of his comments: the division of the text is an ongoing task which he undertakes anew as he comes to each part of the Gospel. To this degree, Thomas is consistent from the first sentence of his lectures to the very end: 'Among the evangelists, Matthew is especially concerned with the humanity of Christ.' However, as one follows his division of the text down to the level of individual pericopae or lines, his single-minded emphasis on the humanity of Christ fades. For example, while he invoked Matthew's special emphasis on Christ's humanity to explain the difference between the Matthaean and the Lukan genealogies, never again does he appeal to this special emphasis to explain differences between the Gospels.

In general, Thomas shows little awareness of Matthew's distinctive teachings or emphases, while such issues as the 'synoptic problem' are not in view at all. In the whole of *Lectura super Matthaeum*, I have found 120 passages where Thomas notes a parallel Gospel passage and comments on it as such. In 68 of these he resolves an apparent discrepancy between the Gospels, and in the

---

[31] As Glorieux notes ('Essai', p. 238), a university master's primary assignment was to lecture daily on Scripture. Hence 'if one wants to retrieve his true teaching, one must go there [the lectures on Scripture] initially to draw it out. There one can seize onto the lively gushing of his thought, the formulation of his doctrines, his progress and his refinements of detail as the problems present themselves to him.'

remaining 52 he brings in the parallel passage to illuminate the text of Matthew with an added detail, an alternative phrasing, or something of the sort. Hence in the majority of cases, Thomas does not attend to differences between the Gospels unless they force themselves upon him in the form of a difficulty to be solved – usually brought to his attention by Augustine's *De consensu evangeliorum*, cited in the *Catena aurea in Matthaeum*.

In short, Thomas consistently pursues Matthew's distinctive features in the macro level *divisio textus*, from the beginning of the lectures to their end, but his more detailed divisions and comments show none of this interest. It is almost as though the *Lectura in Matthaeum* operated at two distinct levels, the broader *divisio* and the detailed comment. Why this apparent dichotomy?

One reason may lie in Thomas' experience of the text of the Gospel, which functions for him as a lens through which one can view reality. In most circumstances, one does not notice a lens while looking through it. If one steps back to see the whole lens – corresponding to the macro level *divisio textus* – then the lens itself becomes an object of attention, and special features of the lens come into view. If a scratch or a particle of dust on the lens obscures one's view – corresponding to apparent internal contradictions or contradictions with other Gospel texts – then once again the viewer becomes aware of the lens as something to be seen in its own right. But in the usual experience of viewing things through a lens – corresponding to Thomas' detailed commentary – one's focus is on the reality seen, while the lens itself vanishes from sight.[32]

Perhaps the best way to describe the progress (as well as the problem) of modern biblical studies is that we have become acutely aware of the text as something standing between us and the facts, as a lens which has its own focal point and areas of magnification. This means that each Synoptic Gospel is its own world, and to comment on any one of them requires an enormous labour to become familiar with a particular presentation of the good news. Not having this perception of the Gospel texts does not make the Synoptic Gospels simply interchangeable, but it does reduce the work involved in commenting on one of them. Of the 678 verses of the Gospel of Mark, for example, only 55 verses are not found in Matthew, and only 187 are not found in Luke. For someone who is focused on the reality described rather than on the text describing it, the slight

---

[32] See Francis Martin, 'Literary Theory, Philosophy of History and Exegesis', *The Thomist*, 52 (1988), pp. 601–2: 'It is clear that in Christian antiquity, the events of the life of Christ were considered as the primary locus of revelation without much consideration being given to the verbal process by which those events reached the audience. There is in this a movement "behind the text".'

differences in detail between parallel verses in Matthew, Mark, and Luke will not stand out.[33]

What such an exegete *will* notice, however, is that Matthew, Mark, and Luke do not present their stories in the same order. While Matthew presents Jesus' rejection at Nazareth immediately after a discourse of parables (Mt. 13.53-58), Mark recounts the same incident immediately after the raising of Jairus's daughter (Mk 6.1-6), and Luke places it at the very beginning of Jesus' ministry (Lk. 4.16-30). This difference in order would stand out even if the texts *were* lenses – even if they were video tapes. Moreover, the logical place for a difference in order of events to show up in a commentary is in the *divisio textus*, which is where we find Thomas paying the most attention to Matthew's special features.

The metaphor of a 'lens' works better with a narrative text such as Matthew's Gospel than with a text composed of arguments, such as Paul's letters.[34] In an argument, the logical interconnection of the premises and conclusions requires that the details of the text serve the larger presentation. The only controlling factor in an argument is the author's purpose. In a narrative, however, there is the author's purpose and then there is also the simple fact of what happened – a fact which is beyond the author's control. This makes it possible for the reader to experience the text as a lens looking onto the facts.

Thomas' experience of the text as a 'lens' is one clue to the seeming two levels in the *Lectura*. We find another clue in the text of the *Catena aurea in Matthaeum*. Thomas' comments early on about Matthew's special emphasis are also found in the *Catena*: Remigius suggests that Matthew and Luke destroy errors about the humanity of Christ, while Mark and John destroy errors about the divinity; Augustine explains the differences between the Matthean and Lukan genealogies in terms of the different intentions of the authors.[35] The patristic sources of the *Catena* do not systematically pursue Matthew's special emphasis thereafter.

---

[33] W.D. Davies and Dale C. Allison, *A Critical and Exegetical Commentary on the Gospel According to Saint Matthew*, International Critical Commentary, vol. 1 (Edinburgh: T & T Clark, 1988), p. 108.

[34] Christopher Baglow has demonstrated that Thomas is a much abler commentator on argumentative texts than narrative texts. See Baglow, *Modus et Forma: A New Approach to the Exegesis of Saint Thomas Aquinas with an Application to the* Lectura super Epistolam ad Ephesios (Rome: Pontifical Biblical Institute, 2002), pp. 23–29, 80–88.

[35] Remigius' comment is the last paragraph of the *Catena aurea in Matthaeum* ch. 1, lect. 1, while Augustine's comment is the first paragraph of the following lecture.

Use of the Catena Aurea

Towards the end of 1262 or the beginning of 1263, Pope Urban IV requested that Thomas assemble a gloss on the four Gospels consisting entirely of quotations from the Church Fathers. The texts were arranged in such a way as to permit a continuous reading, as though the entire gloss were written by one author. With the help of some *florilegia* and a staff of secretaries to collect materials which he then organized and edited, Thomas completed the work rapidly: the volume on Matthew was presented to the pope before his death in October 1264.[36]

Any detailed treatment of Thomas' *Lectura in Matthaeum* must deal with the influence of the *Catena Aurea*.[37] As an illustration of this fact, I have chosen to examine his comments on the Transfiguration (Mt. 17.1-9) – not because they are in any way exceptional, but because they are typical. If Thomas' notes concerning the division of the text are excluded, he gives approximately 45 comments on Mt. 17.1-9. Of these, about 30 use the *Catena* on this passage directly, while 15 do not.[38] Of the available comments in the *Catena*, he skips only 8. Another way to measure the same fact is through word counting: those parts of Thomas' text which are directly dependent on the *Catena* make 70 per cent of the total commentary on Mt. 17.1-9.[39]

However, Thomas does not simply copy from the *Catena* two thirds of the time. Even as he uses his patristic sources, he edits and improves them. He has already edited his sources somewhat simply because he himself compiled the *Catena*: he chose which texts to include in the *Catena*, chose the order of their presentation, and occasionally changed the wording to ensure orthodoxy and

---

[36] Torrell, *Saint Thomas Aquinas*, pp. 136–37.

[37] Beryl Smalley's otherwise wonderful essay on the *Lectura in Matthaeum* in *The Gospels in the Schools c. 1000–c.1280* (London: Hambledon, 1985), pp. 257–71, is marred by her admitted failure to look at the *Catena* (see her comment on p. 257). As a result, she goes far afield to find Thomas' sources, simply commenting on the way that 'perhaps he used the fruits of his own labours in compiling the *Catena Aurea*' (p. 258).

[38] It is difficult at points to decide when a paragraph of text constitutes one comment or two. Also, two of the comments which I have counted as original to Thomas are indirectly dependent on the comments in the *Catena*. Hence these numbers must be taken as roughly accurate.

[39] Again excluding the notes concerning the division of the text, there are 2,525 total words in the Marietti edition for this passage. Of these, 1,769 are in parts of the text where Thomas is directly dependent on the *Catena*. These numbers must also be treated with caution, for reasons which will become clear.

continuity with the surrounding comments.[40] In his lectures, he reworks the patristic texts freely into his own words.

A good example of his rephrasing and organizing activity is his comment on Mt. 17.1 [1418], presented here in parallel with the Chrysostom quotation it paraphrases:

Thomas	Chrysostom
But there is a literal question here, namely why He wasn't transfigured right away when He said [Mat. 16.28]: 'There are some of those who stand here, who shall not taste death, until they see the Son of man coming in his kingdom.' Chrysostom solves it. First, to arouse the Apostles' desire; second, to mitigate their envy, because maybe they had been troubled after this word.	And this is why He did not lead them up immediately after He made the promise, but after six days: that the other disciples might not suffer anything human, that is, some movement of envy; or that, being filled with a more vehement desire by the space of these days, those who were to be taken up might approach with more attentive minds.

Thomas takes Chrysostom's insight and formalizes the presentation. First, he flags the issue raised as a question in the scholastic manner and provides the quotation which gives rise to the question. Then he introduces Chrysostom, who 'solves' the 'question' – terms familiar to his students at the university. Finally, he enumerates Chrysostom's answers: 'first', 'second'. In some cases, when Thomas neglects to mention which patristic source he is drawing upon, or when he combines a number of authorities in one enumeration of solutions, the result can look much more like a *quaestio* originating from the schools than a string of patristic citations. One benefit of Thomas' organizational work is that his lectures are much easier to read and digest than the parallel passages of the *Catena*. His labour to weave patristic citations together so as to read as though from a single author finds its natural culmination in the streamlined presentation of the *Lectura*.

Perhaps even more characteristic of Thomas' treatment of the *Catena* is his tendency to supply biblical citations in support of the insights he finds in the patristic texts. While the *Catena aurea in Matthaeum* has, for our passage, 12 citations or allusions to Scripture, in the *Lectura* Thomas offers 52; while almost none of the uses of Scripture in the *Catena* amounts to a formal citation, Thomas offers at least a partial quotation for nearly all of his uses of

---

[40] See the dedicatory letter to Pope Urban IV which prefaces the *Catena aurea in Matthaeum*.

Scripture. A good example is his comment on Mt. 17.6 [1441], 'the disciples fell on their faces', given here in parallel with the text from Remigius which it expands:

Thomas	Remigius
But one should note that the impious fall down in one way, the saints in another. The impious fall back, as is written in 1Kg. 4:18 of Eli, who when he had heard rumors about the Lord's ark, fell from a chair and died of a broken neck. But the saints fall on their faces: Rev. 7:11, 'who fell on their faces'. And the reason is that we do not see what is behind [us]. Ecc. 2:14, 'The eyes of a wise man are in his head.'	But the very fact that the holy apostles fell on their faces was a sign of sanctity: for those who are holy fall on their faces, while the impious fall back.

As before, Thomas introduces his comment with a familiar scholastic tag, alerting the student that a distinction is about to be made. He then provides examples both of the impious falling back and of the righteous falling forward, illustrating the rule which Remigius asserts. Finally, he goes a step further than Remigius and offers a reason for the rule: the righteous fall but fall wisely, so to speak, as a result of seeing the good, while the impious fall whither they know not, in folly. This too has its accompanying citation, of course.

Thomas appears here as a never-ceasing fountain of Scripture, a 'living concordance', leaving one to wonder how he is able to find a suitable citation for every occasion. In many cases, the answer is through keyword association. As Jean Leclercq describes mediaeval monastic exegesis, 'Each word is like a hook, so to speak; it catches hold of one or several others which become linked together and make up the fabric of the exposé.'[41] A simple example is Thomas' comment on Mt. 17.1 [1420], 'and He led them up on a high mountain apart'. Building from a comment from Remigius in the *Catena*, he supplies biblical citations with the keyword 'mountain':

> Why on a mountain? To indicate that no one is led to contemplation but he who goes up onto a mountain, as in Gen. 19:17, about Lot: 'Save yourself on the mountain'. And He says 'very high,' because of the loftiness of contemplation. Is. 2:2, 'it shall be exalted above the hills, and

---

[41] Jean Leclercq, *The Love of Learning and the Desire for God* (New York: Mentor, 1961), p. 79.

all nations shall flow unto it. And many people shall go, and say: Come and let us go up to the mountain of the Lord.' For that loftiness of glory will be above every loftiness of knowledge and virtue.

At some points it is difficult to see how Thomas arrives at a given text, but the chain of thought can generally be reconstructed. Reworking a comment of Rabanus, Thomas explains that Christ took only three men up the mountain to indicate that only those who hold to faith in the Trinity will enter heaven, and to support this he cites Mk 16.6, 'He who believes and is baptized shall be saved.' The key notion 'faith' is obviously at play, but how does the Trinity enter into Mk 16.6? Why cite this passage when so many other verses with the word 'faith' are at hand? The answer is that Thomas views Mk 16.6 as describing the same scene as Mt. 28.18-20, where Jesus gives the formula for baptism: 'Baptizing them in the name of the Father, and of the Son, and of the Holy Spirit.'[42] Once this connection is made, Mk 16.6 is an apt text to cite for Thomas' purpose.

At other times, certain biblical texts are associated in Thomas' mind with certain topics. In a homily on Mt. 17.3, 'And behold, Moses and Elijah appeared to them,' Chrysostom comments that many had said Jesus was Elijah or Jeremiah or one of the prophets (see Mt. 16.14), and suggests that Moses and Elijah appeared at the transfiguration so that 'at least here the differences between servants and the Lord might be seen'.[43] Thomas fills out this idea with a quotation from Ps. 85.8 (86.8), 'There is none like thee among the gods, O Lord.' He has used the quotation several times before: in a question in the *Prima Pars* on whether any creature can be like to God, and in his commentary on the Divine Names of Dionysius, again concerning whether any creature can be like to God; he will go on to use it again in the *Lectura in Ioannem*, as a refutation of the Jews who thought that Jesus was inferior to Abraham.[44] Neither the text of the Gospel nor Chrysostom's comment offers a keyword connection to Ps. 85.8, but the topic of comparing God with creatures is linked in Thomas' mind with this verse from the Psalms.

Scattered among Thomas' reworkings of the *Catena* we find comments which are original to Thomas. In a couple of cases, these comments are as simple as bringing another verse of Scripture to

---

[42] That Thomas sees Mk 16.6 as reporting the scene in which Jesus gives the formula of Baptism is clear from *ST*, III, 68, 8, obj. 1 and reply.

[43] *Catena aurea in Matthaeum*, ch. 17, lect. 1. The citation is drawn from Chrysostom's homily no. 57 on Matthew.

[44] See *ST*, I, 4, 3; *In Dionysii de divinis nominibus*, ch. 9, lect. 3; *In Io*. 8.53 [1275]. He also uses Ps. 85.8 as his thematic text for the prologue to the *Super Epistolam ad Hebraos lectura*, which is difficult to place in the chronology of Thomas' works.

bear on the present one, as in Thomas' comment on Mt. 17.2 [1422], 'He was transfigured':

> To be transfigured is the same as to be changed from one's own figure, as it is written in 2 Cor. 11:14 that Satan transfigures himself into an angel of light. So it is no marvel if the just shall be transfigured into a figure of glory; and so He was transfigured, because He laid aside what is His own.

Here again the connection is made through a keyword, 'transfigure', and in this case it is a connection which Thomas has made before.[45]

Only once in our passage does Thomas *not* use a biblical quotation offered in his patristic sources. The *Catena* on Mt. 17.4 has a passage from Rabanus, who rebukes Peter for desiring to build tabernacles on the grounds that no such structures will be needed in heaven; after all, Rev. 21.22 says, 'And I saw no temple in the city.' Thomas argues instead that Peter's mistake was to think that the Lord needs a house on earth, when His house is not on earth but in heaven, as Rev. 21.3 states: 'Behold the tabernacle of God with men.' While heavily dependent on the sayings of the Fathers, Thomas is willing on occasion to disagree.

The use of Quaestiones

One important area where Thomas tends to be independent of the *Catena* is in his use of *quaestiones*, a distinctively scholastic element in his commentaries. All the scholastic literary forms – *quaestio, disputatio, summa, articulus* – arose from the activity of lecturing on a text. As the master 'read' or lectured on the designated text, inevitably he would come across an obscure word, or a difficult thought, which raised questions. Over time, the act of answering these questions became more formalized, and became a recognizably separate component of the lecture. As it grew in size, the *quaestio* became independent of the lecture, and gave birth to the *disputatio*. When the lively *disputatio* was simulated as a way of presenting doctrine to students, it became the *disputatio*'s tamer cousin, the *articulus*, which in turn was the building block of the *summa*.[46] There is therefore an evolutionary kinship between the doctrinal discussions of the *Lectura super Matthaeum* and the articles of the *Summa Theologiae*.

One can often discern a formal *quaestio* in the lectures on Matthew. After giving a word-by-word commentary on the text of Matthew's Gospel, Thomas pauses before going on: 'But here a

---

[45] See *Sent.* III, 16, 2, 1, obj. 1.
[46] See M.-D. Chenu, *Towards Understanding St. Thomas* (Chicago: Henrey Regnery, 1964), pp. 79–96.

question arises', 'One should note that ...', 'One should understand that ...', or 'But it is objected that ...' What follows is usually closely related to the text at hand, but goes beyond simply commentary to pursue an issue raised by the text.[47] A couple of times, he closes his discussion with a phrase such as, 'Now let us return to the text.'[48]

Of the approximately forty-five comments Thomas makes on Mt. 17.1-9, our sample passage, four have to do with a *quaestio*. The proportion of four *quaestio*-related comments to forty-five total comments, or 5 per cent, is representative for the commentary as a whole: I find more than forty places in the *Lectura super Matthaeum* where a question is separated out from the course of the commentary in the manner described above. These passages together make up something around 5 per cent of the total text of the *Lectura*.

The *quaestiones* cover all manner of topics: the manner of Christ's conception, the nature of prophecy, fate, the causes of lunacy and the distinction between lunacy and demonic possession, whether demons can work miracles, the justice of eternal punishment, and so on.[49] They are of all different sizes, as well. Some are only three lines long, yet quite clearly a formal *quaestio*, while others cover multiple pages. By far the longest series of *quaestiones* in the lectures are those on the Eucharist.[50] Our discussion of the *quaestio* on the order of the Beatitudes suggested that some of the Matthew *quaestiones* are 'rough drafts' of later *articuli* in the *Tertia Pars*, giving them a particular value for historians of Thomas' thought.

In the comments on Mt. 17.1-9, two *quaestiones* engage the issue of whether Christ took on during His earthly life the properties of a glorified body. Meditating on 1 Cor. 15.42-44, the mediaevals taught that the resurrected body will have four special properties or 'gifts': *claritas*, *agilitas*, *subtilitas*, and *impassibilitas*. According to Thomas, Hugh of St Victor held that Christ took on *subtilitas* when He left the closed womb of the virgin; *agilitas* when He walked on the water; *claritas* when His face shone like the sun at the transfiguration; and *impassibilitas* at the Last Supper, when He broke His eucharistic body without suffering harm.

Thomas opposed this notion early in his career, in his commen-

---

[47] See Smalley's comment in *The Gospels*, p. 261: 'Thomas distinguishes himself from most earlier commentators by keeping to the point, concentrating with a fierce singlemindedness on the text in hand. To read him after Albert is like passing from a Victorian salon, littered with furniture and ornaments, to a white-washed "functional" living room.'

[48] See Marietti edn, n. 150 and n. 413.

[49] The *quaestiones* mentioned can found at numbers 132; 145–150; 170; 1458; 668 and 1945–6; 635.

[50] *In Matt.* 26.26-28 [2169–2201].

tary on the *Sentences* of Peter Lombard.[51] He argued that Christ took on our passible state in order to suffer for us, and possession of the four 'gifts' for even a brief span of time would be incompatible with that passible state. Instead, Christ took on the radiance of *claritas* in a miraculous manner, in such a way that it was not an abiding characteristic of His body but a transient quality.[52] Later on, in the *Tertia Pars*, he will repeat the same arguments, in the same order, using more or less the same authorities.

In the *Lectura super Matthaeum*, commenting on 17.2, Thomas gives the issue a very similar treatment. He begins by noting that Christ had the beatific vision from the moment of His conception, and hence one would expect that this glorious state would overflow into His body. However, because Christ was God as well as man, He was able to control this overflow such that the joy of the beatific vision was retained strictly in the uppermost part of His soul, while all His lower powers were left open to suffering and sorrow. Christ was, therefore, simultaneously and perfectly *viator* and *comprehensor*, one who struggles in the way and one who enjoys the end. The four incidents discussed by Hugh of St Victor (who is not mentioned here by name) would disrupt this arrangement, making Christ more a *comprehensor* than a *viator*. In reality, these things happened by God's power, miraculously, rather than by possession of the four 'gifts' in advance of the resurrection.

A few paragraphs later, commenting on the last part of verse 2, 'and His clothing became as white as snow', Thomas finds occasion to clinch his argument by pointing out that clothes do not receive the four gifts, and so the radiance of Christ on Mount Tabor was not a result of the gift of *claritas*. He had made this point in his commentary on the Sentences, years before.[53]

This short series of *quaestiones* is typical of others in the lectures on Matthew: in general, little is said in the Matthew *quaestiones* which is not found in fuller form elsewhere in Thomas' earlier works, especially in the *Scriptum super Sententiarum* or in the

---

[51] *Sent.*, III, 16, 2, 2.

[52] In the case of the Eucharist, Thomas denies that Christ's 'impassibility' had anything to do with the state of Christ's body: it was rather due to the fact that the breaking of the host takes place in the appearances of bread, not in Christ's own appearances (*species*). Thomas also goes after Hugh's teaching when he comments on the walking on the water, *In Matt.* 14.25 [1265].

[53] *Sent.*, III, 16, 2, 2, obj. 7.

Summa Theologiae.[54] Having already written a commentary on the *Sentences* and the *Summa contra Gentiles*, and in the midst of writing the *Summa Theologiae*, Thomas did not have to expend much energy solving new theological questions.

The unique genius of these *quaestiones* emerges when one looks at the *Lectura super Matthaeum* as a whole. Together, they demonstrate the doctrinal and catechetical potential of Matthew's text, flowing from the extraordinary range of issues a commentator encounters in this Gospel – often called 'the teacher's Gospel'.[55] They give an example of how an exegete can introduce doctrinal discussions without straying from the point of the text or wandering into irrelevancies. Modern commentators are comfortable going beyond the text to introduce historical discussions, but are less sure of themselves when it comes to theological excursuses.[56] Such work requires a set of skills quite different from those of the historian, as well as a certain level of comfort in looking *through* the 'lens' offered by the text rather than around it. Indeed, theological skill or training is closely related to one's comfort in 'looking through the lens': one reason why many commentators are uncomfortable trusting the Gospel's claims is that they are unable to make sense of the realities the text presents to them. They conclude that the text

---

[54] Beryl Smalley (*The Gospels*, p. 262) notes an apparent exception to this at *In Matt.* 10.30 [877], where Thomas discusses whether all the hairs we have cut off during our lives will be returned to us at the resurrection. Because the resulting mass would be unseemly, it does not seem so; but what does the saviour mean by saying that 'All the hairs of your head are numbered'? Some (*quidam*) have suggested that all the hair Adam cut off during his extraordinarily long life would be parcelled out among his descendants at the resurrection, thus giving each resurrected human a reasonable amount of hair. Thomas' own solution is to point out that our Lord said our hairs are *numbered*, which indicates that our hair will be restored at the resurrection as regards its form, not as regards its weight. This *quaestio* is not found in Thomas' other works. Noting that Albert hints at a similar discussion at the same point in his commentary on Matthew, Smalley suggests that this question has become attached to this part of Matthew's Gospel in scholastic discussions, so that Thomas would have let his students down had he skipped it. This is true, but even more importantly, the issue is treated at length by Jerome and Augustine in the *Catena aurea in Matthaeum*, ch. 10, lect. 11. Thomas' own solution to the question is borrowed from Augustine.

[55] Hence the title of Paul S. Minear's book, *Matthew: The Teacher's Gospel* (New York: Pilgrim, 1982). On p. 3, Minear comments that Matthew was 'a *teacher* who designed his work to be of maximum help to *teachers* in Christian congregations' (emphasis original).

[56] See the comments in Luke Timothy Johnson and William S. Kurz, *The Future of Biblical Scholarship: A Constructive Conversation* (Grand Rapids, MI: Eerdmans, 2002), pp. 161–62.

itself must be unreliable: such a reality could not be.[57] Thomas'
sure-footed 'theological criticism' offers a sense of confidence and
competence instructive for contemporary exegesis.

Comment *or* Quaestio?

It is often difficult to tell when to classify a given passage as a
quaestio instead of simple 'comment'. As a form, the *quaestio* began
as comments on a difficult text, slowly became a recognizably
separate part of scholastic commentary, and eventually won
independence in the *disputatio* and the *articulus*. We have focused
on the second stage of this evolution, *quaestiones* recognizable by
their separation from the flow of the commentary and by the
introductory and closing phrases. However, there are innumerable
places in Thomas' lectures where the first stage is in evidence, where
the boundary between comment and *quaestio* is hazy or non-
existent.

An example of this occurs in the commentary on the
Transfiguration, at Mt. 17.5 [1436], 'This is my beloved son'.
Thomas does not mark it as a question with a special phrase, or
separate it from the course of his comments, but the method and
content of the comment could easily have made it a *quaestio*:

> Our love is based on a creature's goodness. For a thing is not good
> because I love it, but rather I love a thing because it is good. But God's
> love is the cause of goodness in things. And as God poured out goodness
> in creatures through creation, so in the Son through generation, since He
> communicates [His] entire goodness to the Son. Hence creatures are
> blessed by participation, but He gave the entire [goodness] to the Son; Jn.
> 3:35, 'The Father loves the Son, and has placed all things in His hands.'
> Hence Love itself proceeds from the Father loving the Son, and from the
> Son loving the Father.

While this comment is quite typical as regards scholastic
approach, its content is surrounded by puzzles. Here, he takes
'This is my beloved son' as applying to Christ in His divinity, and
closes by citing Jn 3.35. But in his lectures on John, he argues that Jn
3.35 is more aptly applied to Christ in His humanity, and ends by
citing Mt. 3.17, 'This is my beloved son'![58] Moreover, it is difficult

---

[57] A classic expression of this discomfort is Rudolf Bultmann's essay 'New
Testament and Mythology', in *Kerygma and Myth* (ed.) Hans Werner Bartsch, trans.
Reginald H. Fuller (New York: Harper and Row, 1961), pp. 1–16. Bultmann remarks
(p. 5) that: 'It is impossible to use electric light and the wireless and to avail ourselves
of modern medical and surgical discoveries, and at the same time to believe in the
New Testament world of spirits and miracles.'

[58] *In Io.* 3.35 [545].

to see how the several sentences in this paragraph relate to one another: is 'God's love is the cause of goodness in things' supposed to apply to the following sentence, 'as God poured out goodness in creatures through creation, so in the Son through generation'? If so, this would have God's love causal with respect to the generation of the Son, which contradicts what Thomas says elsewhere.[59] If not, it is difficult to reconstruct with any certainty what role the sentence 'God's love is the cause of goodness in things' plays in the paragraph. Similarly, it is not clear to what purpose he brings in the procession of the Holy Spirit at the end.

One can explain Thomas' words in such a way as to avoid heresy, if the Father's love for the Son is seen as a natural love such as we have for the final end.[60] One might also see Thomas as presenting a pattern in the various loves mentioned: 1) our love for creatures, which is caused by the creatures we love; 2) God's love for creatures, which causes the creatures He loves; 3) God's love for the Word, which is a response rather than being causative.[61] This pattern offers at least some explanation for the presence of the various elements in the paragraph, although how it would function as a comment on the text of Matthew is not clear.

The difficulty a reader faces in understanding Thomas' remarks reminds us of our limited access to Thomas' *ipsissima verba*. It may be that Thomas offered sound theological reasons for applying the word 'beloved' in a special way to the Son, and the scribe – Leodegar, in this case – simply misunderstood his point. One option, for example, would be to say that Thomas began by distinguishing God's love for creatures from God's love for the Son, including the fact that God's love for the Son does not cause the Son. He may have also mentioned that God gave everything to the Son, which is a sign that God's love for the Son is incomparable with His love for any creature. Thomas then moved on (perhaps) to note that God's love for the Son is so great that it is Love itself, the Holy Spirit. All of which adds a terrific force to the words, 'This is my beloved son'. But Leodegar latched on to the idea that God's love for creatures is a cause of the creatures and that God has given everything to the Son, and combined these thoughts to produce a beautiful, original and – unfortunately – Arian argument.

---

[59] See *ST*, I, 42, 2.

[60] My thanks to Dr Michael Waldstein for this suggestion.

[61] I am indebted to Dr Matthew Levering for the perception of this pattern in Thomas' comment.

Conclusion

Piece by piece, an answer has emerged to our opening question: how did Thomas produce the *Lectura super Matthaeum* during a period already packed with literary output? Each topic covered above contributes something to the solution.

The fact that the *Lectura* are precisely that – *lectura* rather than an *expositio* – indicates that Thomas did not have to take time to write out everything in detail. At most, he wrote out class notes from which to speak. This same fact introduces the possibility that our scribes, Peter and Leodegar, may have filled out the lectures at places beyond what the master originally said. In other words, counting pages is not a reliable way to quantify what Thomas actually produced. The date of the *Lectura* is also very important. It places the lectures on Matthew after the *Catena Aurea* and near the end of Thomas' career as an author of systematic works, so that he has every intellectual tool he needs to assemble his lectures efficiently, if not effortlessly. The use of the *Catena Aurea* throws a great deal of light on the problem. While Thomas has only to provide himself with notes from which to speak, fully two thirds of his comments are provided for him in skeleton form by the *Catena*. In fact, Peter or Leodegar may have used the *Catena* at points to fill out their *reportationes*, although the manner in which the patristic citations are edited indicates that the massive use of the *Catena* represents Thomas' own work.[62] The doctrinal discussions of the *Lectura*, both in formal *quaestiones* and in comments which approach that form, overlap extensively with Thomas' earlier work and with other works he was composing at the time. The fact that there is little original speculation in the lectures on Matthew indicates that Thomas did not have to spend much time preparing his notes for these sections.

In short, Thomas was able to produce the lectures on Matthew without a great deal of preparation because the lectures on Matthew contain little which he did not have close at hand. His mastery of Scripture, patristics, and scholastic theology was such that he could produce a masterful commentary on Matthew on the side, so to speak, even as he tended all his other irons in the fire.

The interest of the *Lectura* for historians of St Thomas is clear: in many places, they are the nearest precursor to the *Tertia Pars*, while

---

[62] An interesting example of this is at *In Matt.* 17.1 [1419]. Thomas' comment is not directly drawn from any patristic source; however, it seems to have been inspired by the *Catena*, because the same comment shows up in *ST*, III, 45, 3, ad 4 as a gloss on something Chrysostom says in the *Catena* on Mt. 17.1. This kind of cross-referencing between the *Lectura in Matthaeum* and the *Summa* indicates that this use of the *Catena* is Thomas' own rather than a scribe's invention.

in others (the eschatological discourse of Matthew 24–25, for example) they represent his final word on a particular subject. But the value of the *Lectura* for students of Scripture may be greater still, because of the way the patristic tradition is brought together, organized, and woven together with a scholastic handling of the theological difficulties presented by the Gospel. While Thomas is right to observe that no one could grasp the Lord's words fully, his effort in gathering together the strengths of Christian thought from the patristic era through high scholasticism makes a good start. After seven hundred years, the *Lectura in Matthaeum* remains not just a valuable historical witness, but a remarkable commentary as well.

4

READING JOHN WITH ST THOMAS AQUINAS

Matthew Levering

In the English translation, Aquinas' *Commentary on the Gospel of St. John* runs to over one thousand pages. Many potential theological readers find the length and variety of topics so daunting that, when combined with the scholastic style and the common presumption that contemporary historical-critical scholarship has superseded Aquinas' exegesis, the Commentary goes unread and its theological insights untapped. Given this situation, this chapter will approach Aquinas' exegesis of the Gospel of John by ranging across the entire Commentary and presenting a variety of his exegetical techniques and sources. I will discuss six excerpts from Aquinas' Commentary, one each from the following roughly distinguishable sections of the Gospel of John: the prologue (chapter 1); the sacramental teachings (chapters 2–7); the attestation to Jesus' divinity (chapters 8–11); the Farewell Discourse (chapters 12–17); the crucifixion of Jesus (chapters 18–19); the resurrection of Jesus (chapters 20–21). By means of this approach, I hope to illumine, in an introductory fashion, the modes and significance of Aquinas' exegesis of the Gospel of John.[1]

---

[1] Jean-Pierre Torrell, in what has become the standard historical study of Aquinas, places the composition of the Commentary on John around the years 1270–72. The Commentary is a *reportatio*, written down by Reginald of Piperno at the specific request of the Dominican friars and Adenulf of Anagni, from Aquinas' class lectures to his students at the University of Paris. It was produced during the same time that Aquinas produced his commentaries on Aristotle's *Nichomachean Ethics* and *Metaphysics* and much of his *Summa Theologiae*. See J.-P. Torrell, *Saint Thomas Aquinas*, vol. 1: *The Person and His Work* (Washington, DC: Catholic University of America Press, 1996), pp. 198–201.

All translations are taken from St Thomas Aquinas, *Commentary on the Gospel of St John* (ed. and trans. James A. Weisheipl and Fabian R. Larcher; vol. 1, Albany, NY: Magi Books; vol. 2, Petersham, MA: St Bede's, n.d.). The commentary is cited in the text according to the paragraph numbers of the Marietti edition: *Super Evangelium S. loannis Lectura*, ed. Raphaelis Cai (Rome: Marietti, 5th edn, 1951).

The Word made flesh: John 1.1-18

Aquinas thinks that John's primary purpose in the Gospel is 'to show the divinity of the Incarnate Word' [§23]. The prologue presents Christ's divinity in a highly condensed fashion, as a preparation for the chapters of the Gospel in which Christ's words and deeds manifest his divinity. Therefore, the prologue can be divided into three sections. Verses 1–5 of the prologue depict the divine existence and divine operation of the Word. Verses 6–13 describe the Incarnation of the divine Word. In verses 14–18, lastly, John teaches succinctly how we come to know the divinity of the incarnate Word.

I will focus upon Aquinas' reading of John 1.16-18, 'And from his fullness have we all received, grace upon grace. For the law was given through Moses; grace and truth came through Jesus Christ. No one has ever seen God; the only Son, who is in the bosom of the Father, he has made him known.'[2]

In interpreting these verses, Aquinas cites the views of Origen, Augustine (twice), John Chrysostom (twice), Denys the Areopagite, and Gregory the Great.[3] His range in the Fathers, furthermore, is complemented by a similar biblical breadth.[4] In short, in addition to

---

[2] Aquinas refers to Jn 1.16 in *ST*, I–II, 108, 1; II–II, 176, 1, obj 3; III, 1, 6; 2, 11, ad 2; 7, 1; 8, 1; 8, 5, s.c.; 19, 4, obj. 2; 24, 3; 27, 5, ad 1; 39, 6, obj. 4; 53, 2, obj. 3; 64, 4, obj. 3; 69, 4 and 5. He refers to Jn 1.17 in *ST*, I, 75, 1 ad 1; I–II, 98, 1; 98, 3, obj. 2; 112, 1, obj, 1; II–II, 12, 2, obj. 3; III, 2, 11; 27, 5; 38, 3; 61, 4, obj. 1; 79, 1. He refers to Jn 1.18 in *ST*, I, 33, 3, ad 2; 41, 3.

[3] By way of comparison, Albert the Great, in his commentary on Jn 1.16-18, quotes Hugh of St Victor and Isidore (and refers to Arius), but does not quote Augustine or Origen. Of the biblical texts, Albert and Aquinas share Gen. 32.30, Exod. 32.20, Zech. 4.7, Mt. 5.8 and 11.27, and Heb. 7.19 – surprisingly few in common, it would seem. Both Albert and Aquinas quote numerous biblical texts that the other does not employ. See Albert the Great, *Opera Omnia*, ed. Borgnet, vol. 24: *Enarrationes in Ioannem* (Paris: Vivès, 1899), pp. 53–56. According to J.A. Weisheipl, Albert composed his Commentary on John originally in 1256 and produced a revised edition sometime between 1272–75: see Weisheipl's article 'Albert the Great, St.' in the *New Catholic Encyclopedia* (New York: McGraw-Hill, 1967), pp. 254–58. Interestingly, Aquinas cites 'modern' (e.g., Hugh of St Victor) authors by name much less than does Albert. In Aquinas' *Catena Aurea* for Jn 1.16-18, he quotes Origen, Chrysostom, Augustine, Gregory, Hilary, and Bede.

[4] As recipients of grace, Thomas refers to Stephen as depicted in Acts and to the Virgin Mary as depicted in Lk. 1.28. In describing the gift of the grace of the Holy Spirit, he employs texts about the Holy Spirit in 1 Cor. 12.11, Joel 2.28, Rom. 8.9, and Wis. 1.7; about grace in Sir. 24.26, Eph. 4.7, Prov. 4.2, Rom. 3.1, Rom. 6.23, Rom. 11.6, and Zech. 4.7. He compares Christ and Moses by means of Deut. 6.4, Deut. 34.10, Isa. 33.22, 2 Cor. 3.9, Heb. 7.19 (twice), Heb. 10.1, and Rom. 6.6, as well as Jn 14.6 and 18.37. He explores the question of whether any human being or angel has ever seen God, through Exod. 33.20, Isa. 6.1, Isa. 45.15, Prov. 30.4, 2 Sam. 6.2, 1 Tim. 6.16, Mt. 5.8, Mt. 18.10, Mathew 22.30, 1 John 3.2, Genesis 18.1-3, Genesis 32.30,

citing five Fathers (three Greek and two Latin), Aquinas cites three of the four Gospels, 11 of the 27 books of the New Testament, and 13 books of the Old Testament, including three of the five books of the Pentateuch as well as texts from the historical books, the Prophets, the Psalms, and the Wisdom literature. All this, it should be emphasized, appears in Aquinas' relatively short discussion of three verses of John's Gospel. As a resource for reading the Bible canonically (employing the analogy of faith) and with attention to the patristic interpreters, Aquinas' exegesis is exemplary.

Interpreting the meaning of the word 'fullness' (Jn 1.16), Aquinas distinguishes three kinds of fullness: that of sufficiency, that of superabundance, and that of 'efficiency and overflow' [§201].[5] Philosophical analysis of the word 'fullness' establishes these three kinds. One can be 'full' by containing what suffices to complete oneself; or by containing even more than what suffices for oneself; or by containing a completion that is not only even more than sufficient for oneself, but also causes fullness in others. Comparing John's use of 'fullness' to the sense applied to the Virgin Mary in the Gospel of Luke, Aquinas then employs this threefold distinction theologically to indicate Christ's uniqueness and Mary's pre-eminence among the saints. When the angel calls the Blessed Virgin 'full of grace', Aquinas suggests, the angel has the second kind of 'fullness' in mind. Mary's superabundant grace exceeds that of any other mere creature, and overflows 'from her soul into her body', since her spiritual relationship to the Holy Spirit bears fruit in her virginal maternity [§201].

In contrast, when the evangelist John says 'from [or 'of'] his fullness we have all received', he is referring, Aquinas reasons, to the third kind of fullness, one that both is complete in itself and causes fullness in others. He remarks that the preposition – 'from' or 'of' – can indicate, in other contexts, this kind of *causal* fullness: 'Note that the preposition *de* [of, from] sometimes signifies efficiency, i.e., an originative cause, as when it is said that a ray is or proceeds "from" the sun' [§202]. The same preposition, he gladly notes, has been used by the Church to express doctrinally the consubstantiality of the Son and the Father. When these meanings of 'from' or 'of' are drawn together, Aquinas finds – now at the highest level of theological speculation – that the *causal fullness* of the incarnate Word is, when understood in light of trinitarian doctrine, none

---

Wisdom 13.5, Romans 1.20, Job 36.25, Job 36.26, Jer. 32.18, 2 Cor. 5.8, and 2 Cor. 12.3, as well as Jn 4.24 and 17.3. He investigates Christ's unique knowledge of God by means of Ps. 2.7, Ps. 109.3, 1 Cor. 2.11, Mt. 11.27, Isa. 52.6, Heb. 1.1, and Heb. 2.3.

[5] Albert the Great does not treat 'fullness' other than by providing parallel biblical texts. He focuses instead on 'law' and 'grace', and on the vision of God. His discussion of the latter appears as a 'quaestio' inserted within his Commentary.

other than the Holy Spirit. Citing a number of biblical texts in defence of this position, he explains, 'In this usage, the fullness of Christ is the Holy Spirit, who proceeds from him, consubstantial with him in nature, in power and in majesty. For although the habitual gifts in the soul of Christ are other than those in us, nevertheless it is one and the same Holy Spirit who is in him and who fills all those to be sanctified' [§202]. Yet, there is a third way of understanding the preposition. It can also signify the receiving of a portion. In this way the expression 'from his fullness have we all received' (Jn 1.16) expresses our (incomplete) *sharing* in Christ's fullness, a sharing that does not make Christ any less full. Thus is the philosophical doctrine of participation, which we find throughout the New Testament, made explicit. As Aquinas states, 'For he [Christ] received all the gifts of the Holy Spirit without measure, according to a perfect fullness; but we participate through him some portion of his fullness; and this is according to the measure which God grants to each' [§202].

By means of analysis of the word 'fullness' and the preposition 'from', Aquinas has thus shed light upon the uniqueness of Christ, the degrees of spiritual fullness, and the reality that the 'fullness' of Christ is the Holy Spirit. Each of these theological theses finds additional confirmation elsewhere in the Bible. Aquinas has theologically deepened our understanding of the meaning of John 1.16: 'And from his fullness have we all received.' He then takes up the phrase 'grace upon grace' (Jn 1.16) in light of the sentence that follows, 'For the law was given through Moses; grace and truth came through Jesus Christ' (Jn 1.17). Citing John Chrysostom, Aquinas proposes that this double 'grace upon grace' may refer to God's twofold gift: his gift to the people of Israel, 'the grace of the Old Testament received in the law', which Aquinas calls 'a great grace' [§204], and his gift of reconciliation in Christ.[6] The theological import of this reading, which has in Aquinas 'fitting' rather than 'demonstrative' status, is the affirmation of the Mosaic law as a grace. Aquinas' is a theology of fulfilment, but not a supersessionist theology; the grace of the Mosaic law, which gives 'true knowledge of the one true God', is not superseded but rather participates in the graced fulfilment brought by Christ.

Aquinas goes on to point out that Augustine interprets the 'grace upon grace' in a different manner, though with equal theological fittingness. According to Augustine, 'grace upon grace' indicates the way that the grace of eternal life, won by merits, is nonetheless a grace since merit has for its principle 'justifying and prevenient grace, which is not given to us because of our works' [§206]. The

---

[6] For Chrysostom's and Augustine's positions see also the *Catena Aurea*.

goal of such exegesis, it will be clear, is not to attain definitive insight into the mind of the human author.[7] Rather, it is to explore, and participate in, the *sacra doctrina* in a way that enables the reader to apprehend more fully the reality being taught, namely, the reality of our receiving 'grace upon grace' from Christ's fullness.

Verse 17, which teaches that 'grace and truth came through Jesus Christ', prompts a similar process of questioning for Aquinas. How, he asks, can 'truth' come 'through Jesus Christ', if, as the evangelist John later says, Christ *is* the truth (Jn 14.6)? [§207].[8] As John has already taught, 'all things were made through him [the Son]' (Jn 1.3). In answer, therefore, one can say both that since Christ is the uncreated word he *is* the truth, and that since all things were made through him, all created truths were made through him. The truth that we are given through Christ, like grace, is a *sharing* in Christ's divine fullness: 'these are certain participations and reflections of the first Truth, which shines out in those souls who are holy' [§207]. Holiness is a participation in God's sheer holiness. Participation in God, Aquinas thus shows through speculative analysis, governs John the evangelist's account of 'grace and truth'.

Taking up the theme that 'No one has ever seen God' (Jn 1.18), Aquinas puts this claim through a similar process of speculative questioning. He cites a number of passages from Scripture that seem to defend the opposite claim.[9] Secondly, he distinguishes three ways in which God might be 'seen': exteriorly through a created, visible image; interiorly through a created image in the imagination; and interiorly in elevated contemplation through a created 'spiritual light' [§211]. These three ways rest upon philosophical analysis of the progression of knowing from exterior to interior. Aquinas then demonstrates that no created (and thus finite) likeness or concept, no matter how elevated, could adequately represent the infinite reality that is God. Yet, this point seems to contradict John 17.3, which states, 'This is eternal life, that they know you, the only true God, and Jesus Christ whom you have sent' [§212]. Aquinas argues that in this life 'seeing' God as God is in himself is impossible, because in this life we depend upon concepts to know. In eternal life, in contrast, God will make himself present to our minds as he is.

---

[7] See John F. Boyle, 'Authorial Intention and the *Divisio textus*', in Michael Dauphinais and Matthew Levering (eds.), *Reading John with St. Thomas Aquinas* (Washington; DC: Catholic University of America Press, 2005), pp. 3–8.

[8] Origen raises this question: see the *Catena Aurea* on this verse. Aquinas follows and develops Origen's solution.

[9] Here Aquinas is following Augustine, who observes that Jacob, Moses, and Isaiah seem to have seen God face to face: see the *Catena Aurea*. The chain of patristic texts put together by Aquinas on this verse is fascinating, but Aquinas' discussion in his Commentary follows a different line.

Even then, however, we will not 'comprehend' God in the technical sense: we will know God as he is, and yet our knowledge will not be comprehensive or exhaustive because of God's infinite nature. Rather than here setting forth the nuanced fashion in which Aquinas develops all these points, for our purposes it suffices to note simply how biblical exegesis requires such metaphysical and theological precisions, once one treats the word 'God' as intelligible and presumes that the *sacra doctrina* in one part of the Bible illumines, rather than contradicts, the true meaning of the *sacra doctrina* in other parts of the Bible. Exegesis, on this view, constitutes an intelligent, doctrinally informed participation in the sacred teaching, and thus cannot be limited to teasing out the sense of the text strictly in terms of the explanatory categories available to the human author of the text.[10]

The Sacraments: John 2–7

Chapters 2–7 of the Gospel of John are filled with sacramental teaching.[11] We will focus here, as a typical example of Aquinas' exegesis of such passages, on John 3.5-6: 'Jesus answered, "Amen, amen, I say to you, unless one is born of water and the Spirit, he cannot enter the kingdom of God. That which is born of the flesh is flesh, and that which is born of the Spirit is spirit." '[12]

Aquinas first discusses this passage in connection with John 3.3, in which Jesus tells Nicodemus the same thing, although in slightly different words: 'Amen, amen, I say to you, unless one is born anew, he cannot see the kingdom of God' (Jn 3.3).[13] Aquinas here undertakes a discussion of what is required to 'see' the kingdom of God.[14] As so often, he begins with a philosophical distinction. As noted above, such deployment of philosophy in biblical exegesis is justified by the continuity, as wisdom, between human teaching (itself a participation in the divine mind) and divine teaching.

[10] See Henri de Lubac, *Exégèse médiévale: Les quatre sens de l'écriture* (Paris: Aubier, 1959–64).

[11] For further analysis see, e.g., Francis J. Moloney, *The Gospel of John* (Collegeville, MN: The Liturgical Press, 1998).

[12] Aquinas cites Jn 3.5 in *ST*, I, 74, 3, ad 4; I–II, 112, 1, ad 2; III, 38, 6; 39, 4; 60, 5, *sc*; 66, 2, ad 3; 66, 3, *sc*; 66, 7, obj. 2; 66, 9; 66, obj. 10, ad 1; 68, 1, *sc*; 68, 2, obj. 1; 68, 9; 80, 1, obj 1; 84, 7, ad 3.

[13] Aquinas quotes Jn 3.3 in *ST*, I–II, 87, 5, obj. 2.

[14] This discussion on 'seeing' and 'the kingdom of God' follows Albert the Great, although Albert's account is less detailed than Aquinas'. See Albert the Great, *In Ioan.*, p. 116. See also Janet E. Smith, 'Come and See', in *Reading John with St. Thomas Aquinas*, forthcoming; Pierre-Yves Maillard, *La vision de Dieu chez Thomas d'Aquin: Une lecture de l'* In Ioannem *à la lumière de ses sources augustiniennes* (Paris: Vrin, 2001).

Aquinas explains that 'since vision is an act of life, then according to the diverse kinds of life there will be diversity of vision' [§432]. Just as sense organs provide sensible vision, so the spiritual soul, as a principle of spiritual life, provides spiritual vision. However, sin has obscured this spiritual vision. Therefore, in order to 'see' or to 'enter' the kingdom of God – the life of pure Spirit – human beings need a 'spiritual regeneration: "He saved us by the cleansing of regeneration in the Holy Spirit (Titus 3:3)"' [§432].

Aquinas then examines the meaning of 'kingdom'. He identifies various attributes that belong to true kingship, among them the power of the throne, dignity, the bestowal of favours, and the establishment of justice. Connecting these elements together theologically, Aquinas proposes that 'the kingdom of God' signifies God's 'glory and dignity', which are 'the mysteries of eternal salvation' [§433].[15] As king of his creatures, God accomplishes to his glory eternal salvation, bestowing his favours (grace and glory) upon his creatures and elevating his creatures to share in his dignity. Yet, this salvation is possible only in justice, because justice is the foundation of a true kingdom. Aquinas remarks that the divine mysteries 'are seen through the justice of faith: "The kingdom of God is not food and drink" (Rom. 14.17)' [§433].[16] The biblical quotation indicates the grounding of Aquinas' analysis of 'kingdom', which does not fail to be philosophical, in the explanations of Scripture. As we have emphasized, the *modes of teaching* are united in Aquinas' exegesis, whose aim is to reach up to the divine teacher.[17]

In order to enter the 'kingdom', therefore, we must be regenerated in justice. There are, Aquinas suggests, three stages to this spiritual regeneration, which correspond to three kinds of vision (sensible, imperfect spiritual, and perfect spiritual). The first two are the Old Law and the New Law, both of which are imperfect. Following St Paul, Aquinas teaches that the Old Law contained visible symbols of spiritual regeneration (e.g., the cloud, the crossing of the Red Sea) which could and did inspire the saving faith of the Israelites: ' "All

[15] See Benedict T. Viviano, 'The Kingdom of God in Albert the Great and Aquinas', *The Thomist*, 44 (1980), pp. 502–22; as well as chapters 4–6 of my *Christ's Fulfillment of Torah and Temple* (Notre Dame: University of Notre Dame Press, 2002).

[16] This is the key point made by Albert the Great in his commentary on the verse.

[17] On this point see, e.g., Michael Sherwin, 'Christ the Teacher in St. Thomas's *Commentary on the Gospel of John*', in *Reading John with St. Thomas Aquinas*, forthcoming; Michael Dauphinais, 'The Pedagogy of the Incarnation: Christ the Teacher according to St. Thomas Aquinas' (Ph.D. dissertation, University of Notre Dame, 2000); chapter 1 of my *Scripture and Metaphysics: Aquinas and the Renewal of Trinitarian Theology* (Oxford: Blackwell, 2004).

were baptized into Moses, in the cloud and in the sea" (1 Cor. 10.2),
i.e., they received baptism in symbol' [§433]. In the New Law these
symbols are fulfilled – not negated, because they permanently retain
their meaning as markers of salvation – by the gift of baptism which
is a visible sign that causes spiritual regeneration. Baptism regen-
erates us 'inwardly by grace, but not outwardly by incorruption'
[§433]. By baptism we are restored to justice, but we still bear the
marks and consequences of sin in our bodies, and so we remain
spiritually weak. Since we are not yet fully regenerated, we 'see' the
kingdom only imperfectly. The third stage marks the completion of
salvation history, the fullness of the restoration to holiness by
sharing in the divine life: 'There is perfect regeneration in heaven,
because we will be renewed both inwardly and outwardly. And
therefore we shall see the kingdom of God in a most perfect way'
[§433].[18] He goes on to point out that this spiritual regeneration, or
being 'born again' (Jn 3.3), is a 'generation from above' and
therefore 'in the likeness of the Son of God' [§435]. When we are
perfectly conformed in wisdom to Christ the Teacher, we will
perfectly 'see' God's kingdom which is his dignity, glory, and divine
favours.[19] Once again exegesis climbs to speculative heights.

   Arriving at direct consideration of John 3.5, 'unless one is born
again of water and the Holy Spirit, he cannot enter the kingdom of
God', Aquinas notes that 'see' and 'enter' here mean the same thing
[§441].[20] He then explores, from within the context of *sacra doctrina*,
the reasons why it would make sense for Jesus here to add 'of water
and the Holy Spirit' (not present in John 3.3) to 'born again'.
Aquinas first seeks to identify the role of the Holy Spirit.[21] Having
already shown that spiritual generation means conformity to the
Son, he notes that conformity or likeness to the Son comes about
above all by 'our having his Spirit' [§442]. He confirms this
statement with various biblical quotations; and we might recall his
earlier point, in interpreting John 1.16, that the Son's 'fullness' is the
Holy Spirit. He then addresses possible – not probative – reasons for
the water.[22] Were solely the Spirit present in the sacrament of

---

[18] As Albert the Great notes, Hugh of St Victor details three stages of human
history: before the Mosaic Law, the Law, and the period of grace (each stage
participating in the next: Hugh's vision is not a Hegelian supersessionist understanding of linear time). See Albert, *In Ioan.*, p. 117.

[19] Aquinas develops the interpretation of Chrysostom, found in the *Catena Aurea*
on this verse.

[20] As does Albert the Great: *In Ioan.*, p. 119.

[21] See for further discussion Bruce D. Marshall, 'What Does the Spirit Have to
Do?', in *Reading John with St. Thomas Aquinas*, pp. 62–77.

[22] See Gilbert Narcisse, *Les raisons de Dieu: Argument de convenance et esthétique
théologique selon saint Thomas d'Aquin* (Fribourg: Éditions universitaires, 1997).

baptism, there would be no physical sign to make visible the event of regeneration. Experientially, in terms of what Robert Sokolowski calls the 'theology of disclosure', this lack of a physical sign would make it difficult for us to apprehend the event of God's presence regenerating the sinner.[23] Not only the fact that our knowledge relies upon sensibles, but also water's characteristic attribute as cleansing, makes water a fitting sign to express God's regenerative presence in the sacramental event. Water suits God's purposes because 'we understand that just as water washes and cleanses the exterior in a bodily way, so through baptism a man is washed and cleansed in a spiritual way' [§443].

The lack of a sensible sign would be deleterious also, and indeed for Aquinas primarily, on theological grounds. First, it would imply that the event was solely spiritual, as if the body were not involved. Aquinas expresses this point Christologically, because baptism gives us a likeness to the Son: since baptism has its spiritual effect through the cross of the *Word made flesh*, the sacrament of baptism images this union of spiritual and bodily through the union of a divine aspect (the Holy Spirit) and a bodily aspect (the water). He unites these Christological grounds with the theology of creation, since the Redeemer is none other than the Creator. In the account of creation in Genesis 1.2, he notes, the Spirit and water are united in bringing forth things into physical life. Christ's baptism in the Jordan indicates that the same conjunction now brings forth souls into spiritual life [§443]. Aquinas also remarks that the action of the Holy Spirit reveals the Holy Spirit's divine nature. Citing John 1.13, he argues syllogistically, 'He from whom men are spiritually reborn is God; but men are spiritually reborn through the Holy Spirit, as it is stated here [Jn 3.5]; therefore the Holy Spirit is God' [§444]. The whole Trinity, Father, Son (Word), and Holy Spirit, thus finds a place in Aquinas' reading of both John's Prologue and John 3, illuminating the union between trinitarian theology and the theology of the sacraments.[24]

Aquinas goes on to make clear that Jesus' words are consistent with recognition that persons who have not been baptized with

[23] See Robert Sokolowski, *Eucharistic Presence: A Study in the Theology of Disclosure* (Washington, DC: Catholic University of America Press, 1993).

[24] For analysis that exposes the interconnectedness of Aquinas' treatment of diverse theological themes, see, e.g., the essays in *Aquinas on Doctrine* (eds. Thomas Weinandy, Daniel Keating and John Yocum; London: T & T Clark, 2004); A.N. Williams, *The Ground of Union: Deification in Aquinas and Palamas* (Oxford: Oxford University Press, 1999).

water can nonetheless 'see' or 'enter' the kingdom of God.[25] In addition to those people who have died while desiring baptism or who have died as martyrs (baptism of blood), Aquinas gives the example of the ancient Israelites. As regards the latter, they shared in the effects of baptism by participating in its symbol, and received the full fruit of baptism (eternal life) after Christ's Paschal mystery fulfilled the symbol: they 'were reborn with a symbolic rebirth, because they always had a sense perceptible sign in which true rebirth was prefigured. So according to this, thus reborn, they did enter the kingdom of God, after the ransom was paid' [§445]. In other words, there are ways of receiving the effects of baptism without receiving the sacrament itself. Having thus excluded the erroneous view that only those who actually receive the sacrament can be saved, he addresses another error, namely the Pelagian idea that the baptism of children is not for the removal of sin but is solely so that children can 'see' or 'enter' the kingdom. Following Augustine, he points out that only a spiritual obstacle – sin – could prevent someone from entering the kingdom, and thus children would only need to be baptized if (contra the Pelagians) they were in a state of sin [§446].[26]

Aquinas very briefly treats John 3.6, 'That which is born of the flesh is flesh, and that which is born of the Spirit is spirit.' He has already noted that only God can produce spiritual life, in the full sense of 'seeing' the divine mysteries, in us. Left to our natural principles, we could not have such life in us, and thus we need to be 'born of the Spirit', as Aquinas discussed in the context of John 3.3.[27] To the earlier discussion, Aquinas adds a philosophical comment on the preposition 'of' or 'from' in which he remarks that the preposition can generally indicate either efficient or material causality. In the case of birth 'of the flesh', it means both. In the case of birth 'of the spirit', it means solely efficient causality; and this special efficient causality differentiates rational creatures who participate in God's life by grace from rational creatures who do not. He concludes with a Christological clarification: the efficient cause of *both* Christ's material generation and his spiritual generation in grace (as man) is the special agency of the Holy Spirit.

---

[25] This point is addressed similarly by Albert the Great in his commentary on the verse. Albert notes that Lombard takes it up in Book IV of his *Sentences*. See Albert, *In Ioan.*, p. 120.

[26] See also the quotation from Augustine in the *Catena Aurea* on this verse. Albert focuses his treatment of Jn 3.6 upon the removal of original sin: *In Ioan.*, pp. 120–21.

[27] For further discussion see Carlo Leget, 'The Concept of "Life" in the *Commentary on St. John*', in *Reading John with St. Thomas Aquinas*, pp. 153–72. See also Carlo Leget, *Living with God: Thomas Aquinas on the Relation between Life on Earth and 'Life' after Death* (Leuven: Peeters, 1997).

Christ's humanity, in short, is a unique case as regards the doctrine of John 3.6 [§448].

Christ's divinity: John 8–11

These chapters contain a set of testimonials by Jesus to his divinity. We will examine a central one of these testimonials, John 10.27-30:

> My sheep hear my voice, and I know them, and they follow me; and I give them eternal life, and they shall never perish, and no one shall snatch them out of my hand. My Father, who has given them to me, is greater than all, and no one is able to snatch them out of the Father's hand. I and the Father are one. (RSV)[28]

In Aquinas' Latin Vulgate version, the text of John 10.29 reads slightly differently: 'What my Father has given to me is greater than all...'[29] The difference does not cause fundamental exegetical problems, because Aquinas takes up themes present in the RSV version when interpreting 'the Father is greater than I' (Jn 14.28).

Aquinas first comments on the pattern of 10.27-28, which contains two things which Jesus' 'sheep' (that is, those who follow him as the royal good shepherd – see John 10.11, 14) do, and two things which Jesus, in response, does.[30] Aquinas' interjections in his quotation of the biblical text deserve attention: 'The first thing we do is to obey Christ. Concerning this he says, "my sheep", through predestination, "hear my voice", by believing and obeying my precepts: "O that today you would hearken to his voice! Harden not your hearts" (Ps. 95:7)' [§1446]. Recalling an anti-Pelagian point made at length earlier in the Commentary (see Jn 6.44, 65, 'No one can come to me unless the Father who sent me draws him'), Aquinas reminds us that Christ's followers, those who obey him, do so ultimately not because of their own goodness, but because of the grace of God. 'Predestination' describes the providence of God in which his undeserved, completely gratuitous gift of sanctifying grace elects those who enjoy the relationship of faith in Christ.[31] Aquinas

---

[28] Aquinas refers to Jn 10.27 in *ST*, I–II, 108, 4, ad 3. He refers to Jn 10.30 in III, 17, 1, obj. 5.

[29] 'Pater meus, quod dedit mihi, maius omnibus est.'

[30] Albert the Great speaks of a 'special grace' given to the 'sheep' so that they will be able to know the Shepherd and obey him. Like Aquinas, Albert discusses 'predestination' and free will in this regard, although more briefly. See Albert, *In Ioan.*, pp. 424, 426. See also J.C. Smith, 'Christ as "Pastor," "Ostium" et "Agnes" in St. Thomas Aquinas', *Angelicum*, 56 (1979), pp. 93–118.

[31] See *ST*, I, 23; see also Daniel A. Keating, 'Justification, Sanctification and Divinization in Thomas Aquinas', in *Aquinas on Doctrine*, pp. 139–58, especially pp. 142–48.

likewise draws out a theological point in his interjected comment on the meaning of 'hearing' Christ's voice. He points back to similar use of 'hearing' in the psalms, in which 'hearing' God's voice means trusting and obeying God's commandments. The obedience of faith constitutes the same kind of 'hearing', although this time the voice is Christ's, indicating Christ's divinity.

Aquinas' interjections thus link 'hearing' and doing Christ's word, while rejecting the suggestion that this 'doing' – our works – belongs primarily to our own will rather than primarily to God's grace. Hearing Christ's voice (believing his words in faith) involves doing works of love (obeying his commandment – see Aquinas' commentary on John 15.12-14), but such works of love have as their fundamental source God's election, his gift of sanctifying grace.

In the first parallelism, Christ's sheep hear his voice, and in turn Christ knows his sheep. Aquinas draws two theological implications out of Christ's 'knowing', both of which explore further the interjection he has already made regarding predestination. Of Christ's statement that 'I know them' (Jn 10.27), he writes, 'This is like saying: The very fact that they hear me is due to the fact that I "know them" by an eternal election' [§1447]. God's gracious election causes faith in us, since Christ's words, as the revelation of divine mysteries that surpass the ability of human reason's demonstrative powers, require a *divinely given* intellectual ability (the virtue of faith) to know divine mysteries.[32] This point receives fuller treatment in Aquinas' interpretation of John 15.16, 'You did not choose me, but I chose you ...'. Aquinas secondly holds that Christ's saying 'I know them' indicates Christ's love and approval of his followers. Love is the source of divine election. If we are known by Christ *as his followers*, that means that we have, by his love, been made his followers.[33] Aquinas quotes 2 Timothy 2.19, 'The Lord knows those who are his' [§1447]. Such knowing indicates intimacy.

If this parallelism expresses divine election, however, what about human freedom? If we 'hear [Christ's] voice' ultimately because Christ 'knows' us, are those who reject Christ's voice culpable for this rejection? It would seem that their only fault, or at least the causal source of their faults, is that they have not been elected by God. Before moving on to the second parallelism, Aquinas raises this theological difficulty: 'But if a person cannot believe unless God gives this to him, it seems that unbelief should not be imputed to anyone' [§1447]. His response is that human sin, not God, is the

---

[32] See Romanus Cessario, *Christian Faith and the Theological Life* (Washington, DC: Catholic University of America Press, 1996).

[33] See *ST*, I, 20, 2.

ultimate cause of separation from Christ.[34] Sin, original and actual, separates human beings from God. If God gratuitously draws some persons, moving them to enter by their own free will into his friendship, that does not mean that God is at fault for the condition of those who do not share in this gratuitous election – precisely because the election is gratuitous. Aquinas explains that 'sin, for example, original sin, and in some persons actual sin, is the cause why we are not enlightened by God through faith' [§1447].

The cause that separates each human being from God's merciful love is sin. God does not owe anyone the special gift by which God moves them so that they freely turn away from sin and toward him, and if he gives this undeserved gift to some, it cannot be viewed as an injustice to the others who have condemned themselves by their own ongoing sinful rejection of God's merciful love: 'Thus, all who are left by God are left by reason of the just judgment of God, and those who are chosen are lifted up by God's mercy' [§1447]. Note that Aquinas, as he always does in the controversies that surround the Church's answer to Pelagianism, refuses to seek further reasons than God's judgment and mercy. God does not draw all sinners (human and angelic) to himself. The justice of this can be shown, but the reason for it awaits the revelation of the fullness of God's wise Providence for creation at the end of time. While we can recognize and celebrate God's mercy and justice, we cannot pry further without harm.[35]

The second parallelism is 'they follow me, and I give them eternal life' (Jn 10.27-28). Citing Job 23.11 and 1 Peter 2.21, Aquinas comments that to 'follow' Christ consists in 'our imitation of Christ' [§1448].[36] The imitation of Christ consists in leading a cruciform life, by which we are turned away from self-centred cleaving to this world, and turned toward God's mercy. Recognizing our need for God's mercy, we become merciful and meek as Christ was. As Aquinas puts it, we follow Christ 'by walking the path of gentleness and innocence in this life' [§1449].[37] Through this sharing in Christ's meek and innocent suffering, we receive his reward: 'eternal life'.[38]

[34] See *ST*, I–II, 79.

[35] See Robert V. Wharton, 'Evil in an Earthly Paradise: Ivan Karamazov's "Dialectic" against God and Zossima's "Euclidean" Response', *The Thomist* 41 (1977), pp. 567–84.

[36] Albert the Great remarks that we must be 'configured to the Shepherd' by following and participating in him. We receive 'the form of the Shepherd'. See Albert, *In Ioan.*, p. 424. See also Jean-Pierre Torrell, *Saint Thomas Aquinas*, vol. 2: *Spiritual Master* (trans. Robert Royal; Washington, DC: Catholic University of America Press, 2003), pp. 102ff.

[37] Aquinas quotes Alcuin to this effect in the *Catena Aurea*.

[38] Albert emphasizes that this gift occurs sacramentally, through the Eucharist. See Albert, *In Ioan.*, p. 425.

Probing the meaning of 'eternal life', Aquinas suggests that its three key aspects can be located by examining Christ's full promise in John 10.28, 'I give them eternal life, and they shall never perish, and no one shall snatch them out of my hand.'[39] First, the life that Christ gives those who truly follow him is 'eternal'. To be truly and definitively eternal, life cannot be corruptible. Furthermore, it is an incorruptible enjoyment of God, as Aquinas confirms by quoting John 17.3, 'This is eternal life, that they know thee the only true God, and Jesus Christ whom thou hast sent.' Second, he notes that the incorruptibility of eternal life requires the incorruptibility of its recipient: 'they shall never perish'. Here he takes the opportunity to point out the misinterpretation of Origen. Third, Aquinas notes that eternal life, even if incorruptible in itself and in us, could still come to an end 'by being snatched by force' [§1449]. But God's power, as Aquinas affirms through quotations from Wisdom 3.1 and St Augustine, prevents this: 'no one shall snatch them out of my hand'.

Yet, Jesus says 'my hand'. Were Jesus solely a human being, could the power signified by Jesus' 'hand' be a sufficient guarantee that we are not going to lose eternal life? Clearly the answer is no. Aquinas thus suggests that the purpose of the remainder of the passage (Jn 10.29-30) is to demonstrate our eternal life by proclaiming the divinity of the Son, on which our eternal life depends.[40] In Jesus' teaching, Aquinas recognizes not merely a testimony to Jesus' divinity, but a testimony to Jesus' divine sonship as the guarantee of our salvation ('eternal life'). In exposing this connection between Jesus' proclamation of his divinity and Jesus' soteriological teaching, Aquinas observes that Jesus' words have a syllogistic logic. Jesus intends, Aquinas suggests, to make the following argument: 'No one can snatch what is in the hand of my Father; but the Father's hand and mine are the same; therefore, no one can snatch what is in my hand' [§1450]. We can only know 'eternal life' when we know the true nature of Jesus Christ.

As noted above, Aquinas' text for John 10.29 reads, 'What my Father has given to me is greater than all, and no one is able to snatch them out of the Father's hand.' He therefore interprets 'what my Father has given to me' as signifying not Jesus' followers, but rather the Son's divinity as begotten. This reading fits with 'is greater than all', because the divine nature is greater than all. The RSV text, in contrast, reads 'My Father, who has given them to me,

---

[39] See the work of Carlo Leget, as well as Luc-Thomas Somme, *Fils adoptifs de Dieu par Jésus Christ: La filiation divine par adoption dans la théologie de saint Thomas d'Aquin* (Paris: Vrin, 1997).

[40] This direction is taken by Augustine and by Hilary of Poitiers in the *Catena Aurea*.

is greater than all ...'. In both cases, the emphasis lies upon the reality that God the Father is greater than all, and is therefore a sure guarantee for our eternal life; and in both cases the Father grants this authority to the Son.

Aquinas' text and the RSV accord in the second half of John 10.29, 'and no one is able to snatch them out of my Father's hand'. In commenting on this text, Aquinas carefully shields the Father's 'power' from the realm of pure will or arbitrariness.[41] It is not solely because of the omnipotence of the Father that no one can undermine the Father's will to draw Christ's followers into eternal life. Rather, it is ultimately due to his divine wisdom, which providentially orders all things according to the pattern that he knows in his wisdom. Aquinas adduces a text from Job to make this point about Providence: 'Now "no one is able to snatch out of my Father's hand", because he is the almighty One who is not subject to violence, and he is all-wise from whom nothing is hidden: "He is wise in heart, and mighty in strength" (Job 9.4)' [§1450].[42]

In short, the 'eternal life' of Christ's followers has its source in the wisdom of the Father. Christ can say that 'I give them eternal life, and they shall never perish, and no one shall snatch them out of my hand', because he expresses the one divine wisdom as the only-begotten Son. There is no difference between Christ's 'hand' and the Father's 'hand' because their power is radically one: 'Thus he says, "I and the Father are one".' As if to say: 'no one shall snatch them out of my hand', because I and the Father are one, by a unity of essence, for the Father and the Son are the same in nature' [§1450]. In expressing the divine wisdom for our salvation, Christ guarantees that his word of 'eternal life' will come to pass. Wisdom and power are united, providing a sure basis for the promise of eternal life.

In accord with his practice of using heresies as guideposts for how not to read Scripture, Aquinas places his interpretation in contra-distinction to the positions of the two key trinitarian heresies, Arianism and Sabellianism.[43] Aquinas' 'lectura', whose full extent

---

[41] As nominalist theology does not. See, e.g., Michael Allen Gillespie, *Nihilism before Nietzsche* (Chicago: University of Chicago Press, 1995).

[42] See Aquinas' *Commentary on Job* as well as Martin D. Yaffe's 'Interpretive Essay' in Thomas Aquinas, *The Literal Exposition on Job: A Scriptural Commentary Concerning Providence* (Atlanta, GA: Scholars Press, 1989).

[43] See Gilles Emery, *Trinity in Aquinas* (Ypsilanti, MI: Sapientia Press, 2003), especially chapter 7, 'Biblical Exegesis and the Speculative Doctrine of the Trinity in St. Thomas Aquinas' Commentary on St. John', also forthcoming in *Reading John with St. Thomas Aquinas*. Pace various attempts to read Aquinas' biblical commentaries in opposition to the *Summa Theologiae*, Emery demonstrates that 'the principal difference of the Trinitarian doctrine of the commentary and that of the *Summa Theologiae* does not reside in the themes treated nor in the aim which consists in exposing the truth, neither in the conceptual tools, but simply in the organization of

we have not traced, begins with John 10.19 and concludes with verse 30. The verse that sets the tone for Aquinas' interpretation is John 10.24, in which Jesus' audience in the temple asks him, 'How long will you keep us in suspense? If you are the Christ, tell us plainly.' Jesus claims his messianic stature by proclaiming that because of his unity with God, he gives eternal life to his followers. The Sabellians affirm this unity by conflating the two divine persons, but this position is untenable in light of Jesus' distinction between himself and the Father ('I and the Father'). In denying the unity, by contrast, the Arians 'say that a creature can in some sense be one with God, and in this sense the Son can be one with the Father' [§1451]. Aquinas concludes his discussion of the text from John 10 by pointing out the soteriological, as well as exegetical, failure of the Arian position: 'For our Lord proves that no one will snatch the sheep from his hand precisely because no one can snatch from the hand of the Father. But this would not follow if his power were less than the power of the Father. Therefore, the Father and Son are one in nature, honour and power' [§1451]. If Christ possesses the divine power – which is the key to his promise regarding his followers' 'eternal life' – then he must, given the radical transcendence of God, be God.

The Farewell Discourse: John 12–17

In contrast to his usual procedure, Aquinas devotes a distinct 'lecture' in his Commentary solely to half a verse from Jesus' Farewell Discourse, namely the first half of John 14.27, in which Jesus tells his disciples, 'Peace I leave with you; my peace I give to you; not as the world gives do I give to you.' Aquinas explains why he has separated this verse to treat in itself: the previous section of John 14 had detailed what the disciples would receive from the Holy Spirit's coming, while in John 14.27 Jesus promises 'a gift they will obtain from his own [Jesus'] coming and presence' [§1961]. The gift is 'peace'.

Aquinas first proposes a difficulty. The Holy Spirit is usually associated with love, which causes peace. Why, then, would Jesus associate himself, the Son, with 'peace'? Why not make clear instead that peace is among the blessings given by the Holy Spirit (see John

---

the matter. Whereas the *Summa Theologiae* presents the Trinitarian doctrine according to the *ordo disciplinae* which manifests the internal arrangement and coherence (the order of exposition where the different aspects and concepts of the Trinitarian doctrine are connected according to their mutual implications), the commentary on St. John presents the same teaching following to the letter the biblical text' (*Trinity in Aquinas*, p. 318).

20.19-22)? The reason, Aquinas suggests, consists in Christ's intention to teach the disciples about the relationship of the Son and the Spirit. Since the Spirit proceeds from the Son, whatever the Spirit gives or does is also from the Son. The Son gives us his peace by giving us his Holy Spirit.

According to Augustine's famous definition, employed here by Aquinas, 'Peace is nothing else than the tranquillity arising from order' [§1962].[44] In order to understand peace, therefore, we must recognize that human beings exhibit a threefold 'order'. The soul and body should be properly ordered, as happens when the intellect directs the will and the intellect and will direct the sense appetites; the person should be rightly ordered to other created persons by the bond of love; and the person should be rightly ordered to God by loving God above all things. 'Order' signifies the just relationship of one thing to another.[45] Given this threefold order, 'peace' is also threefold, as Aquinas affirms through biblical quotations: interior (with oneself), with one's neighbour, and with God. It might seem that we could enjoy 'peace' on earth. In a certain sense, Aquinas grants, this is possible, indeed requisite, for followers of Christ. Yet in its full meaning, it is clear that even the followers of Christ, on earth, do not enjoy perfect 'peace'. Aquinas recognizes this tension: 'The saints [true Christians] have this peace now, and will have it in the future. But here it is imperfect because we cannot have an undisturbed peace either with ourselves, or with God, or with our neighbour. We will enjoy it perfectly in the future, when we reign without an enemy and there can never be conflicts' [§1962].

When Jesus describes 'peace' in two ways – 'Peace I leave with you, my peace I give to you' – he may, Aquinas thinks, be describing these two degrees of peace, imperfect and perfect. Without peace, the fruit of the grace of the Holy Spirit, Jesus' followers would be unable to be sanctified on earth, and would remain entirely unjust (disordered) in themselves, in relation to other created persons, and in relation to God. In leaving 'peace' with his followers, Jesus leaves interior tranquillity and simplicity, love of neighbour, and love of God above all things. We recognize these attributes of 'peace' as the marks of human holiness. This peace is the characteristic of the new covenant established by Jesus. Such peace enables us to 'conquer the enemy [sin] and love each other. This is a kind of covenant

---

[44] See *ST*, II–II, 29, 2.

[45] For further discussion see Carlos-Josaphat Pinto de Oliveira, 'Ordo rationis, ordo amoris: La notion d'ordre au centre de l'univers éthique de S. Thomas', in *Ordo sapientiae et amoris* (ed.) C.-J. Pinto de Oliveira (Fribourg: Éditions universitaires, 1993), pp. 285–302.

established by Christ which we should keep: "A covenant of peace was established with him" (Sir. 45:24)' [§1962].[46]

Without such peace, believers could not arrive at the goal of eternal life promised by Jesus, since their sins, grounded in their lack of charity, would prevent them. Citing Augustine, Aquinas notes that 'one cannot gain the inheritance of the Lord who is unwilling to observe his covenant, nor can he have a union with Christ if he lives in strife with a Christian' [§1962]. And yet Aquinas is well aware that strife occurs in Christian life. Who could be saved if Jesus' words meant that Jesus has provided his followers with perfect peace, since all believers know how far we are from such peace, either in ourselves or in relation to others? 'Peace' in this sense is a real fruit of grace, and a mark of sanctification, but is imperfect in this world. On this reading, the second way of describing 'peace' – 'my peace I give to you' – indicates a second sense of 'peace', namely the perfect peace that we will enjoy in heaven. Jesus characterizes this peace as 'my peace' because it is perfect, just as his peace has always been perfect. As Aquinas notes, 'He always had this second kind of peace, because he was always without conflict' [§1963].[47]

Yet, this interpretation poses a problem: surely the 'peace' that Jesus leaves with us (the first way of describing peace) is also his peace? In other words, is it not theologically erroneous to suggest that 'my peace' refers solely to the perfect peace of heaven, since any peace that followers of Jesus enjoy on earth also comes from Jesus and is a real sharing in his peace? Drawing the connection between this text and John 16.33, 'in me you shall have peace', Aquinas affirms the unity of Christian peace. He notes, indeed, that the distinction between imperfect and perfect peace may well not be Jesus' meaning: 'According to Augustine, both statements can refer to the peace of this time. Then Christ is saying, "Peace I leave with you", by my example, but "my peace I give to you", by my power and strength' [§1963].

Aquinas thus grants the interpretation that the repetition of 'peace' may serve solely to instruct Jesus' followers that their imitation of Christ (their 'peace') will be possible only by relying upon Christ's power, not their own. In Augustinian fashion, however, he also affirms that a distinction must be made between our enjoyment of Christ's 'peace' on earth and in heaven. He expresses the distinction by stating that while Christ is the author of

---

[46] Albert the Great describes this 'peace' as the 'reconciliation to God which the Son establishes in going to the Father' and as 'true tranquillity of conscience in the testimony of the Holy Spirit'. See Albert, *In Ioan.*, p. 549. Albert's comments on this verse are quite brief.

[47] Aquinas is following and expanding upon Augustine: see the lengthy quotation from Augustine in the *Catena Aurea* on this verse.

our peace in both this life and the next, in the next life we enjoy peace in the same way that Christ possesses it, whereas in this life we do not enjoy peace in this way. For Aquinas, then, it is important to recognize variations on the meaning of 'peace' in interpreting the text. Otherwise, one will end up being forced either to deny that followers of Christ receive peace – deny that any real sanctification occurs at all – or else, imagining that we are expected as Christians to display on earth Christ's perfect peace, to despair at our pitiful condition and to fear that no one is saved because all are hypocrites.

In interpreting the concluding section of Jesus' sentence, 'not as the world gives do I give to you', Aquinas holds that Jesus intends to distinguish his peace from what passes for peace in the 'world', that is, in the human condition outside the redemptive relationship with Jesus. Aquinas proposes that Jesus' peace differs from the world's in at least three ways. First, Jesus gives peace with a different end in view, and the 'end' separates the two kinds of peace. In this sense, Jesus' meaning would be as follows: 'The world gives peace so exterior goods can be possessed undisturbed; but I give peace so that you can obtain eternal things' [§1964]. Citing Wisdom 14.22, Aquinas notes that the world's peace can be put to wrong use, since, being undisturbed, the sinner may find the commission of sin to be easier.[48] Christ's peace, in contrast, cannot be mistaken for a state of gentility in which sin may flourish. Instead, Christ's peace has a radical character, because it orders the person to eternal goods. Christ's peace could therefore include disturbing an unjust worldly 'peace'.[49]

The other two ways in which Jesus gives peace differently from the world take up the distinction between true peace and superficial peace, which masks interior conflict. Aquinas first makes a distinction between real and apparent peace. Jesus' peace informs the heart as well as outward acts. Such peace contrasts with the worldly peace described in Psalm 27.3, quoted by Aquinas: 'The wicked ... who speak peace with their neighbours, while mischief is in their hearts' [§1964]. A second distinction consists in possessing peace imperfectly or perfectly. Peace that shapes only exterior acts is radically imperfect in its ability to render the whole person 'peaceful'. Aquinas quotes Isaiah 57.21, 'There is no peace, says my God, for the wicked' [§1964]. In contrast, Christ's peace shapes

---

[48] Aquinas quotes Chrysostom to this effect in the *Catena Aurea*.

[49] For further discussion, articulating a Christian case against pacificism, see John Milbank, 'Violence: Double Passivity', in *Must Christianity Be Violent? Reflections on History, Practice, and Theology* (eds.) Kenneth R. Chase and Alan Jacobs (Grand Rapids, MI: Brazos Press, 2003), pp. 183–200 and, in the same volume, 'Addendum: Testing Pacificism: Questions for John Milbank', pp. 201–6, and 'Christian Peace: A Conversation between Stanley Hauerwas and John Milbank', pp. 207–23.

all aspects of the human person, and in this sense Christ's peace is 'perfect': 'the peace of Christ brings tranquillity both within and without. "Great peace have those who love your law" (Ps. 119:165)' [§1964].[50]

Aquinas' meditation on the 'peace' described in John 14.27 thus seeks to bring out the depths of Jesus' teaching about his peace. He considers Jesus' peace in two ways: as participated by us in this world as distinct from the next, and as distinct from the world's. Both of these distinctions belong to Jesus' own teaching, in the Gospel of John, about the 'abiding' in God that constitutes 'eternal life'. By carefully probing Jesus' teaching for the theological implications present in it, Aquinas performs the task of sharing in the *sacra doctrina* of Christ the Teacher.[51]

The Crucifixion: John 18–19

In order to see how Aquinas presents fulfilment of prophecy, as well as allegorical and anagogical interpretation, we will examine Aquinas' commentary on John 19.34: 'But one of the soldiers pierced his side with a spear, and at once there came out blood and water.'

Reading anagogically, Aquinas proposes that the word 'pierced' provides an eschatological meaning, teaching us about our eternal life. By employing the word 'pierced', not 'wounded', the evangelist indicates the new reality of a direct opening into the body of Christ, that is to say the body of the Son of God. In other words, human beings, through Christ's death, now possess a direct opening or entrance into the life of the Trinity. Aquinas combines this insight with evocative texts about openings from the Genesis account of Noah's ark – the primordial account of new creation, read allegorically here – and from the book of Revelation's proclamation of access to the trinitarian worship through the slain Lamb who lives. He writes, 'It deserves notice that he does not say "wounded" but "pierced", that is "opened", because in his side the door of eternal life is opened to us: "After this I looked, and lo, in heaven, an open door!" (Rev 4:1). This is the door in the side of the ark through which those animals entered who were not to perish in the flood (Gen. 7)' [§2458].[52] For Aquinas the opening in Christ's body,

[50] This account of 'peace' shapes Romanus Cessario's *Introduction to Moral Theology* (Washington, DC: Catholic University of America Press, 2001).

[51] See also my 'The Pontifical Biblical Commission and Aquinas' Exegesis', *Pro Ecclesia* 13 (2004), pp. 25–38.

[52] Francis Moloney reads Jn 19.34 sacramentally, but does not draw out the ecclesiological significance of the 'pierced' or opened side. The interpretation is from Augustine. See, for Augustine's remarks, Aquinas' *Catena Aurea* on this passage.

understood as an opening into the living Body of the Son in whom we share in the trinitarian life ('eternal life'), signals the salvation that Christ has won for us.

Given that the opening in Christ's body is a sign of salvation, one can understand the outflow of blood and water. On a first level, Aquinas suggests, the outflow was a miracle, since even if the blood came out because it was still warm (rather than congealed as in the general case of corpses), the pure water flowing from a human corpse indicates a miracle.[53] However, Aquinas is not primarily concerned with the question of whether it was a miracle, a question that continues to be debated scientifically today. Rather, Aquinas sees in the outflow not primarily a sign of Christ's divinity, but a sign of Christ's full humanity.[54] Blood and water are integral to human bodies. Aquinas has recourse to the science of his day to make this argument: 'The outpouring of blood and water happened so that Christ might show that he was truly human. For human beings have a twofold composition: one from the elements and the other from the humours. One of these elements is water, and blood is the main humour' [§2458]. Christ saves us in his humanity. Aquinas places this point first because of his knowledge of docetist views that denied the humanity of Christ on the Cross, a position reflected in the Quran's denial that Jesus, in his real human body, suffered and died on the Cross.[55]

It is the salvation accomplished by the incarnate Son in his full humanity that we receive through the sacraments, which mediate to us, in an incarnational fashion, the fruit of his salvific actions in the flesh.[56] After pointing out the character of the blood and water as signalling Jesus' full humanity, Aquinas turns to the sacramental symbolism present in the outflow.[57] First, the outflow of blood manifests the salvific power of the Passion of Christ, which when the

[53] Albert the Great also remarks on the congealing of the blood in corpses. See Albert, *In Ioan.*, p. 663.

[54] See Paul Gondreau, 'Anti-Docetism in Aquinas' *Super Ioannem*: St. Thomas as Defender of the Full Humanity of Christ', in *Reading John with St. Thomas Aquinas*, pp. 254–76.

[55] See Joseph Ellul, 'Thomas Aquinas and Muslim–Christian Dialogue: An Appraisal of *De rationibus fidei*', *Angelicum* 80 (2003), pp. 177–200.

[56] On the sacraments and Christ's Passion, see *ST*, III, 62, 5. On the relationship of the Eucharist and the Mystical Body in Aquinas, see Martin Morard's rebuttal of Henri de Lubac's *Corpus Mysticum*: Morard, 'Les expressions "*corpus mysticum*" et "*persona mystica*" dans l'oeuvre de saint Thomas d'Aquin', *Revue Thomiste*, 95 (1995), pp. 653–64. For Aquinas' theology of sacramental representation, see Thierry-Dominique Humbrecht, 'L'eucharistie, "représentation" du sacrifice du Christ, selon saint Thomas', *Revue Thomiste* 98 (1998), pp. 355–86; Dom Anscar Vonier, *A Key to the Doctrine of the Eucharist* (Eugene, OR: Wipf and Stock, 2002 [1925]). See also John Yocum's excellent 'Sacraments in Aquinas', in *Aquinas on Doctrine*, pp. 159–81.

[57] As does Albert, albeit much more briefly. See Albert, *In Ioan.*, p. 664.

soldier pierces Christ's side has only just been completed (see Jn 19.30). Christ's suffering, his sacrificial spilling of his lifeblood, constitutes a reversal of the proud selfishness of fallen humanity, and thereby restores, in expiatory fashion, the just order between creature and Creator. Through Christ's blood, a path of justice is reopened between human beings and God. As Aquinas states, 'we are cleansed from our sins by his blood, which is the price of our redemption: "You know that you were ransomed from the futile ways inherited from your fathers, not with perishable things, such as silver or gold, but with the precious blood of Christ, like that of a lamb without blemish or spot" (1 Pet. 1:18)' [§2458].[58]

Similarly, the outflow of water recalls the central imagery by which the prophets describe the new creation, the forgiveness of sins, that is to come upon Israel. Aquinas notes, 'And we are cleansed from our stains by the water, which is the bath of our rebirth: "I will sprinkle clean water upon you, and you shall be clean from all your uncleannesses" (Ez. 36:25); "On that day there shall be a fountain opened for the house of David and the inhabitants of Jerusalem to cleanse them from sin and uncleanness" (Zech. 13:1)' [§2458]. This prophetic imagery has now been fulfilled.[59] The outflow of blood signifies both the source of the power of all the sacraments (i.e., Christ's Passion) and the sacrament of the Eucharist, in which we receive the saving blood of Christ. The outflow of water signifies the sacrament of baptism, which cleanses us from sin; and it may also signify the sacrament of the Eucharist, in which the priest mixes water with wine.[60]

In sum, the piercing of Christ's body is not tangential to Christ's Passion. Rather, the piercing of Christ's body, and the resulting outflow of blood and water, belong to the teaching that Christ does from the cross. Aquinas had earlier quoted Augustine with regard to Christ's teaching: 'As Augustine says, Christ hanging on the cross is like a teacher in his teaching chair' [§2441].[61] In this light, the place in which Christ's body is pierced also belongs to Christ's teaching of new creation from the cross. Adam's side is opened to create his bride Eve; Christ's side is opened to bring forth the sacraments which build Christ's bride the Church. Reading allegorically,

---

[58] See *ST*, III, 46–47. See also Romanus Cessario, 'Aquinas on Christian Salvation', in *Aquinas on Doctrine*, pp. 117–37.

[59] For further analysis, see my *Christ's Fulfillment of Torah and Temple*.

[60] The sacramental mixing of water and wine is emphasized by Theophylact (eleventh century), cited in the *Catena Aurea* on this passage.

[61] See the studies of Michael Sherwin and Michael Dauphinais noted above, as well as my 'Does the Paschal Mystery Reveal the Trinity?', in *Reading John with St. Thomas Aquinas*, 78–91 (an expanded version of this essay appears as Chapter 4 of my *Scripture and Metaphysics: Aquinas and the Renewal of Trinitarian Theology*).

Aquinas states, 'This event [the piercing] was also prefigured: for just as from the side of Christ, sleeping on the cross, there flowed blood and water, which makes the Church holy, so from the side of the sleeping Adam there was formed woman, who prefigured the Church' [§2458].[62] Such allegorical reading is possible because God teaches both through history and through Scripture. One would expect Christ's teaching on the cross to correspond to, and fulfil, God's earlier teaching.

The piercing of Christ's body, then, teaches us about the full humanity of Christ, about the sacramental mediation of the salvific power of Christ's passion, and about the bringing forth of Christ's bride the Church.

The Resurrection: John 20–21

As a final example of Aquinas' exegesis, let us turn to his commentary on John 20.17: 'Jesus said to her [Mary Magdalene], "Do not hold me, for I have not yet ascended to the Father; but go to my brethren and say to them, I am ascending to my Father and your Father, to my God and your God." '[63]

In interpreting this complex text, Aquinas seeks assistance from the Fathers: Gregory the Great, Augustine (twice), and John Chrysostom. The greatest difficulty lies in understanding why Christ told Mary Magdalene not to hold him. After all, Aquinas points out, the very opposite is found in other post-resurrection accounts, for example Luke 24.39, 'Handle me, and see; for a spirit has not flesh and bones' [§2516].[64] In Matthew 28.9, Mary Magdalene and other women were allowed to take hold of the risen Christ's feet. One way to address this difficulty would be to dismiss the historicity of the other accounts, but Aquinas rejects that possibility, preferring to suppose that Mary Magdalene met Christ twice on that Easter morning.

Why then would Christ tell Mary Magdalene, at this meeting, not to hold him? Drawing as usual upon the exegesis of the Fathers, particularly Augustine,[65] Aquinas presents three possible explanations, two of which he deems 'mystical reasons' [§2517]. All the explanations depend upon understanding Christ as a teacher (which Mary Magdalene proclaims him to be in the preceding verse, Jn

---

[62] Aquinas cites Augustine to this effect in the *Catena Aurea*. Albert the Great makes the same point in his *In Ioan.*, p. 663.

[63] Aquinas refers to Jn 20.17 in *ST*, III, 20, 2, *sc* 3; 23, 2, obj. 2; 23, 2, ad 2; 55, 6, obj. 3; 57, 1, obj. 4, and *sc*; 80, 4, ad 1.

[64] This difficulty is discussed by Augustine in a passage quoted by Aquinas in the *Catena Aurea*.

[65] See the *Catena Aurea* on this verse.

20.16), who therefore speaks here in order to teach Mary Magdalene, and/or us, an important truth.[66] The first explanation, from Augustine, presents Christ as teaching through mystical symbolism, as Christ does often in the Gospel of John. If we read Christ's words, in their context, as mystical teaching, Mary Magdalene could symbolize 'the Church of the Gentiles, which was not to touch Christ by faith until he had ascended to the Father' [§2517]. Jesus could intend, therefore, to teach us through mystical symbolism a truth about the Church, whose permanent centre is Israel to whom Christ preached in the flesh.

Augustine's second explanation, in Aquinas' view, also requires reading the text mystically, on the assumption that Jesus is teaching a spiritual truth that can only be understood in faith. Augustine suggests that 'touch is the last stage of knowledge: when we see something, we know it to a certain extent, but when we touch it our knowledge is complete' [§2517]. Mary Magdalene may know Jesus to a certain extent, but not yet know him fully as the divine Son. Jesus would then be teaching her how to know him. She should not think that she already knows him fully ('hold' or 'touch' him) in the limited sense that she now sees him; she must seek to see him spiritually.[67] Augustine in this way presents the encounter between Jesus and Mary Magdalene as a spiritual or mystical instruction, understandable (and therefore interpretable) only in faith, that has to do with how Mary Magdalene must learn to know Jesus. Aquinas summarizes Augustine's second interpretation:

> Thus Christ says, 'Do not hold me', that is, do not allow what you now believe of me to be the limit of your faith, 'for I have not yet ascended to my Father', that is, in your heart, because you do not believe that I am one with him – yet she did believe this later. In a way Christ did ascend to the Father within her when she had advanced in the faith to the point of believing that he was equal to the Father. [§2517]

Such interpretations, Aquinas makes clear, presuppose that Jesus' teaching intends to make a spiritual point that will only be understood with spiritual eyes.

The third possible explanation that Aquinas gives, from John Chrysostom, is not a mystical interpretation. Rather, Chrysostom

---

[66] For discussion of Mary Magdalene, see Michael Sherwin, 'Christ the Teacher in St. Thomas's *Commentary on the Gospel of John*', as well as Pim Valkenberg, 'Aquinas and Christ's Resurrection: The Influence of the *lectura super Ioan.* 20–21 on the *Summa Theologiae*', in *Reading John with St. Thomas Aquinas*, pp. 173–93 and 277–92.

[67] Citing Augustine, Gregory the Great, and Chrysostom, Albert the Great thus suggests that Mary Magdalene had to be prepared to elevate Christ in the devotion of her heart: see Albert, *In Ioan.*, p. 678.

supposes that Mary Magdalene, seeing Jesus, thinks of him simply as a man who, having died, has now risen from the grave to return to his former bodily life.[68] Such a response on Mary Magdalene's part would not be surprising. On this reading, Jesus' instruction to Mary not to hold him 'was like saying: Do not think that I have a mortal life, and can associate with you as before: "Even though we once regarded Christ from a human point of view, we regard him thus no longer" (2 Cor. 5:16)' [§2518]. Similarly, Jesus' explanation that 'I have not yet ascended to my father' would explain why he was in this transitional state, visible to her as if continuing his mortal life. The transitional state belonged to his desire to teach his followers: 'For before he ascended he wanted to strengthen in the hearts of the apostles their faith in his resurrection and in his divinity' [§2518].

Aquinas next interprets Jesus' command to Mary Magdalene to 'go to my brethren'. He interprets this command in terms of the dignity given to human beings by Christ.[69] Thus he first points out that the apostles are Jesus' brethren in two ways, by sharing human nature with him and by being adopted sons of the Father by grace. He then directs attention to the particular dignity of Mary Magdalene, which involves 'three privileges' [§2519]: that of being a prophet, since she serves as the prophets did as an intermediary between angelic teachers and other human beings; that of sharing the rank of the angels, because she was able to gaze upon the risen Lord, as the angels do; and that of possessing 'the office of an apostle' and serving as an 'apostle to the apostles' in her task of proclaiming Christ's resurrection to the apostles [§2519]. Following Gregory the Great, Aquinas suggests that her role, in God's plan, teaches us about the dignity of woman: 'Thus, just as it was a woman who was the first to announce the words of death, so it was a woman who would be the first to announce the words of life' [§2519].[70] Jesus' instruction to Mary Magdalene – 'go to my brethren', the command of evangelization – thereby teaches us about the dignity of all his followers, a dignity based upon both creation (sharing human nature) and new creation (sharing the life of grace).

Commenting upon Jesus' instruction that Mary Magdalene 'say to them [the apostles], I am ascending to my Father and your

---

[68] See the *Catena Aurea* for Chrysostom's full remarks. Aquinas develops Chrysostom's interpretation by emphasizing Jesus' desire to teach.

[69] For further discussion see Serge-Thomas Bonino, 'The Role of the Apostles in the Communication of Revelation according to the *Lectura super Ioannem* of St. Thomas Aquinas', in *Reading John with St. Thomas Aquinas*, pp. 318–46.

[70] See the *Catena Aurea* on this verse. Albert the Great also mentions the point about Eve announcing death and Mary Magdalene announcing life: *In Ioan.*, p. 678.

Father, to my God and your God', Aquinas recognizes that the words could be taken to indicate that Jesus, like his brethren, is merely a creature.[71] He notes that Arius reads the text in precisely this way. Before presenting Arius's interpretation, therefore, he contextualizes John 20.17 canonically by quoting Ephesians 4.10, 'He who descended is he who also ascended far above the heavens', as well as John 14.12, which belongs within a discourse that treats the relationship of Christ to the Father [§2520]. Arius, Aquinas explains, assumed that 'my Father and your Father' meant that God was Christ's Father in the same way that God is the Father of other human beings. Aquinas offers two possible answers to Arius. The first is that Jesus could be speaking to his 'brethren' as their brother, which in his human nature he is. On this reading, the text would refer to his unity in human nature with his followers, a unity which makes possible the salvific inclusion of all human beings within Christ's relationship to the Father.[72]

The second answer comes from Augustine, who proposes that 'Christ is speaking of himself and referring to each of his natures' [§2521]. According to Augustine, the clause with 'Father' refers to Christ's status as the divine Son, and the clause with 'God' refers to Christ's humanity. Thus, speaking of 'my Father and your Father', Christ indicates the dignity to which he is bringing his followers: his Father by nature, our Father by grace. Christ ascends in order to draw us into this relationship with his Father, as St Paul, quoted by Aquinas, attests: ' "God sent forth his Son ... so that we might receive adoption as sons" (Gal. 4:4); "For those whom he foreknew he also predestined to be conformed to the image of his Son, in order that he might be the first-born among many brethren" (Rom. 8:29)' [§2521]. Speaking of 'my God and your God', Christ indicates his role as the mediator, in his humanity, between human beings and God: his God in his humanity, our God in so far as we are united to God by the human mediator Christ.[73] Aquinas again explains this position using texts from St Paul descriptive of our salvation:

For God is our God because through Christ we are pleasing to him: 'Having then been justified by faith, we have peace with God through our Lord Jesus Christ, through whom also we have obtained access by faith to this grace in which we stand; and we exult in the hope of the glory of the children of God' (Rom. 5:1); 'God was in Christ reconciling the world to himself' (2 Cor. 5:19). [§2521]

---

[71] St Hilary of Poitiers makes this point, and Augustine expands upon it: see the *Catena Aurea* on this verse.

[72] Without mentioning Arius, Albert the Great emphasizes this aspect of adoptive sonship: *In Ioan.*, p. 679.

[73] Albert the Great makes this point in *In Ioan.*, p. 679.

Augustine's reading assumes that Christ, in teaching Mary Magdalene, is teaching her and us about the structure of salvation.[74]

Conclusion

For Aquinas, it will be clear, Scripture is God's *teaching* through human words.[75] Once the text is understood as God's teaching, one recognizes that the theologian who probes questions arising from the text in a mode that goes beyond the explanatory categories that would have been possessed by the human author is not practising 'eisegesis'. Rather, the words of the human author of a biblical text require explication that acknowledges the place of the particular text within the whole of God's teaching, which takes place in various modes. Furthermore, as a sharer in sacred teaching, receiving in faith by the grace of the Holy Spirit the truths of revelation taught by the Church, the exegete does not set out to determine, from a 'blank slate' as it were, the meaning of the Scriptures.[76] Instead, exegesis should enhance our ecclesial insight into God's inexhaustibly rich teaching and thus contribute to the Church's ongoing proclamation of the divine mysteries.

If the divinely inspired words of the human author of a biblical text participate in and reveal divine wisdom, as Aquinas believes they do, then the biblical words must be appropriated by a variety of sapiential practices. We have seen examples of such practices in Aquinas' exegesis of the Gospel of John. First and foremost, Aquinas manifests a broad familiarity with the canon of Scripture, enabling him to treat Scripture as divine teaching that possesses an intelligible unity as well as diversity. Second, Aquinas demonstrates awareness of the exegesis of the Fathers, whose suggestions he draws upon particularly at difficult exegetical points. The Fathers' interpretations, which often differ from each other, are never presented as proof-texts, but rather assist the reader in contemplating God's teaching under the inspiration of the Holy Spirit. Third, Aquinas accepts the viability of what he calls the 'mystical' sense of

---

[74] See also Richard Schenk, '*Omnis Christi Actio Nostra Est Instructio*: The Deeds and Sayings of Jesus as Revelation in the View of Thomas Aquinas', in *La doctrine de la révélation divine de saint Thomas d'Aquin* (ed.) Leo J. Elders (Vatican City: Libreria Editrice Vaticana, 1990), pp. 104–31.

[75] For further discussion see Leo J. Elders, 'Aquinas on Holy Scripture as the Medium of Divine Revelation', in *La doctrine de la révélation divine de saint Thomas d'Aquin*, pp. 132–52; Marc Aillet, *Lire la Bible avec s. Thomas: Le passage de la* littera *à la* res *dans la Somme théologique* (Fribourg: Éditions universitaires, 1993).

[76] For further insight see Luke Timothy Johnson and William Kurz, *The Future of Catholic Biblical Scholarship: A Constructive Conversation* (Grand Rapids, MI: Eerdmans, 2002).

Scripture: God may at times be teaching through the human words
in a way that can be understood most fully only by those who have
the eyes of faith. Fourth, Aquinas employs the doctrinal determin-
ations of the Church, as well as the errors that the Church has
excluded (e.g., Arianism, Pelagianism), as guideposts for interpretation, since these doctrinal judgments, guided by the Holy Spirit
who inspired Scripture, indicate the true content of God's teaching
and expose where interpreters can go astray. Fifth, Aquinas includes
philosophical analysis within his exegesis, although without making
philosophical analysis the sole ground of particular interpretations.
He seeks insight into divine teaching by means of the tools of human
wisdom, which itself is a created participation in the divine mind.[77]
Sixth, in parsing the meaning of the biblical words, Aquinas often
does not identify a definitive interpretation, but instead presents
various options that are consistent with the faith without deciding
among them, in order to respect the biblical text's capacity to
contain various meanings. Seventh and lastly, Aquinas' exegesis
exhibits his ability to think together the mysteries of faith, and
thereby to attain balanced insight into the whole. In the midst of his
exegesis he often pauses upon a passage in order to explore complex
and difficult theological problems that arise from the biblical text
and that cannot, as modern exegesis has proven despite itself, be
elided. As Gilles Emery has eloquently put it, 'Biblical exegesis is
speculative as Holy Scripture is speculative; it leads one to the
contemplation of truth, because such is the aim of Scripture itself.'[78]

---

[77] On this point see also David B. Burrell, 'Act of Creation with Its Theological
Consequences', in *Aquinas on Doctrine*, pp. 27–44; Rudi A. te Velde, *Participation and
Substantiality in Thomas Aquinas* (Leiden: Brill, 1995).
[78] Emery, *Trinity in Aquinas*, p. 314.

5

AQUINAS ON 1 AND 2 CORINTHIANS:
THE SACRAMENTS AND THEIR MINISTERS

Daniel A. Keating

Aquinas' commentaries on First and Second Corinthians, rich in theological content, present us with special textual difficulties. An exegetical 'fault-line' runs through the extant manuscript (i.e. an early and late edition appear to be combined), and a significant strata of text is simply missing (commentary on 1 Cor. 7.15–10.33). The leading hypothesis for this state of affairs is the following: Aquinas appears to have commented on the Pauline epistles early in his career (either from 1259–65 or 1265–68). Then towards the close of his life (either at the end of his time in Paris, 1271–72, or during his period in Naples, 1272–73), he undertook a revision of his commentary on Paul's letters, but only completed Romans through 1 Corinthians chapter 10. Finally, in the process of the collecting and handing on of his commentaries, the portion from 1 Cor. 7.15–10.33 was lost, and a commentary on these verses from Peter of Tarentaise was inserted as a substitute in order to complete the commentary.[1] On this account, what we now possess is a more developed *expositio*

---

[1] For recent treatments of the dating of Thomas' commentaries on the Pauline epistles, see Eleonore Stump, 'Biblical Commentary and Philosophy', in N. Kretzmann and Eleonore Stump (eds.), *The Cambridge Companion to Aquinas* (Cambridge: Cambridge University Press, 1993), pp. 254–55; Christopher T. Baglow, '*Modus et Forma': A New Approach to the Exegesis of Saint Thomas Aquinas with an Application to the Lectura super Epistolam ad Ephesios* (Rome: Editrice Pontificio Istituto Biblico, 2002), pp. 115–17; and Gilbert Dahan, 'Introduction', in Thomas Aquinas, *Commentaire de la première épitre aux Corinthiens* (Paris: Les Éditions du Cerf, 2002), pp. xii–xiii. Dahan presents the two leading hypotheses on the dating of the Pauline commentaries, the first from Weisheipl (building on the thesis of Mandonnet), and the second from Torrell: J.A. Weisheipl, *Friar Thomas D'Aquino: His Life, Thought and Works* (Washington, DC: Catholic University of America Press, 1974), pp. 246–49; Jean-Pierre Torrell, *St. Thomas Aquinas,* vol. 1: *The Person and his Work* (Washington, DC: Catholic University of America Press, 1996), pp. 327–29, 337–41. Though the two accounts differ respecting the precise date of the original series on the Pauline commentaries, both argue for an initial set of commentaries in the 1260s, and then a more detailed redaction of Romans (and part of 1 Corinthians) late in Aquinas' career.

for 1 Cor. 1.1–7.14, probably revised by Thomas himself toward the end of his life, and a slightly less developed *reportatio* for 1 Cor. 11.1–2 Cor. from an earlier point in his career, and a lacuna in the commentary from 1 Cor. 7.15–10.33.[2]

Despite these textual difficulties, and despite a measure of uncertainty about how the parts of the commentary relate to each other within the span of Aquinas' career, it seems clear that Aquinas never wavered in his overall estimate of Paul's epistles and the place of the Corinthian correspondence within them. If indeed the Prologue to the Romans commentary – where Thomas offers his outline of the Pauline letters in some detail – dates from the very end of his life, and if the commentary on 1 Cor. 11 through 2 Corinthians comes from his early years of lecturing in Rome, then we have very strong evidence that he remained firm from first to last concerning the place of 1 and 2 Corinthians within the Pauline corpus. His statements on theme, outline and development found in 1 Cor. 11–2 Cor. coincide exactly with those found in 1 Cor. 1– 7.10b, and in this sense there is a seamless perspective that runs through the commentaries on both letters.

Confident of this, I will consider these commentaries within the one overarching framework that Thomas himself provides, and read them as exhibiting in two redactions a single, consistent perspective on Paul's letters to the Corinthians.[3] For each epistle, I will ask and attempt to answer two questions: (1) What is for Thomas the central theme and the macro-outline of the letter? (2) How does he expand and develop the key themes within the letter? In addition, I will point to other potentially significant or interesting features of the commentaries (most of which cannot be investigated here), and I will attempt along the way to link his topical discussions in these

---

[2] For the distinction between *reportatio* and *expositio* in Aquinas' biblical commentaries, see Terence McGuckin, 'Saint Thomas Aquinas and Theological Exegesis of Sacred Scripture', *New Blackfriars*, 74 (1993), pp. 202–4; and Donald K. McKim, 'Aquinas, Thomas', *Historical Handbook of Major Biblical Interpreters* (Downer's Grove, IL: Intervarsity Press, 1998), pp. 86–87. For the probable origin of the *reportatio* in medieval practice, see Beryl Smalley, *The Study of the Bible in the Middle Ages* (Notre Dame, IN: University of Notre Dame Press, 2nd edn, 1964), pp. 200–8.

[3] Given that we do not possess the early *reportatio* of Thomas on 1 Cor. 1–7, which presumably was disposed of in favour of the new redaction, it is impossible to determine whether and where Thomas altered his judgment on particular points of exegesis. But it is clear that his overall view of the letters remained the same in both versions.

commentaries with similar treatments in the *Summa Theologiae*, in the hope that the two accounts may be mutually illuminating.[4]

Commentary on 1 Corinthians

Theme and Outline

The overarching framework that Thomas supplies for the Pauline epistles appears in the Prologue to his *Commentary on Romans*. The fourteen letters (Hebrews is included by Aquinas) present teaching that 'bears entirely on Christ's grace':[5] first, as grace appears in the Head who is Christ (Hebrews); second, as it appears in its principal members (1–2 Timothy, Titus, Philemon); and finally, as it appears in the mystical body, the Church (the remainder of the letters). Within this last category, Christ's grace is 'susceptible of a triple consideration': grace in itself (Romans); the sacraments of grace (1–2 Corinthians, Galatians); and the work of unity that grace realizes in the Church (Ephesians, Philippians, Colossians, 1–2 Thessalonians). Notably, he further subdivides the two epistles to the Corinthians: 'the first treats of the sacraments themselves and the second of the dignity of their ministers'.[6]

It is just this thematic schema that reappears in the Prologue to his *Commentary on 1 Corinthians*. Following the pattern of mediaeval exegesis in general, Aquinas employs a key text from elsewhere in the Scripture to describe the dominant theme of a biblical book.[7] The text he chooses for 1 Corinthians is Wis. 6.24 (Vulgate): 'I will not hide from you the mysteries (*sacramenta*) of God, but will seek her out from the beginning of her birth, and bring the knowledge of her to light, and will not pass over the truth.' He provides this further comment:

> Thus the above text discloses to us the subject matter of this epistle, in which the Apostle treats of the sacraments of the Church. For since in the epistle to the Romans he had discussed God's grace, which works in the seven sacraments, here in the first epistle to the Corinthians he treats

[4] Aquinas makes ample use of 1 and 2 Corinthians in the *Summa*. He cites the former approximately 400 times and the latter approximately 130 times. And though certain chapters are quoted most frequently (e.g. 1 Cor. 12, 13 and 15), quotations can be found from every chapter of both letters.

[5] Translation by Baglow, '*Modus et Forma*', pp. 124–25. Dahan, 'Introduction', p. ix, observes that no author before the end of the thirteenth century composed a commentary on 1 Corinthians in isolation – in every case it was part of a series of commentaries on Paul's epistles taken together.

[6] Baglow, '*Modus et Forma*', pp. 124–25.

[7] For the scholastic practice of employing a scriptural text to define the subject matter of a biblical book, as part of an overall introduction called the *accessus*, see Dahan, 'Introduction', pp. x, xxvi–xxvii.

of the sacraments themselves, and in the second epistle to the Corinthians the ministers of the sacraments.[8]

By identifying an overarching theme, Aquinas is following (whether consciously or not) in the Greek Patristic tradition of identifying the *skopos* of a biblical book as a prerequisite for line-by-line commentary.[9]

Aquinas provides us with the macro-outline of the letter as he begins his commentary on the main body of the letter in 1.10, and he is unerringly faithful to this outline throughout the commentary.[10] In keeping with the concentric ordering of texts common in the scholastic period, he first divides the text between a general teaching pertaining to all concerning the sacraments (chapters 1–15) and a special and particular teaching aimed at the Corinthians themselves (chapter 16). The topic of the sacraments is then subdivided into three parts: (1) the sacraments themselves (chapters 1–11); (2) the reality signified and contained in the sacraments, namely, grace (chapters 12–14); and (3) the reality signified in the sacraments, but *not* contained, that is, the glory of the resurrection (chapter 15). Finally, he divides the section on the sacraments into a discussion of baptism (chapters 1–4), matrimony (chapters 5–7), and the Eucharist (chapters 8–11). Placed in schematic format, the outline appears as follows:[11]

I. General teaching on the sacraments (chaps. 1–15)
   A. The sacraments themselves (chaps. 1–11)
      1. Baptism (chaps. 1–4)
      2. Matrimony (chaps. 5–7)
      3. Eucharist (chaps. 8–11)
   B. The reality contained and signified: grace (chaps. 12–14)

---

[8] *In 1 Cor.*, prol. [1–2]. It is clear that Aquinas was giving lectures on the Pauline epistles in succession, because at the beginning of the commentary on 1 Corinthians he refers to what he had said earlier in treating Romans (*In 1 Cor.* 1.1-9 [4]). Translations of Aquinas' commentaries on 1 and 2 Corinthians are taken from an unpublished translation by Fabian Larcher, modified and adjusted by the author. The number in brackets refers to the paragraph number in the Marietti edition of the commentaries: *Super Epistolas S. Pauli Lectura* 2 vols, 8th edn; ed. Raphaelis Cai (Rome: Marietti, 1953).

[9] For the notion of *skopos* (aim or intent) in the Greek Fathers, see Frances Young, *Biblical Exegesis and the Formation of Christian Culture* (Cambridge: Cambridge University Press, 1997), pp. 21–27; and Robert W. Wilken, 'Cyril of Alexandria as Interpreter of the Old Testament', in Thomas G. Weinandy and Daniel A. Keating (eds.), *The Theology of St. Cyril of Alexandria* (London/New York: T & T Clark, 2003), pp. 14–19.

[10] *In 1 Cor.* 1.10-17a [19].

[11] For a minutely detailed outline of the commentary, see Stroobant de Saint-Éloy, *Commentaire de la première épitre aux Corinthiens*, pp. 49–70.

C. The reality signified, but not contained: the resurrection (chap. 15)
II. Particular teaching for the Corinthians (chap. 16)

We may well ask: Isn't this a rather forced outline, a structure artificially imposed upon the whole letter? It appears that Aquinas was not the first to identify the sacraments as the central theme of 1 Corinthians; he is probably building on an exegetical tradition that he accepted and developed.[12] It may be admitted that there is a certain artificiality in this way of conceiving the whole of the letter. It is doubtful that Paul understood himself as providing a treatise on the sacraments. He was responding to a set of questions and issues put to him by the Church (or parties within it), several of which pertained to the sacraments. But once this is admitted, there is a certain genius in Thomas' way of depicting the letter. It is a framework that does shed light on the content of the letter, and helps to position the various parts in relation to each other.

We should also recognize that 'the sacraments' function primarily for Thomas as a kind of formal outline for the whole, giving it order and perspective. But he does not attempt to relate every topic explicitly to the sacraments, and he frequently handles exegetical issues on their own terms with no reference to the sacraments.[13] In other words, the theme and macro-outline provide a helpful framework for the whole commentary, but they are not overly invasive, and there is no attempt at the conclusion of the commentary to summarize the whole in terms of the theme and its parts.

The Sacraments

As might be expected in his careful line-by-line study of the text, Thomas does not provide an extended treatment of the sacraments in general, but instead offers brief comments here and there in the text. I will begin by drawing attention to two of his more significant comments about the sacraments in general and their interrelation, and then go on to examine what he says about each of the three

---

[12] Dahan, 'Introduction', p. xii: 'Beaucoup de commentateurs du XIIIe siècle mettent, tout comme Thomas d'Aquin, l'accent sur les questions liées au sacrament.' He cites John of La Rochelle (d. 1246) as one example of a thirteenth-century author who identifies the sacraments as the pivotal theme of 1 Corinthians.

[13] McGuckin, 'Saint Thomas Aquinas and Theological Exegesis of Sacred Scripture', p. 210, observes: 'Even though in the general introduction to his exegesis of St. Paul, St. Thomas suggests a basic systematic approach to the Pauline commentaries in relation to the theology of grace, many of the deeper questions emerge here and there, without obvious organization, on the prompting of a word or phrase from Sacred Scripture.'

sacraments featured in 1 Corinthians: baptism, matrimony, and the Eucharist.

In a comment on the eucharistic prayer in 1 Cor. 11.23-24, Aquinas gives us his own explanation for why the sacraments were instituted in the first place:

> So it should be noted that the sacraments were instituted on account of a need in the spiritual life. And because bodily things are likenesses of spiritual things, it is fitting that the sacrament be proportionate to things which are necessary to bodily life, in which generation comes first, to which baptism is proportionate and through which one is reborn into spiritual life. Secondly, for bodily life is required growth, by which one is brought to perfect size and power. To this is proportionate the sacrament of Confirmation, in which the Holy Spirit is given for strength. Thirdly, for the spiritual life food is required, by which man's body is sustained, and likewise the spiritual life is fed by the sacrament of the Eucharist.[14]

The sacraments are instituted by Christ for the purpose of spiritual life, and notably, this spiritual life follows the pattern of bodily, natural life: generation (baptism); growth (confirmation); food (Eucharist).[15] These are, for Thomas, the 'sacraments of faith' that together effect and strengthen in us the very life of God.[16]

The second text to consider on the sacraments in general is Aquinas' commentary on 1 Cor. 5.7, 'For Christ our paschal lamb has been sacrificed.' Here we see his biblical typology at work, displaying the relation between the sacraments of the Old Law and those of the New. The Passover, for Thomas, is 'the most excellent sacrament of the Old Law'.[17] The lamb is a figure of Christ, the innocent 'lamb of God' (Jn 1.36); the passing through the Red Sea is a type of our baptism; and the unleavened bread is a type of the Eucharist. The entire event of the exodus and deliverance from Egypt is a type of the 'sacraments of faith' by which we are reborn and strengthened in true spiritual life. And importantly, Thomas concludes by calling his readers to 'celebrate the feast', not only sacramentally through partaking of the Eucharist, but 'also

---

[14] *In 1 Cor.* 11.23-24 [650].

[15] In the *Summa* (III, 65, 1), Thomas offers this exact explanation of the ordering of the sacraments and their conformity to the bodily pattern of growth. The likeness between bodily and spiritual growth is a characteristic feature of his theology of grace: for this likeness applied to growth in charity, see *ST*, II–II, 24, 9; for its application to daily reception of the Eucharist, see *ST*, III, 80, 10.

[16] For references to the 'sacrament(s) of faith', see *In 1 Cor.* 5.9-13 [263]; *In 1 Cor.* 6.1-6 [265]; see also *In 1 Cor.* 4.1-5 [186] where Thomas speaks of 'the sacraments of the Church, in which divine power secretly works salvation', and *In 1 Cor.* 6.7-13a [285] for baptism and Eucharist as the sacraments by which we are saved.

[17] *In 1 Cor.* 5.6-8 [246]. For Aquinas' exposition of this verse in the *Summa*, see III, 73, 6.

spiritually by relishing his wisdom'.[18] Aquinas' commentary on this key verse shows us how he unites a typological exegesis with a description of the sacramental economy, maintaining throughout his emphasis on the impartation of, and growth in, true spiritual life.

Baptism.[19] As noted above, the sacrament of baptism serves as the formal heading for chapters 1–4, but it is noteworthy that once he begins the commentary itself, Thomas immediately joins baptism with catechetical teaching as defining these opening chapters: 'In the first part the Apostle deals with doctrine along with baptism; thus he follows the example of the Lord, who gave the disciples the injunction to teach and to baptize in one command (Matt. 28:19)'. By joining baptism to teaching about the Gospel and treating them together, Aquinas specifies the subject matter in a way much more in keeping with the actual content of chapters 1–4, and at the same time shows the intrinsic connection between the sacrament of baptism and teaching about the faith.

The dominant concern regarding baptism that Thomas returns to at several points in the commentary arises directly from the text of 1 Corinthians itself: What is the relation between Christ and the ministers of baptism? The sharp demarcation that Paul makes in 1 Cor. 1 between Christ and the minister of baptism affords Thomas the opportunity to underscore the unique role of Christ. It is 'the grace of Christ alone' that works in baptism, and not the virtue of the minister.[20] This is why, Aquinas tells us, Paul is so insistent that we belong to Christ, and not to Apollos, Peter, or Paul himself (1 Cor. 1.12). He goes on to say that there are two powers proper to Christ in baptism: one is the divine power (by which the triune God cleanses us inwardly) and the other is the power proper to his human nature. The divine power cannot be communicated to any creature. The second power, the excellence proper to his human nature, could *in principle* be communicated to others, but in fact Thomas claims that it is not. Here is his description of this power proper to Christ's human nature:

> The other is the power proper to His human nature, which is the power of excellence in the sacraments and consists of four things: one is that He instituted the sacraments; the second is that He can produce the effect of the sacraments without the sacraments; the third is that the merit of His passion works in baptism and the other sacraments; the fourth is that the

[18] For the distinction between partaking of the Eucharist sacramentally or spiritually, see also *In 1 Cor.* 11.27-34 [698]. Thomas develops this distinction extensively in his commentary on the Gospel of John, *In Io.* 6.53-60 [969–976]; 6.61-72 [992], and in the *Summa* (III, 80, 1–4).

[19] For baptism in the *Summa*, see III, 66–71.

[20] *In 1 Cor.* 1.10-17a [24]. *ST*, III, 64.

sacraments are conferred by calling on His name. Now he could have shared this power of excellence with His ministers and particularly the fourth, namely, that baptism be consecrated in their names, but He reserved it for Himself; otherwise schism would arise in the Church, for people would suppose that there are as many baptisms as baptizers.[21]

Aquinas concludes this section of commentary with a striking statement about the sole sufficiency of Christ for salvation as effected in baptism:

> Therefore, if the sufferings of Christ alone [*si solius Christi passio*], if the name of Christ alone [*si solius Christi nomen*], confers the power to be saved on the baptized, then it is from Christ specially [*verum est proprium esse Christo*] that baptism has the power to sanctify. Consequently, anyone who attributes this to others divides Christ into many parts.[22]

If such is the case with baptism, this principle does not hold for the effectiveness of preaching and teaching. Though the two activities – baptism and teaching/preaching – are for Thomas essentially linked, they do not operate identically. The particular and personal virtue of the preacher does contribute significantly to the effectiveness of his words:

> The diligence or virtue of the baptizer contributes nothing in baptism, for it is indifferent whether baptism be given by a greater or lesser personage. But in the preaching of the gospel the wisdom and virtue of the preacher contributes a great deal; consequently, the apostles, being better qualified, exercised the office of preaching in person. In the same way it is said of Christ …[23]

Matrimony.[24] Just as he expanded the topic area of baptism to include teaching and preaching, so here Aquinas understands chapters 5–7 to be concerned, not just with matrimony *per se*, but with fornication, matrimony and virginity – which indeed are the main subjects Paul raises in these chapters. In Thomas' reading, Paul first attacks the sin which is contrary to marriage, namely fornication (chapters 5–6),[25] and then modifies with wisdom the zeal of those who, because of their detestation of fornication, concluded that marriage itself was a sin (chapter 7).[26] In the context of showing

---

[21] *In 1 Cor.* 1.10-17a [29].

[22] *In 1 Cor.* 1.10-17a [34].

[23] *In 1 Cor.* 1.10-17a [39].

[24] Aquinas' teaching on matrimony appears in *ST*, suppl., 41–68. This was compiled and edited by one of his pupils from his early *Commentary on the Sentences*, written at the beginning of his career. For a later treatment of the sacraments in Thomas, see *ScG*, IV, 78.

[25] *In 1 Cor.* 5.1-5 [228].

[26] *In 1 Cor.* 7.1-9 [313].

the fundamental goodness of marriage, he provides a summary of the purposes for marriage as ordained by God.

> Thus, therefore, matrimony has three goods. The first is that it is a function of nature in the sense that it is ordered to the production and education of offspring; and this good is the good of offspring. The second good is that it is a remedy for desire, which is restricted to a definite person; and this good is called fidelity, which a man preserves toward his wife, by not going to another woman, and similarly the wife toward the husband. The third good is called the sacrament, inasmuch as it signifies the union of Christ and the Church, as it says in Ephesians (5:32).[27]

In the comments immediately following, Thomas states the fundamental equality of husband and wife with respect to conjugal rights, offering a spiritual interpretation of the creation of woman from man in Gen. 2.21.

> Hence the woman was not formed from the feet of the man as a servant, nor from the head as lording it over her husband, but from the side as a companion, as it says in Genesis (2:21). Hence, they must pay the debt to one another according to what it says in Romans (13:7).[28]

Though constraints of space do not allow for a full discussion, Aquinas' statement here on the equality of husband and wife respecting conjugal rights should be read together with his exegesis of 1 Cor. 11.3ff., where Paul states that 'the head of a woman is her husband', and that a woman ought to veil herself in church because the man 'is the image and glory of God, but woman is the glory of man'. In brief, Aquinas distinguishes the sense in which man and woman are equally the image of God (Gen. 1.27; Gal. 3.28), from the sense in which the man is the principal glory of God because of the order of creation (Gen. 2.23). The woman is fully the image of God in dignity, but because she was 'taken out of man', she is in a special sense 'the glory of man'.[29]

Because of the section of commentary that is missing, beginning with 1 Cor. 7.15, we unfortunately do not have access to Thomas' full treatment of the relationship between marriage and virginity. What we do possess shows us that he follows the traditional understanding that virginity is the greater good (though not

---

[27] *In 1 Cor.* 7.1-9 [318].
[28] *In 1 Cor.* 7.1-9 [321]. In the *Summa* (I, 92, 3), he offers the very same exegesis of Eve being taken from Adam's side.
[29] His treatment of this question in the *Summa* (I, 92–93) is entirely consistent with his handling of the issue here in the *Commentary on 1 Corinthians*.

commanded), and marriage the lesser good (though not prohibited or sinful in itself).

Eucharist.[30] We lack Thomas' commentary on chapters 8–10, and so possess commentary on only one chapter concerned with the Eucharist (chapter 11). But from his topic statement at the beginning of chapter 11, it is clear that up to this point he has been concerned primarily with a practice contrary to the Eucharist (namely, partaking of food offered to idols); now he is going to take up Paul's instruction on the Eucharist *per se* (which in fact he does beginning with v. 17).

Aquinas' commentary on the Eucharist is difficult to summarize but makes for very interesting reading. Once again, he follows the text carefully and offers shorter or longer comments on each verse. Among the various topics he addresses are: the need for fasting before the Eucharist;[31] a recommended penance before receiving the sacrament;[32] how one can become inebriated from the consecrated wine when the substance of wine no longer remains;[33] and how the Eucharist may serve as a sacrifice for those who do not receive it.[34] The most developed section of his commentary treats the presence of Christ in the Eucharist (thus, transubstantiation) and the various issues that arise from this understanding of what it means when Christ says, 'This is my body ... this is my blood.'[35]

Among the many possible points of interest concerning Aquinas' teaching on the Eucharist here, I will identify three for special mention. The first is his account of why the Eucharist is given under two species (bread and wine; body and blood). He offers three reasons. First, since the Eucharist is designed for the perfection of our spiritual growth, it is fitting that it be given in the form of both food and drink – this is appropriately parallel to the means we have for bodily growth. Again we see the way Aquinas views the sacraments as accomplishing in the spiritual realm what physical food and drink accomplish in the bodily realm. Second, the two species are suited to the Passion of Christ which they signify. Just as Christ's blood was separated from his body on the cross, so in the sacrament the blood is offered separately from the body. Third, the two species correspond to our dual constitution of body and soul. The body of Christ is offered for the health of our bodies; the blood is offered for the health of our souls. Thomas invokes Lev. 17.11,

---

[30] For the Eucharist in the *Summa*, see III, 73–83.

[31] *In 1 Cor.* 11.17-22 [631–32].

[32] *In 1 Cor.* 11.27-34 [690]. For a short treatise on the sacrament of Penance, see *In 2 Cor.* 7.9b-11 [269].

[33] *In 1 Cor.* 11.17-22 [640–43].

[34] *In 1 Cor.* 11.25-26 [682].

[35] *In 1 Cor.* 11.25-26 [662–85]. *ST*, III, 75–77.

'For the soul of the flesh is in the blood', in order to show the relation between blood and the soul.[36]

The second point of interest is how Thomas presents the relationship between the Eucharist and the other sacraments (especially baptism). We have already seen how he regards the sacraments as providing a divine means of spiritual birth, growth and maturity in Christ. Immediately following this ordering of the sacraments, he adds:

> It should be understood that the cause of generation is not joined according to its substance to the one generated, but only according to its power; but food is joined according to its substance to those who are fed. Hence in the sacrament of baptism, by which Christ regenerates us to salvation, it is not Christ according to His substance but only according to His power. But in the sacrament of this Eucharist, which is spiritual food, Christ is there according to His substance.[37]

In the other sacraments, the consecrated matter (water, oil, chrism) needs to be put to effective use if the sacrament is to effect the work of grace. But in the case of the Eucharist it is different: 'This sacrament is completed in the very consecration of the matter, in which Christ himself is contained, who is the end of all sanctifying grace.'[38] The special quality of the Eucharist for Thomas is the manner in which Christ is substantially contained in it. This being said, it is still the case that Thomas understands the Eucharist to have its proper effect in us only if we partake of it worthily, that is, spiritually and with faith.

This brings us directly to the third point for special mention, namely, Aquinas' pastoral approach to the Eucharist as a means of spiritual refreshment and growth. This pastoral concern arises from 1 Cor. 11.27-34, where Paul speaks about worthy and unworthy ways to receive the Eucharist, and asserts that it is possible for one 'to eat and drink judgement upon himself'. Consistent with his treatment throughout, Thomas identifies 'the fruit of this sacrament' as 'spiritual refreshment'. We can sin against proper reverence for the Eucharist venially by approaching it with a mind distracted by worldly concerns. This for Aquinas impedes the actual spiritual refreshment we gain by partaking. But we can also sin mortally if we show contempt for the sacrament or approach with the intention of

---

[36] *In 1 Cor.* 11.23-24 [653]. In the *Summa* (III, 74, 1), Thomas offers just these three reasons for the use of the two species, and adds a fourth, namely, that the bread and wine each demonstrate that the Church is made up of many members (many grains make the bread, many grapes make the wine).

[37] *In 1 Cor.* 11.23-24 [651].

[38] *In 1 Cor.* 11.23-24 [660].

sinning mortally.[39] It is in this way that we eat or drink judgment upon ourselves. The goal, then, is to partake of the Eucharist, not just sacramentally, but sacramentally and spiritually. By this we receive the *res* of the sacrament, which is charity.[40]

Aquinas concludes by addressing the question of frequency of reception. Some, he says, are drawn to receive the Eucharist frequently because they acquire spiritual life from it. Others, through fear of receiving it unworthily, partake more rarely. 'Both are commendable', Thomas concludes, because the one case exhibits charity and the other honour and reverence towards Christ. In his closing comment, Aquinas shows at once his profound appreciation for the Eucharist as daily life-giving nourishment and his sensitivity to the pastoral needs of those who receive:

> But because of themselves love is preferred to fear, it seems more commendable to receive more frequently rather than more rarely. Yet because something more choiceworthy in itself can be less choiceworthy in regard to this or that person, each one should consider in himself which effect the frequent reception of this sacrament would have in him. For if someone feels that it helps him make progress to the fervour of his love of Christ and in his strength to resist sins, he ought to receive frequently. But if someone feels in himself less reverence for this sacrament by receiving it frequently, he should be advised to receive it rarely.[41]

A temple of the Holy Spirit

There are many potentially interesting topics within Aquinas' *Commentary on 1 Corinthians* that readers may wish to explore: for example, the contrast between human and divine wisdom (1 Cor. 1.17–2.16);[42] the relationship between male and female in Christ (1 Cor. 11.1-16);[43] the place of spiritual gifts and their relation to charity (1 Cor. 12–14);[44] or Paul's magnificent treatment of the resurrection of the dead (1 Cor. 15.1-58).[45] Given limitations of

---

[39] *In 1 Cor.* 11.27-34 [687–89].

[40] *In 1 Cor.* 11.27-34 [698].

[41] *In 1 Cor.* 11.27-34 [699]. In the *Summa* (III, 80, 10), Thomas offers the same explanation for frequency of reception: it is praiseworthy and recommended to receive daily, but each should receive according to the frequency that serves his spiritual good. The account in the *Summa*, however, appears to place greater weight on daily reception. If indeed his commentary on 1 Cor. 11 predates the *Summa*, it is at least possible that Thomas came to place greater emphasis on daily reception of the Eucharist late in his life.

[42] *In 1 Cor.* 1.17b–2.16 [40–121].

[43] *In 1 Cor.* 11.1-16 [582–620].

[44] *In 1 Cor.* 12–14 [709–887]. *ST*, I–II, 68; II–II, 171–78.

[45] *In 1 Cor.* 15.1-58 [888–1023]. *ST*, suppl., 69–99.

space, I have selected just one subject to sketch out in brief: Aquinas' treatment of the Christian as a temple of the Holy Spirit (1 Cor. 3.16-23; 1 Cor. 6.19).

The text that prompts Thomas' discussion of the Christian as a temple of the Holy Spirit is 1 Cor. 3.16: 'Do you not know that you are God's temple and that God's Spirit dwells in you?' He begins by stating a general principle: 'Everything in which God dwells can be called a temple.'[46] He then identifies three senses in the Scripture in which a temple is understood as God's dwelling place. First, in the sense that God dwells within himself (Rev. 21.22, 'Its temple is the Lord God'). Second, in the sense that God dwells in a building consecrated by the worship offered to him there (Ps. 5.7, 'I will worship toward your holy temple'). Finally, in the sense that God dwells in us by faith working through love (Eph. 3.17, 'That Christ may dwell in your hearts through faith'). The reference to the Spirit dwelling in us (v. 16b) only proves that the Spirit indeed is God: 'This shows that the Spirit is God, by whose indwelling [*inhabitationem*] the faithful are called God's temple, for only God's indwelling [*inhabitatio*] makes a thing God's temple.'[47]

Thomas goes on to specify what it means to say that God dwells in us as in a temple. We know, Thomas reminds us, that God exists in all things by means of his essence, power, and presence, but his indwelling as in a temple is distinct from this manner of presence.

> God is said to dwell spiritually as in a family dwelling in the saints, whose mind is capable of God by knowledge and love, even though they may not be actually thinking of Him or loving Him, provided that by grace they possess the habit of faith and charity, as is the case with baptized infants. However, knowledge without love does not suffice for God's indwelling [*inhabitationem Dei*] ... That is why many persons know God either by natural knowledge or by unformed faith, yet God's Spirit does not dwell in [*inhabitat*] them.[48]

For Thomas, then, the indwelling of the Spirit is the prerequisite and ongoing condition for the operative habit of faith formed by love in the Christian.

Further on in the commentary, when considering 1 Cor. 6.19, 'Do you not know that your body is a temple of the Holy Spirit within you, which you have from God?', Aquinas links the idea of the temple of the Holy Spirit explicitly with Rom. 5.5, thus demonstrating the link between the indwelling of the Spirit and charity:

---

[46] *In 1 Cor.* 3.16-23 [172].
[47] *In 1 Cor.* 3.16-23 [172].
[48] *In 1 Cor.* 3.16-23 [173].

God's house is called a temple. Therefore, because the Holy Spirit is God, it is correct to say that anyone in whom the Holy Spirit exists is called a temple of God. But the Holy Spirit is chiefly in the hearts of men, in whom the love of God is poured out by the Holy Spirit, as it says in Rom. 5:5. But secondarily, He is also in the bodily members, inasmuch as they perform acts of charity.[49]

It may be useful to compare this discussion of the indwelling of God through the Holy Spirit with Aquinas' commentary on 2 Cor. 6.16, 'For we are the temple of the living God.' If the proposed dating of the commentaries is correct, then his commentary on this text actually predates by several years his discussion of 1 Cor. 3.16 and 6.19. Though the details of the exegesis differ, Aquinas states in all three texts the same basic understanding of what it means to say that God dwells in us as in a temple.

He begins his discussion of 2 Cor. 6.16 by identifying the reason for the use of temple imagery: 'For the use of a temple is that God dwell in it, because a temple is a place consecrated for God to dwell in.'[50] Then in a neat piece of intertextual commentary, Thomas interprets the dwelling of God in us through the words of Lev. 26.11-12, taking each phrase in turn: 'I will place my dwelling [*tabernaculum*] in your midst ..., I will walk among you, I will be your God, you shall be my people.' The first phrase, Thomas tells us, pertains to 'operating grace', which refers to God being in someone by grace.

> For although God is said to be in all things by his presence, power, and essence, he is not said to dwell in [*inhabitare*] them, but only in the saints through grace; the reason being that God is in all things by his activity, inasmuch as he joins himself to them as giving being and conserving them in being, but in the saints by the activity [*operationem*] of the saints themselves, by which they attain to God and in a way comprehend him, which is to love and to know. For those who know and those who love have within themselves the thing known and loved.[51]

Aquinas makes here the same distinction he made above between God existing in all things by his presence, power, and essence on the one hand, and his indwelling in the saints by grace on the other. But there is a noteworthy addition: the indwelling of God as in a temple causes us to act in faith and love, enabling us to know and love God *because* he dwells within us. The indwelling of God through the Holy Spirit in the saints is not a passive presence; on the contrary,

[49] *In 1 Cor.* 6.13b-20 [309].
[50] *In 2 Cor.* 6.11-18 [240].
[51] *In 2 Cor.* 6.11-18 [240]. For a parallel text in the *Summa* on God dwelling in us as in a temple, see I, 43, 3.

for Thomas it is the active principle by which we know and love God.

The second phrase from Lev. 26.11-12, 'I will walk among them', is applied by Thomas to 'co-operating grace' which enables us to make progress with God's help:

> I will promote them from virtue to virtue, for this progress is impossible without the grace of God: 'By the grace of God I am what I am' (1 Cor. 15:10). For just as operating grace makes us to be something in the being [esse] of justice, so co-operating grace makes us progress in that being [esse].[52]

The third phrase, 'I will be their God', is referred to the providential protection of God or to the reward awaiting the saints, which is nothing other than God himself. Finally, the last phrase, 'they shall be my people', applies to the worship and service that the faithful give to God.

From this simple text in which the Christian people are identified as the temple of the living God, Aquinas develops a very full picture of what it means to have God dwelling in us. We are given grace to know and love God and to progress from virtue to virtue in the new life given to us; we are granted the reward of having God as our recompense, and are enabled to worship him rightly in Spirit and truth. All this because God has come to dwell effectively in us through the Holy Spirit.

Aquinas has sometimes been faulted for having an instrumental doctrine of grace that minimizes the indwelling of God through the Holy Spirit, and it has been noted that his treatise on grace in the *Summa* appears to eschew the language of indwelling.[53] But here in his biblical commentaries we find a rich account of the Christian as a temple of the living God and of the indwelling of the Spirit producing in us all the fruits of faith and love. This is entirely

---

[52] *In 2 Cor.* 6.11-18 [240].

[53] For this latter observation, see A.N. Williams, *The Ground of Union: Deification in Thomas Aquinas and Gregory Palamas* (Oxford: Oxford University Press, 1999), p. 81. In the entire *Summa*, Aquinas only twice cites these texts on our being temples of the Holy Spirit: 1 Cor. 3.16 (*ST*, I–II, 109, 9, ad 2); 1 Cor. 6.19 (*ST*, I, 27, 1). But for an account of the centrality of the indwelling of the Holy Spirit in Aquinas' theology, see my article, 'Justification, Sanctification and Divinization in Thomas Aquinas', in Thomas G. Weinandy, Daniel Keating, and John Yocum (eds.), *Aquinas on Doctrine: A Critical Introduction* (London/New York: T & T Clark, 2004), pp. 148–51.

consistent with his constantly repeated principle that the gift of the Holy Spirit is the chief mark of the New Covenant in Christ.[54]

Commentary on 2 Corinthians

Theme and Outline

As the theme verse for 2 Corinthians, Aquinas chooses Isa. 61.6, 'Men shall speak of you as ministers [*ministri*] of our God.'[55] This verse admirably suits his purpose because, as he reminds us, 'In the first epistle the Apostle discussed the sacraments, in this one he discusses the ministers, both good and bad, of these sacraments.' He then expands on the purpose and theme of this letter:

> The reason he wrote this epistle was that he had preached to the Corinthians, but they had welcomed certain false apostles, whom they preferred to the Apostle. Therefore he writes them this epistle, in which he commends the apostles and the dignity of the true apostles, and discloses and reproves the falseness of the false apostles.[56]

Again, this may seem to us an overly narrow estimation of what Paul is doing in this letter, but Thomas immediately widens the subject by defining the role of God's ministers as threefold: (1) they dispense the sacraments (1 Cor. 4.1, 'Stewards of the mysteries of God' [*dispensatores mysteriorum Dei*]); (2) they govern the people of God (Wis. 6.4); and (3) they labour for the salvation of all through the preaching of the gospel (1 Cor. 3.5).[57] By means of this elaboration of what a minister of God is, Thomas broadens the theme of the letter to include not only the dispensation of the mysteries, but the governing of God's people and the ministry of the gospel. Seen from this broadened vantage point, Aquinas' definition of the theme very nicely captures the heart of 2 Corinthians, namely, Paul's extended defence of his ministry of the gospel in the face of criticism levelled against him by the so-called false apostles and by the Corinthians themselves.

Thomas outlines the epistle according to his stated theme. Following introductory material (chapters 1–2), the first main section concerns the dignity of the ministers of the New Covenant

---

[54] Aquinas makes this point explicitly in his commentary on the New Covenant, *In 2 Cor.* 3.6-11 [90]: 'So it is clear that the Old Law is a covenant of words, but the New Covenant is a covenant of the Holy Spirit, by whom the love of God is poured out in our hearts, as it says in Rom. 5.5. Consequently, when the Holy Spirit produces charity in us, which is the fulness of the Law, it is a New Covenant.' See also *ST*, I–II, 106, 1–3.

[55] *In 2 Cor.*, Prol. [1].

[56] *In 2 Cor.*, Prol. [1].

[57] *In 2 Cor.*, Prol. [2].

(chapters 3–9), and the second main section the guilt of the evil and false apostles who distort the gospel (chapters 10–13). This fundamental division is then further delineated by Thomas in the following way:[58]

I. Introduction (chapters 1–2):
   A. The comfort shown to God's ministers (1.1-14)
   B. Paul's explanation for not visiting the Corinthians (1.15–2.17)
II. The dignity of the good ministers of the New Covenant (chaps. 3–9)
   A. The ministry of the New Covenant (chaps. 3–5)
      1. The dignity of ministry in the New Covenant (chap. 3)
      2. The exercise of ministry in the New Covenant (chap. 4)
      3. The reward for ministry in the New Covenant (chap. 5)
   B. The carrying out of this ministry by the Apostle (chaps. 6–9)
      1. Commendation for the Corinthians (chap. 7)
      2. Exhortation to almsgiving (chaps. 8–9)
III. The guilt of false ministers (chaps. 10–13)

Ministers of Christ

Aquinas' teaching on Christ's ministers appears intermittently in the text, like rare and precious gems. Here we find no systematic treatment, but rather brief discussions on this point or that, as the biblical text prompts him and provides occasion for comment. For example, faced with Paul's claim to be 'an apostle of Jesus Christ' (2 Cor. 1.1), Thomas tells us that the apostles are succeeded principally by the bishops, while priests are the successors to the 72 disciples. By addressing Timothy as his 'brother', Paul demonstrates that the bishops are brothers to one another, and this is why 'the Pope calls all bishops brothers'.[59] Or again, to justify Paul's escape by night from his enemies in Damascus (2 Cor. 11.32-33), Aquinas offers the following judgment on what leaders should do when persecuted. First, they should take advantage of any human help offered, and not tempt God by scorning it. Second, if the leader alone is sought, he ought to flee and save himself for the benefit of the people (which is what Paul did). But if both the leader and his people together are sought, the leader should remain with his people, preferring their good to his own.[60]

One thread that runs throughout the commentary is Thomas' depiction of the fundamental task of the Christian preacher and

---

[58] For the primary texts that give the thematic outline of the letter, see *In 2 Cor.* 3.1-5 [78]; 6.1-5 [203]; 7.1-3 [245]; 8.1-8 [280]; 10.1-6 [343].

[59] *In 2 Cor.* 1.1-2 [4–5]. For Aquinas' treatment of bishops and prelates in the *Summa*, see II–II, 184, 5–6; 185.

[60] *In 2 Cor.* 11.27-33 [439]. He offers the very same explanation in *ST*, II–II, 185, 5.

governor. As a foil, it may be useful to examine Thomas' depiction of a Christian leader by first seeing how he identifies and characterizes the false apostles who are opposing Paul. According to most contemporary scholarly accounts, Paul faces two different sets of opponents in 1 and 2 Corinthians respectively.[61] Those he opposes in 1 Corinthians are the so-called *pneumatikoi*, a set of Christian teachers, possibly representing a Wisdom tradition within Hellenistic Judaism, who boasted of a claim to superior wisdom and preached a highly realized eschatology. In contrast, the 'false apostles' that Paul faces in 2 Corinthians (named in 11.13) are teaching that the Law of Moses must be kept along with the gospel. They are Judaizers who claim authority from the 'superlative apostles' (2 Cor. 11.5) for their insistence on the ongoing role of the Law.

Aquinas merges these two sets of opponents together, calling them all 'false apostles'. In the context of 1 Corinthians, he identifies them as distorting the gospel by appeal to traditions of human wisdom, and as denying the future resurrection of the dead.[62] In the context of 2 Corinthians, he views them as insisting on the legal observance of the Law along with the gospel, and as despoiling the Corinthians by exacting payment for their services.[63] Thomas in fact suggests that Peter and John themselves regarded Paul as inferior because he had not been with Christ as they had been, and he defends Paul against what he considers to be their error in thinking this way.[64] But the chief fault of the false apostles, for Aquinas, is that they fail to serve for the good of their subjects; instead of feeding them with the truth, they oppress them for their own gain.[65] Commenting on the text, 'What we preach is not ourselves, but Jesus Christ as Lord, with ourselves as your servants for Jesus' sake' (2 Cor. 4.5), Aquinas presents the primary task of the Christian leader:

> We preach Jesus as Lord, but ourselves as servants, the reason being that we principally seek the praise of Christ and not our own. For a servant is one who exists for the profit of the master. That is why a minister of the Church, who does not seek the honour of God and the welfare of his subjects, is not a true ruler, but a tyrant. For whoever rules well should be as a servant seeking the honour and profit of his subjects.[66]

---

[61] See e.g. Gordon D. Fee, *The First Epistle to the Corinthians* (Grand Rapids, MI: Eerdmans, 1987), pp. 7–15; Ralph P. Martin, *2 Corinthians*, Word Biblical Commentary vol. 40 (Dallas: Word, 1986), pp. xxx–xxxiii, liii–lxiii.

[62] *In 1 Cor.* 1.17b-25 [40]; 4.6-13 [206]; 15.53-58 [1023].

[63] *In 2 Cor.* 2.12-17 [76]; 6.11-18 [231]; 10.7-12 [358]; 11.1-3 [379].

[64] *In 2 Cor.* 11.4-8 [384]; 12.11-13 [489].

[65] For a catalogue of the five ways that the false apostles oppressed the Corinthians, see *In 2 Cor.* 11.16-21a [416].

[66] *In 2 Cor.* 4.3-6 [128].

This basic description is repeated and enlarged upon at several points in the commentary. Speaking of Paul's role in spreading the gospel (2 Cor. 2.14), Thomas says that the twofold task of a preacher is to exhort the faithful in sacred doctrine (*in doctrina sacra*) and to refute those who contradict it.[67] Later in the commentary, he draws from Paul's words, 'I will most gladly spend and be spent for your souls', a threefold charge for Christian leaders: 'feed them by word, feed them by example, feed them by temporal subsidies'.[68] Plainly, Thomas takes seriously the overarching theme of the letter that he has identified, namely, the ministers of Christ, especially in their role as preachers of the gospel and servants of God's people.

Paul's Pastoral Strategy

There are also many potentially interesting topics within Aquinas' *Commentary on 2 Corinthians* that readers may wish to explore: for example, the relationship between the Old and New Covenants (2 Cor. 3);[69] the transformation of our mortal nature (2 Cor. 4–5);[70] the Christological exegesis of Christ becoming poor that we might become rich (2 Cor. 8.9);[71] and the nature of Paul's visions (2 Cor. 12.1-6).[72] In keeping with the dominant theme of the letter, however, I have chosen for particular development Aquinas' treatment of Paul as Pastor.

One of the more striking features of the *Commentary on 2 Corinthians* is the way that Thomas uses Paul's defence of his own ministry to guide and shape pastoral strategy for Christian leaders. If one sat through all of Thomas' lectures on this epistle – which his hearers presumably did – one would come away with something like a pastoral handbook for leading and shepherding God's people, especially those who are most recalcitrant and shallow in their faith. Here we see one of the clear advantages of reading Aquinas' biblical commentaries alongside the *Summa*: the rich pastoral wisdom that he draws from this epistle does not appear in anything like the same depth in the *Summa* itself.

In order to gain an appreciation of the depth and consistency of Thomas' pastoral strategy, I will stitch together several texts from

---

[67] *In 2 Cor.* 2.12-17 [72].

[68] *In 2 Cor.* 12.14-19 [500]. See also *In 2 Cor.* 11.27-33 [432].

[69] *In 2 Cor.* 3.1-18 [78–115]; *ST*, I–II, 106–8.

[70] *In 2 Cor.* 4.1–5.21 [116–202].

[71] *In 2 Cor.* 8.9-15 [294–95]. Curiously, Thomas cites this text once only in the *Summa* (III, 40, 3) in the context of defending Christ's bodily poverty. He makes no further Christological use of it.

[72] *In 2 Cor.* 12.1-6 [440–70].

disparate parts of the commentary. This is by no means an artificial procedure or unfaithful to the epistle: Paul himself scatters his apologies for his actions throughout the letter, and Thomas follows suit by offering comment whenever appropriate. For instance, when Paul says that 'it was to spare you that I refrained from coming to Corinth' (2 Cor. 1.23), Aquinas explains it thus:

> He knew that they were incorrigible. Hence, if he had gone then, he would either have punished them, and they perhaps would have left the faith altogether, or he would not have punished them, and then he would have been giving them occasion to sin more.[73]

When Paul defended his failure to come on the grounds that he wanted to spare them another painful visit, Thomas likens his action to that of Christ:

> The reason he did not wish to grieve them is the same one whereby the Lord did not wish his disciples to fast, namely, in order that they be drawn to Christ and be joined to him not by fear but by love. For the Lord wished to strengthen and nourish them in the faith in all sweetness and heartfelt desire, so that, being thus established in love, they would not easily turn away from him because of tribulations.[74]

Thomas considers that Paul is being appropriately lenient in 2 Cor. 2.6 when he calls on the Corinthians to forgive the one who has caused pain to all. This was 'expedient for the time and the person. For it is better to observe such a spirit of leniency in correcting, so that the fruit of correction follow on the penance, than to correct so harshly that the sinner despairs and falls into worse sin.'[75] For Thomas it is the *fruit* of correction that the Christian leader must always seek above all. The hallmark of his pastoral counsel as presented in this commentary is the appeal to mercy and forbearance for the sake of leading God's people to mature faith.

Thomas' penetrating understanding of sin, grief and sorrow enables him to recognize the pastoral strategy needed to correct those who are on the brink of despair.

> For some are sometimes so steeped in sorrow because of sin and punishment of sin, that they are overcome, when they have no one to comfort them; and this is bad, because it does not result in the hope for

---

[73] *In 2 Cor.* 1.15-24 [47].
[74] *In 2 Cor.* 2.1-4 [48].
[75] *In 2 Cor.* 2.5-11 [59].

the fruit of repentance, namely reformation, but in despair he delivers himself over to all sins.[76]

The 'advantage over us' that Satan seeks to gain (2 Cor. 2.11) is not only to lead us into sin; additionally 'he destroys those he already has by the severity of prelates who drive to despair by not correcting them in a compassionate way'.[77] Because the Corinthians were both weak in faith and stubborn in their disobedience, Paul was humble and gentle towards them in order to win them.[78] For Aquinas, Paul is a spiritual physician who rejoices, not in the bitterness of the medicine, but in the eventual effect of the medicine which is spiritual health.[79] He is even willing to 'play the madman' in order to humble the false apostles and shame the Corinthians. His apparently foolish talk (2 Cor. 11.21) was in reality deep pastoral wisdom, according to Thomas. In a striking example of flexible pastoral application, Aquinas concludes that 'subjects frequently compel their prelates to do things which seem unwise to do, although considering the time and place, they were done wisely'.[80]

In two moving passages, Thomas points to the root and cause of this pastoral concern in Paul. When Paul says, 'I feel a divine jealousy for you', he is acting as the groomsman who espouses the Corinthians to Christ through faith and love.

> Now a person is sometimes jealous for his wife, to keep her for himself. This is the way the Apostle was jealous on behalf of his people, whom he saw prepared for a fall and, although espoused to Christ, wished to be prostituted to the devil. Consequently, he would not permit Christ, the true spouse, to suffer their being shared with the devil; hence he says, 'a divine jealousy'.[81]

And finally, Thomas shows that Paul's ministry is grounded in the love of God and neighbour. In a surprising and delightful exegesis of 2 Cor. 5.13, 'If we are beside ourselves, it is for God; if we are in our right mind, it is for you', Thomas shows the essential link between experiential prayer and sober governance of the people of God. With this extended citation we close in a fitting way this brief examination of Thomas Aquinas' commentaries on 1–2 Corinthians, as a study of the sacraments and their ministers.

---

[76] *In 2 Cor.* 2.5-11 [62]. In the *Summa* (II–II, 20, 4, ad 2; 35, 1; III, 9, 9, ad 3), Thomas draws the same conclusion (citing 2 Cor. 2.7) regarding sorrow leading to despair.
[77] *In 2 Cor.* 2.5-11 [66].
[78] *In 2 Cor.* 10.7-12 [362].
[79] *In 2 Cor.* 7.4-9a [264].
[80] *In 2 Cor.* 12.11-13 [485].
[81] *In 2 Cor.* 11.1-3 [375–76].

Hence it should be noted that the apostles were midway between God and the people: 'While I stood between the Lord and you at that time' (Deut. 5:5). Therefore, they were required to draw from God whatever they poured out upon the people. Hence it was necessary that sometimes they raised themselves to God by contemplation to obtain heavenly things, and sometimes conformed themselves to the people to deliver what they had received from God; and all this tended to their profit. Hence he says, 'for if we are beside ourselves' i.e., raised to the state of receiving gifts of graces, and this in order to be united to God, which is done by means of temporal things: 'I said in my vision' (Ps. 116:11, Vulgate); Dionysius: 'Divine love causes ecstasy.' 'If we are in our right mind', i.e., adapt ourselves to you by delivering God's precepts, 'it is for you', i.e., for your benefit. This sobriety is not opposed to inebriation in wine, which brings wars on earth, but to that inebriation which is from the Holy Spirit and draws men to divine things and about which Song of Songs (5:1) says: 'Eat, O friends, and drink: drink deeply, O lovers!' For that sobriety is for the benefit of our neighbour, but the inebriation is for the love of God.[82]

---

[82] *In 2 Cor.* 5.11-15 [179].

6

AQUINAS ON EPHESIANS AND COLOSSIANS[1]

Mark Edwards

The century preceding the birth of Aquinas in 1225 is often regarded as an age of resurgent vigour and curiosity, in which the Church played little part except when it inadvertently promoted the fertilization of the European mind through universities at home and crusades abroad. Insolent, sceptical, scientific and ruthlessly concupiscent – a man, in short, who would not have read the fourth chapter of Ephesians with much patience – the Emperor Frederick Hohenstaufen consummates the 'renaissance of the twelfth century' for the eminent historian Charles Homer Haskins.[2] Modern European thought, however, perhaps owes less to this great infidel than to one of his nominal subjects – one, moreover, who was no poet but a philosopher, no layman but a friar, not even a turbulent Franciscan but a studious Dominican, fully orthodox by conviction and by temperament as much of a humanist as a friar could be in an age when the classical spirit flowered in the vernacular and the best Latin was no longer classical.

In the commentaries of Aquinas on Ephesians and Colossians we see at once a vindication and a critique of humanism. While they borrow the instruments of philology, and do not disdain the study of created things (*scientia*), both commentaries share Paul's belief in the primacy of *sapientia,* the knowledge of things eternal, over all the fruits of human curiosity.[3] The questions to be resolved by *sapientia* are primarily metaphysical: Who is Christ? Whence comes the Spirit? Is the government of the natural world by angels a devolution or a usurpation of the divine prerogative? To deny oneself the world without denying its creator is more, perhaps, than

---

[1] All citations taken from the internet version of the *Textum Taurini* (1953), typed by R. Busa and edited by E. Alarcon.
For Ephesians: <http:www.corpusthomisticum.org/cep.html> .
For Colossians: <http://www.corpusthomisticum.org/ccl.html> .
[2] See especially C.H. Haskins, *The Renaissance of the Twelfth Century* (Cambridge, MA: Harvard University Press, 1927, reprinted Cleveland, OH: World Publishing Co., 1957), p. 248.
[3] For the distinction see *In Col.*, cap. 2, lect. 1.

can be expected in the lay academy, and I will not try here to convince the modern scholar that he ought to read Aquinas. I venture to hope, on the other hand, that modern theologians can be persuaded to take an interest in a predecessor of undisputed greatness, whose fidelity to the Church and its traditions was combined with erudite candour in the interrogation of a sacred text.

Ephesians and Colossians as Scripture

The order of St Dominic taught the Church that the sword and the keys would not suffice as tools of government if the pen was resigned to Cathars, troubadours and absconding clerics; it saw no reason, however, to cultivate any tongue but Latin, which in Italy at least was still without rival as a literary medium. And if the tongue of scholars was also that of the infallible Scriptures, the rules by which one had learned to parse any other text could be applied without scruple to the letters of St Paul. To us it seems a paradoxical artifice, but to Aquinas it was simply good style, to embellish the Apostle's denigration of human wisdom with an echo of the *Aeneid*.[4] For him the old Rome had been so fully digested in the new that it seemed natural to characterize the heretics of his day in words that had once been employed by pagans as a pretext for the suppression of the Church.[5] Classical Latin rhetoric distinguishes three factors that contribute to goodwill or *benevolentia*[6] – the occasion, the speaker's person and the character of his audience; when, therefore, Paul blesses God at the beginning of Ephesians, Aquinas suggests that his three causes of gratitude are his own ministry, the salvation of the Ephesians and the goods that abound in Christ.[7] Ancient readers (Chrysostom excepted[8]) had confessed that Paul lacked grace of style, and had even made a virtue of it. Up to a generation ago, most scholars endorsed this estimate; today,

---

[4] *In Eph.*, cap. 1, lect. 3: *sapientia nostra non est ut sciamus naturas rerum et siderum cursus* etc.. ("Our wisdom does not consist in the knowledge of natural things and the courses of the stars"). This echoes Virgil, *Aeneid* 6.850, and his disavowal of Lucretian physics at *Georgics* 2.490. Augustine in his definition of *scientia Dei* (knowledge of God) at *On the Trinity* 4.1 makes a similar allusion to Lucretius, *On the Nature of Things* 1.73.

[5] See at *In Eph.*, cap. 1, lect. 4: *vana et illicta religio superstitio est* (vain and illicit religion is superstition), alluding both to the pagan branding of Christianity as *vana or prava superstitio* (Minucius Felix, *Octavius 9;* Pliny, *Letters 10.96*), and to the status of Christianity before it was made *religio licita* in 306.

[6] As e.g. in Cicero, *Ad Herennium* 1.4.8–1.69, if we discount the possibility of deriving *benevolentia* from forensic adversaries.

[7] *In Eph.*, cap. 1, lect. 1.

[8] See J. Fairweather, 'The Epistle to the Galatians and Classical Rhetoric', part 1, *Tyndale Bulletin*, 45.1 (1994), pp. 1–22.

however, it may be that those who refuse to employ the scalpel of rhetorical criticism on his bristling periods are in a minority. What the modern exegete does in pursuit of historical understanding, Aquinas did in the confidence that timeless truths should be interpreted by timeless rules.

Aquinas himself, against those who denounce rhetoric as an affront to the simplicity of the gospel, replies that doctors such as Ambrose, Leo and Gregory had not been ashamed to marry truth with artifice.[9] He regards it as a virtue in Paul that he practises the formalities which were expected of a literary artist: Colossians, for example, he divides into the salutation, the matter and the closing benedictions, and he finds this division foreshadowed in the proem, where the signatories come first, then the Colossians (as recipients of the matter), then an invocation of grace.[10] In what follows, however, the disparity between the mediaeval and the modern way of reading becomes apparent: no critic of our own day would imagine that Philippians, Ephesians and Colossians were instalments in a pedagogic trilogy, Ephesians cementing the ecclesiastical unity which is commended in Philippians, while Colossians was designed to preserve it against the attrition of heresy.[11] It is possible that this passage hints at a likeness between the apostle of *sapientia* and the wisest prophet of the old dispensation, for Origen's disciples in the West had preserved his theory that King Solomon wrote Proverbs, Ecclesiastes and the Song of Songs as a triad, so that the reader might ascend from ethics to physics (that is, the knowledge of creation), thence to the mysteries of faith.[12]

As Origen presumes that all the works ascribed to Solomon in the Hebrew canon are genuine, so Aquinas takes it for granted that the fourteen letters ascribed to Paul, including even the pastorals and Hebrews, were the true offspring of his pen. The majority of scholars now deny that Paul was the author of Ephesians,[13] on the grounds that it lacks the characteristic greetings, does not seem to have been written in response to any question or particular circumstances, is the only letter ascribed to him that employs the

---

[9] *In Col.*, cap. 2, lect. 1.

[10] My interpretation of *In Col, prooemium*, on Col. 1.1.

[11] *In Col.*, proem, citing Gen 32.2 to prove that the Church resembles a military encampment and Ephesians 6.17 to suggest that the word is the living sword of the apostle.

[12] Origen, proem to *Commentary on Song of Songs*, through Jerome, *In Ecclesiastem*, proem (*PL* 23.1011–12). On the survival of Origen's teachings in the West see H. De Lubac, '*Exégèse Mediévale* vol. 1.1 (Lyons: Aubier, 1949), pp. 207–38. Aquinas would not, however, have drawn this knowingly from Origen, on whose heresies see below.

[13] C.L. Mitton, *The Epistle to the Ephesians* (Oxford: Clarendon Press, 1951) has not been superseded as a clear and comprehensive survey of the relevant data.

noun *ecclesia* to denote the Church universal (3.10, 5.32), and in one place presupposes the ascension of Christ, of which he seems to be ignorant elsewhere. No other Pauline letter makes such frequent use of the formula 'in high places',[14] or admonishes its readers at such length against the subterfuge of demons (6.11-17). The letter to the Colossians offers modest parallels in doctrine and imagery, while the 'household code' in which it expounds the complementary duties of wives and husbands, slaves and masters, is all but identical with that of the letter to Ephesus.[15] Yet since it is not Paul's habit to repeat himself so faithfully, the conclusion now most commonly drawn from these observations is that only one of the letters (at most) can be original. Even the Colossian letter strikes a peculiar note when it alludes to Christ's pre-existence,[16] his discomfiture of powers and principalities on the cross (2.13-14), and the completion of his sufferings in the body of the Church (1.24-9).

Aquinas, of course, suspected nothing of this, but, since his method in exposition is to corroborate Paul from Paul wherever he can, he cannot fail to show incidentally how much the Ephesian letter has in common with the rest of the Pauline corpus. As he draws most frequently on texts whose authorship remains undisputed – and as we may be sure that his logical mind would have demanded inconsistency, and not merely idiosyncrasy, as proof that works ascribed to Paul were in fact by different authors – it is unlikely that any critic of our own day could have made him doubt that the letter to the Ephesians was both Pauline and inspired. The provenance of canonical texts was in any case of little account in an age when it was still supposed that the authors had been vessels of infallible and uniform inspiration. On this principle any two occasions when the omniscient Spirit avails himself of the same words can be assumed to convey the same meaning, and Aquinas is thus inclined to juxtapose passages which seem to us to exhibit only a tenuous or accidental likeness. What has the field that Matthew calls 'the world' to do, for example, with the wall that separates Jew from Greek at Ephesians 2.14?[17] How could the man who scorned to know Christ after the flesh have meant to say that the stature of a 'perfect man', the form of the body in the resurrection, is attained by everyone at thirty-three, the age that Christ chose for his death?[18] At

---

[14] Eph. 1.20, 2.6, 3.10; see also 6.12.

[15] Eph. 5.19–6.9; see also Col. 3.17–4.3.

[16] The common reading of Col. 1.15-18 (see also Eph. 3.9), challenged, e.g. by J. Ziesler, *Pauline Christianity* (Oxford: Clarendon Press, 1990), pp. 128–30. Aquinas, *In Col.* 1.4 employs the traditional reading against the Manichees, who deny the original goodness of creation, and the Arians, who subordinate the image to the Father.

[17] *In Eph.*, cap. 2, lect. 5, citing Mt. 13.38.

[18] *In Eph.*, cap. 4, lect. 4 on Eph. 4.13. See also 2 Cor. 5.16.

the same time, it remains true that the past and current associations of an image make an important contribution to its meaning in a new context; Paul himself, had he tried to unknit the pattern of his own thoughts when he exhorted the Ephesians to come together as stones in the Saviour's temple, might have found it hard to improve on the catena of citations which his commentators adduces from the Scriptures, old and new.[19] Citations from the Old Testament are legion, and not always beside the purpose: thus a latter-day historian of morals might adduce the same prohibitions from the Old testament to explain the presence of blasphemy and calumny in the catalogue of vices at Colossians 3.8.[20] While he often hears the voice of Christ in the psalms, he seldom attempts to improve on the literal sense of the historical books: the drunkenness of Lot is for him a warning to the bibulous, not (as others thought) a religious ecstasy in symbolic dress.[21] If at other times the citations seem to us redundant and artificial, we must remember that the reader of a mediaeval work had fewer books to hand than we do, and that consequently the author would never miss an opportunity to instruct him in the principles of faith.

Wisdom and Ecclesiastical Truth

Aquinas was always conscious that his order had been set up to refute the dualists – or, as the papal church preferred to style them, Manichees[22] – who allegedly maintained that the ills of the world were ineradicable, the handiwork of a dark power which can only desire but never comprehend the truth and love revealed in Christ. Manichees – the Manichees of Augustine at least, who were better known to Aquinas than his own contemporaries – held that every human being enters the present world as a child of light or darkness, with his destiny written upon him, and that the actions which the Old Testament ascribes to God are in fact those of the dark lord in his purblind emulation of divine justice. It was consequently the duty of any Dominican commentator on Ephesians to show that predestination, as Paul had taught it, did not imply that heaven and hell were reserved for beings of different natures, or that the world was a flawed creation from the outset. If the 'prince of the air'[23] is

[19] *In Eph.*, cap. 2, lect. 6, on Eph. 2.20-22, including pertinent references on Christ as rock or stone.

[20] *In Col.*, cap. 3, lect. 2, citing Lev. 24.14 and Prov. 13.5.

[21] *In Eph.*, cap. 5, lect. 7, following Jerome, *Letter* 69.9 and amplifying the prohibition of drunkenness at Eph. 5.18.

[22] See S. Runciman, *The Medieval Manichee* (Cambridge: Cambridge University Press, 1947, reprinted 1982).

[23] Eph. 2.2; see below on angels.

wicked, he made himself so, and if we are now enslaved to him, it is not because he made us but because he induced us to imitate his fall.

In commenting on the opening verses Aquinas has to prove, against the Pelagians,[24] that the eternal predestination of the saints is determined only by the will of God, and not by any human works accomplished or foreseen. On the other hand, he must argue that the grace of God is not constrained, or circumscribed by any inherent property in his creature, and that, far from being overruled, the will of the saint is disenthralled from sin and taken up into the fellowship of good works. To this end he distinguishes between grace and glory, between the grace that saves and the grace that inspires the works which make us dear to God.[25] No reader of the time would fail to identify his opponent here as the fatalistic Manichee, and hence there is no need to defile the word of God by naming him. On the other hand, the more abstruse conceit that earthly bodies were created by the evil god and heavenly ones by the Father of Jesus Christ is expressly imputed to the Manichees in the commentary on Colossians.[26] With some regret, we may also detect an uncharitable allusion to their posterity when Aquinas repeats the maxim that it is not the death but the cause that makes the martyr.[27] The crusade against the Albigensians culminated in victory and massacre in 1215; the suppression of the Knights Templar was still to come in 1306; the years between saw the birth of the Inquisition, in which the Dominicans played a leading role.[28]

Aquinas was not a persecutor: he made this comment, not to kindle fires, but to announce that he was writing on behalf of Christendom, rather than indulging a private feud. The Manichees, like all heretics, were enemies of the Church, and must be refuted from the Fathers who had shaped the mind of Christendom and continued to furnish norms for the interpretation of Scripture. Augustine – who, after routing the Manichees, rescued the Church from the contrary and more seductive error of Pelagius – is cited freely and always with approval. It is he – the same man who tells us that the vision of God is the whole reward of faith[29] – who also explains that the primordial act of God was to endow the minds of

[24] The *Pelagiani* are censured at *In Eph.*, cap. 1, lect. 1.
[25] *In Eph.*, cap. 1, lect. 1. See *ST* I.23.3 and 5.
[26] *In Col.*, cap. 1, lect. 4.
[27] *In Eph.*, cap. 3, lect. 1. See Augustine, Letter 185.9; *On Enduring* 10.
[28] H.C. Lea, *The Inquisition of the Middle Age: Its Organization and Operation* (London: Eyre and Spottiswood, 1963, reprinted New York: Harper Torchbooks, 1969), 77ff.
[29] *In Eph.*, cap. 1, lect. 1.

angels with the 'principles of the natural creation'.[30] He was also the scourge of pagan fatalism, and Aquinas accepts his judgment that the drawing of lots, in contrast to astrology, is a pious act which seeks God's will without trespassing on the mysteries that he has chosen to reserve for another day.[31] In passages such as these we find the key to the idiosyncrasies of Ephesians: it is not our impotence but the loving omnipotence of God that is revealed in the doctrine of predestination, and if for a time we wage unequal warfare with the powers and principalities, it is because they know the bliss from which we have fallen. That is to say, they are perfect representatives of *scientia* without charity, of purely mundane and temporal understanding which is not informed by wisdom.[32] Aquinas borrows his definition of wisdom from Augustine,[33] tacitly applauding his predilection for the deutero-canonical Wisdom of Solomon. Although this was a Greek composition, and therefore of inferior authority to the Hebrew canon according to the rule laid down by Jerome, the African Church of Augustine's day had refused to admit that any book of the Septuagint was less inspired than another.[34] The book of Wisdom had been for Augustine an indispensable weapon against the Manichees, since no other work – not even the other four ascribed to Solomon[35] – had testified so clearly to the uniform operation of the same wisdom in the framing of the heavens, the inspiration of the Scriptures and the call of the elect.

In the prologue to the commentary on Colossians, it is wisdom that completes the drill of the soldier in the camp of God; the first words that Aquinas writes in his own voice in the Commentary on

[30] *In Eph.*, cap. 3, lect. 3. On the knowledge of the angels see Augustine, *City of God* 11.29 and *On Genesis according to the Letter* 4.29–32.

[31] *In Eph.*, cap. 1, lect. 4, citing *Discourses on the Psalms* 34.17. For Augustine's polemic against astrology see *City of God* 5.1–8. Aquinas condemns all forms of divination, but allows that lots may be cast to divide a property and to consult God's will where nothing is disclosed to human reason.

[32] See especially *In Eph.*, cap. 3, lect. 5 on the possibility of charity without *scientia*, though at cap. 3, lect. 2 *scientia* is almost a synonym for wisdom (*sapientia*), in keeping with the usage of Paul at Rom. 11.33. At cap. 1, lect. 3 we are told that wisdom (*sapientia*) does not consist in knowledge of natural phenomena (*non est ut sciamus* etc.), and that the *scientia* of the apostles is not of the mundane order.

[33] Citing *On the Trinity* 4 at *In Eph.*, cap. 5, lect. 6. For Augustine's distinction between *scientia* and *sapientia* see also *On the Trinity* 12.14 (22) ff., and for his principle that charity governs the understanding of Scripture see *On Christian Doctrine* 1.35–40.

[34] See Jerome, *Praefatio in Librum Sapientiae Salomonis* (*PL* 23.1242–3); C. Munier (ed.), *Concilia Africae* (Turnhout: Brepols, *CSEL* 149), p. 108 (*Canones in Apiarium* 24).

[35] Proverbs, Ecclesiastes, The Song of Songs and Sirach (Ecclesiasticus), according to *On Christian Doctrine* 2.12.

Ephesians are *sicut dixit sapiens*, 'as the wise man says'. Paul, he goes on, declares the true 'preacher of wisdom' to be 'an Israelite in the contemplation of God, a Christian in devoutness of faith, an apostle in the authority of his office'.[36] It is indeed the glory of the apostles, and of those who rule the Church as their successors, to abound in all divine wisdom,[37] but laity and priesthood alike enjoy a foretaste of this dispensation when they forswear the counterfeit wisdom of the world.[38] It is proved from the Wisdom of Solomon that true Wisdom must be imparted by the Spirit,[39] and in the same paragraph a Christological turn is given to Solomon's aphorism that a wise son is the glory of his father.[40] Paul's asseveration at Col. 2.3 that all the treasuries of wisdom and knowledge (*scientia*) are hidden in Christ is reinforced by a verse from another Solomonic writing: 'Who will fathom the wisdom of God who precedes all things?'[41] Wisdom of Solomon 8.1 is applied to him as the 'wisdom who spans the frontiers of the world'.[42] The antithesis of wisdom is idolatry, which is traced to the fallen angels on the authority of Wisdom of Solomon 14.27.[43] The same book is cited to illustrate the frailty of our perceptions,[44] and when Paul speaks of the 'manifold wisdom of God' it is left to Solomon to explain that it owes this character to the 'holy, single and manifold spirit of understanding'.[45] And again the same book is cited to show how God 'refines the elect like gold', in contrast to the smith who forges a perishable idol.[46] Long before Paul, then, Solomon had divined the association between idolatry, false wisdom and the defection of the angels; he had shown that folly is multiplied if we blame the Creator for sores that his fallen acolytes have inflicted on the world.

The Image of God

From ancient times the Solomonic books had been adduced, by writers whom we now call orthodox, to corroborate Christ's divinity and illustrate the mode of his procession from the Father. When

[36] *In Eph.*, proem, citing 1 Cor. 11.22.

[37] Eph. 1.8, at *In Eph.*, cap. 1, lect. 6, with citation of Luke 21.15.

[38] *In Eph.*, cap. 1, lect. 6, citing Rom. 1.22 and the Latin Gloss.

[39] Wis. 9.17 at *In Eph.*, cap. 1, lect. 6.

[40] Prov. 10.1 at *In Eph.*, cap. 1, lect. 6.

[41] Sirach (Ecclesiasticus) 1.3 at *In Eph.*, cap. 3, lect. 2. See also *ST*, pt. 1. 32.2, 34.1 etc.

[42] *In Eph.*, cap. 4, lect. 2, after finding an allusion to the Trinity in Eph. 4.5-6, and citing one of Augustine's favourite verses, Wis. 11.22.

[43] *In Eph.*, cap. 2, lect. 1; see also the citation of 1 Cor. 2.6 at *In Eph.*, cap. 3, lect. 2.

[44] Wis. 9.14 at *In Eph.*, cap. 2, lect. 1.

[45] *In Eph.*, cap. 3, lect. 3, citing Wis. 3.6 to illustrate Eph. 3.10.

[46] Wis. 3.6 at *In Eph.*, cap. 3, lect. 4., explaining Eph. 3.13.

Paul states at Col. 1.15 that Christ is 'the image of the invisible God, the firstborn of every creature', the first clause might be thought to entail the 'anthropomorphite' view that the Second Person of the Trinity is visible by nature, with the 'Arian' corollary (to use Aquinas' term[47]) that he is inferior and subordinate to the First. The second clause might seem to endorse the notorious tenet – held by Arius himself, and perhaps by him alone[48] – that the Son is a creature of the Father. Against such pedantic readings Aquinas first appeals to the saying of Dionysius the Areopagite,[49] that while the intellect grasps the essence of every other being through participation, no created intellect can participate in the essence of Good, and consequently relations within the Godhead, while they may be represented to our weak senses by analogy, remain strictly beyond our knowledge. And since it is the nature of the subject that determines the application of the analogy, we cannot say (for example) that because an earthly image is always inferior to its original and distinct in kind, the Son must be inferior to and distinct in nature from God. It is in fact the title 'Word' that precludes this reckless inference, if we allow ourselves to be guided by Ecclesiasticus 24.1-12. This teaching, which implies unity of original, hence unity of nature, between the Son and the Father, is couched in a different metaphor at Heb. 1.3 (itself a reminiscence of Wis. 7.25): 'the brightness of his glory and the impressed mark of his substance'. Since Origen's time this text had been employed, with all the necessary caveats against the ascription of material properties to the Godhead, as a proof that Father and Son are of one substance – *homoousios* or 'consubstantial', as the Nicene Creed of 325 proclaimed.[50] In calling the Son the image of the Father, Aquinas adds, we affirm two things: first that the two are alike, and

---

[47] *In Col.*, cap. 1, lect. 3, where the spelling, as elsewhere, is *Arriani*. It is not clear that the first opponents of Arius were in fact concerned to maintain a strict equality between the Son and the Father, though they certainly argued for unity of nature, and hence the essential invisibility of the Son.

[48] Theodoret, *Church History* 1.5; Epiphanius, *Panarion* 69.7.

[49] See below. Aquinas cites Dionysius frequently in *ST*: (e.g. I, 1, 9) on the propriety of applying incongruous metaphors to God because their metaphorical function will be more evident.

[50] On Origen (whose opinion may have reached the west through Pamphilus' *Apology*, translated by Rufinus), see M.J. Edwards, 'Did Origen Apply the Word *Homoousios* to the Son?', *Journal of Theological Studies* 49 (1998), pp. 558–70. At *ST*, I, 32, 1, Aquinas accuses Origen of having fathered the notion of two substances in the Godhead, but at I, 34, 1, when arguing that 'Word' is a personal name, he is prepared to meet an objection derived from Origen's *Commentary on John*.

secondly that the relation of dependence is unilateral: we do not call the Father the image of the Son.[51]

The divinity of the Son is thus not compromised by the first clause of Col. 1.15. Now as both the text from Hebrews and the prologue to the Gospel of John associate the Word with the creation, Aquinas argues that the individuation of Son and Father was entailed, not by any difference in their natures, but by the father's desire to make the Son a foundation for other beings.[52] He is not described as the 'firstborn of creation' because he was made like other creatures, for we have already seen that biblical passages prove him to be of one substance with the Father from whom he radiates or proceeds. The locution can be fully interpreted only when we observe that Paul goes on in Col. 1.16-18 to describe the Son in relation to the world and then to the Church. In relation to the world, he is 'firstborn' for no other reason than that he is its creator and the sustaining cause of everything within it. In relation to man he is 'firstborn' because he took our own condition upon himself and went so far as to suffer death, then rose again – and again as man – to be an earnest of the general resurrection. 'Firstborn of all creation' at Col. 1.18 can thus be affirmed as a literal truth, as can the first half of the teaching that the Son of man is exalted to the right hand of the Father; but to say that Christ was truly man is not to deny, as the Arians suppose, that he is God.

As Aquinas points out in the *Summa Theologiae*,[53] Christ was no less the image of God when he became man, for man himself is declared to have been created in God's image. Paul at Ephesians 5.32 declares the love of Christ for his Church a 'great mystery', adding 'nevertheless, let every one of you in particular love his wife as he loves himself'. In his Commentary[54] Aquinas understands this to imply that every husband is a type of Christ, and that it is not enough that Christ himself should condescend to our lowliness, maintain an abiding fellowship with us and join us to himself unless we manifest the same love toward our neighbour. Whether v. 33 would be best described as an example of typology or of allegory we need not pause to determine; to Aquinas it was less important to

---

[51] At *ST*, I, 35, 2, Aquinas argues that we do not apply the term 'image' to the Spirit because he does not share the Father's generative function. See below on the errors of the Greeks.

[52] The argument here summarized occurs chiefly at *In Col.*, cap. 1, lect. 4. On the creature-regarding character of the name 'Word', see *ST*, I, 34, 3.

[53] *ST*, I, 35, 2, where it is explained, in answer to the third objection, that the Son is properly the image which shares the nature of the original, while humanity is the image that does not share the nature – a reference to Aristotle's remarks on statues, *Categories* ch. 1.

[54] *In Eph.*, cap. 1, lect. 10.

characterize than to justify a figurative reading[55] – which was easy enough in this case, as it was Paul himself who had authorized it, not to innovate upon his own meaning but to bring a mystery home to common life.

In these comments Aquinas characteristically fuses verses from the Old Testament and the New, not to arrive at any new doctrine, but to substantiate what he believes to have been the doctrine of the Church from the beginning. To prove at once the antiquity and the philosophical cogency of the orthodox reading, he cites the most ancient mouthpiece of the Church available to him outside the New Testament. The appeal to Dionysius (of whose authority in this period I shall say more in the following section) is particularly apt, because Paul measures the glory of Christ by his superiority to the angelic powers. The ranking of the angels, whether fallen or unfallen, is one matter on which he halts between two opinions, thus disturbing the consensus of the Fathers.[56] At a time when even educated worshippers were conscious of no hyperbole in professing to join with 'angels and archangels and all the company of heaven', his inconsistency raised a difficulty that only a companion of the apostles could resolve.

The Lore of Angels

No one in the thirteenth century ventured to doubt that a ninefold hierarchy was divided into three triads, or that in the first triad Seraphim took precedence over Cherubim. It was also agreed that in the third triad the middle rank (the eighth in all) was occupied by the archangels, and the lowest of all by angels. But if it was also true that every triad has its own properties, and that every angel enjoys the vision of glory that is fitted to his station, it was evidently the duty of theologians to know the order of the five other species – 'thrones, dominations, princedoms, virtues, powers', as Milton styles them *metri gratia*[57] – who have titles but no proper names in Scripture. In Ephesians we have the descending sequence 'domin-

---

[55] On the sufficiency of the literal sense in Thomas see M.L. Lamb, *Commentary on St Paul's Epistle to the Ephesians by St Thomas Aquinas* (Albany, NY: Magi Books, 1966), pp. 11–17; on the presence of allegory in this passage see idem., p. 303, n. 154.

[56] *In Eph.*, cap. 1, lect. 7. See also *ST* I, 108.

[57] *Paradise Lost* 5.600, quoted by B. Colgrave, *The Earliest Life of Gregory the Great* (Lawrence, KS: University of Kansas Press, 1968), p. 120 in connection with chapter 25 of the anonymous Monk of Whitby's life of Gregory. In fact, Milton comes closest to the order in which the angelic ranks are *named* by Isidore of Seville, *Etymologies* 7.5.16–21.

ations, virtues, powers, principalities',[58] while in Colossians thrones are followed by principalities, dominations and powers.[59] Which was the more considered view of Paul?

The witnesses on either side could hardly have been more eminent. The order of Colossians had been followed by Pope Gregory I,[60] under whose brief tenure Saxons, Visigoths and Lombards had accepted the pastoral leadership of Rome. The great pontiff is quoted frequently in Aquinas' 'Golden Chain' (*Catena Aurea*) of comments on the gospels, and was at no time to be lightly contradicted. On the other hand, the order of Ephesians had been endorsed before Gregory (though without his being aware of it) by the author who professed to be Paul's convert, Dionysius the Areopagite. Now dated by most scholars to the fifth century, the false Dionysius possessed an authority second only to that of Scripture in the thirteenth century, and was duly made the subject of a commentary by Aquinas. It is his scheme[61] that is rehearsed at length in the commentary on Ephesians. While the Seraphim, Cherubim and thrones behold the mystery of the Godhead, the angels of the second triad administer the general laws of nature in accordance with this mystery, although special interpositions are entrusted to the principalities, angels and archangels of the third triad. By contrast there is only the barest account of Gregory's system in the commentary on Colossians – not only (we may surmise) because this work is more concise than its predecessor, but because Gregory's angelology is untenable as dogma, whatever its merits as exegesis.[62] Dante, an admirer of Aquinas but not such a friend to the papacy, imagines that when Gregory entered heaven he learned the truth from Dionysius – whereupon he laughed, as scholars do in heaven when their labours are undone.[63]

No one mistake, of course, can rob a pope of his authority, and Gregory's ebullition, 'Oh, the love of God!' is quoted twice in the commentary on Ephesians.[64] A third of the Church's four great

---

[58] By inversion of Eph. 1.21: *Supra omnem principatum et potestatem et virtutem et dominationem* (Vulgate).

[59] Col. 1.16: *sive throni, sive dominationes, sive principatus, sive potestates* (Vulgate).

[60] *Homilies on the Gospels* II.34.7 at *PL* 76, 1249–50. Gregory cites both the Pauline testimonies.

[61] *Celestial Hierarchy* 8, pp. 32–5 in the edition of G. Heil (Berlin: De Gruyter, 1991).

[62] *In Col.*, cap. 1, lect. 4, endorsing Gregory's caveat that the ranking of angels represents a difference in office only, and not in nature (*Homilies* II.34.8 at *PL* 76, 1250).

[63] *Paradiso* 28. 130–5. In Convivio 1.6, Dante follows his tutor Brunetto Latini and Isidore of Seville (n. 57) in adopting the order Powers, Dominations, Virtues, Princedoms, Thrones.

[64] *In Eph.*, cap. 2, lect. 2 and cap. 3, lect. 5, from the Easter vigil.

doctors, Ambrose of Milan, is cited rarely but with reverence;[65] where, however, the halo of antiquity is lacking, any comment may be open to correction. Even the illustrious Peter Lombard, the 'Master of the Sentences', is found to have erred by attributing to mortal saints the knowledge that Augustine reserves for angels, while excluding lesser angels from the knowledge that Dionysius grants to all.[66] Aquinas frequently turns to the Latin Gloss which had been compiled in the previous century from the writings of the Fathers to elucidate the obscurities of the Vulgate.[67] He endorses its pronouncements that the Doctors of the Church receive an 'increment of glory', and that the wall between the Jews and Gentiles is cemented on one side by Jewish law and on the other by Gentile folly;[68] he agrees that it is better to speak of an 'earnest' than of a 'pledge' of our salvation, since a pledge would be a mere substitute, to be returned in exchange for the thing itself.[69] He favours its conjecture that, when the wisdom of God is said to be imparted through the Church, this means through the preaching of the apostles, citing Augustine to prove that the content of this preaching was imparted by the angels.[70] On the other hand, when he cites the gloss on Ephesians 1.4-5 he protests that the distinction between the elect and the predestined which it implies was not in the mind of the Apostle.[71] The deference that we owe to the Fathers cannot be claimed by any recent commentator, though no received opinion should be lightly set aside.

Fathers East and West

Perhaps we ought to say, no received opinion of *Latin* Christendom. With the exception of Dionysius (whom he no doubt read in the

---

[65] I have noticed only one citation, at *In Eph*, cap. 1, lect. 4.

[66] *In Eph.*, cap. 3, lect. 3, commenting on *Sent.* II.3.2 (14).2 in *Magistri Petri Lombardi Sententiae in IV Libros Divisae*, Spicilegium Bonaventurae IV (Rome: Pontifical Institute, 1971), 342.13–17. On angelic knowledge in Dionysius see *In Eph.* cap. 3, lect. 3.

[67] On the contribution of Anselm of Laon to the *Glossa Ordinaria*, and on Aquinas' debt to this twelfth-century predecessor, see B. Smalley, *The Study of the Bible in the Middle Ages* (Oxford: Blackwell, 1952), pp. 146–66. For further citations see *In Col.*, cap. 1, lect. 6; cap. 2, lect. 1; cap. 2, lect. 4; and especially the picturesque quotation at *In Eph.*, cap. 6, lect. 3 (glossing 6.12): 'bad men are horses, demons their riders. Slay the rider and you possess the horse'.

[68] *In Eph.*, cap. 1, lect. 6 (on Eph. 1.17-18) and cap. 2, lect. 5 (on Eph. 2.14).

[69] *In Eph.*, cap. 1, lect. 5 on Eph. 1.14.

[70] Not to, but within the apostles, at *In Eph.*, cap. 3, lect. 3.

[71] *In Eph.*, cap. 1, lect. 2, where the exegesis is described as 'forced' (*extorta*). See also *ST* I, 23.4.

Latin of the heretic John Scotus Eriugena)[72], Aquinas borrows little from Greek authors in these commentaries. Where a name is used, it is almost always to inoculate the reader against some heresy. Arius can teach us the fate of those who slight the divinity of Jesus,[73] while the condemnation of Origen should deter us from maintaining the pre-existence of the soul or the salvation of the demons.[74] John Damascene, a touchstone of catholicity in the *Summa Theologiae*, is quoted once, and no disparagement seems to be implied by the conjecture that it was the Platonists who taught him to regard Satan as the viceroy of God in all things earthly before his fall.[75] The *Platonici* can be believed, since they concur with the Areopagite, when they assert that God communicates certain blessings through intermediaries;[76] and it is certainly to their credit that Augustine found some rumour of the Trinity in their writings.[77] On the other hand, their belief that the first creation was a world of noetic entities, and that these entities, or angels, made the present world, is not to be entertained.[78] Aquinas writes not only as a Christian but as a student of Aristotle, whose philosophy he labours to reconcile with catholic doctrine in the *Summa*.[79] Nevertheless, there is no appeal to his name in either commentary, perhaps because the exposition of Scripture was not a discipline in which anyone, however proficient in ethics, physics, metaphysics or politics, could have anticipated the wisdom of the Church.

We hear little in either commentary from the eloquent John Chrysostom, a favourite in the *Catena Aurea*. His view that the consummation foretold by Jesus at Matthew 24.4 was the sack of

---

[72] For his commentary on *Celestial Hierarchies* 8, see *PL* 122, 194–208. Dionysius is also cited at *In Eph.*, cap. 1, lect. 8; cap. 3, lect. 3 and cap. 4, lect. 4.

[73] *In Col.*, cap. 1, lect. 4. The allusion to him at *In Eph.*, cap. 4, lect. 5 is merely opprobrious. See also *In Col.*, cap. 1, lect. 5. on Photinus, who fused the Father with the Son; cap. 2, lect. 2 on Nestorius, who was held to have divided the human Jesus and the Word into two persons.

[74] *In Eph.*, cap. 1, lect. 3 and cap. 1, lect. 8. The references are from hearsay (e.g. Augustine, *City of God* 11.23), and are only partially verified in Origen, *First Principles* 1.3, 1.4.1, 1.8.1, etc.

[75] *In Eph.*, cap. 2, lect. 1. See also John Damascene, *On the Orthodox Faith* 2.4.1. On the putatively Platonic origin of this notion see n. 78.

[76] *In Col.*, cap. 2, lect. 2, with the caveat that angels are only occasional ministers of divine largesse.

[77] *In Col.*, cap. 1, lect. 6, alluding to Augustine, *Confessions* 7.9. For examples of Platonic texts baptized by Augustine see *City of God* 10.23, 10.29.

[78] *In Col.*, cap. 1, lect. 4. At *City of God* 12.24, Augustine equates the angels with the lesser gods of Plato's *Timaeus*, to whom the Demiurge entrusts the creation of humanity.

[79] On Aristotle in the Middle Ages see E. Gilson, *La Philosophie au Moyen Age* (Paris: Payot, 1941), pp. 550–70.

Jerusalem in AD 70 is countermanded at once by Augustine's argument that the gospel had not yet been preached to all nations by this date.[80] To us it seems regrettable that Aquinas did not learn from the 'Antiochene' school of Chrysostom to look into the soul of Paul, or ask himself what events and circumstances might have quickened the Apostle's pen and shaped his mode of writing. While he can pause to annotate an allusion to Jewish festivals,[81] or explain that the 'writing against us' was a legal indictment, torn up according to custom when the defendant is acquitted,[82] Aquinas is apt to treat the words of Paul as though their sense was determined more by the situation of the reader than by that of the author and his correspondents. Such practices are now condoned in academic circles with the maxim that 'the unity of a text lies not in its origin but in its destination'.[83] It was surely, however, his churchmanship, not his hermeneutical bias that caused Aquinas to neglect his Greek precursors. The papal church of his time believed that her Eastern sister, severed from the root of orthodoxy by the German occupation of Rome, had lapsed into numerous heresies, the most heinous of which – the denial that the third person of the Trinity proceeds jointly from the other two – had justly led to her excommunication in 1054. In 1204, when the Franks redeemed the expenses of the Fourth Crusade by sacking Constantinople, Rome not only endorsed the conquest but installed her own creature as patriarch.[84] The city had barely ceased to be a Latin fief when Aquinas wrote his treatise *Against the Errors of the Greeks*, in which he taxed both Athanasius and the great Basil with indiscretions in their teaching on the procession of the Spirit.[85] The rebuttal of the Greeks and their Western sympathizers was after all another acknowledged duty of the Dominicans, and one that prompted

---

[80] *In Col.*, cap. 1, lect. 2. Augustine, *Letter* 166.9 is quoted in *Catena Aurea*, vol. 1 (Oxford: J.H. Parker, 1841; reprinted London: St Albans Press, 1997), pp. 808–9, and is followed by an excerpt from the Latin Gloss that attempts to harmonize the two opinions.

[81] *In Col.*, cap. 1, lect. 4, asserting of the Law what he does not assert of Scripture in these commentaries – that the literal sense is inferior to the allegorical and the anagogic.

[82] *In Col.*, cap. 2, lect. 3, where the writing at Col. 2.14 is also identified as the 'handwritten scripture', i.e. the letter that kills in contradiction to the Spirit.

[83] E. Clark, *Reading Renunciation* (Princeton: Princeton University Press, 1999), citing Roland Barthes, *Image, Music, Text* (Glasgow: Fontana, 1977), p. 148, with reference to Augustine.

[84] S. Runciman, *The Eastern Schism* (Oxford: Clarendon Press, 1955), p. 156.

[85] Translated (and dated to 1264) by J. Likoudis, *Ending the Byzantine Greek Schism* (New Rochelle, NY: Catholics for the Faith, 1992), pp. 125–89. See e.g. Book 1, ch. 11 and 12 on Athanasius and Basil, though the citations are (as usual) inauthentic, and the older Greeks are (as always) acquitted of any substantial error.

Aquinas to exceed the bounds of paraphrase when he came to explain how our access to the Father through the Spirit is prepared by the work of Christ:

> We have access to the Father through Christ [Eph. 2.18] because Christ acts through the Holy Spirit. See Rom. 8.9: 'If anyone has not the spirit of Christ, he is none of his'. And thus whatever is done through the Spirit is likewise done through Christ. And when he says 'to the Father', this is to be understood as applying also to the whole Trinity, since on account of the unity of essence the Son and the Holy Spirit are in the Father, and the Father and the Son in the Holy Spirit. (*In Eph.*, cap.2, lect.5)

As in an earlier passage, where the Spirit is the bond or *nexus* of Father and Son,[86] the Latin view that the Spirit proceeds from both the other persons is maintained against the Greeks who hold that the Spirit, like the Son, proceeds uniquely from the Father. Nor, we may add, is this an arid point of metaphysics, for without this spirit of love it is impossible to grasp the revelation of the Word.[87] None of the Eastern Fathers adduced as witnesses to the origin of the Spirit in *On the Errors of the Greeks*[88] appears in the Commentary on Ephesians. The difference between the two works is the difference between a history of dogma and a dogmatic exegesis; history and exegesis for their own sake we cannot demand of a theologian in the thirteenth century – not even, perhaps, of a theologian in the twenty-first. This passage on the Trinity deserves quotation because it is at once so characteristic of Aquinas and so foreign to the principles of modern commentary. But if, as many will feel, the neglect of history is a shortcoming in his commentaries, while his efforts to corroborate the dogmas of Latin Christendom are chimerical, we should also be prepared to see that these defects – if defects they are – are inseparable corollaries of his merits. The commentaries on Ephesians and Colossians are the work of a mind unparalleled in philosophical rigour and endowed with all the hermeneutical arts that it was possible to acquire in a thirteenth-century university. Aquinas has the Bible by heart (albeit only in Latin); he reveres the acknowledged doctors of the Church, but never allows respect to overpower his judgment; he looks in the

---

[86] *In Eph.*, cap. 1, lect. 1. At *In Col.*, cap. 1, lect. 3 'Augustine in the Gloss' is said to have characterized the Spirit as the mutual love of the Father and the Son. See also *On the Trinity* 9.1-3 and 9.17.

[87] *In Eph.*, cap. 1, lect. 5, where it is clear that the word of truth proceeds from Christ.

[88] See e.g. Book 2, chapters 9–27 (pp. 166–176 Likoudis), where, however, the citations from authorities other than Cyril are almost always apocryphal.

epistles for what is in them, not for opportunities to amuse the learned or trouble the devout. Humility, circumspection and unwillingness to commend one's own opinions are not virtues inculcated in modern scholarship; they are Christian virtues none the less, and even today perhaps not wholly unserviceable to those who aspire to read the mind of Paul.

7

THOMAS' COMMENTARIES ON PHILEMON, 1 AND 2 THESSALONIANS AND PHILIPPIANS

Francesca Aran Murphy

The Church

Although Thomas is held to have written no single article, let alone a treatise, about the Church,[1] his commentary on Paul's letters can be seen to fashion a thorough survey of his ecclesiology. As Thomas states in the Prooemium to the Pauline letters as a whole, the material to hand is the grace of Christ: 'the teaching bears entirely on Christ's grace'. This initial Prooemium, cross-referenced and elaborated in the 'Prooemii' to the individual letters,[2] spells out Paul's 'teaching' as describing the expression of Christ's grace in the Church: 'according to its existence in the Head himself, Christ', in Hebrews, 'as it is in the principal members of the mystical body' in the epistles to the 'prelates', that is, the Pastoral epistles, and 'as it is in the mystical body itself, which is the Church', in Galatians. The same matter can be analysed in three other ways: Christ's grace can be exhibited first, 'in itself', as in Romans, second, in the 'sacraments', positively in Corinthians and negatively in Galatians, and third, 'according to the work of unity that it realizes within the Church'. Thomas finds yet another 'triplet' in the Pauline corpus: the 'institution' or 'foundation' of 'ecclesial unity' in Ephesians, the 'progress' of such unity in Philippians, its defence 'against errors' in Colossians, and its defence against 'present' and 'future persecutions', in 1 and 2 Thessalonians. '*Prelatos*', sometimes given in translations of these commentaries as 'bishop', can refer to anyone 'set over' other people. A final way of analysing the letters divides the letters directed to spiritual from those to temporal 'overseers': Timothy and Titus fall into the first, Philemon into the second, category. The Paul commentary is an organic expression of

---

[1] Yves Congar, *Thomas d'Aquin: Sa vision de théologie et de l'église* (London: Variorium Reprints, 1984), p. 523.

[2] P.C. Spicq, *Esquisse d'une histoire de l'exégèse latine au moyen age* (Paris: J. Vrin, 1944), p. 306.

the theme of the grace of Christ in the Church; each commentary articulates an angle of the entire artefact.

Paul's salutation to the Thessalonians elicits an initial definition of the Church: 'Paul greets the Church, which is the assembly of believers. And [he does] this "in God the Father and the Lord Jesus Christ", that is, in the faith of the Trinity and the divinity and humanity of Christ, because our beatitude will consist in knowing them.'[3] The 2 Thessalonians commentary notes that this 'congregatio' 'ought to be in God, otherwise it is evil'.[4] Where he defines the Church as congregatio fidelium, Thomas is envisaging it in its God-given faith. The congregatio fidelium is the Church as the body of the baptized, those sanctified in the grace of Christ, the 'Communion of Saints'.[5]

Paul can call Timothy his brother (Phlm. 1.1), Thomas says, because 'they are brothers as to the perfection of faith'.[6] Whereas sanctifying grace unites us to God, 'freely bestowed grace' enables someone to 'co-operate' in bringing others to God.[7] This 'permits one to act "in persona Christi"'.[8] The visible, hierarchical Church thus exhibits freely bestowed grace. The empirical Church appears in the commentaries when a spiritual 'prelatos' hoves in view, as when Paul mentions 'Archippus, our fellow soldier' (Phlm. 1.2): Thomas remarks that 'he had been so powerful at Colossae that all the Christians had been under his shelter. And this brings in the Church, for he was a Bishop ... And he says, Archippo commilitoni, because all the Church leaders are spiritual soldiers of the Church.'[9] The salutation to Archippus is followed by 'and to the Church which is in thy house': Thomas says 'He introduces them as well, so that they are moved by him to obey'.[10]

---

[3] In 1 Thes., cap. 1, lect. 1; Thomas Aquinas, Commentary on Saint Paul's First Letter to the Thessalonians and the Letter to the Philippians, trans. F.R. Larcher and Michael Duffy (Albany, New York: Magi Books, 1969).

[4] In 2 Thes., cap. 1, lect. 1. There is no current translation of the 2 Thessalonians commentary. The translation given here was made by Morton Gauld, fellow in Ecclesiastical Latin at Aberdeen University, and myself.

[5] Congar, Thomas d'Aquin: Sa vision de théologie et de l'église, p. 527.

[6] Thomas Aquinas, In Phlm., cap. 1, lect. 1; trans. Ralph McInerny in Thomas Aquinas: Selected Writings (London: Penguin, 1998). The one I use here was made by the Aberdeen Latin Reading Club, led by Nick Thompson, Peter Williams and Robb Price.

[7] ST, I–II, 111, 1.

[8] Congar, Thomas d'Aquin: Sa vision de théologie et de l'église, pp. 527–28.

[9] In Phlm., cap. 1, lect. 1.

[10] In Phlm., cap. 1, lect. 1.

Thessalonians

In the 1 Thessalonians commentary, the ark is a symbol for the Church in its storm-tossed unity. The Bible verse introducing the commentary is 'The waters increased, and bore up the ark and it rose above the earth' (Gen. 7.17). The water surrounding the ship is a metaphor for the tribulations of the historical Church. Although 'water extinguishes fire', and, analogously, 'tribulations diminish . . . desire', the Church's sufferings 'do not diminish the true charity of the Church: "Many waters cannot quench love, neither can floods drown it" (Song of Songs 8.7)'.[11]

The two Thessalonians commentaries deal with the unity for which the Church struggles on earth, as it approaches the last times. In 1 Thessalonians, Paul 'urges the Thessalonians to prepare for the coming judgment', and, sternly quenching the fonts of millennial fervour, Thomas emphasizes that Christians cannot time the End-times. The Lord's 'day' 'will come like a thief' (1 Thes. 5.2; see Rev. 3.3) and 'at night because of the uncertainty': 'Now is the time to escape from the wrath of God to the mercy of God, for the end of the world will not be a time of mercy but of justice.'[12]

Where 1 Thessalonians speaks to the Church of the present, 2 Thessalonians addresses the Church as standing on the threshold of the millennium. The biblical sampler for this pre-millennial Church is Genesis 49.1: 'Gather yourselves together that I may tell you that which may befall you in the last days.' This letter deals with the 'dangers of the Church in the time of Antichrist'.[13] It calls for unity of mind in its congregation: first, because 1 Thessalonians had inadvertently set the calendralizers off their marks, second because the awareness of the perishability of temporal things should encourage them in the 'will' to 'gather together with a view to seeking one thing, the prize of heaven' and, third, this should direct their 'thoughts' to the 'one stable truth' on Whom the Church is founded.[14] Chief among the future dangers is to be shaken ('moved', 2 Thes. 2.2) by 'false revelations', 'false ratiocination or exposition of Scripture' and 'by authority which has been influenced by misunderstanding'.[15]

The first issue arose because 1 Thes. 4.17, 'Then we which are alive and remain shall be caught up into the clouds' had, in Paul's time, as in the Middle Ages and today, led some to await a pre-emptive 'rapturing'. Thomas douses such millennialist expectations.

---

[11] *In 1 Thes.*, Prooemium.
[12] *In 1 Thes.*, cap. 5, lect. 1.
[13] *In 2 Thes.*, Prooemium.
[14] *In 2 Thes.*, Prooemium.
[15] *In 2 Thes.*, cap. 2, lect. 2.

The reason why the apostle removes this, concerning the advent of the Lord, is, because the *Prelatos* ought in no way to wish that any good be procured through a lie. Also because the thing believed will be dangerous, that is that the day of the Lord is near. First because it would create the occasion for greater deception, because after the time of the Apostles there would be some who said they were the Christ ... And this the apostle did not wish. Also the Devil frequently pretends to be Christ ... Augustine puts another reason, that a danger would threaten the faith. When someone might say: the Lord will come late, and then I will prepare myself for him. Another one will say: he will come soon, and so I will prepare myself now. Another will say: I don't know. And this one speaks best, since he agrees in Christ. But he will err the more, who says: soon, since, with the elapse of the time limit, men will despair, and they will believe that the scriptures are false.[16]

Thomas' exegesis follows Augustine's interpretation of Revelation and other biblical eschatological texts, as against the heterodox exegetical traditions, renewed in the previous century by Joachim of Fiore.[17] Where Joachim and his epigones read Revelation as a sequence of predictions which could be used to 'cast the horoscope' of the End Times, the Augustinian tradition stressed, first, that Revelation depicts recurrent events in the Church in the 'Sixth Day' of history, from the birth of Christ until the Second Coming, and, second, that apparent signs of the End are to be treated with scepticism. In his Commentary on the *Sentences*, Thomas reiterated the Augustinian formulae for interpreting the 'thousand years' of Revelation 20.1-6 allegorically,[18] noting that 1 Thessalonians 5.2 says 'the day of the Lord will come like a thief in the night' 'because there is no certainty of [when] the day of the last judgment will be'.[19] Persecution was commonly held to herald the Antichrist. Joachim had synchronized the tribulations of the Old Covenant with those immediately to precede the millennium.[20] Against this, the *Sentence* commentary observes that

---

[16] *In 2 Thes.*, cap. 2, lect. 2.

[17] For discussions of the 'Augustinian versus Joachimite' traditions, see Richard K. Emmerson and Bernard Mcginn (eds.), *The Apocalypse in the Middle Ages* (Ithaca and London: Cornell University Press, 1992); Bernard McGinn, *The Calabrian Abbot: Joachim of Fiore in the History of Western Thought* (New York: Macmillan, 1985); Norman Cohn, *The Pursuit of the Millennium* (London: Secker & Warburg, 1957); Jonathan Alexander, 'The Last Things: Representing the Unrepresentable: The Medieval Tradition', in Frances Carey, *The Apocalypse and the Shape of Things to Come* (London: British Museum Press, 1999), pp. 43–98.

[18] IV *Sent.*, 43, 1, 3, qc. 1, ad 4.

[19] IV *Sent.*, 47, 1, 1, qc. 3, *sc* 2; see also *ScG*, IV, 83, 22.

[20] See Bernard McGinn, *The Calabrian Abbot*, pp. 148–49.

Augustine answers certain persons who wished to liken the number of persecutions suffered by the Church to the number of the plagues of Egypt, in these words: 'I do not think that the occurrences in Egypt were in their signification prophetic of these persecutions, although those who think so have shown nicety and ingenuity in adapting them severally the one to the other, not indeed by a prophetic spirit, but by the guess-work of the human mind' (City of God, 18.52) ... The same remarks would seem applicable to the statements of Abbot Joachim, who by means of such conjectures about the future foretold some things that were true, and in others was deceived.[21]

But, writing many years later on 2 Thessalonians 2.3 (which says that 'division' will preface the coming of 'the man of sin') Thomas pinpoints 'discessio' or 'division' in the Church as a sign of the proximity of the Antichrist. As Thomas dryly notes, the word discessio had been 'much expounded in the Glosses'. Augustine had referred the 'division' to the dispersal of the Roman Empire. Thomas finds this questionable: why is it that 'long ago the peoples fell away from the Roman empire, and yet the Antichrist still hasn't come? What must be said', Thomas thinks, is that the Roman Empire

has not yet ceased to be, but has been transformed from the temporal into the spiritual, as Pope Leo said in a sermon on the apostles. And therefore one must say that the division from the Roman empire ought to be understood, not only temporally, but in a spiritual way, that is in reference to the faith of the Roman Catholic Church. And this is an appropriate sign, because just as Christ came when the Roman empire dominated all people, so conversely the sign of the Antichrist is division from it.[22]

Writing in the Summa Theologiae on the grace of Christ as head of the Church, Thomas had seen a counterpart to Christ's fullness of grace in the Antichrist, the 'man of sin': 'he is the head of all the wicked by reason of the perfection of his wickedness'. Hence on 2 Thes. 2.4, 'Showing himself as if he were God', a gloss says, 'As in Christ dwelt the fullness of Godhead, so in Antichrist the fullness of all wickedness'. Not indeed as if his humanity were assumed by the devil into unity of person, as the humanity of Christ by the Son of God; but that the devil by suggestion infuses his wickedness more copiously into him than into all others. And in this way the wicked who have gone before are signs of Antichrist, according to 2 Thes.

---

[21] IV Sent., 43, 1 qc. 2, ad 3. The identical remarks have been translated into the Supplement to the Summa Theologiae, I–II, 77, 2, ad 3. For other negative comments on Joachim see, for instance ST, IaIIae, 106, 4.

[22] In 2 Thes., cap. 2, lect. 2.

2.7, 'For the mystery of iniquity already worketh.'[23] Thomas repeats this analysis in the 2 Thessalonians commentary. He adds in reference to 'that wicked one shall be revealed' (2 Thes. 2.8): 'it says *revelabitur*, because just as all the goodness and virtues of the saints, who preceded Christ, were the figure of Christ, so in all the persecutions of the Church, tyrants have been as it were figures of the Antichrist, and the Antichrist was latent in them: and thus the totality of that malice, which lies in them, will be revealed in that time.'[24]

If 'division' or 'revolt' (*discessio* can be translated both ways) is the mark of the Antichrist, its counterpart is the unity and peace to be found in God alone. Paul means two things when he calls God 'the Lord of peace' (2 Thes. 3.16):

> that man is in agreement with himself, and with others. And neither can be had sufficiently except in God: since he cannot sufficiently agree with himself except in God, and still less with others because the affections of man only then agree in themselves when that which is sought as regards the one suffices as regards all, which nothing can be except God, 'Who satisfieth thy desire with good things' (Ps. 102:5). For anything else, apart from God, is not sufficient to all, but God is sufficient. ... And men are not united amongst themselves, except in that which is common amongst them, and God is this maximally.[25]

Philippians

In comparison to the shadowy historical travails of Thessalonians, the Church of Philippians seems lifted on high, iridescent with the light of Christ. Thomas finds his key note for this exemplary Church in Proverbs 4.18: 'The path of the righteous is like the light of dawn, which shines brighter and brighter until full day.' The way of the Philippians is called a 'path' because they chose the 'narrow gate' (Mt. 7.14), because of its 'splendour' – 'for the just shine, and so their way shines' – and because it progresses; 'it is always growing'.[26] It is 'fitting', Thomas says, 'that those who best preserved' the 'unity of the Church' 'should be held up as an example'.[27] He notes three forms of 'unity' amongst these saints: 'the unity of love', the 'unity of concord', or their being of 'one will and one soul' and their 'unity of co-operation'.[28] In reference to the mutual help which the Philippians give one another, Thomas cites a

[23] *ST*, III, 8, 8.
[24] *In 2 Thes.*, cap. 2, lect. 2.
[25] *In 2 Thes.*, cap. 2, lect. 2.
[26] *In Phil.*, Prooemium.
[27] *In Phil.*, Prooemium.
[28] *In Phil.*, cap. 1, lect. 4.

text from Proverbs which runs like a refrain through his Pauline commentary: 'A brother that is helped by his brother is like a strong city' (Prov. 18.19).

Proverbs 18.19 is apposite to the service of preaching, which Thomas understands as the work of a '*societas* of *socii*',[29] a society of friends. The text comes up again at the end of Philippians when Thomas notes that Paul calls one member of the church 'yokefellow' (Phil. 4.3) '*quia socius erat praedicationis eius*', 'because he was his fellow preacher'.[30] Preachers are brethren because they share a single ministry within the Church, forming a fellowship with the same source and goal. Thomas sees the ecclesial service of preaching as distinct from the priesthood.[31] Preachers are not a 'church within the church', a clerisy. The first preachers, the Apostles 'received the first fruits of the Spirit (Rom. 8:23) ... prior to others ... and more abundantly too,'[32] so that they could transmit this 'freely bestowed grace' to others. It is the Apostles' 'preaching of the faith', their true doctrine, which makes them founders of the Church.[33] Thomas picks out a practical, rhetorical feature which indicates to him that 'Paul's preaching is not corrupt, but sound': he 'did not employ flattery, that is, only speaking of pleasant things to them'.[34]

'The ministers of God', Thomas says in his Thessalonians commentary, 'are preachers. Preaching is from Christ, who is its principle, "figured" by the prophets and executed by the Apostles.'[35] Paul was the 'model of the theologian' for Thomas, and he sees the theologian's 'service' of the Church as a 'participation' in the light of the Word of God, given to him so that his words can 'enlighten the minds of the faithful'.[36] Thomas had used the idea of a 'downward flow' of knowledge or divine light from God to teacher to people ever since his 1256 Inaugural Lecture on Psalm 103.13.[37] Based in a theology of participation in the body of Christ and articulated through a philosophy of exemplary causality, the idea reappears in Thomas' notes on the effects of Paul's preaching. Thomas sees Paul's converts as mirroring his preaching. Paul 'says, you have

[29] Congar, *Thomas d'Aquin: Sa vision de théologie et de l'église*, p. 54.

[30] *In Phil.*, cap. 4, lect. 1.

[31] *In 2 Thes.*, cap. 3, lect. 1: 'And thus out of the Gospel there are two kinds of men who have the power to live by being maintained by others, who are those who serve the altar, and preachers.'

[32] *ST*, I–II, 106, 4. Thomas is citing the Gloss.

[33] Congar, *Thomas d'Aquin: Sa vision de théologie et de l'église*, p. 213.

[34] *In 1 Thes.*, cap. 2, lect. 1.

[35] *In 1 Thes.*, cap. 2, lect. 2.

[36] M.J. Le Guillou, *Christ and Church: A Theology of the Mystery* (New York: Desclee, 1966), pp. 179 and 166.

[37] Thomas' 'Inaugural Lecture' is translated in Simon Tugwell (ed. and trans.), *Albert and Thomas: Selected Writings* (New York: Paulist Press, 1988), pp. 253–360.

imitated us so perfectly that "you became an example ... the word of the Lord sounded forth from you", that is, the Lord has been preached'. When others commend the Thessalonians, 'they praise in you my preaching and your conversion'.[38] Preachers are a 'fellowship' but one which looks beyond itself for its source – 'That ... is sound preaching when someone teaches in that course and end in which Christ taught'[39] – and beyond itself for its fruits: 'It is the practice of a sound preacher to use as an example the blessings coming to others.'[40]

According to the *Summa*, one can know that one has grace in two ways: through direct divine revelation and by inference from perceptible, God-given signs. In the latter sense

> someone can know that he has grace, for example by perceiving that he takes delight in God and despises worldly things, and by not being conscious of any mortal sin in himself. We may understand in this sense the text of Revelation, 'To him who overcomes I shall give a hidden manna, which no one knows except him who receives it'; for in fact he who receives it knows by an experience of sweetness which is not experienced by him who does not receive it. Yet this knowledge is imperfect.[41]

On earth, experiential 'knowledge' that one is united to Christ by grace is 'imperfect' because our sanctification is incomplete until it achieves the vision of God in heaven.

Thomas is thus connoting 'imperfect' knowledge via 'perceptible signs' when, commenting on 'Knowing, brethren, beloved of God, your election' (1 Thes. 1.4), he states that Paul implies 'I am certain that you are among the elect ... And I know this because God granted me abundant evidence of this in preaching, that is, that those to whom I preach are chosen by God, for God gives them the grace to listen profitably to the word preached to them; or else, God gives me the grace to preach rewardingly to them.' Information of this type is not a human construct: 'Paul's preaching to them was authenticated not by arguments but the power of signs.'[42] His converts are likewise a sign to Paul of the measure of his own 'hope' of eternal reward: 'For the greatest reward of the preacher comes from those whom he has converted.'[43]

---

[38] *In 1 Thes.*, cap. 1, lect. 1.
[39] *In 1 Thes.*, cap. 2, lect. 1.
[40] *In 1 Thes.*, cap. 1, lect. 1.
[41] *ST*, I–II, 112, 5.
[42] *In 1 Thes.*, cap. 1, lect. 1.
[43] *In 1 Thes.*, cap. 2, lect. 2.

Grace

If the 'entire doctrine' of Paul's letters 'deals with the grace of Christ',[44] what does Thomas mean by grace? He claims that 'the grace of the Holy Spirit is a kind of interior disposition infused into us which inclines us to act rightly',[45] 'an effect of God's gratuitous will' present in us, whereby we are 'moved by him sweetly and promptly towards obtaining the eternal good'. [46]

Only God can render us Godward: 'since it is a participation in the divine nature ... it is necessary that God alone should make godlike, by communicating a share in his divine nature by participation and assimilation'.[47] By virtue of his ontological or personal union with the divine Word, 'all of the acts' of the humanity of Christ were 'acts of the *suppositum* (or person)': 'So he was full of grace.'[48] The plenitude of grace in Christ's humanity is the 'instrumental' means causing other human beings to 'participate' in his deifying grace: 'his humanity was the instrument of his divinity.'[49]

This doctrine flows into Thomas' ecclesiology: as 'an individual man', Christ 'had grace to such an extent that it would flow to others'.[50] Functioning 'as a kind of universal principle of grace for men',[51] this 'eminence of grace' falls 'under the notion of headship'.[52] Christ exhibits 'gratia capita', the grace of the head of the body of the Church: the grace personal to 'the soul of Christ' is identical to 'the grace which makes him the head of the Church'.[53] Thus, for Thomas, the Church is 'God saving and divinizing humanity through the mystery of Christ', a 'mystery' which 'unites Christ and Christians'.[54] The 2 Thessalonians commentary observes that one finds 'the desire and love of the whole congregation of the saints ... where Christ is'.[55] Thomas works out the theory of 'gratia capita' and the analogy of the Church as one body with Christ as its head in the *Summa Theologiae* III, q. 8, and in his John commentary. The John commentary finds that

---

[44] Aquinas, Prooemium, Paul's Letters.

[45] *ST*, I–II, 108, 1, ad 2.

[46] *ST*, I–II, 110, 2.

[47] *ST*, I–II, 112, 1.

[48] Aquinas, *In Io.*, cap. 1, lect. 8, commenting on John 1.14, 'And we have seen his glory, the glory of the Only Begotten of the Father, full of grace and truth.'

[49] *ST*, III, 8, 1, ad 1.

[50] *ST*, III, 7, 1, ad 3.

[51] *ST*, III, 7, 11.

[52] *ST*, III, 8, 5.

[53] *ST*, III, 8, 5.

[54] Congar, *Thomas d'Aquin: Sa vision de théologie et de l'église*, p. 530.

[55] *In 2 Thes.*, cap. 2, lect. 1.

just as there is one sense common to all the parts of the body, namely the sense of touch, while all the senses are found in the head, so in Christ, who is the head of every rational creature (and in a special way of the saints who are united to him by faith and charity), all virtues and graces and gifts are found superabundantly; but in others, i.e. the saints, we find participation of the graces and gifts, although there is a gift common to all the saints, and that is charity.[56]

Charity, the Spirit's gift of love, is 'common to all the saints', or to every person united in grace to Christ. Thomas gives the reason for this in his *Sentence* commentary. Just as a human body with 'numerically' diverse members has a single 'root' in the soul, so,

all the members of the Mystical Body have as their final perfection the Holy Spirit who is numerically one in all. And charity itself, spread among them by the Holy Spirit, though different according to essence in the diversity of persons, is nonetheless united in its root and numerically one, for the specific root of an operation is the object from which it receives its specification. And that is why, as all believe in and love one and the same object, the faith and charity of all are united in one and the same root ...[57]

Thus, commenting on Philemon 1.5, 'Hearing of thy charity and faith, which thou hast in the Lord Jesus and towards all the saints', Thomas notes that Paul prays to God for Philemon's 'necessities and goods ... that is, charity and faith ... But in what do you have faith and charity? "In the Lord Jesus" ... And this is amongst the necessities, for the more sweetly Christ is loved the more his members are loved; because he who does not love the head, does not love the members.' Here Thomas passes into alliteration: '*Et hoc est necessarium, quia ex Christo dulcius dilecto derivatur dilectio ad membra; quia non diligit caput, qui non diligit membra.*' The love with which the members love Christ and one another issues from the grace of the Holy Spirit within the body of Christ, which he unifies in love.

In the *Summa Theologiae*, the great kenotic passage in Philippians 2.1-7 is read evidentially, as 'build[ing] up faith in the Incarnation'. It was fitting that Christ underwent 'physical disabilities' because, 'since human nature is unknown to us except as burthened by these bodily disabilities, if the Son of God had taken on a human nature without them it would seem as if he were not a real man ... This is why, as Philippians says, "he emptied himself, taking the form of a

---

[56] *In Io.*, cap. 1, lect. 8.
[57] III *Sent.*, 13, 2, 2, qc. 2, ad 1.

servant".'[58] The Philippians commentary interprets the text 'evidentially-experientially', with reference to the humanity of Christ.

Thomas' teaching on *gratia capita*, Christ's grace as head of the Church stresses 'not the imitation of Christ so much as Christ's role in our deification'.[59] The soul of the one who has grace 'participates, by way of a kind of likeness, in the divine nature', and that through the mediation of 'the humanity of Christ' acting as a 'living instrument with a spiritual soul'.[60] Whereas most interpretations of the Pauline 'kenosis' text start at verse 2, Thomas takes it from the top. The English translation of Philippians 2.1-9 which best renders Thomas' approach is perhaps the NEB: 'Let your bearing towards one another arise out of your life in Christ Jesus. For the divine nature was his from the first; yet he did not think to snatch at equality with God, but made himself nothing, assuming the nature of a slave. Bearing the human likeness, revealed in human shape, he humbled himself, and in obedience accepted even death – death on a cross.' Thomas takes the passage as an 'exhortation': Paul is 'urging them to the virtue of humility by the example of Christ'.[61] But this is not simply a 'moralizing' reading of Philippians. The 'example' which Thomas sees Paul as presenting is that of the humanity of Christ as head of the Church. Christ's headship in relation to the 'body' can be seen in terms of order, perfection and efficacy or 'power-source'. 'Under the relationship of perfection,' Thomas says, 'it is in the head that one finds all the internal and external senses which are in the other members, whereas in the other members there is only touch ... Under the relationship of power, the dynamism and movement of the other members, together with the direction of them in their acts, is from the head by reason of the sensible and motive power ruling there.'[62] Not only the factual 'being' of the humanity of Christ, but 'his actions through the power of his divinity, give us salvation by causing grace in us, simultaneously by merit and by a certain efficacity'.[63] Thus, in Thomas' reading of Philippians 2.1, Jesus' humility shapes our own experience:

> Therefore, he says, be humble ... hence 'have this mind among yourselves', i.e. acquire by experience the mind 'which you have in Christ Jesus' ... We should experience this in five ways, that is in five

[58] *ST*, III, 14, 1.
[59] Aidan Nichols, *Discovering Aquinas: An Introduction to his Life, Work and Influence* (London: Darton, Longman & Todd, 2002), pp. 116–17.
[60] *ST*, III, 7, 1, ad 3.
[61] *In Phil.*, cap. 2, lect. 2.
[62] *ST*, III, 8, 1.
[63] *ST*, III, 8, 1 ad 1.

senses. The first is to see his charity, so that being enlightened we may be conformed to him: 'Your eyes shall see the king in his beauty' (Is. 33:17); 'And we all with unveiled face, beholding the glory of the Lord, are being changed into his likeness, from one degree of glory to another' (2 Cor. 3:18). Secondly, to hear his wisdom, in order to be blessed: 'Happy are these your servants who continually stand before you and hear your wisdom' (1 Kgs. 10:8) ... Third, to smell the grace of his meekness, that we may run to him: 'Your anointing oils are fragrant ... draw me after you' (Song of Songs 1:3). Fourth, to taste the sweetness of his mercy, that we may always be delighting in God: 'Taste and see that the Lord is good' (Ps. 34:9). Fifth, to touch his power, that we may be saved. Mt. 9:21: 'If I only touch his garment, I shall be made well.' And thus by imitation of this action you will feel as if touched.

The ability to 'experience' Christ's humility requires the Pneumatic gift of wisdom, that is, the supernatural 'inclination' to,[64] or connaturality with, Christ's goodness infused by grace. According to Thomas, 'there is a twofold knowledge of God's goodness or will. One is speculative ... The other ... is effective or experiential, and thereby a man experiences in himself the taste of God's sweetness and complacency in his will.'[65]

The Philippians commentary interprets 'being in the form of God' as meaning that Christ is 'true God'. Thomas understands 'he emptied himself' to mean, not that he emptied himself of the divinity with which he was 'filled', but, rather that he assumed that which he 'had not', a human nature: 'he emptied himself, not by putting off his divine nature, but by assuming a human nature'. Thomas says that

> It is beautiful that he says 'he emptied himself'. For the empty is opposed to the full. For the divine nature is sufficiently full, because every perfection of goodness is there. ... But human nature and the soul is not full, but in potentiality to fullness, because it was made as a blank slate. Therefore, human nature is empty. Hence he says, 'he emptied himself', because he assumed a human nature.[66]

Thomas reads 'the *form* of a servant' as intending to avoid the substantive term 'servant': Christ didn't assume a fully-fledged human nature (adoptionism), but 'nonetheless the Son of God was made man'.[67] Christ was 'made in the likeness of men, and in habit found as a man' (Phil. 2.7) because a habit (*habitus*) is something one 'has' or possesses, 'like a garment', effecting no alteration in the

---

[64] *ST*, I, 1, 6, ad 3.
[65] *ST*, II–II, 97, 2, ad 2.
[66] *In Phil.*, cap. 2, lect. 2.
[67] *In Phil.*, cap. 2, lect. 2.

wearer, but improving the apparel. The divine nature 'had' the human nature, the humanity enrobed the 'divine person without changing him': the human 'nature itself was changed for the better, since it was filled with grace and truth'.[68]

With Philippians 2.8, 'He humbled himself, becoming obedient unto death, even to the death of the cross', Thomas turns to the humility exercised by Christ's human will:

> The manner and sign of his humility is obedience, because it is characteristic of the proud to follow their own will ... In order to show the greatness of Christ's humility and passion, he says that He 'became obedient'; because if he had not suffered out of obedience, His passion would not be so commendable, because obedience gives merit to our sufferings. But how was he made obedient? Not by his divine will, because it is a rule (*regula*) but by human will, which is ruled in all things by the will of the Father. ... And it is congruous that he bring obedience into his passion, because the first sin was accomplished by disobedience.[69]

In tackling Philippians 2, Thomas connects the personal unity of the human-divine nature in Christ to our sanctifying conformity to that divine-human nature.

In Thomas' ecclesiology, 'the body of Christ has as its law the grace of the Holy Spirit';[70] 'Since ... the Holy Spirit proceeds as Love ... he proceeds as being the first Gift. This is what Augustine means when he says that "through the Gift who is the Holy Spirit, a multitude of gifts are distributed to Christ's members".'[71] The Holy Spirit is not present to the human soul *substantially*, as the Word was united to Christ, but as a supernaturally infused '*accidental form*'.[72] This 'being-in' us of the Spirit is not substantial but 'modal', the 'gait' of the Spirit acting within our way of being. Humans are re-created to the mode of the Spirit: 'in this sense grace too is said to be created, in that men are created modally according to it, that is, are established in a new being, out of nothing, that is, not by their merits'. [73] In the 2 Thessalonians commentary, Thomas says that, of 'these gifts of God, the first is faith, through which God lives in us ... The second is charity, through which God is in us as to effects. "God is love, and who lives in love, lives in God and God in him" (1 Jn. 4:16).'[74]

---

[68] *In Phil.*, cap. 2, lect. 2.
[69] *In Phil.*, cap. 2, lect. 2.
[70] Congar, *Thomas d'Aquin: Sa vision de théologie et de l'église*, p. 533.
[71] *ST*, I, 38, 2, citing Augustine *De Trinitate*, XV.19.34.
[72] *ST*, I–II, 110, 2, ad 2.
[73] *ST*, I–II, 110, 2, ad 3.
[74] *In 2 Thes.*, cap. 1, lect. 1.

One metaphor for this intentional being of God in humans is light: 'grace is a kind of light of the soul'.[75] Again, citing the Gloss, he says 'grace is the radiance of the soul, attracting holy love. But radiance is a quality, just like beauty of body.'[76] He can thus gloss 'you shine as lights in the world' (Phil. 2.15) as meaning that they 'are luminous, not in essence, since God alone is light like that. ... But they are light inasmuch as they have some of the light which was the light of men, that is, of the Word of God irradiating us.'[77] Since grace is a 'created reality', it is the recipient human being who changes on reception of it, not the Holy Spirit.[78] Hence, 'Do not extinguish the Spirit' (1 Thes. 5.19) does not mean extinguishing the 'divine, incorruptible and eternal person' of the Holy Spirit. Rather, 'someone is said to quench the Spirit either in himself or in somebody else ... For when somebody wishes to do something generous as a result of the impulse of the Holy Spirit, or even when some generous inclination arises, and the person impedes it, he extinguishes the Holy Spirit.' This can also be achieved by 'mortal sin' and 'by concealing him': so 'if you have the gift of the Spirit, make use of it for the benefit of your neighbours'.[79]

Just as the theoretical doctrine of 'created and uncreated grace' has a pragmatic and pastoral follow-on in Thomas' scriptural reading, so does the apparently arcane theory of the co-existence of grace and human free will. It's worth Paul's time to warn the Thessalonians, Thomas thinks, because 'the good deeds that we do are the result of free will, and so a man could profit from a warning. And since these deeds are also the result of grace, man needs prayer as well.'[80] Free will is a prerequisite of moral judgement: 'guilt is not imputed to him who does not have the use of free will'.[81] Thomas outlines the four potential potholes of the topic of grace and free will in his Philippians commentary:

Then when he says, 'for God is at work in you, both to will and to work' (Phil 2:13), he strengthens their confidence, and he excludes four false opinions. The first is the opinion of those who believe that man can be saved of his own free will without God's help ... The second are those who deny free will altogether and say that man is necessitated by fate or by divine providence. He excludes this when he says, 'in you', because He

[75] *ST*, I–II, 110, 1, *sc.*

[76] *ST*, I–II, 110, 2, *sc.*

[77] *In Phil.*, cap. 2, lect. 4.

[78] Jean-Pierre Torrell, *Saint Thomas Aquinas*, vol. 2, *Spiritual Master* (Washington: Catholic University of America Press, 2003), pp. 189–190.

[79] *In 1 Thes.*, cap. 5, lect. 2.

[80] *In 1 Thes.*, cap. 1, lect. 1.

[81] *In 2 Thes.*, cap. 2, lect. 2.

moves the will from within to act well: 'Thou hast wrought for us all our works' (Is. 26:12). The third ... is that of the Pelagians who say that the choices are in us, but the performing of works in God, because willing comes from us, but accomplishing comes from God. He excludes this when he says, 'both to will and to work': 'It depends not upon man's will', i.e. without God's help, 'or exertion, but upon God's mercy' (Rom. 9:16). The fourth is the opinion that God accomplishes every good in us and does this through our merits. He excludes this when he says 'for his good pleasure', and not our merits, because before we get God's grace there is no good merit in us ...[82]

It is the graced human being herself who acts in faith and love; otherwise 'we would be excluded from the act of love of God and neighbour ... we would only be the theatre in which they occurred'.[83] The method by which God moves any being is construed to its nature, and thus God 'moves men by the characteristics of human nature, one of which is free choice. So the motion from God towards justice', that is, justification, 'does not take place without a movement of free choice'.[84] A force whose movement is purely physical, like gravity, cannot be oriented toward grace; so far from excluding it, the human characteristic of free will is what makes it possible for us to walk with a graced gait. Thomas observes that Paul's confidence in his converts 'depends on the one who gives grace, and on men who are free willed in order that they may be directed in grace'.[85]

Thomas holds this view of the co-operation of free will with grace together with the opinion that all Christians, and indeed 'all men' are in some sense members of the body of which Christ is the head. Being 'in Christ' is not identical to being predestined or elected to salvation. In the first place, all Christians, present, past and future are 'in Christ': 'the body of the Church', Thomas says in the *Summa Theologiae*,

> is made up of people from the beginning to the end of the world. Nor are they all together in grace, because at any given moment there are people who do not have grace just then but may have it later on; and there are others who already have it. So people can be classed as members of the mystical body because of their potentiality ... Some members have a potentiality that will never be actuated. Others are eventually actuated ...

---

[82] *In Phil.*, cap. 2, lect. 3.
[83] Torrell, *Spiritual Master*, p. 182.
[84] *ST*, I–II, 113, 3.
[85] *In 2 Thes.*, cap. 3, lect. 1.

Moreover, every human being is in some way ontologically oriented toward Christ. Within history as a whole,

> Christ is the head of all men, but in different degrees. First ... he is head of those who are united to him in glory; secondly of those who are actually united to him by charity; thirdly, of those who are actually united to him by faith; fourthly, he is head of those who are only potentially united to him, with a potency that has not yet been activated, although it is to be, according to divine predestination; fifthly, he is head of those who are potentially united to him with a potency that will never be actuated. These last are people on earth who are not predestined. When such people leave the world they cease entirely to be members of Christ, because they are no longer even in potency to be united with him.[86]

Commenting on 2 Thes. 2.13-14, Thomas draws this together with a distinction between God's eternal election and the temporal call made by God to human beings:

> The benefits of God which he puts are two, that is the election of God, which is eternal, and calling, which is temporal, here '*in qua et vocavit vos*' ... Therefore he says, 'he hath ... chosen us', that is, the apostles, and you, that is the faithful. Ephesians 1:4: 'According as he hath chosen us in him before the foundation of the world, that we should be holy.' He touches on three things around election, that is the ranking of the elect, the purpose of election, and the means of attaining the end. The elect are all the saints from the beginning of the world. ... But the first fruits are especially the apostles. ... And so he says 'first fruits unto salvation.' And the end of election is eternal salvation; and so he says 'unto salvation' ... This will be done, first, on the part of God, through sanctifying grace; whence he says '*in sanctificatione spiritus*'; second, on our part, that is the consent of free will through faith; thus he brings in '*et in fide veritatis*'. Next when he says 'whereunto he hath called you', he puts the second benefit, which is the temporal calling to Christ, since it follows from election.[87]

Although our knowledge of their number is imperfect, the Church itself encompasses 'the universal or cosmic assembly of the elect, those who will see God'. The Church is an ordering, putting all of those whose enjoyment of God is a real possibility on parade: 'Angels and men are ordered to ... the glory of enjoying God. So the Church's mystical body consists not of humans alone but also of angels: Christ is the Head of this entire multitude, the whole

---

[86] *ST*, III, 8, 3.
[87] *In 2 Thes.*, cap. 2, lect. 2.

caboodle.'[88] Following Augustine, Thomas' Philippians commentary defines 'peace' ('And the peace of God, which surpasseth all understanding,' Phil. 4.7) as 'the tranquillity of order'. This can be seen in three ways:

> first, in so far as it exists in the principle of order, namely, in God ... From that profound source in which peace exists it flows first into the beatified, in whom there is no disturbance either of guilt or punishment; then it flows into saintly men: the holier he is, the less his mind is disturbed ... But it is more perfect in the beatified ... Now because God alone can deliver the heart from all disturbance, it is necessary that it come from Him; hence he says, 'of God': and this, inasmuch as peace considered in that source 'passes all created understanding' ... As it exists in heaven, it surpasses all the knowledge of the angels; but as it exists in the saints on earth, it surpasses all the knowledge of those who lack grace: 'To him who conquers I will give some of the hidden manna, and I will give him a white stone' (Rev. 2:17).[89]

The Christological conception underlying such 'Platonic', trickle-down analyses is the Biblical principle that, just as the grace of Christ is the 'first fruits' and 'cause' of our grace, so 'his resurrection is the cause of our resurrection'.[90] As the Philippians commentary notes, 'Christ rose by his own power, but man not by his own power, but by the grace of God.'[91] Considered as God, Christ caused his own resurrection, for 'the divine power and activity of Father and Son are the same'.[92] As the *Sentence* commentary has it, 'the resurrection of Christ has the divinity as its immediate cause; but the resurrection of others is mediated by the risen man in Christ'.[93] Still more technically, the 'power of Christ's own divinity', as common to Christ and the Father, is the 'univocal efficient cause' of our resurrection; but the 'instrumental cause' of our resurrection is the 'flesh of Christ acting as it were like an organ' of the deity.[94] Since it is mediated through the resurrection of the humanity of Christ, our resurrection takes the same embodied shape as his: he will 'reduce' our body 'to his form'.[95] The 1 Thessalonians commentary notes that 'Christ's resurrection is not only the cause, but also the *pattern* (*exemplar*) of our resurrection. The Word made flesh revives our bodies, while the Word as such revives our souls.

---

[88] Nichols, *Discovering Aquinas*, p. 121.
[89] *In Phil.*, cap. 4, lect. 1.
[90] IV *Sent.*, 43, 1, 2, qc. 1 co.
[91] *In Phil.*, cap. 3, lect. 2.
[92] *ST*, III, 53, 4, ad 1.
[93] IV *Sent.*, 43, 1, 2, qc. 1, ad 3.
[94] IV *Sent.*, 43, 1, 2, qc. 1 co.
[95] *In Phil.*, cap. 3, lect. 3.

Christ is the pattern of our resurrection in that Christ assumed flesh, and also rose embodied in flesh.'[96]

Paul had instructed the Thessalonians that

> we who are left alive until the coming of the Lord shall not precede those who have fallen asleep. For the Lord himself will descend from heaven at the word of command, at the sound of the archangel's voice and the trumpet call of God; and the Christian dead will rise first, then we who are left alive shall be caught up, along with them, in the clouds, to meet Christ in the air. Thus we shall always be with the Lord. (1 Thes. 4.14-17)

Augustine deplored the fact that this passage had given rise to 'continuous' speculation 'whether those whom Christ is to find living in this world ... are never to die at all, or whether in that precise moment of time when they are caught up in the clouds, along with those rising again, to meet Christ in the air, they will pass with marvellous speed through death to immortality'.[97] Like the Bishop of Hippo, Thomas thinks that Paul is speaking of a universal resurrection of the dead, not of a rapturing of the living. Thomas describes the current notion of 'rapturing' as entailing that 'the living will be taken up into the clouds and ... will die and rise while they are being taken up'. As against this, Thomas holds that those still alive at the Second Coming, 'will all die and all will rise at the same time'. His view of the universal resurrection is a sober, Augustinian one:

> In order to show that Christ is the cause of the resurrection, he shows that all the dead shall rise in the presence of Christ. Three causes co-operate in the accomplishment of the general resurrection: the principal cause is the divine power; the second cause is instrumental, that is the power of the humanity of Christ. The third cause might be termed a ministering cause in that the power of the angels will have some effect in the resurrection. For Augustine shows that things occur through God, by their mediation. In the resurrection, some things shall be done by angels, such as the collection of the dust. But the restoration of the bodies and the soul's reunion with the body will be accomplished immediately through Christ.[98]

Paul speaks of the general resurrection as heralded by 'the trumpet call of God'. Gregory the Great had seen the trumpet's sounding as a demonstration of the Son's coming in judgment. Thomas' *Sentence* commentary notes that Paul's use of the Old Testament symbol is congruent here, since it was used to 'gather

[96] *In 1 Thes.*, cap. 4, lect. 2.
[97] Augustine, *City of God*, XX. 20.
[98] *In 1 Thes.*, cap. 4, lect. 2.

people together in Council, to move to war, and to call to festival. The resurrected themselves are gathered to a Council of judgement, to the war in which "the whole world will fight against the wise" (Wisdom 5:21), and to the festival of eternal solemnity.[99] His 1 Thessalonians commentary reiterates this trail of allusions,[100] adding by way of how to identify the last trumpet, that 'if it is a physical sound' that is, one we can hear, it's just a 'trumpet', but if 'it is not a physical voice then it is the divine power of Christ present and manifest to the whole world'.[101] The trumpet is thus an effective symbol of the 'resurrection's coming by divine power', 'called a trumpet because of its resonance ... derived from God who raises from the dead'.[102]

The Last Judgment will be effected by Jesus Christ in his glorified humanity: 'when the Lord Jesus shall be revealed from heaven with the angels of his power' (2 Thes. 1.7) means that 'he will appear to all in human form'.[103] The *Summa Contra Gentiles* notes the parallelism: 'Since by His humanity in which He suffered and rose again Christ earned for us both resurrection and eternal life, it is to Him that universal judgement belongs.'[104]

From Hilary on, interpreters of Philippians had spoken of the 'two states' of Christ, the 'state of obedience' (*status obedientis*) and the 'state of glory' (*status gloriae*). 'In the first coming', Thomas says in his 1 Thessalonians commentary, 'he came as obedient' (Phil. 2.8), but the second coming 'will be the coming of glory'.[105] Thomas sees a 'necessary' parallelism in the movement from the obedient state to the glorified: it was 'necessary' that Christ rise from the dead because 'divine justice' requires that those who humble themselves are exalted.[106] In our earthly lives 'one reaches glory by sufferings endured here';[107] 'let me be found not only having justice but also conformed to his death';[108] 'it is very praiseworthy to be chained for Christ; in this is our beatitude'.[109]

The glorification of the saints is brought about through Christ's instrumental headship: 'Christ's soul was moved by God through grace in such a way that not only he himself should arrive at the

[99] IV *Sent.*, 43, 1, 2 qc. 2 co.
[100] *In 1 Thes.*, cap. 4, lect. 2.
[101] *In 1 Thes.*, cap. 4, lect. 2.
[102] *In 1 Thes.*, cap. 4, lect. 2.
[103] *In 2 Thes.*, cap. 1, lect. 2.
[104] *ScG*, IV, 96, 2.
[105] *In 1 Thes.*, cap. 4, lect. 2.
[106] *ST*, III, 53, 1, ad 1.
[107] *In Phil.*, cap. 3, lect. 2.
[108] *In Phil.*, cap. 3, lect. 2.
[109] *In Phlm.*, cap. 1, lect. 1.

glory of eternal life but should bring others to it too, in his role as head of the Church and author of human salvation.'[110] Discussing the 'rewarding of the saints' at the Last Judgment, Thomas states that 'glorified in his saints' (2 Thes. 1.10) could mean 'that the good of itself is communicated', and signifies further that the saints 'are his members, on whom he lives, and in whom he is glorified, in so far as his glory, that is of the head, extends right up to his members'.[111] Thus the saints of 1 Thessalonians 4 are 'caught up' into 'the clouds, to meet Christ' 'to show their deiformity'.[112]

Spiritual egalitarians respond negatively to Dante's *Paradiso*; Dante's ranking of the beatified is not to their taste. Saint Thomas shared Dante's ecclesial aesthetic. He felt that there is more grace in some than in others, partly because some prepare themselves better, but primarily because God 'dispenses the gifts of his grace diversely, in order that the beauty and perfection of the Church should emerge from the array of these different degrees'.[113] The beatitude of the blessed in heaven will be 'equal' in the sense that all will see *God*, but it will not be shared out amongst the *blessed* in the same way. Quantitatively, each saint will obtain the 'shared beatitude' 'to a greater or less extent, according to how more or less ardently he loves God'. The outcome will nonetheless be 'proportionate' or 'fitting' 'because as it is the glory of Peter to his gift and merit, so is the glory of Linus to his'[114] (just deserts: 'it seems fitting that God should make return, in proportion to the excellence of his power, to a man who works in the degree of his own power'[115]). Like theological aesthetics, merit comes down to 'divine ordination':[116] 'not all have equal happiness: because some see more clearly, just as some will love more ardently and will rejoice more. Hence each person will have a definite amount according to God's predestination'.[117]

The heavenly Church has the three elements attributed to beauty in scholastic teaching: proportion, order and 'light'. For Thomas, 'the beauty of the Church principally consists in its interior',[118] that is, in 'the comeliness of grace aris[ing] from the shining of divine light'[119] in its members, to be perfected in heaven. The evidence that

---

[110] *ST*, I–II, 114, 6.

[111] *In 2 Thes.*, cap. 2, lect. 2.

[112] *In 1 Thes.*, cap. 4, lect. 2.

[113] *ST*, I–II, 112, 4.

[114] *In 2 Thes.*, cap. 1, lect. 2.

[115] *ST*, I–II, 114, 3.

[116] *ST*, II–I, 114, 4.

[117] *In Phil.*, cap. 3, lect. 2.

[118] IV *Sent.*, 15, 3, 1, qc. 4, ad 1.

[119] *ST*, I–II, 109, 7.

'beauty consists in due proportion' is, as Thomas remarks, that 'beautiful things ... please when seen'.[120] Since 'eternal life consists in the possession and enjoyment of God',[121] joy is a recurrent theme of these letters. So 'when Paul says, "and so we shall always be with the Lord" (1 Thes. 4:16) he shows the beatitude of the saints, for they shall always be with the Lord and derive constant enjoyment from him'.[122]

Thomas' view of the Church as stretching between heaven and earth is summed up in the lines, 'it is not only the efficaciousness of Christ's Passion that is communicated to us, but also the merit of his life. And all the good that all the saints do is communicated to those who live in charity, for all are one ... This is why he who lives in charity enters into participation with all the good that is done in the whole world.'[123] Thus, for example, 'the goodness of the disciples is the glory of the Bishop'.[124]

The Theological Virtues

Grace is the seed-bed of the virtues. It is the way in which the soul is re-formed so as to be receptive to virtuous dispositions. Whereas grace is a qualitative 'gait,' the virtues are its acts, as it were, its 'legs': 'faith active through love is the first act in which sanctifying grace is displayed'.[125] The three theological virtues, 'the blessings' in Paul's readers 'for which he offers thanks' are 'faith, hope and charity'.[126] Just as the theological virtues are planted in grace, so all other virtuous behaviour patterns are outgrowths of faith, hope and love: 'Nothing else is possessed well unless the man himself is possessed by faith and charity.'[127] The Thessalonians are *filii lucis ... et filii diei'* (1 Thes. 5.5): 'This light,' Thomas says, 'is the faith of Christ', and 'out of the faith of Christ comes the day which is the brilliance of good actions'.[128] Faith, hope and charity are the principal virtues to which Thomas responds in his reading of these letters, as being the efflorescence of the Church.

[120] *ST*, I, 5, 4, ad 1.
[121] *ST*, I–II, 114, 4.
[122] *In 1 Thes.*, cap. 4, lect. 2.
[123] Thomas Aquinas, *Expositio in Symbolum Apostolorum*, 10, cited in Torrell, *Spiritual Master*, p. 106.
[124] *In 2 Thes.*, cap. 1, lect. 1.
[125] *ST*, I–II, 110, 3, ad 1.
[126] *In 1 Thes.*, cap. 1, lect. 1.
[127] *In 2 Thes.*, cap. 3, lect. 3.
[128] *In 1 Thes.*, cap. 5, lect. 1.

Faith

Whereas the normal meaning of 'faith' in modern languages is psychological or existential, referring to a subject's act of belief in something unknown, in Thomas' usage, the term's primary meaning is something objective, referring to a knowledge of God sustained by an act of God. Faith is 'like a transplant of the knowledge of God in us';[129] 'in the manifestation of faith, God is the active cause',[130] human beings the recipients. The Church for Thomas is not constructed horizontally, through the sharing of a common story of belief, but by participation in God as First Truth. The 'mystical Body is primarily constituted through unity of true faith'[131] given by the one God. According to Thomas, the 'fruit' of 'the righteousness which comes from faith in Christ' (Phil. 3.9) 'is knowledge of him, and the power of his resurrection, and to be in the society of his saints'.[132]

The objective content of faith gives rise to and structures a subjective phenomenology of faith, one to which Thomas attends with pastoral seriousness. The mosaics at Ravenna depict Christ the teacher as a young man; in the upward course of the revelation of the faith, from Old to New Testaments, the 'ultimate consummation' of the giving of faith, by Christ to John the Baptist and the Apostles is like the fresh 'time of ... youth'.[133] In its divine object, faith is, as it were, in the pink of youth. And so, in its human subjects, a living faith is marked by growth. Considering the practical psychology of faith, Thomas remarks that 'spiritual blessings ... are not safely guarded except a man progress among them. Out of these gifts of God, the first is faith, through which God lives in us, and in this we grow intellectually ... And so man progresses through knowledge, devotion and inhesion (*inhaesionem*).'[134] Paul can pray for his converts to increase 'in faith'[135] because God, the First Truth on which the Church is founded is not just stable but bubblingly active. Faith will eventually be outgrown: the heavenly, eschatological Church will be no longer *congregatio fidelium*: in its final state, the Church will become a *congregatio comprehendentium*, a congregation of comprehenders of God.

[129] Congar, *Thomas d'Aquin: Sa vision de théologie et de l'église*, p. 219.
[130] *ST*, II–II, 1, 7, ad 3.
[131] IV *Sent.*, 13, 2, 1, sol.
[132] *In Phil.*, cap. 3, lect. 2.
[133] *ST*, II–II, 1, 7, ad 4.
[134] *In 2 Thes.*, cap. 1, lect. 1.
[135] *In 1 Thes.*, cap. 3, lect. 2.

Hope

Hope is likewise an objective, structured intentional relation, relating God and human beings. A realistic hope is one which intends an attainable outcome outside the hoper's grasp. As Thomas says in reference to the Philippians' hope of future happiness,

> Hope is a movement of the appetite toward an arduous good. And this can occur in two ways: sometimes a person hopes to obtain something by himself, and then there is hope without expectation; but sometimes he hopes to obtain something through someone else, and then there is hope with expectation. This is the way we expect, when we have the hope of obtaining something through someone else: 'With expectation I have waited for the Lord, and he was attentive to me' (Ps. 40:1); 'For in this hope we were saved' (Rom. 8:24).[136]

Because their objective, transitive source is the immutable God, the 'bright hope' (*spem bonem*) of which Paul speaks to the Thessalonians is 'the *infallibility* of eternal reward'. Paul the preacher can 'encourage' and admonish them 'to will' this good, 'externally', but the hope 'will not be efficacious, unless the Spirit of God is in the interior'.[137]

Charity as Friendship

Charity is the 'top virtue': one reason the *Summa Theologiae* gives for this is that the other virtues are gestated in charity's Godward desire: 'Charity is called the mother of the other virtues because, by commanding them, it conceives the acts of the other virtues, by desire of the end.' Charity is the 'efficient cause' of the other virtues, imposing 'the form on all': 'what gives an act its order to the end must give it its form'.[138]

The Philippians commentary states that 'man's perfection consists in adhering to God through charity'.[139] A second reason why charity is the 'most excellent of the virtues', is that a remnant of the 'instrumental' clings to faith and hope, whereas charity hits the target itself. Whereas faith is used as a means to the end of truth, charity 'attains God himself that it may rest in him' – it desires God for God's sake alone.[140] Higher even than the truths of faith is what Thomas in the Thessalonians commentary calls 'the truth of love' (*charitatis veritatem*): Thomas swings Paul's phrase, 'love of truth'

---

[136] *In Phil.*, cap. 1, lect. 3.
[137] *In 2 Thes.*, cap. 2, lect. 3.
[138] *ST*, II–II, 23, 8, reply, ad 1 and ad 3.
[139] *In Phil.*, cap. 3, lect. 2.
[140] *ST*, II–II, 23, 6.

(*charitatem veritatis*, 2 Thes. 2.10) around, swapping the genitives to make the point that 'unless faith is formed through charity it is nothing'.[141]

Love is superior in a third way: even virtuous 'works are not good unless they are directed to the end of charity',[142] because any apparent 'proximate' good which is not related to the 'ultimate end of man', the 'enjoyment of God' in which charity rests, is spam morality, 'a counterfeit virtue'.[143] Thomas gives a practical discussion of how this 'truth of love', a 'kind of intuitive affinity for God',[144] affects our reasoning and moral judgments in reference to Paul's prayer that 'your charity may more and more abound in knowledge and in all discernment' (Phil. 1.9):

> But does knowledge arise from charity? It seems so, because ... charity is the Spirit, of whom it is said in John (16:13): 'When the Spirit of truth comes, he will guide you into all truth.' The reason for this is that when a person has a habit, if that habit is right, then right judgement of things pertaining to that habit follows from it; but if it is corrupted, then false judgement follows. Thus the temperate person has good judgement in regard to sex, but an intemperate person does not, having a false judgement. Now all things that are done by us must be informed by charity. Therefore, a person with charity has a correct judgement both in regard to things knowable (hence he says, 'with knowledge', by which one recognizes truth and adheres to the truths of faith) ... and in regard to things to be done, hence he says 'all discernment'.[145]

Thomas sees charity as creating a society, but his way of doing so does not privilege 'external action', or visible social behaviour. To the contrary, as Thomas sees it, the 'new law of love', in which the gospel consists, does not operate through external motives but 'intrinsically'.[146] The 'love of the brethren' (1 Thes. 4.9) which Paul enjoins upon the Thessalonians is given them 'by an interior teaching' of the Holy Spirit;[147] it is the 'interior affections which are perfected by charity'.[148] Thomas responds to Paul's strong metaphorical expression of the idea of charity as interior desire when, reflecting on 'how I long after you all in the bowels of Jesus Christ' (Phil. 1.8), he writes that it's as if Paul had said, 'How I long after

---

[141] *In 2 Thes.*, cap. 2, lect. 3.
[142] *In 2 Thes.*, cap. 2, lect. 3.
[143] *ST*, II–II, 23, 7.
[144] Pamela M. Hall, *Narrative and the Natural Law: An Interpretation of Thomistic Ethics* (Notre Dame: University of Notre Dame Press, 1995), p. 76.
[145] *In Phil.*, cap. 1, lect. 2.
[146] *ST*, I–II, 107, 1, ad 2.
[147] *In 1 Thes.*, cap. 4, lect. 1.
[148] *In Phil.*, cap. 1, lect. 2.

your salvation and participation in the merciful heart of Christ. . . . the power of love reaches to the inmost depths of the heart. Or else he means, I long for you to be in the heart of Jesus Christ, i.e., that you may love him intimately and be loved by him.'[149]

Thomas gets from the interiority of love to communal charity by creating a nexus of Pauline language and trinitarian thought. The New Law 'is the law of charity, which Paul calls the "bond of perfection" (Col. 3.14)':[150] the Holy Spirit is the 'bond' of love between Father and Son. 'Wherever there is God's work, He Himself must be found as the author. Given that the charity with which we love God is found in us by the act of the Holy Spirit, it is necessary that the Holy Spirit Himself dwell in us as long as we have charity.'[151] It is the 'charity' of 'the Holy Spirit' which 'establishes among all the members' of the body of Christ 'an organic connection that makes them interdependent in the same communion'.[152] When Paul exhorts his readers to 'be of one mind' (Phil. 2.2), he is enjoining them to 'charity', which requires 'consensus of two persons in the same thing on the part of the affections, and their judging mentally in concord'.[153] Paul is asking the Philippians to 'complete my joy' (Phil. 2.2), and Thomas connects this to 'fraternal charity'. Backing up a line to, 'if any fellowship of the Spirit' (Phil. 2.1), Thomas extends the 'fraternity' to the 'special fellowship which prevails among men who share various things, as soldiers share the arms of warfare'.[154]

Thomas uses the idea of 'communication' – or conversation – to turn Aristotle's idea of friendship to theological use. Asking how there can be friendship between God and humans – something the Greek had not envisaged – Thomas says that 'friendship is between friend and friend' and such 'well-wishing is founded on some kind of communication': given that 'there is a communication between man and God, inasmuch as He communicates His happiness to us, some kind of friendship must needs be based on this same communication'.[155] The 'opportunity for conversation', Thomas notes in response to Paul's despondent 'being taken away from you' (1 Thes. 2.17) 'requires the presence of a friend'.[156] Conversely, 'the Lord is near' (Phil. 4.5) 'touches on a cause of joy, for a man rejoices

[149] *In Phil.*, cap. 1, lect. 1.
[150] *ST*, I–II, 107, 1.
[151] *ScG*, IV, 21.
[152] Torrell, *Spiritual Master*, p. 194.
[153] *In Phil.*, cap. 2, lect. 1.
[154] *In Phil.*, cap. 2, lect. 1.
[155] *ST*, II–II, 23, 1.
[156] *In 1 Thes.*, cap. 2, lect. 2.

when his friend is near', and Christ 'is near through indwelling grace'.[157]

Deploying this Aristotelian notion, Thomas articulates his thinking on the charity sustaining the Church: 'friendship creates a community of affection and makes, so to speak, one heart from two'.[158] To hear and obey the new law of the gospel is to follow 'the councils' of a 'wise friend', Christ.[159] The New Law of charity is characterized by friendship because a 'property of friendship is harmony of will';[160] one practises its commandments as an act of 'friendship', springing from the 'community of affection' which the Spirit creates between God and ourselves.

Under the direction of Hugh of St Cher, the early thirteenth-century Dominicans had worked co-operatively to elicit more accurate versions of the Vulgate, complete with chapter and verse numbers, and the Concordances which enabled every biblical reference to evoke a series of analogous expressions.[161] Thomas' own scriptural commentaries were the end result of a massive team effort in biblical scholarship; this is one of the practical experiences which underlies his idea of mutual love as friendship. 'Socii', or brother Dominicans – often interchangeable terms – always played some role in the production of scholarly works;[162] we would not have these Pauline commentaries without the faithful 'reportatio' of the brothers. They are themselves the fruit of the brotherly help to which they so frequently refer. As Thomas relied on his forebears in biblical scholarship and on his reporters, so Paul depends on Timothy, 'the one who was most in accord with the Apostle': 'Our brother', in the Thessalonians commentary means 'sustained by charity': 'A brother helped by a brother is like a strong city' (Prov. 18.19).[163]

Mutual co-operation within the Church does not result from finding one another likeable, delightful, or even useful. Charity can only be friendship which extends to love of enemies because it begins as love for God: the *Summa Theologiae* explains that one can love a friend 'for himself', and such love is directed solely at him; but friendship can also spread beyond him when someone who

---

[157] *In Phil.*, cap. 4, lect. 1.

[158] *ScG*, IV, 21.

[159] *ST*, I–II, 108, 4, *sc*.

[160] *ScG*, IV, 22.

[161] Beryl Smalley, *The Study of the Bible in the Middle Ages* (Oxford: Basil Blackwell, 1952), p. 270.

[162] Congar, *Thomas d'Aquin: Sa vision de théologie et de l'église*, pp. 49–52.

[163] *In 1 Thes.*, cap. 3, lect. 2.

has a friendship for a certain person, for his sake loves all belonging to him, be they children, servants, or connected with him in any way. Indeed, so much do we love our friends, that for their sake we love all who belong to them, even if they hurt or hate us; so that ... the friendship of charity extends even to our enemies, whom we love out of charity to God, to Whom the friendship of charity is chiefly directed.[164]

To 'rejoice in the Lord' (Phil. 4.4) is to create a wave effect: 'if you rejoice in the Lord, it topples over into rejoicing in his Incarnation' and 'if you rejoice in your good, you will topple over into rejoicing in the good of others'.[165]

'Unlike Paul', then, Thomas prefers to think of Christians as God's friends than as God's slaves.[166] But, he is also 'perhaps subverting ... Aristotle's ethics'. Thomas 'seems to contravene Aristotle's notion of friendship' in that the Greek writer 'denies to the affiliation of unequals the title of complete friendship', and therefore, lacking a doctrine of human deification in Christ, did not imagine God and human beings as capable of friendship.[167] Thomas' account is not wholly original. Drawing on John 14, Saint John Chrysostom had seen John the Evangelist as 'a friend of the Emperor, ... speaking with Him, and from Him hearing all things'.[168] In Hellenistic times, the Greek idea of friendship as pertaining between equals had been stretched to include client-patron relationships; Chrysostom had overturned the customary view of this by seeing the wealthy as supplicants and clients of God's closest friends, the poor.[169] Thomas will cite an apposite instance of Chrysostom's attitude: in reference to Paul's instructing Philemon to 'prepare me a lodging', 'Chrysostom asks what we are to make of this remark in which a poor man commands a rich man by letter from across the expanse of the earth to prepare a lodging for him.'[170] Following on from his idea of the 'friendship' between God and Christians, Thomas' idea of charity within the Church as 'friendship' is also somewhat socially and ecclesially subversive.

The umbrella concept of charity as extending first down its shaft from God and spreading its spokes over God's Church, impacts on Thomas' opinions concerning both spiritual and temporal *'prelati'*. In his letter to the Philippians, Paul addresses himself 'to all the

---

[164] *ST*, II–II, 23, 1, ad 2.
[165] *In Phil.*, cap. 4, lect. 1.
[166] Torrell, *Spiritual Master*, p. 172.
[167] Hall, *Narrative and the Natural Law*, pp. 76–77.
[168] Chrysostom, *In John*, Hom. 1, cited in Michael Sherwin, 'Friends at the Table of the Lord: Friendship with God and the Transformation of Patronage in the Thought of John Chrysostom', *New Blackfriars* 85 (2004), pp. 387–98 (390).
[169] Sherwin, 'Friends at the Table of the Lord', pp. 397–98.
[170] *In Phlm.*, cap. 1, lect. 1.

saints in Christ Jesus who are at Philippi, with the bishops and deacons' (Phil. 1.1). The saints are 'the lesser ones', 'call[ed] saints on account of their baptism'. Thomas asks 'Why does he mention the lesser ones before the greater? Because the people are prior to the Bishop.' The ministry of the bishop exists for the service of the laity: 'the flocks are to be fed by the shepherds, and not vice versa'.[171] The first bishops were, in Thomas' view, the apostles. Paul does not advert to his 'title' in saluting the Thessalonians because 'since we are all equal if we do not fail in our duties, the Apostle, in writing to these good people, ... supplies only his humble name which is *Paul*'.[172]

Thomas takes on board the fact that there are 'special classes of people' within the visible Church: the people's disposition to the bishops differs from that to their 'equals'.[173] Bishops 'bear the full weight of the group' on their shoulders. The 'work' which 'properly belongs to their office' is 'correction'.[174] This goes so far as expelling miscreants from the Church.[175] The purpose of the episcopal admonition of a misbehaver 'ought to be his correction, which charity intends', and which 'ought not to be done out of the malice of hatred, but out of concern for charity ... And likewise he says "but admonish him as a brother" (2 Thes. 3.15). In which charity is shown.'[176]

Within the principle that our friendship opens out from God to other people, Thomas notes that the bishop 'should not be imitated in everything, but in those things which are according to the rule of Christ'.[177] When Paul praises the Thessalonians for becoming 'imitators of us', he means, Thomas thinks, that 'you imitated me not in my human failings but in those points in which I imitated Christ in the midst of suffering'.[178] In short, the people should 'respect' their bishops 'on behalf of God' and 'on your own behalf, because they are useful to you'.[179]

Philemon

The original context of Paul's letter to Philemon occasions an analysis of the relationship of temporal 'overseers' to slaves: Onesimus, a slave belonging to Philemon had been baptized, and

---

[171] *In Phil.*, cap. 1, lect. 1.
[172] *In 1 Thes.*, cap. 1, lect. 1.
[173] *In 1 Thes.*, cap. 5, lect. 1.
[174] *In 1 Thes.*, cap. 5, lect. 1.
[175] *In 2 Thes.*, cap. 3, lect. 1.
[176] *In 2 Thes.*, cap. 3, lect. 3.
[177] *In 2 Thes.*, cap. 3, lect. 1.
[178] *In 2 Thes.*, cap. 1, lect. 1.
[179] *In 2 Thes.*, cap. 5, lect. 1.

had taken the opportunity to skip Colossae, escaping to Paul's protection at Rome. Paul now returns Onesimus the slave to his 'prelate', with reluctance. Thomas' task, in a sense, is to justify or explain Paul's action. The biblical citation which heads off Thomas' discussion is: 'If the slave is faithful, let him be to you as your soul' (Sir. 33.31). This fits 'the material of the letter' because 'here he shows how temporal lords should be to temporal servants, and how a faithful servant should be to his master'.[180] 'Faithfulness is required on the part of the servant; this is the slave's good, for all that he is he must give to the master.' In exhibiting such faithfulness, the servant is 'like a friend in disposition' to the master: for 'this is proper to friendship, that they should be of one mind in what they will and what they do not will'.[181] Such 'servile' friendship has its counterweight: the servant or slave 'should be managed' by the master 'like a brother; for he is a brother, as to the generation of nature, having the same author'. He is likewise a brother within the Body of Christ: 'as to the generation of grace it goes the same', as is indicated by Galatians 3.27 ff.[182]

Paul himself is Onesimus' baptismal 'father', having given 'birth' to 'this son' 'in chains'. It was nonetheless right for him to send the man back to his master, because Philemon would not 'seek his death'.[183] Paul would have preferred to keep Onesimus, and indeed had the 'maximal' right to this son's fellowship and ministration 'because he was in chains on behalf of Christ'. He gave the escapee back into the hands of his master in the knowledge that Philemon ought to return Onesimus to himself: but he 'wished that this should come about voluntarily'.[184] Thus, as Thomas seems to see it, Paul's letter is a roundabout request for the return of Onesimus to himself, a means of getting Philemon to practise the New Law through his own inclination and free will. As spiritual prelate, Paul is able to tell 'Philemon, that although he might be great, he should nonetheless get used to ministering to the apostle'. The purpose of his request for a lodging, is 'to insinuate familiarity and love; in this way he will be prompt to obey'.[185]

The idea that one loves other people through one's love of God rests in Augustine's distinction between use and enjoyment, *uti* and *frui*. We should, Augustine says, 'use' things as means to happiness, and enjoy those things which make us happy. 'Father, Son and Holy

---

[180] *In Phlm.*, cap. 1, lect. 1.
[181] *In Phlm.*, cap. 1, lect. 1.
[182] *In Phlm.*, cap. 1, lect. 1.
[183] *In Phlm.*, cap. 1, lect. 2.
[184] *In Phlm.*, cap. 1, lect. 2.
[185] *In Phlm.*, cap. 1, lect. 2.

Spirit' are the only 'true objects of enjoyment'.[186] It follows, for Augustine, that in 'loving his neighbour as himself, a man turns the whole current of his love ... into the channel of the love of God'.[187] Therefore,

> when you have joy of a man in God, it is God rather than man that you enjoy. For you enjoy Him by whom you are made happy, and you rejoice to come to Him in whose presence you place your hope of joy. And accordingly, Paul says to Philemon, 'Yea, brother, let me have joy of thee in the Lord.' For if he had not added, 'in the Lord', but had only said, 'Let me have joy of thee', he would have implied that he fixed his hope of happiness upon him, although even in the immediate context to 'enjoy' is used in the sense of use with delight'. For when the thing that we love is near us, it ... bring[s] delight with it. And if you pass beyond this delight, and make it a means to that which you are permanently to rest in, you are using it ... But if you cling to it, and rest in it, finding your happiness complete in it, then you may be truly and properly said to enjoy it. And this we must never do except in the case of the Blessed Trinity, who is the Supreme and Unchangeable Good.[188]

Thomas' concluding exegesis of Philemon tracks Augustine closely:

> Therefore he says, thus 'May I too make use (*fruar*) of thee' (Phlm. 1:20), since you are contrary to me in nothing. And if you satisfy me in this, there will be nothing in my heart concerning you which saddens me, and thus you will delight me. But if we take enjoyment as something final, this ought not to be enjoyment of man, but of God alone. ... He adds, *in domino* [in the Lord] that is, I will enjoy you in the delectation of God, delighting in the divine goodness in you, since his action is love, the fruition of the effect, that is, charity. Thus he adds 'refresh my bowels in this' (1:20). For the spiritual man is refreshed, when he satisfies the desires of his soul. And as if he said: fulfil the intimate desire of my heart. And not with respect to evil, but *in Christo* (1:23), and thus the fulfilment of desire is good.[189]

---

[186] Augustine, *On Christian Doctrine*, I.5.5.
[187] Augustine, *On Christian Doctrine*, I.22.21.
[188] Augustine, *On Christian Doctrine*, I.33.37.
[189] *In Phlm.*, cap. 1, lect. 2.

8

THE GRACE OF CHRIST IN HIS PRINCIPAL MEMBERS: ST THOMAS AQUINAS ON THE PASTORAL EPISTLES

John Saward

Introduction

According to one of his biographers, St Thomas Aquinas had a 'special devotion' to the Apostle of the Gentiles.[1] William of Tocco tells us that Brother Thomas 'wrote on all the epistles of Paul, which he valued above all writings, the Gospels alone excepted; and [that] while engaged on this work at Paris, he is said to have had a vision of the Apostle'.[2] Bernard Gui likewise admired St Thomas for the privilege divinely given him of sharing in the wisdom of the apostles: 'O happy master, to whom Heaven's key-bearer opened the gate of the Scriptures, to whom the heaven-climbing master of marvels, Paul, showed secrets of heavenly truth!'[3] Francesco Traini's fourteenth-century masterpiece, 'The Triumph of St Thomas', represents this celestial instruction in visual form: the painter shows St Peter and St Paul, alongside the four Evangelists, pouring out the light of their writings on the mind of St Thomas.[4] The convergent testimony of Thomistic hagiography and iconography

---

[1] St Thomas 'had a special devotion (*specialem devotionem*)' to St Paul; William of Tocco, *Vita S. Thomae Aquinatis*, cap. 60; (ed.) D.M. Prümmer, *Fontes vitae S. Thomae Aquinatis notis historicis et criticis illustrati* (Toulouse: Privat, 1911), p. 133.

[2] William of Tocco, *Vita S. Thomae Aquinatis*, cap. 17, p. 88; translation in Kenelm Foster (ed.) *The Life of St Thomas Aquinas: Biographical Documents* (London and Baltimore: Longmans, 1959), p. 70. Tocco is doubtless referring to the incident described by Bernard Gui: 'Once at Paris, when writing on Paul's epistles, he came to a passage which quite baffled him until, dismissing his secretaries, he fell to the ground and prayed with tears; then what he desired was given him and all became clear.' ('The Life of St Thomas Aquinas', n. 16 in Foster, *The Life of St Thomas Aquinas*, p. 38).

[3] Bernard Gui, 'Life of St Thomas Aquinas', n. 16 in Foster, *The Life of St Thomas Aquinas*, p. 39.

[4] The painting can be found in the Church of Santa Caterina in Pisa.

suggests a fruitful principle for historical research and theological understanding: *mens Thomae totaliter Paulina.*[5]

For anyone investigating St Thomas's debt to St Paul, the commentary on the Pastoral Epistles has an interest proportionate to the special character of the epistles themselves.[6] In his prologue to the commentaries on the fourteen epistles of St Paul, St Thomas tells us that 'nine of them instruct the Church of the Gentiles; four instruct the prelates and princes of the Church, as well as kings; and the last is addressed to the Hebrews, the sons of Israel'.[7] The subject of all fourteen is the grace of Christ: as it is found, first, in Christ the Head (Hebrews); secondly, in the principal members of the Mystical Body, that is, Christians in positions of authority (*praelatos*), whether spiritual or temporal (the Pastorals and Philemon); and, thirdly, in the totality of the members of the Mystical Body (the nine other epistles).[8] Thus, if Aquinas is right, then the order in which the Pauline epistles are printed in our Bibles corresponds to the order in dignity of their subject matter; in a certain way, we ascend from Romans to the Pastorals and Hebrews. If this is so, then we should expect St Thomas's treatment of the Pastorals, concerned as they are with the grace of Christ in His principal members, to have a particular richness; and indeed scholarly opinion confirms our

[5] Commenting (in 1959) on Tocco's account of Thomas' vision of the Apostle, Fr Kenelm Foster made the understated observation: 'This special devotion of St Thomas to St Paul has been somewhat ignored, I think. It is one of the links between St Thomas and St Dominic' (Foster, *The Life of St Thomas Aquinas*, p. 70). Some years before, I.M. Vosté concluded an article on St Thomas' Pauline exegesis with the robust assertion that St Thomas' commentaries on the Pauline epistles are 'major works of his theology', and that 'he who would ignore and neglect them would not have a perfect familiarity with the Thomistic genius' (I.M. Vosté, 'S. Thomas Aquinas epistularum S. Pauli interpres', *Angelicum* 20 (1942), p. 276). Much more recently, André Dupleix, in his analysis of St Thomas' spiritual doctrine, has written: 'At first sight, the Pauline vein is the most striking. When he is emphasizing the Christ-conforming character of grace or the imitation of Christ, Thomas finds material in Paul that he can immediately employ, and most often he is content to put it into theological form. And were one inclined to think that this primacy [of Paul] may be only a matter of perspective – after all, Thomas' commentary on the entire Pauline corpus has a major place in his works – one would still have to explain why he was so attached [to Paul] with such predilection. At the very least we must recognize an affinity between these two authors' (André Dupleix, 'Saint Thomas maître spirituel'; (ed.) S.-T. Bonino, *St Thomas au XXe siècle*, Actes du colloque du centenaire de la 'Revue thomiste' (Paris: Éditions Saint-Paul, 1994), pp. 504–5.

[6] The commentary on the two letters to Timothy and the one to Titus are part of the *reportatio* made by Reginald of Piperno from a course that St Thomas may have given between 1265 and 1268 (see also Jean-Pierre Torrell, *Initiation à saint Thomas d'Aquin: Sa personne et son oeuvre* (Fribourg and Paris: Éditions universitaires, 1993), p. 372).

[7] *Expositio et lectura super epistolas Pauli apostolic*, prol. (translations are my own.)

[8] *Expositio et lectura super epistolas Pauli apostolic*, prol.

expectation. In the words of Père Spicq: 'The commentary on the Pastorals ... constitutes not only one of his best Scriptural works, but also a masterpiece of medieval exegesis.'[9]

The Pastorals can be further divided as follows: in 1 Timothy, Thomas instructs Christian pastors (in the person of Bishop Timothy) about the maintenance of the Church's unity; in 2 Timothy, he urges them to be steadfast in the face of persecution; and in Titus, he warns them of the need to defend the Church against heresy.[10] Prelates must govern the Church (1 Timothy), be ready to suffer for the people entrusted to their care (2 Timothy), and to take coercive action against the wicked, especially those who corrupt the faith (Titus).[11] In the Pastoral Epistles, the Apostle provides his spiritual sons with a kind of *pastoralis regula*,[12] an instruction on the ministry that is his and theirs – his through direct appointment as apostle by Christ (see 1 Tim. 1.12-13; 2.7), theirs as successors of the apostles through the laying on of hands (see 2 Tim. 1.6). And in the commentary on the epistles, St Thomas not only presents an extensive discussion of the pastoral ministry of the bishop, but also anticipates some of the chief themes of the *Summa Theologiae*. Indeed, to some extent, the content and order of the three epistles correspond to the content and order of the three parts of the *Summa*. The exposition of 1 Timothy contains important teaching on 'God not only as He is in Himself, but also as beginning and end of creatures'; the 2 Timothy commentary seems to be more concerned with 'the movement of the rational creature to God'; while the *Super epistolam ad Titum* contains precious doctrine on the person of Christ, 'who, as man, is our way to God'.[13]

In what follows, I shall consider the three Thomistic commentaries on the Pastoral Epistles in relation to their doctrine, respectively, of God as the beginning and end of his creatures, of the moral life of man, and of the Incarnation of the eternal Word. In each case, it will become apparent that they contain anticipations of the teaching to be found in the three parts of the *Summa*.

---

[9] C. Spicq, *Les épîtres pastorales*, t. 1 (Paris: Gabalda, new edn, 1969), p. 15.

[10] *Expositio et lectura super epistolas Pauli apostoli*, prol.

[11] *In 1 Tim.*, prol.

[12] Of 1 Timothy, St Thomas says that 'it is a kind of pastoral rule, which the Apostle imparts to Timothy, giving him instruction on everything concerned with the governance of prelates' (*In 1 Tim.*, cap. 1, lect. 2).

[13] See *ST*, I, 2, prol.

Deus omnes homines vult salvos fieri: *1 Timothy and the mystery of God's saving will*

In his commentary on the first epistle to Timothy, as in the First Part of the *Summa*, St Thomas shows us how good things come from God to men. The specific difference is that, whereas in the *Prima Pars* St Thomas is concerned with the natural order of creation, in the commentary on 1 Timothy the emphasis is on the priestly mediation of God's gifts in the supernatural order of the new creation. Now, it is above all in the public prayers of the Church's liturgy, especially the Holy Sacrifice of the Mass, that the priest, participating in the mediation of Christ,[14] brings the supernatural gifts of God to His people. Before doing anything else, then, the Apostle gives Timothy this command: 'I desire therefore, first of all, that supplications, prayers, pleas, and thanksgiving be made for all men' (1 Tim. 2.1).[15] He goes on to give the theological reason for this command: 'This is good and acceptable in the sight of God our Saviour, who will have all men to be saved, and to come to the knowledge of the truth' (1 Tim. 2.3-4). St Thomas discusses this last clause on several occasions, especially in the *Prima Pars* of the *Summa* in the treatise on the will of God. He quotes the Apostle's words as a difficulty when he is asking whether God's will is always fulfilled:

> It seems that the will of God is not always fulfilled, for the Apostle says: 'God will have all men to be saved, and to come to the knowledge of the truth' (1 Tim. 2:4). But this does not happen. Therefore, the will of God is not always fulfilled.[16]

---

[14] St Thomas explains that the uniqueness of the mediation of Christ does not 'exclude others in a certain respect being called "mediators" between God and men, namely, inasmuch as they co-operate in the uniting of men with God, whether dispositively or ministerially' (*ST*, III, 26, 1). Just as the baptized are sons-in-the-Son, so those ordained to the ministerial priesthood are mediators-in-the-Mediator, by participation in His mediation.

[15] In a remarkable passage, St Thomas shows that all the forms of prayer mentioned by St Paul in 1 Tim 2.1 are found in the varying orations of the Mass, and indeed in the fixed Ordinary of the Mass: '[T]his is the manner of praying in the Church of God: *Almighty, everlasting God* (this is the ascent of the mind, which is prayer (*oratio*)), who has given to the Church this or that benefit (thanksgiving, *gratiarum actio*), grant, we beseech thee (plea, *postulatio*) ... Through [our] Lord [Jesus Christ] (supplication, *obsecratio*).' In the Ordinary of the Mass, there is supplication up to the consecration; the consecration itself is a prayer, because it is a 'meditating on those things that Christ did'; from the consecration to Communion comes a plea for the living and the dead, and for [the priest] himself; at the end comes thanksgiving (*In 1 Tim.*, cap. 2, lect. 1). According to Tugwell, '[t]his application of the text to the Mass comes from the Marginal Gloss' (*Albert and Thomas: Selected Writings*, (ed.) Simon Tugwell (New York: Paulist Press, 1988), p. 438n).

[16] *ST*, I, 19, 6, obj. 1.

In his reply, he says that the Apostle's words can be explained in three ways. The first two of his glosses come directly from St Augustine: God wills all men to be saved in the sense that no one is saved whom He does not will to be saved; and God wills all men to be saved in the sense that He wills the salvation of men of all sorts and conditions: male and female, Jew and Gentile, small and great. However, Thomas adds, God 'does not will every man of every sort to be saved'. The third interpretation, and the one to which he gives most attention both in the *Summa* and the commentary on 1 Timothy, is based on a distinction derived from the Greek Father whom St Thomas cites more frequently than any other apart from Denys and Chrysostom, namely, St John Damascene.[17]

[A]ccording to Damascene, [the words of the Apostle] refer to the *antecedent* will, not the *consequent* will. This distinction does not apply to the divine will itself, in which there is no before or after, but to the things willed. To understand what this means, we should consider the fact that each and every thing, insofar as it is good, is willed by God. Now something can be good or bad at first sight, and as considered absolutely, but then turn out to be the opposite, when considered alongside some additional factor; this is its 'consequent' consideration. Thus, considered absolutely, it is good for a man to live, and evil for him to be killed. However, if there is an additional factor, if the man in question is a murderer or dangerous to society, then it is good for him to be killed and evil for him to live. Accordingly, we can say of a just judge that *antecedently* he wants every man to live, but *consequently* he wants the murderer to be killed. Similarly, *antecedently* God wills all men to be saved, but *consequently* He wills some to be damned, according to the requirements of His justice. Now what we will antecedently we do not will simply, but only in a certain respect; for the will is related to things as they are in themselves, and as they are in themselves, they exist under particular conditions. Thus we will something simply when all particular circumstances are considered; this is what we mean by willing consequently. Hence it can be said that a just judge wills, simply speaking, the hanging of a murderer, yet in a certain respect, when the murderer is considered as a human being, he wills him to live. Such willing can be called a velleity rather than an absolute will. Thus it is clear that whatever God wills simply takes place, though what He wills antecedently may not take place.[18]

[17] See St John Damascene, *De fide orthodoxa*, lib. 2, cap. 29; *PG* 94. 968. See the classic article by Louise-Marie Antoniotti, 'La volonté antécédente et conséquente selon saint Jean Damascène et saint Thomas d'Aquin', *Revue Thomiste* 65 (1965), pp. 52–77.
[18] *ST*, I, 19, 6, ad 1.

In the commentary on 1 Timothy, St Thomas offers several precisions that assist our understanding of the arguments in the *Summa*. First, he makes a distinction between God's 'will of sign' (*voluntas signi*) and God's 'will of good pleasure' (*voluntas beneplaciti*).[19] The former is called 'God's will' by way of metaphor; the latter is God's will in the proper sense. The will of sign is the will as indicated by a command, as, for example, in the *Pater noster* when we pray, 'Thy will be done', as if to say, 'May we obey the commandment that expresses thy will.'[20] Now according to the will of sign God does indeed will the salvation of all men, because, in one way or another, 'He has proposed to all men the precepts, counsels, and remedies of salvation.'[21] The trouble is that consideration of the divine will of sign does not resolve any enigma about mankind's actual attainment of salvation through divinely proposed 'precepts, counsels, and remedies'. Some men heed them; others reject or ignore them.

St Thomas goes on to expound the four senses in which God can be said to will the salvation of all men according to His will of good pleasure, which is the *eudokía* of which St Paul so often speaks (see Eph. 1.5). The first is that God wills the salvation of all by making His saints will the salvation of all. 'There has to be this willing in the saints, because they do not know who are predestined, and who are not.'[22] The second and third interpretations are the Augustinian ones summarized in the *Summa*. Thomas does not linger over them. The fourth and most detailed argument, manifestly his preferred solution, is the one that draws on the distinction of St John Damascene, already mentioned, between antecedent and consequent will.

St Thomas first of all explains, as he does in the *Summa*, that Damascene's distinction does not imply any 'before or after' in the will of the eternal and immutable God, as if at first He willed one thing and later willed another. No, the order of antecedent and consequent applies to the things willed rather than to the will willing. Taking account, then, of what is willed, we can say that the will can be looked at in two ways: as bearing upon things 'in general and absolutely', or 'according to certain circumstances and in particular'.[23] Now an absolute and general consideration is prior to one that is particular and circumstantial. We can, therefore, fittingly call the absolute will *quasi antecedens*, and the will as bearing upon

---

[19] *In 1 Tim.*, cap. 2, lect. 1.
[20] *ST*, I, 19, 11; see also *De Ver.* 23, 3.
[21] *In 1 Tim.*, cap. 2, lect. 1.
[22] *In 1 Tim.*, cap. 2, lect. 1.
[23] *In 1 Tim.*, cap. 2, lect. 1.

something in particular as *quasi consequens*.[24] St Thomas gives the example, not of a just judge (as in the *Prima Pars*), but of a merchant, who, absolutely speaking, wants to save all his wares, but who, in particular circumstances, is not willing to save them, if keeping them on board leads to the sinking of the ship transporting them.[25] The first, absolute kind of willing is by antecedent will; the second, circumstantial kind is consequent. St Thomas now applies the distinction to the salvation of all men as willed by God:

> Thus, in God, the salvation of all men, considered in itself, has the aspect of something that can be willed (*habet rationem ut sit volibilis*). That is the way the Apostle is speaking here, and in this sense His will is antecedent. But if we consider the good of justice, and the fact that sinners are punished, then He does not will in this way [the salvation of all men]. This is His consequent will.[26]

Here, like St John Damascene before him, Thomas gives us the response of what Garrigou-Lagrange once called 'Christian common sense' to the question of God's universal salvific will: 'God in His goodness wants all men to be saved by His antecedent will, the will, namely, that precedes His foresight of sin. But, after foreseeing the sin of final impenitence in many men, God by His consequent will wills the infliction on them of the punishment they deserve.'[27] In His justice, God will not save those unwilling to repent and accept His mercy. Valid and valuable though this argument is from the moral point of view, as harmonizing the infinite goodness of God with the loss of the damned, it does not resolve the deeper metaphysical and theological difficulty, namely, of seeing how God's will is fulfilled in those who die unrepentant and are therefore lost eternally. Is He impotent to preserve them from the sin of final impenitence? Surely not: since He preserves some from that fate, He has the power, *de potentia absoluta*, to preserve all. Presumably, the omnipotent God only permits this irrevocable last sin for the sake of some greater good. But what is that greater good, and how is the divine permission of final impenitence to be reconciled with God's universal salvific will? These questions inevitably arise when we consider St Thomas's position, whether in the *Summa* or in the commentary on 1 Timothy, in light of what the Church, responding to the errors of Gottschalk, Calvin, and Jansen, has defined concerning God's universal salvific will: God sincerely wills the

---

[24] *In 1 Tim.*, cap. 2, lect. 1.
[25] St Thomas also uses this example in *ST*, I–II, 6, 6.
[26] *In 1 Tim.*, cap. 2, lect. 1.
[27] R. Garrigou-Lagrange, *De Deo uno: Commentarium in Primam Partem S. Thomae* (Turin and Rome: Marietti, 1950), p. 413.

salvation of all men, not just of the predestined;[28] God does not will
the moral evil committed by His creatures either *per se* or *per
accidens*, but only permits it;[29] the Lord Jesus sheds His precious
blood on the cross for the salvation of all men without exception.[30]

From a consideration of the magisterial decrees directed against
heretical predestinationism, it follows that it cannot be by His
antecedent will that God wills the eternal punishment of the
reprobate. God's antecedent will is one of fatherly blessing, His
desire for the whole race of man, albeit considered absolutely and in
general, to share in His own Trinitarian life by grace in this life and
in glory in the life to come. By contrast, God's consequent will, by
which He wills the eternal punishment of certain men, bears upon
them in their particular circumstances and personal choices, and
thus in their actual obstinacy here and now.[31] As Antoniotti says:

> Antecedent will manifests the primacy of mercy. As regards what is from
> Him, God shows mercy. If He punishes, it is by reason of us, because of
> what He finds in us, what can only come from us, namely, sin, which He
> only permits, and for a greater and totally mysterious good. Punishment
> is, as it were, outside the first and truly fundamental intention of the
> divine will.[32]

---

[28] In condemning the errors of Gottschalk, the Council of Quiercy (853) decreed the
following: 'Almighty God "wants all men" without exception "to be saved" (1 Tim
2.4), even though not all be saved. The fact that certain ones are saved is the gift of the
One who saves; the fact that certain ones are lost is the fault of those who are lost'; *De
libero arbitrio hominis et praedestinatione*, cap. 3; H. Denzinger and A. Schönmetzer,
Enchiridion symbolorum, definitionum et declarationum de rebus fidei et morum
(Barcelona, Freiburg and Rome: Herder, new edn, 1976), n. 623.

[29] Against Calvin, the Council of Trent teaches: 'If anyone says that it is not in the
power of man to make his ways evil, but that God does the evil works just as He does
the good ones, not only by permitting them, but also properly and *per se*, so that
Judas's betrayal no less than Paul's vocation was God's own work, *anathema sit*' (The
Council of Trent, sixth session (1547), *Decretum de iustificatione*, can. 6; Denzinger
and Schönmetzer, *Enchiridion symbolorum, definitionum et declarationum de rebus
fidei et morum*, n. 1556). St John Damascene is emphatic that by neither antecedent
nor consequent will does God will the sins of His creatures (see also Antoniotti, 'La
volonté antécédente et conséquente selon saint Jean Damascène et saint Thomas
d'Aquin', p. 57).

[30] See the Jansenist thesis condemned by Pope Innocent X in *Cum occasione* (1653):
'It is Semi-Pelagian to say that Christ died or poured out His blood for absolutely all
men (*pro omnibus omnino hominibus*)' (Denzinger and Schönmetzer, *Enchiridion
symbolorum, definitionum et declarationum de rebus fidei et morum*, n. 2005).

[31] See Garrigou-Lagrange, *De Deo uno: Commentarium in Primam Partem S.
Thomae*, pp. 421–2. '[R]eprobation is called a preparation with regard to punishment,
which God also wills by consequent will, not antecedent' (St Thomas, *De Ver.* 6, 1, ad
5).

[32] 'La volonté antécédente et conséquente selon saint Jean Damascène et saint
Thomas d'Aquin', p. 70.

Neither in the treatise on the divine will nor in the commentary on 1 Timothy does St Thomas allow us to descend with precipitate ease into what must remain a chasm of mystery. However, a little more light is shed in some later questions in the *Summa*: for example, in the discussions of reprobation in the *Prima Pars*, and of sin in the *Prima Secundae*. As regards the first, St Thomas argues that the diversity of destinies for intellectual creatures (eternal glory for some, eternal perdition for others), like diversity in grades of being for all creatures, shows forth the divine goodness in the infinite richness of its simplicity. The *bonitas Dei*, in its myriad reflections in creatures, displays not a dull uniformity, but a dramatic multiplicity, including the fact of reprobation alongside of predestination. Such 'theo-aesthetic' or 'theo-dramatic'[33] considerations are *a posteriori*; they presuppose the fact of reprobation and display its fittingness, but they do not, indeed cannot, go further towards the reason for reprobation. Why God chooses some for glory (predestination), and wills to permit others to remain impenitent in their sin, and to inflict eternal punishment upon them for that sin (reprobation), 'has no reason, except the divine will'.[34]

The impenetrability of the mystery of reprobation derives from the incomprehensibility of the divine will. Even our own wills are relatively inaccessible to our apprehension, for the intellect understands its own operations better than those of the faculty of intellectual appetite.[35] How much more, then, will the workings of the will of the Supreme and Infinite Good surpass the grasp of our mind. Sin, including the sin of final impenitence that God sometimes mysteriously permits, is also impenetrable, though for very different reasons. The good God is incomprehensible through an excess of intelligibility, but sin is a mystery, the *mysterium iniquitatis*, by a defect of intelligibility. As a kind of evil, sin is something negative, the dis-order in a human action. In the words of Matthias Scheeben: 'Sin is not being, but non-being; and therefore it has no proper efficient cause, but a deficient cause (*causa deficiens*). Thus sin is essentially darkness, which appears blacker and murkier the more it

---

[33] These terms adapt expressions coined by Hans Urs von Balthasar, who, in a theological trilogy, considers divine revelation from the perspective of three transcendentals of beauty, goodness, and truth: *Herrlichkeit: eine theologische Ästhetik* (Einsiedeln: Johannes Verlag, 1961), *Theodramatik* (Einsiedeln: Johannes Verlag, 1973), and *Theologik* (Einsiedeln: Johannes Verlag, 1985).

[34] *ST*, I, 23, 5, ad 3; for the definition of reprobation, see I, 23, 3.

[35] In his treatise on the Blessed Trinity, Père Garrigou, in discussing the name 'Love' as applied to the Holy Spirit, says that 'anything to do with love is less known to us than things to do with the intellect'. He then gives as one of three reasons for this ineffability of love the fact that 'the intellect knows more of what is in itself than what is in another faculty, the will': see also Garrigou-Lagrange, *De Deo trino et creatore* (Turin: Marietti, 1951), p. 147.

is illuminated by reason.'[36] Even for God, above all for God, sin is opaque to the intellect. As St Thomas says, when discussing evil in general in relation to the divine ideas: 'God knows evil, not by its own reason, but by reason of the good. Evil, therefore, has no idea in God, neither as exemplar nor as reason.'[37] This truth needs to be remembered in any discussion of the divine permission of moral evil. Sin has no positive meaning or value of itself. God did not, therefore, as it were, write it in advance into the scenario of the universe; as Jacques Maritain puts it, it arises entirely out of the improvisations of the creaturely actors.[38] The all-holy God only permits moral evil because He can bring good out of it; angelic and human wickedness cannot thwart the happy ending of the divine drama. In the words of Jacques Maritain:

> He whose name is above every name, the eternally Victorious One, is sure of winning the game in the end. He wins at every moment, even when He seems to be losing. Each time a free creature unmakes for its part the work that God makes, God to that extent remakes this work – for the better – and leads it to higher ends. Because of the presence of evil on earth, everything on earth, from the beginning to the end of time, is in perpetual recasting. However real the risks may be, much more real still is the strength of arm that causes them to be surmounted by creation and repairs the damages creation has incurred.[39]

When discussing the causes of sin, St Thomas presents further arguments that illuminate God's permission of final impenitence. First, he makes it clear that God is not the author of the sinfulness of the sinful act. Inasmuch as it is an act and therefore a being (*ens*), it derives from God, the First Being, as every other being does. However, as regards the sinfulness of the act, the defect or disorder

---

[36] Matthias Joseph Scheeben, *The Mysteries of Christianity* (St Louis and London: Herder, 1946), p. 243.

[37] *ST*, I, 15, 3, ad 1. Jean-Miguel Garrigues, on the basis of this same text in the treatise on the divine ideas, has argued that God 'cannot foresee [evil], cannot even see it, because He is ontologically, infinitely alien (*étranger*) to evil. He has *nothing*, absolutely nothing, to do with it'; *Dieu sans idée du mal: La liberté de l'homme au Coeur de Dieu* (Limoges: Éditions Criterion, 1982), p. 17. Moreover, 'God, in His creative plan, did not include this possibility [of sin] in terms of foreseeable probability' (ibid., p. 89). This argument is excessive, as J.-H. Nicolas pointed out in a review: if God does not know evil *in any way*, then He does not know the world He has created (see *Revue Thomiste*, 83 (1983), p. 651). My claim, following St Thomas, is more modest, namely, that, since God knows evil differently from the way He knows the good, and since the mode of willing something presupposes the mode of knowing it, the order of the reprobation is different from the order of predestination, that is, the latter is *ante praevisa merita*, while the former is not *ante praevisa demerita*.

[38] Jacques Maritain, *Dieu et la permission du mal*; Jacques et Raïssa Maritain, *Oeuvres complètes*, vol. 12 (Fribourg: Éditions universitaires, 1992), p. 86.

[39] Maritain, *Dieu et la permission du mal*, p. 92.

in the act, we have to say that it comes from the created cause alone, the free will of the rational creature.[40] The effect, the sinful act, is a deficient act, and the cause, the sinful will, is a deficient cause. As Thomas points out, citing Augustine, the defect is comparable to 'silence or darkness, because it is solely a negation'.[41]

The Augustinian–Thomistic concept of the deficient cause confronts us with the lack of symmetry between the causality of the good act (whether natural or supernatural) and the causality of the evil act, and therefore between predestination and reprobation. Those theologians who insist upon an unconditional reprobation pay insufficient attention to this lack of symmetry by assuming that, since predestination is an utterly gratuitous gift, without consideration of the rational creature's merits (*ante praevisa merita*), reprobation must likewise take no account of his demerits (*ante praevisa demerita*). The trouble with this assumption is that it overlooks the fact that merits and demerits relate to the divine (fore)knowledge and will in essentially different ways. God, the First Cause, is at work, by concurrence, in whatever is positive and good in the actions of His creatures, even in the natural ones,[42] a fortiori in the supernatural, meritorious ones.[43] Only in the deficiency, the destructive negativity, of their evil actions can they say, 'All my own work'.[44] As Maritain points out, without God we can do nothing, but without God we can do nothing, that is, we can '*nihilate*', by blocking and impeding, the supernatural motion of the Holy Spirit

---

[40] *ST*, I–II, 79, 2.

[41] St Thomas, *De malo* 1, 3; see also St Augustine, *De civitate Dei*, lib. 12, cap. 7; *PL* 41.355.

[42] See *ST*, I, 105, 4.

[43] God's gratuitous gifts of sanctifying grace and charity are the principle of merit (see *ST*, I–II, 114, 4).

[44] As St Augustine says: ' "There the workers of iniquity are fallen; they are cast out, and could not stand" (Ps. 35:13). In impiety each one attributes to himself what is of God, and by that impiety he is cast out into his own darkness, which is what the "works of iniquity" are. It is plainly he himself who performs *these* works, and *for carrying them out he is self-sufficient*. But he does not do the works of justice unless he receives help from that fount and that light in which there is a life that wants for nothing, and where there is "no change, nor shadow of alteration" (Jas 1:17)' (*De spiritu et littera*, cap. 7, n. 11; *PL* 44, 206–7). Herbert McCabe makes the same point: 'The sinner's failure to choose happiness is just that – a failure, a not-doing, and this not-doing is not the work of God. The only thing there is is the sinner's own failure. Sin and Hell, because they are failures, absences, undoings, are the only things that are uniquely and solely the work of human choice with which God has nothing whatever to do. *They are purely and simply the result of private enterprise and initiative*'; *God Still Matters* (London and New York: Continuum Press, 2002), pp. 185–86).

in actual grace.[45] This self-sustained resistance of the created will to the uncreated, including the ultimate, irrevocable refusal that lands the creature in Hell, comes from nowhere but his finite and fallible will. God has the initiative in the line of good, but the creature has the initiative in evil, 'not the initiative of an act', but 'the free initiative of a non-act, a nihilation, a non-consideration of the rule'.[46] God can and does give the grace of final repentance even to the most obstinate of sinners, a grace which scatters the darkness of the stubborn will; but that grace is, at least condignly, unmerited and indeed unmeritable, the outcome of God's prodigal mercy alone.[47] The damned cannot complain of injustice in not receiving the grace of final repentance. God did not owe it to them, and their impenitence was not forced upon them; it was their own wilful choice. As Cardinal Journet says:

> [I]f someone is not among the predestined, it is by consequence of a refusal for which he himself takes, and will never cease to take, responsibility. He persists in his refusal, in his hatred – and that will be his torment – but he will not disavow his first choice.

It is this refusal, freely maintained to the sinner's last breath, that God 'foresees', or rather, as Journet explains, simply sees in the serenity of His succession-less eternity:

> We do not say: 'God does not predestine, God abandons, God reprobates those He knows in advance will or would refuse His prevenient graces.' We say: 'God does not predestine, God abandons, God reprobates those He sees, from all eternity, taking the first initiative of definitively refusing His prevenient graces.'[48]

God predestines to glory those in whom He does not see, from all eternity, this destructive first move on the part of the creature. There

---

[45] 'Without me you can do nothingness, without me you can introduce into being that nothingness or that non-being of the due good, that privation, which is evil. And it is this, this initiative of evil, that you can only have without me (for with me you can only do good). Here we have the line of non-being or of evil, where created liberty has the first initiative'; Maritain, Dieu et la permission du mal, p. 44. The 'first initiative of evil' comes from the creature alone, whereas in the good act, though the creature has the initiative of its freedom, the creature does not have the metaphysically first initiative, which is proper to the Creator'; Jacques Maritain, St Thomas and the Problem of Evil (Milwaukee: Marquette University Press, 1942), pp. 35–36.

[46] Maritain, Dieu et la permission du mal, p. 48. 'If I do evil, it is because I have myself taken a first initiative to shatter, by nihilating, the shatterable motion by which God inclined me to do good, and to introduce into my acts the nothingness that vitiates them. All the evil that I do comes from me' (idem., p. 51).

[47] The grace of final actual repentance is the form the grace of perseverance takes in those who, before their conversion on the threshold of death, have been in the state of mortal sin (see ST, I–II, 114, 9).

[48] Charles Journet, Entretiens sur la grâce (Paris: Desclée, 1957), p. 67.

is no reprobation before the foreseeing of demerits, whereas predestination comes solely from the generosity of the Father of mercies, that is, before any foreseeing of merits.[49]

Damascene's distinction, as expounded by Aquinas in the commentary on 1 Timothy, therefore, retains its validity. It is by His consequent will, as it confronts in His eternity the obstinacy of the persistently and finally impenitent sinner here and now, that God wills his eternal forfeiting of supernatural beatitude.[50] The merciful Father, who wills the salvation of all men, sent His Son to be the mediator of God and men (see 1 Tim. 2.5), that is, says St Thomas, the mediator 'between God and all men, which would not have been the case had He not wanted to save all'.[51] If the incarnate Son's propitiation for our sins, though sufficient for all, is efficacious only for some, that lack of efficacy is 'on account of some impediment' in the sinners concerned.[52] 'God turns away from man no more than man turns away from God.'[53] Thus fidelity to St Thomas's doctrine of predestination, whether in the *Prima Pars* or the commentary on 1 Timothy, does not require adherence to the thesis of *reprobatio ante praevisa demerita*.[54] What Maritain called 'the absolute innocence of God' is uncompromised.[55]

Bonum certamen certavi: *2 Timothy and the battle for beatitude*

In his first epistle to Timothy, St Paul speaks of the bishop as the governor ensuring good order among his people; in the second

---

[49] See *ST*, I, 23, 5.

[50] 'Reprobation begins when, *starting with infidelity to grace*, God determines by consequent will to abandon the sinner to his sin, by reason of His goodness, which is to be manifested by way of a justice that punishes'; Antoniotti, 'La volonté antécédente et conséquente selon saint Jean Damascène et saint Thomas d'Aquin', p. 74 (my italics).

[51] *In 1 Tim.*, cap. 2, lect. 1.

[52] *In 1 Tim.*, cap. 2, lect. 1.

[53] *ST*, II–II, 24, 10.

[54] In addition to Maritain and Journet, already quoted above, see the works of the following Thomists: F. Marín-Sola, 'El sistema tomista sobre la mocion divina', *La ciencia tomista* 32 (1925), pp. 5–55; Mark Pontifex, *Freedom and Providence* (New York: Hawthorn Books, 1960); William G. Most, *Grace, Predestination, and the Salvific Will of God: New Answers to Old Questions*, (Front Royal: Christendom Press, new edn, 1997). Towards the end of his life, Jean-Hervé Nicolas, with whom Maritain debated these questions over the course of many years, modified his hitherto Bañezian position in line with some of Maritain's concerns ('La volonté salvifique de Dieu contrariée par le péché', *Revue Thomiste* 92 (1992), pp. 177–96). More recently, in a spirited defence of 'Thomism of the strict observance', David Berger has argued for reprobation *ante praevisa demerita*; see *Thomismus: Grosse Leitmotive der thomistischen Synthese und ihre Aktualität für die Gegenwart* (Cologne: Editiones thomisticae, 2001), pp. 242–3. The debate continues even among Thomists.

[55] See Maritain, *Dieu et la permission du mal*, p. 17.

epistle, he sees him more as a shepherd caring for his flock, and ready, if need be, to lay down his life for them, in imitation of Christ the Good Shepherd.[56] Writing to his 'dearly beloved son' for a second time, the Apostle, from his opening words, turns his attention to the final supernatural end gratuitously given to men by God, the end towards which all the official actions and personal sufferings of the Church's sacred ministers are directed: 'the promise of life, which is in Christ Jesus' (2 Tim. 1.1), that is, says St Thomas in his commentary, 'the eternal life promised by Christ'. 'This', he adds, 'must be the goal of prelates.'[57] Thus, in a certain way, 2 Timothy and its commentary correspond in content to the Second Part of the *Summa*: the subject matter is heavenly beatitude and the way to attain it. The note that distinguishes the treatment found in the commentary from the one in the *Secunda Pars* is that St Thomas, in his exposition of St Paul, gives more emphasis to the struggle that inevitably accompanies the pursuit of Christian virtue and holiness in a world that is hostile to Christ and His Church. 'All that will live godly in Christ Jesus shall suffer persecution' (2 Tim. 3.12). Whether he be pastor or layman, the believer who reaches eternal life in Heaven is one who, like St Paul himself, has 'fought the good fight' (2 Tim. 4.7).

Whereas in the *Secunda Pars* St Thomas begins with the exposition of beatitude, considering the goal before the means by which it is attained, in the commentary on 2 Timothy, following the order of the Apostle's argument, he places beatitude at the end and reaches it only after a discussion of the suffering and persecution to be endured by the Church's pastors, and of the grace that will sustain them. As regards the latter, the Apostle's emphasis is chiefly on the specific sacramental grace of Holy Order, 'the grace of God which is in thee by the imposition of my hands' (2 Tim. 1.6), a grace that he admonishes Timothy to 'stir up' (ibid.). As he usually does, St Thomas refers to this sacramental form of sanctifying grace as 'the grace of the Holy Spirit'.[58] The use of this phrase prepares the way for his discussion of the Apostle's contrast between 'the spirit of fear' and 'the Spirit of power, and of love, and of sobriety' (2 Tim. 1.7).

Now there is a twofold spirit: the spirit of the world, and the Spirit of God. And the difference between them is as follows. 'Spirit' signifies love, for the term 'spirit' implies impulsion, and love impels. Now there is a twofold love, namely, the love of God, which is through the Spirit of

---

[56] See *In 2 Tim.*, prol.

[57] *In 2 Tim.*, cap. 1, lect. 1.

[58] *In 2 Tim.*, cap. 1, lect. 3. On the phrase 'grace of the Holy Spirit', see *ST*, I–II, 108, 1; 114, 3; II–II, 24, 3.

God, and the love of the world, which is through the spirit of the world: 'For we received not the spirit of this world, but the Spirit that is of God' (1 Cor 2:12). Now the spirit of the world makes us love the goods of this world, and to fear temporal ills, and so [the Apostle] says: 'For God hath not given us the spirit of fear, but of power, and of love, and of sobriety' (2 Tim 1:7) ... There is another spirit, the spirit of the fear of the Lord, the Holy Spirit, and this makes us fear God; it is without punishment and without offence, and it comes from God.[59]

In the *Prima Secundae*, in the treatise on the new law, St Thomas likewise contrasts the unholy spirit of this world with the Holy Spirit of God. Summarizing a tradition of ascetical wisdom reaching back to the Desert Fathers, he says that 'contempt of the world' is needed if one is to become 'receptive (*capax*) to the grace of the Holy Spirit', for 'the world, that is, the lovers of the world "cannot receive the Holy Spirit" (Jn 14:17)'.[60] The world in this bad, grace-resisting sense must, of course, be distinguished from the world as a good gift of God. In his commentary on St John's Gospel, St Thomas says that the world has three meanings in Scripture, of which the first two are positive and the third negative. The first meaning is the world as created, as, for example, when St John says, 'through Him [the Word] the world was made' (Jn 1.10). The second is the world as perfected by Christ: 'God was, in Christ, reconciling the world to Himself' (2 Cor. 5.19). Thirdly, there is the world in its perversity, as when St John says that 'the whole world is in the power of the Evil One' (1 Jn 5.19). In this bad sense, the world is the same thing as the worldly, that is, the human beings who love the world inordinately and oppose themselves to God: 'The friendship of this world is the enemy of God' (Jas 4.4).[61] The head or prince of the world thus understood is the devil: 'The devil is called the prince of this world, not by natural dominion, but by usurpation, inasmuch as the worldly, in their contempt for the true Lord, have submitted themselves to him [the devil].'[62]

The world, under the sway of its prince, is unfailingly hostile to the Church of Christ. From his baptism and confirmation, every Christian is committed to fight a spiritual battle against this tireless foe, and from their ordination, bishops such as St Timothy are commissioned to lead the battle: 'Labour as a good soldier of Christ Jesus ... [H]e also that striveth for the mastery is not crowned except he strive lawfully' (2 Tim. 2.4-5). Commenting on this

---

[59] *In 2 Tim.*, cap. 1, lect. 3.
[60] *ST*, I–II, 108, 4.
[61] *In Io.*, cap. 1, lect. 5.
[62] *In Io.*, cap. 12, lect. 5.

passage, St Thomas says that spiritual warfare and bodily warfare differ in their ends:

> The goal of bodily warfare is obtaining victory over the enemies of the fatherland, and so soldiers have to abstain from those things that divert them from the fight, namely, business and pleasure. 'Everyone that fights in the struggle abstains from all things' (1 Cor 9:25). But the goal of spiritual warfare is to be victorious over the men who are against God, and so one must abstain from all those things that distract us from God. Now these are 'secular businesses' (2 Tim 2:4), because concern for this world chokes the Word. And so he says: 'No man ... entangles himself' (ibid.). Against this, someone might say that secular businesses are temporal ones, and that the Apostle did such things, when he lived by the work of his hands. My reply would be that the Apostle says 'entangles', not 'exercises'. Now a man is entangled in the things with which his cares and concerns are connected. Soldiers of Christ, then, are banned from getting entangled with things with which their minds manifestly do not need to be entangled. Likewise, he does not say 'is entangled', but 'entangles himself', for one entangles oneself when one takes on business without piety and necessity. However, when the necessity of the duty of piety and authority is involved, then one does not entangle oneself, but rather is entangled by such necessity. ['I commend to you Phebe ... that] you assist her in whatsoever business she shall have need of you' (Rom 16:2). The reason why they must not entangle themselves is 'that he may please Him to whom he has engaged himself' (2 Tim 2:4). 'If any man love the world, the charity of the Father is not in him' (1 Jn 2:15). For he who is a soldier of Christ has committed himself to waging war for God; and so he must try to please Him to whom he has committed himself.[63]

In the *Secunda Secundae*, when discussing activity suitable to religious, St Thomas makes the same point more briefly and more clearly:

> [M]onks are forbidden to handle worldly business [conducted] out of cupidity, but not out of charity ... It is not curiosity, but charity, if someone gets involved in business out of necessity.[64]

Involvement in business required by charity does not, as it were, make the soldier of Christ guilty of 'fraternizing with the enemy'.

There is no disguising the fact that, for St Thomas, as for the Fathers, the world in its negative sense is one of the three traditional enemies of the soul. The flesh attacks virtue from within, while the devil, operating externally as an agent, entices us into wickedness by persuasion, terror, and flattery. The world also gets at us from

---

[63] *In 2 Tim.*, cap. 2, lect. 1
[64] *ST*, II–II, 187, 2, ad 1 and 2.

outside, though here the attack is 'by way of object' in the sense that it is 'by the things [of the world] that men's hearts are attracted to sin'.[65] Now St Thomas, like St Paul, recognizes that refusing the blandishments of this subtle enemy is a dangerous thing to do. The *mundani* of pagan Rome felt challenged by the preaching of the gospel and responded by subjecting the preachers to dungeon and sword. 'I labour', says the Apostle, 'even unto chains, as if an evildoer' (2 Tim. 2.9), because, when he wrote this epistle, he was already in chains in Rome, a prisoner for Christ. Nevertheless, Paul remains resolute: 'Therefore, I endure all things for the sake of the elect, that they also may obtain the salvation, which is in Christ Jesus, with heavenly glory' (2 Tim. 2.10). By these words, says St Thomas, he reveals the cause of his suffering witness to Christ, 'for it is not the punishment, but the cause that makes the martyr', and the cause (the final cause) is twofold, 'for the honour of God, and for the salvation of one's neighbour'.[66]

In the *Summa*, martyrdom is discussed as the highest act of the virtue of fortitude. It is also an act of faith and charity. Faith is the goal, the good to which the martyr holds firm in his tribulations, while charity is his martyrdom's principal motive, the virtue that commands his action. Still, the immediate motivation eliciting his readiness to suffer for the true faith is fortitude.[67] Moreover, the martyr shows himself to be not only courageous, but also temperate, just, and prudent in the face of the world's allurements.[68] Thus all the virtues, theological and moral, come to their flowering in martyrdom.

The example of martyrdom is a reminder that the rational creature's movement towards God – the subject of the *Secunda Pars* – is not a gentle stroll, but a gruelling march, a journey beset with dangers and difficulties. Even when baptism has washed away the guilt of original sin, its effects remain as wounds in the powers of his soul.[69] The sons of Adam are vulnerable pilgrims on the road to Heaven, with hostile forces at work both within and without. The Christian life is a battle for beatitude. As the Apostle says at the end of 2 Timothy: 'I have fought the good fight, I have finished the

---

[65] II *Sent.*, 21, 1, 1.

[66] *In 2 Tim.*, cap. 2, lect. 1.

[67] See *ST*, II–II, 124, 2, ad 1 and 2.

[68] 'The martyrs in their torments received something of divine glory, not as if drinking at its fount, as those who see God by essence do, but as being refreshed by a sprinkling of that glory. Hence Augustine says: "There", where they see God by essence, "the life of blessedness is drunk at its fount. Hence something is sprinkled on this life, so that in the temptations of this world one lives temperately, justly, courageously, and prudently"' (*De Ver.* 13, 3, ad 9).

[69] See *ST*, I–II, 85, 3.

course, I have kept the faith. As to the rest, there is laid up for me a crown of justice, which the Lord, the just judge, will render to me in that day, and not only to me, but to them also that love His coming' (2 Tim. 4.7-8).

'Our beatitude ... is God'.[70] The perfect supernatural happiness to which the Christian's moral striving is directed is to be found in the vision of the Trinitarian Godhead. Now the one who brings us into that beatitude is Christ,[71] the incarnate Son of God, through His death and resurrection. But we cannot lay hold of what the crucified and risen Christ has done for us without being united most intimately with Him, as members with their Head: 'If we have died with Him, we shall also live with Him; if we endure, we shall also reign with Him' (2 Tim. 2.11-12). If we are to know the power of Christ's resurrection, we must share His sufferings (Phil. 3.10-11), first, sacramentally in baptism, by being plunged into His death (see Rom. 6.3ff), and then practically in our lives, by 'patiently sustain[ing] afflictions and reproaches',[72] and 'suffer[ing] for justice and truth'.[73] It is by 'resisting evils, advancing in the good, and making good use of God's gifts',[74] that we merit the reward of eternal glory, first in our souls in the Beatific Vision and then, on the last day, in the resurrection of the flesh.

Expectantes beatam spem: *Titus and the defence of the truth of Christ*

In the epistle to Titus, St Paul instructs his 'beloved son in the common faith' (Tit. 1.4) on the latter's duty as a bishop to combat heresy and teach orthodoxy. Now the doctrines of the orthodox faith to which the Apostle gives most attention concern the person of the incarnate Word and His redemptive work. That is why verses from Titus have long had an honoured place in the Latin Church's liturgical celebration of the Incarnation. For example, at Christmas, in the epistle of the Midnight Mass, we hear how 'the grace of God our Saviour has appeared to all men' (Tit. 2.11), and at the Mass of the Dawn the reading is taken from the next chapter, which speaks of 'the goodness and kindness (*humanitas, philanthrôpía*) of God our Saviour's appearing (Tit. 3.4). In the ordinary of the Mass, as part of the so-called 'Embolism', which follows the *Pater noster*, the Church includes words from Titus: *expectantes beatam spem*, 'looking for the blessed hope and coming of our great God and

[70] *In 2 Tim.*, cap. 4, lect. 1.
[71] *In 2 Tim.*, cap. 4, lect. 1.
[72] *In 2 Tim.*, cap. 2, lect. 2.
[73] *In Phil.*, cap. 3, lect. 2.
[74] *In 2 Tim.*, cap. 4, lect. 2.

Saviour Jesus Christ' (Tit. 2.13). Given this liturgical use of Titus for Christological purposes, and given, too, St Thomas' habitual sensitivity to liturgical expressions of faith,[75] it should not surprise us to discover that, in his commentary on the third of the Pastoral Epistles, as in the Third Part of the *Summa*, St Thomas has much to say about the incarnate Word and the Sacraments that 'derive their efficacy from the incarnate Word'.[76]

Thomas has Christmas in mind when he expounds the words, 'the grace of God our Saviour has appeared to all men' (Tit. 2.11). He says that in the Nativity of Christ grace can be said to have appeared in two ways: first, in Christ Himself (as the grace of union and the grace of Christ as individual man); secondly, through Christ's mission as 'instructor'.

> The first way is because it was through the greatest grace of God that [Christ] was given to us. And so His conception, though it is an operation of the whole Trinity, is nevertheless attributed in a special way to the Holy Spirit, who is the source of graces.[77]

This is the same doctrine that we find in the *Tertia Pars*. Like all divine operations *ad extra*, the work of fashioning a body for the Son of God from the pure blood of the Virgin is the work of the whole Trinity. However, says St Thomas, this common work is 'attributed in some way to the individual Persons', and 'to the Holy Spirit is attributed the formation of the body assumed by the Son', for that assumption did not take place because of any preceding merits on anyone's part, but 'by grace alone, which is attributed to the Holy Spirit, [for] "there are diversities of graces, but the same Spirit'.[78] The Holy Spirit is the Person who is Gift in the Godhead;[79] it is therefore fitting that the Father should give us His Son in human nature by the overshadowing of the Holy Spirit.

In the commentary on Titus 2.11, having spoken of the appropriation of Christ's conception to the Holy Spirit as the source of all graces, St Thomas goes on to say that 'this grace appeared to all men, and especially to the man Christ, "full of grace and truth" (Jn 1:14)'.[80] Now this statement must not be misinterpreted, in the manner of the Adoptionists, to mean that Christ was a mere man no more than specially endowed with the grace of the Holy Spirit. In his discussion of Christ's conception in the

---

[75] See David Berger, *Thomas von Aquin und die Liturgie* (Cologne: Editiones thomisticae, 2000), passim.
[76] *ST*, III, 60, prol.
[77] *In Tit.*, cap. 2, lect. 3.
[78] *ST*, III, 32, 1, ad 1.
[79] See *ST*, I, 38.
[80] *In Tit.*, cap. 2, lect. 3.

commentary, St Thomas has just referred, at least implicitly, to the
'grace of union', that is, to the hypostatic union of human nature to
the eternal Son as the supreme and unmerited grace of graces.[81]
Now he moves on to the consideration of the 'grace of Christ as an
individual man', that is, to the immeasurable fullness of habitual
grace to be found in the human soul of the Son as a consequence of
the hypostatic union.[82] In his commentary on the next chapter of
Titus, St Thomas will mention the third way in which grace belongs
to Christ as man, namely, 'as Head of the Church': in His human
nature, 'Christ received the supreme plenitude [of the grace of the
Holy Spirit], so that through Him it might flow to all ... "From His
fullness have we all received, grace upon grace" (Jn 1:16).'[83]

   The second sense in which God's grace appears in the Nativity of
Christ is that, through the habitual grace filling and adorning the
human nature of Christ, the human race is to be instructed, 'since
before Christ the world was in ignorance and heresy. "The people
that walked in darkness have seen a great light" (Is 9:2).'[84] And so
the Apostle adds that the grace of our God and Saviour has
appeared in order to 'school' us, 'that, renouncing impiety and
worldly desires, we should live soberly, and justly, and godly in this
world' (Tit. 2.12). The phrase 'impiety and worldly desires' shows
that 'all sins consist either in those things that are directly against
God, which are called sins of impiety ... or in the abuse of temporal
things, and these are worldly desires'.[85] By His 'instruction', Christ
delivers us from both kinds of fault. We should not think, though,
that the saving influence of the incarnate Son is restricted to the
imparting of such external graces of teaching. The Apostle goes on,
therefore, to remind us of the sacrifice of Christ on the cross, by
which He merited the grace that saves us through an inward
transfiguration: 'He gave Himself up for us, that He might redeem
us from all iniquity, and might purify for Himself an acceptable
people, zealous for good works' (Tit. 2.14). St Thomas offers this
commentary:

---

[81] '[I]f by "grace" we mean the gratuitous gift of God itself, then the very fact that
human nature is united to a divine person can be called a grace, inasmuch as this was
done without any preceding merits. But we cannot call it a grace in the sense that
habitual grace was the means by which the union took place' (ST, III, 2, 10). '[T]he
grace of union is the very personal existence (ipsum esse personale) gratuitously given
by God to the human nature in the person of the Word' (ST, III, 6, 6).

[82] '[T]he habitual grace is seen to follow this union as splendour follows the sun'
(ST, III, 7, 13).

[83] In Tit., cap. 3, lect. 1. On the 'capital' grace of Christ, see ST, III, 8.

[84] In Tit., cap. 2, lect. 3.

[85] In Tit., cap. 2, lect. 3.

[W]hen he says, 'Who gave Himself up', he shows the working of grace. First, he shows the benefit of the grace of His Passion; secondly, the fruit of the Passion, when he says, 'to redeem us'. He says, therefore, [in effect]: I say that He is our Saviour, but in what way? He is our Saviour, because 'He gave Himself up for us'. 'Walk in love, as Christ also loved us, and delivered Himself up for us as an oblation and sacrifice to God' (Eph 5:2). The fruit of His love is called liberation and sanctification. [He mentions] the liberation when he says, 'to redeem us from all iniquity' (Titus 2:14). 'He who commits sin is a slave of sin' (Jn 8:34). For by his sin the first man was reduced to the slavery of sin, by which slavery he was inclined to yet another sin (*ad aliud peccatum*). But Christ made satisfaction by His Passion. Therefore, we are redeemed from slavery ... and not only from Original Sin, but also from all sins that by his own will anyone adds on top of that (*superaddidit*). Sanctification is placed in the good, when he says, 'that He might purify for Himself a people', that is, that He might sanctify the people in such a way, namely, that we would be His people, consecrated to Him ... '[an] acceptable [people]', that is, acceptable to God by right faith and intention.[86]

In the *Tertia Pars*, St Thomas makes distinctions that ease our entry into this thicket of argumentation. The Passion of Christ, which saves us by way of satisfaction and redemption (or liberation), is a 'universal cause', which needs to be 'applied' to men individually.[87] In other words, the members, who with their Head are 'like one mystical person', need to make what He has done for them their own.[88] This application or appropriation takes place through the 'grace of the virtues and gifts', that is, sanctifying grace, accompanied by the infused virtues and the Gifts of the Holy Spirit, which is poured into men's souls by the Holy Spirit and 'perfects the essence and the powers of the soul'.[89] The inwardly transfiguring grace of the Holy Spirit, with all its accompaniments, is conferred, restored, or increased in all of the Sacraments. In addition, each Sacrament applies the saving power of Christ's Passion through the bestowal of a specific sacramental grace, which both heals any remaining sin-inflicted defects and causes 'certain special effects required in Christian life'.[90] Thus 'the Passion of Christ obtains its effect, in those to whom it is applied, through faith and charity, and through the Sacraments of faith'.[91]

---

[86] *In Tit.*, cap. 2, lect. 3.
[87] *ST*, III, 52, 1, ad 2.
[88] *ST*, III, 48, 2, ad 1.
[89] *ST*, III, 62, 2.
[90] *ST*, III, 62, 2.
[91] *ST*, III, 49, 3, ad 1.

In his commentary on Titus 3, St Thomas speaks of the deifying effects of the grace of Christ poured out in the Sacraments of His Church. The Apostle says that 'the goodness and kindness of God our Saviour' made its appearance not because of any 'works of justice' we had done, but because, 'according to His mercy, He has saved us, by the laver of regeneration and renovation in the Holy Spirit, whom He has poured forth upon us abundantly through Jesus Christ our Saviour' (Tit. 3–6). Thomas offers the following exposition of these verses:

> In the state of ruination (*perditionis*), man needed two things, which he attained through Christ, namely, participation in the divine nature, and the laying aside of oldness (*vetustatis*). For he had been separated from God ... and had grown old (*inveteratus*): 'Thou art grown old in a strange country' (Bar 3:11). The first of these [things that fallen man needed], participation in the divine nature, we attain through Christ: '[B]y these you have been made partakers of the divine nature' (2 Pet 1:4). Now a new nature is only acquired through generation. However, this nature is so given to us that our own remains; [the new nature] is added over and above (*superadditur*) [our own]. Participation as a son of God is so generated that man [himself] is not destroyed ... Through Christ man also laid aside the oldness of sin, being renewed for the making whole of nature, and this is called 'renovation'.[92]

As for the power that produces these effects of adoption and divinizing renewal, St Thomas says that it comes from the 'Holy and Undivided Trinity', and he quotes two Pauline texts that bring out the Trinitarian shape of our transformation: 'God has sent the Spirit of His Son into your hearts, crying, "Abba, Father"' (Gal. 4.6); 'You have not received the spirit of slavery again in fear, but you have received the Spirit of the adoption of sons, in whom we cry: "Abba, Father"' (Rom. 8.15). Renovation comes from God the Father, in the Holy Spirit, through Christ, for it pertains to both of His natures, the divine and the human, that He gives the Holy Spirit.

> As for the divine nature, since He is the Word, from whom, as also (*simul et*) from the Father, [the Holy Spirit] proceeds as Love ... As for the human nature, since Christ received the supreme plenitude [of the grace of the Holy Spirit], so that through Him it might flow to all.[93]

In the *Tertia Pars*, Thomas makes the same point with a little more metaphysical precision: 'It belongs to Christ as God to give grace, or the Holy Spirit, authoritatively, but it belongs to Him as

---

[92] *In Tit.*, cap. 3, lect. 1.
[93] *In Tit.*, cap. 3, lect. 1.

man to give grace, or the Holy Spirit, instrumentally, inasmuch as His humanity was an instrument of His divinity.'[94] Now the sacred humanity is an 'animate' and 'united' (*coniunctum*) instrument of Christ's divinity. The saving power of grace flows from the Trinitarian Godhead, through the manhood hypostatically united to the Son, into the Sacraments of the Church. The Sacraments, too, are instruments, instruments of the Instrument, one might say, though the Sacraments, unlike Christ's sacred humanity are neither animate nor united. However, the minister of the Sacraments, though he is not a united instrument, is an animate one; he is an intelligent and free human person, who, by consecration in Holy Order, has the power to lend his hands and voice to Christ for the achievement of the supernatural effects of the Church's sanctifying rites. Indeed, according to St Thomas, the ordained man is something even beyond an instrument; he is a kind of 'icon' of Christ, who acts in His person and by His power.[95]

Christ, whom the priest represents as His icon and instrument, is not only the Eternal High Priest but also the Bridegroom of the Church. We might even say that He is Bridegroom-Priest, for His priestly self-offering on the Cross is a husbandly act of love for His Bride, the Church: 'Husbands, love your wives, as Christ loved the Church and gave Himself up for her' (Eph. 5.25). From this it would seem to follow that the bishop or priest who 'images' and acts in the person of Christ is, in a subordinate and participatory way, the bridegroom of the Church, as it were, *a sponsus in Sponso*. This is exactly what we find St Thomas arguing in a number of places. For example, he says that the ring that bishops wear symbolizes the Sacraments of faith, by which the Church is married to Christ, because the bishop is the bridegroom of the Church in place of Christ.[96] Indeed, 'the Pope, who represents the Bridegroom for the whole Church, is called the bridegroom of the Church universal, the bishop of his diocese, and the priest of his parish'.[97] This does not mean that the Church, Christ's Bride, has several husbands, because the priest co-operates with the bishop, the bishop with the pope, and the pope with Christ. Thus 'Christ and the Pope and the bishops and the priest are reckoned as one single Bridegroom of the Church'.[98]

According to St Thomas, the spousal ministry of the bishop is revealed in a most telling way in the epistle to Titus, when he says that the bishop must be 'a husband of one wife' (Tit. 1.6; see also 1

---

[94] *ST*, III, 8, 1, ad 1.
[95] The 'priest is the image of Christ (*gerit imaginem Christi*), in whose person and by whose power he pronounces the words [of consecration]'; *ST*, III, 83, 1, ad 3.
[96] IV *Sent.*, 24, 3, 3.
[97] *Contra impugnantes Dei cultum et religionem*, pars 2, cap. 3, ad 22.
[98] *Contra impugnantes Dei cultum et religionem*, pars 2, cap. 3, ad 22.

Tim. 3.2), a text that in the subsequent canonical tradition of the Church has barred ordination to men in the state of 'digamy', that is, those who have re-married after the death of their first wife. St Thomas says that the reason for this is not moral, as if the Church suspected the twice-married man of incontinence; after all, says Thomas cheerfully, there would be no impediment to his ordination if he had had many prostitutes in the past. No, the profound reason for the impediment of a second marriage is the bishop's sacramental dignity as a representative of Christ the Bridegroom:

> He is the dispenser of the Sacraments, and so there must be no defect of the Sacraments in him. Now the Sacrament of Matrimony signifies the union of Christ and the Church. Therefore, so that the sign may correspond to what is signified, just as Christ is one man and the Church one woman, so also must these bishops be; it would be a defect, if the bishop had had several wives.[99]

This teaching of St Paul, as expounded by St Thomas, has many implications. It confirms indirectly not only the doctrine of the universal Church on the absolute necessity of maleness in the candidate for ordination, but also the discipline of both Christian East and West in admitting only celibate priests to the episcopate. In the person of Christ, the bishop is 'married' to the Church and must therefore be, in truth, the husband of one wife.

Conclusion

In this essay, I have appropriated the theological themes in St Thomas' commentary on the three Pastoral Epistles to the content of the three parts of the *Summa*. Like the divine appropriations, this one is not exclusive: there are important moral themes in 1 Timothy and Titus, while there is Christological teaching in 1 Timothy and much doctrine *De Deo uno et trino* in all three epistles and their Thomistic commentaries. Moreover, so far as I know, there is no evidence to suggest that St Thomas consciously and deliberately composed the commentaries along these lines. However, my appropriation is not without foundation in reality: the preponderant stress in each commentary seems to correspond to the structure of the *Summa*. Whenever the triad of themes – God, man, God-made-man – makes its appearance in the Church's theological tradition, whether here or anywhere else, the reason for that appearance is to be found in the realities of the Creed and the history of salvation. This is how things are. God, who created us in His image, did not abandon us after the fall of our first father, but rather, since He wills

---

[99] *In Tit.*, cap. 1, lect. 2.

all men to be saved and to come to the knowledge of the truth, He sent His Son in human nature to be the one mediator of God and men. Such is the preaching of the Apostle of the Gentiles in the Pastoral Epistles (1 Tim. 1.3ff.); such, too, is the sacred doctrine of Thomas Aquinas. *Mens Thomae totaliter Paulina.*

9

THE SUPREMACY OF CHRIST: AQUINAS' *COMMENTARY ON HEBREWS*

Thomas G. Weinandy, OFM, Cap

Introduction: Scripture, hermeneutics and themes

Aquinas begins his *Commentary on the Letter to the Hebrews* by quoting Psalm 86.8 (Vulgate): 'There is none like you among the gods, O Lord, nor are there any works like yours.'[1] Initially this passage may take the reader by surprise, for its relationship to Hebrews is not immediately evident. Yet, here at the very onset of his *Commentary*, we find the first of numerous examples of Aquinas creatively drawing upon passages from the whole Bible to illustrate more fully, to develop more broadly, or to sanction more convincingly truths contained within Hebrews itself.[2] For Aquinas, the various biblical books, with their distinctive revelational content, help to clarify and to complement one another and so this interplay

---

[1] In all probability Aquinas taught his course on Hebrews in Rome sometime between 1265–68. This would have been during the time that Aquinas wrote the first part of his *Summa Theologiae*. See J.-P. Torrell, *Saint Thomas Aquinas* vol. 1, *The Person and His Work*, (Washington, DC: The Catholic University of America Press, 1996), p. 340.

Aquinas notes that even at the Council of Nicaea some doubted the Pauline authorship because, first, 'it does not follow the pattern of his other epistles'; secondly, its style is different in that 'it is more elegant'; thirdly, it proceeds, more than any other work of Scripture, in 'an orderly manner in the sequence of words and sentences'. In refutation Aquinas states that Paul did not write his name because he was the Apostle to the Gentiles and not to the Jews and so did not want to prejudice his audience against him. The reason that this epistle is more elegant is that Paul was writing in his native tongue, Hebrew, and it was translated into Greek by the great Greek stylist, Luke (see *In Heb.*, Prol. [5]). Because Aquinas refers to Paul as the author, so I, in this essay, will use that designation as well.

All translations of Aquinas' *Commentary on the Letter to the Hebrews* are taken from an unpublished translation by Fabian Larcher. The number in brackets refers to the paragraph number in the Marietti edition of Aquinas' 'Commentary on Hebrews': *Super Epistolas S. Pauli Lectura* ed. Raphaelis Cai (2 vols; Rome: Marietti, 8th edn, 1953).

[2] Aquinas also quotes from a variety of patristics sources as well: Augustine (42 times), Gregory the Great (12 times), Dionysius (9 times), Jerome (8 times), Chrysostom (7 times), Bernard of Clairvaux (twice), and Basil, Boethius, and Lactantius each once.

advances one's understanding of the individual books themselves. Thus, the variety and the scope of the Scripture passages Aquinas weaves within his *Commentary* on Hebrews is staggering in number and impressive in content. This is important for, while he obviously recognizes that each book of the Bible possesses it own genre and its own unique revelational and theological focus, it clearly demonstrates that Aquinas perceives the whole biblical narrative, Old and New Testaments together, as proclaiming the one complete gospel, and thus it is only in the interrelationship, and so the interweaving, of the whole biblical content that one is able to come to a full understanding of that gospel.

Now Aquinas' employment of the above passage from the Psalms is not random. Rather it highlights what he considers the central theme of Hebrews, that is, that Christ, as the Son of God incarnate, is supreme among all others who might be called gods, significantly within the Letter – angels, prophets and priests. 'Christ, therefore, is the great God above all the gods, because he is the splendor [of God], the Word, and the Lord' (*quia Splendor, quia Verbum, quia Dominus est*).[3] Moreover, his supremacy is manifested in his works. He is above the angels because unlike them, who are creatures, he is the Creator. While prophets are enlightened, Christ is the 'enlightener'. Priests do not justify, but, as the supreme High Priest, Christ does.[4] Thus, Aquinas states that Christ's transcendence, who he is and what he does, is what distinguishes this epistle from all of the others.[5] Paul wrote this letter then to correct

the errors of those converts from Judaism who wanted to preserve the legal observations along with the Gospel, as though Christ's grace were not sufficient for salvation. Hence it is divided into two parts: in the first he extols Christ's grandeur to show the superiority of the New Testament

---

[3] *In Heb.*, Prol. [2]. The Latin text is taken from *Sancti Thomae Aquinatis: Opera Omnia, Expositia in Omnes S. Pauli Epistolas, Tomus XIII* (New York: Masurgia Publishers, 1949).

[4] See *In Heb.*, Prol. [3].

[5] See *In Heb.*, Prol. [4]. Aquinas sees some epistles teaching about grace in so far as it extends to the whole mystical body, the Church: Roman, Galatians, Corinthians, etc. Others treat of grace as it extends to individuals: Timothy, Titus, and Philemon. Hebrews 'treats of this grace, in as it pertains to the head, namely, Christ' (*In Heb.*, Prol. [4]). Because this letter treats of the centrality of Christ and his salvific work, Aquinas holds that 'almost all of the mysteries of the New Testament are contained in this epistle' (*In Heb.* 13.17-25 [772]).

over the Old; secondly, he discusses what unites the members to the head, namely, faith.[6]

For Aquinas it is faith in the incarnate Son that is salvific. 'For faith in the Godhead is not enough without faith in the Incarnation.'[7] How Aquinas, therefore, perceives the intention of the Letter is important, for he employs it as the hermeneutical guide to his commentary.

Failing to grasp this hermeneutical principal with its subsequent reading and understanding, a reader's initial impression of Aquinas' *Commentary* may be one of disappointment, for it might first appear that he is merely providing an even more logical and systematic presentation of a treatise that expounds already the most sustained and coherent argument of all the New Testament books. Moreover, unlike his treatment within the *Summa Theologiae*, Aquinas does not seem to develop the sacrificial nature of Christ's priesthood beyond the most rudimentary level. However, it must be remembered that Aquinas' *Commentary* is principally a set of lectures presented to student theologians, and thus he wishes them not to speculate on or develop further theological issues that arise from the text, but rather to master the inherent logic and content of the Letter itself. Thus, as will be seen, what Aquinas does do is take seriously the inbuilt logical structure of the Letter to the Hebrews and in so commenting on the first part of the Letter (chapters 1–10) he clearly articulates two interrelated aspects that are essential to the Letter's argument: first, the fulfilment of Old Testament revelation as found in the supremacy of the Incarnation and, secondly, the ensuing fulfilment and supremacy of Christ's priestly sacrifice. To fully appreciate, then, how Aquinas conceives the relationship between God's revelatory words and actions as narrated in the Old Testament and their fulfilment within the person and work of the incarnate Christ, his *Commentary on the Letter to the Hebrews* is essential reading.[8]

Moreover, in keeping with the theme of the second part of the Letter (chapters 11–13), Aquinas maturely advances his understanding of faith as the only authentic and legitimate response to the

---

[6] *In Heb*. 1.1-2 [6]. It should be noted that Aquinas uses the terms 'Old Testament' and 'New Testament' not simply to designate two groupings of biblical books, but more so to designate the two distinct, though interrelated, covenants, with their various revelational contents – the New Testament/Covenant fulfilling and so surpassing what is prefigured in the Old Testament/Covenant.

[7] *In Heb*. 10.19-25 [502].

[8] For a study on the relationship between the Old and New Testaments as found in Aquinas' teaching on salvation, see Matthew Levering's excellent work, *Christ's Fulfillment of Torah and Temple: Salvation according to Thomas Aquinas* (Notre Dame: Notre Dame University Press, 2002).

finality of God's revelation made manifest in Christ, and that it is such faith that gives rise to and is embodied within the Church. Thus, contained within Aquinas' *Commentary*, as within the Letter itself, there resides the centrality of the gospel message of the Incarnation and Jesus' redemptive death and life-giving resurrection as well as an ecclesiology, that is, the subjective response of faith by which one appropriates the salvific work of Christ and so becomes a member of Christ's body, the Church. It is around these central themes of the Letter and Aquinas' *Commentary* that this essay will revolve.

Hebrews 1.1-3: Introducing the supremacy of Christ

Aquinas recognizes that the first three verses of Hebrews provide a summary proclamation of the whole content and argument of the Letter, for it furnishes the foundation of Christ's supremacy both in who he is and in what he did. Moreover, as within the remainder of the Letter, there is in these initial verses an inherent and necessary bond between Christology and soteriology. Only because of who Christ is as the Son incarnate is he able to accomplish the work of salvation, but equally his work of salvation testifies to who he is, for he could only accomplish such mighty deeds if he were the Son incarnate. What distinguishes then the New Covenant from the Old resides precisely in the manner of God's revelation.[9]

As Hebrews begins, in various times past, God, in various ways, enlightened the minds of many prophets who, in turn, spoke God's many words. However, God now has spoken to us through his Son (see Heb. 1.1-2). For Aquinas, God eternally speaks only one eternal Word who is the Son. All other 'words', spoken at various times, found either in the beginning within the wonders of the created order that manifest the truth of God or through the various prophets, are but manifestations of that one eternal Word. Thus, the Son, as the one eternal Word of the Father, in becoming man now himself speaks the truth, and thus this manner of revelation far exceeds and is actually different in kind from all previous manner of revelation.[10]

> Others are called sons inasmuch as they contain within themselves the Word of God ... But he is the true Son who carries all things by the word of his power. Therefore, Christ's preeminence is clear from his unique

[9] For Aquinas, 'the greatest wonder was that God became man (*Praecipium vero portentum est quod Deus factus est homo*)' (*In Heb.* 2.1-4 [99]).
[10] Aquinas states in *ST* that 'The apostles were instructed immediately by the Word of God, not according to his divinity, but according as he spoke in his human nature' (I, 117, 2, obj. 2 and ad 2). Translation taken from *The Summa Theologica*, Fathers of the English Dominican Province (New York: Benziger Brothers, 1947).

origin and from his relationship to other sons of God. It is these things, which make the New Testament greater than the Old.[11]

Christ's pre-eminence, for Aquinas, is thus twofold. First, it resides, not surprisingly, in his unique origin as the eternally begotten Son of the Father, which accounts for his full divinity. Secondly, Aquinas astutely observes, it resides also in his relationship to other sons in that they are sons only to the extent that they too share in and are so conformed by the word of the Son, for sonship resides in one taking on the very likeness and image of the God of truth, that is, the Father.

For Aquinas, the Letter then, by way of introduction, professes why Christ is supreme and so heir of all things both as God and as man. First, he reflects the glory of God 'because he is not only wise but is Wisdom itself (*ipsa sapientia*)'. Secondly, he is not only noble 'but nobility itself because he bears the very stamp (figure) of his [the Father's] substance (*sed ipsa nobilitas: quia est figura substantiae ejus*)'.[12] Aquinas, following Nicaea, perceives Hebrews as professing that the Son is the same substance as the Father and thus, while distinct subjects or persons, they are, nonetheless, the one God.[13] Thirdly, Christ is supreme by the power of his activity in that the Father created the world through him and upholds all things by his powerful word.[14] Aquinas summarizes Hebrews' testimony as follows:

Consequently, by those three characteristics he (Paul) shows three things of Christ: for by the fact that he is the brightness, he shows his co-eternity with the Father; for in creatures splendour is coeval, and the Word is co-eternal ... But when he says, the image of his substance, he shows the consubstantiality (*consubstantialitate*) of the Son with the Father. For since splendor is not of the same nature as the resplendent thing, then lest

[11] *In Heb*. 1.1-2 [18]. See also 1.9-18. As stated above, Aquinas provides throughout his *Commentary* a wealth of supporting Scripture passages taken from both the Old and the New Testaments. While we will, at times, quote some of them, unfortunately, all of these passages cannot be quoted because of limitations of space. However, the reader is encouraged to refer to the text itself in order to obtain the fullness of Aquinas' argument and so equally obtain the full flavour of his commentary.

[12] *In Heb*. 1.3 [25].

[13] See *In Heb*. 1.3 [27–29]. Unlike many contemporary theologians and Scripture scholars, Aquinas sees the conciliar doctrines of the Trinity and the Incarnation residing within Scripture itself. In a sense there is not even a development of doctrine, for Scripture itself proclaims the doctrine and the Councils themselves merely uphold and clarify and so sanction the doctrine already contained within the sacred text. This is why Aquinas in his opening discussion on Sacred Doctrine in his *ST* equates Sacred Doctrine and Sacred Scripture in that Sacred Doctrine is contained within Sacred Scripture (see *ST,* I, 1, 3 and I, 1, 8).

[14] See *In Heb*. 1.1-2 [22] and 1.3 [32–33].

anyone suppose that it is not similar in nature, he says that it is the image or figure of his substance. But because the Son, even though he is of the same nature with the Father, would be lacking power, if he were weak, he adds, supporting all things by the word of his power. Therefore, the Apostle commends Christ on three points, namely, co-eternity, consubstantiality and equality of power (*a coaeternitate, a consubstantialitate, et ab aequalitate potestatis*).[15]

Now what is important for Aquinas is not simply that the Son or Word of God as truly divine is supreme, but equally that his supremacy resides within his incarnate glorified state as well. In fact, the whole Letter is an argument as to why Christ has achieved his supremacy as the risen, glorious, incarnate Lord and so is written from this perspective. In conformity with Hebrews itself, it was 'indeed as man (*sed inquantum homo*), [that] he has been appointed heir of all things'.[16] Thus, for Aquinas, Christ is also the worthy heir of all things because of the 'strenuousness and industry in acting (*strenuitas et industria*)', that is, by overcoming sin through his passion, death and resurrection.[17] As the Letter to the Hebrews itself will argue, it is the glorious, risen Son of God incarnate, and not simply the Son as God, who is superior and so inherits everything. For, it is as incarnate that the Son accomplished the strenuous work of redemption, that is, the fullness of revelation – the vanquishing of sin and the providing of a new and perfect covenant through his priestly sacrificial death and glorious resurrection.

Here Aquinas, by way of introducing what will become the themes of the Letter's subsequent chapters, creatively links the attributes of the divine Son with his work of salvation as man, and thus displays why it is appropriate for the Son to become man and, as man, accomplish the work of salvation. First, Aquinas, following Anselm, notes that sin is 'a transgression of the eternal law and of God's rights'. 'Therefore, since the eternal law and divine right stem from the eternal Word (*sit a Verbo aeterno*), it is clear that cleansing from sins is Christ's prerogative, inasmuch as he is the Word.' This is an insightful comment by Aquinas. The eternal law embodies all that is true, just and good in relationship to God, that is, the law of love, and it is the Word himself who eternally embodies and so lives out this law. Moreover then, the divine right which demands that such a law be lived out equally stems from the Word, for only as others live in conformity to this law of truth, goodness and justice,

[15] *In Heb.* 1.3 [36].
[16] *In Heb.* 1.1-2 [20].
[17] *In Heb.* 1.3 [37].

this law of love, do they conform themselves to the Word. Thus, when human beings transgress God's divine right by sinning against the eternal law, it appropriately falls to the Word to rectify this defective and unrighteous situation. Secondly, 'sin involves a loss of the light of reason and consequently of God's wisdom in man, since such a light is a participation of divine wisdom'. While employing multiple Scripture passages to sanction such claims, Aquinas also refers to 'the Philosopher (Aristotle)' who confirms that 'all evil is ignorance'. 'Therefore, to set aright according to divine wisdom belongs to the one who is divine wisdom.' Thirdly, since sin is 'a deformity of the likeness of God in man ... it belongs to the Son to correct this deformity, because he is the image of the Father'. It is precisely because human beings were first created in his image that the Son possesses those attributes that authorize him to re-create human beings in his image, and he does so in becoming human himself. Fourthly, since sin deprives humankind of eternal life, 'it is obvious that it belongs to Christ to purge sins both by reason of his human nature and by reason of the divine (*et ratione humanae, et ratione divinae*)'.[18] As God the Son possesses all righteousness he can thus purge away sin, but equally, and importantly for Hebrews, this is primarily accomplished through his humanity, for it was as man and out of love for humankind that the Son purged sin by the loving offering of his humanity to the Father as a sacrifice for sin. The manner in which all of this was accomplished was, for Aquinas, fourfold.

First, since sin is a 'perversity of will by which man withdraws from the unchangeable good', Christ 'bestowed sanctifying grace', by which the will would be healed and so empowered to do what is unchangeably good. Secondly, since the perversity of will leaves a stain upon the soul, Christ removes this stain by the shedding of his blood through which our souls are cleansed. Thirdly, since sin incurs 'debt of punishment', 'to satisfy this debt he (Christ) offered himself as a victim on the altar of the cross'. Fourthly, since sin enslaves us to the devil, Christ redeemed us from such slavery.[19]

---

[18] *In Heb*. 1.3 [39].

[19] *In Heb*. 1.3 [40]. Aquinas states in his *ST*, that through the priesthood of Christ the stain of sin is blotted out by grace, 'by which the sinner's heart is turned to God', and the debt of punishment is removed in that he 'satisfied for us fully ... Wherefore it is clear that the priesthood of Christ has full power to expiate sins' (III, 22, 3).

Moreover, what Aquinas is doing here at the very onset of his *Commentary* is succinctly, but systematically, outlining the various causal effects of Christ's death on the cross which Hebrews itself will later delineate. Nonetheless, it is only within the *ST*, III, 48–49 that he will fully articulate them in a systematic manner. There he treats of the efficiency and the effects of Christ's passion. The latter of which, corresponding to various aspects of the passion – atonement, sacrifice, redemption,

While we have focused a good deal of discussion on Aquinas'
understanding of the first three verses of Hebrews, we did so in
order to do what Aquinas himself did – establish the basic
Christological and soteriological truths that govern the entire
Letter.

Greater than the angels and Moses

Aquinas, having shown from Hebrews that Christ excels in a
fourfold manner, that is, (1) in origin, as the Son of God, (2) in
dominion, as heir of all things, (3) in power, as the creator of all, (4)
in honour, as sitting gloriously at the right hand of the Father,
proceeds now, along with the Letter, to apply this excellency so as to
demonstrate his superiority to the angels. Aquinas argues that
Christ was made superior to the angels not in so far as he was God,
because as Son he was not 'made (*factus*)' but 'begotten (*genitus*)'.
His superiority resides precisely within the Incarnation, 'inasmuch
as by effecting that union [of divine and human natures] he became
better than the angels, and should be called and really be the Son of
God'.[20] While the Son was eternally the Son, yet he retained this
name as man since it is truly the Son who came to exist as man, and
so it is as man that the Son is still superior to the angels. Thus, the
name Son, even when applied to the incarnate Christ, is superior to
that of the angels.[21]
Aquinas interprets Hebrews' employment of Old Testament
passages to affirm this twofold superiority of the Son, that of
being God and man. For example, Psalm 2.7 (Vulgate) speaks of the
ever-present eternal day, as if the Father addresses the Son: 'You are
perfect, Son; and yet your generation is eternal and you are always
being engendered by me, as light is perfect in the air and yet is
always proceeding from the sun.'[22] Yet the passage from 2 Samuel

---

etc. – are: deliverance from sin, freedom from the power of Satan, freedom from
punishment, reconciliation with God, obtaining of eternal life, and the meriting of
Christ's own exaltation. All of these ultimately find mention within his commentary
on Hebrews. Aquinas beautifully summarizes the above when he states:

Christ's passion, according as it is compared with his Godhead, operates in
an efficient manner; but in so far as it is compared with the will of Christ's
soul it acts in a meritorious manner; considered as being within Christ's very
flesh, it acts by way of satisfaction, inasmuch as we are liberated by it from
the debt of punishment; while inasmuch as we are freed from the servitude
of guilt, it acts by way of redemption; but in so far as we are reconciled with
God it acts by way of sacrifice. (*ST*, III, 48, 6, ad 3)

[20] *In Heb*. 1.4-7 [46]. See also *ST*, III, 22, 1, ad 1.
[21] See *In Heb*. 1.4-7 [47–48].
[22] *In Heb*. 1.4-7 [49].

7.14: 'I will be a father to him and he a son to me', refers, for Aquinas, to the future Incarnation whereby the Father will be Father to his incarnate Son and his incarnate Son will be his son.[23] Moreover, this dual application is found in that the angels worship the Son not merely as God but equally as incarnate. Again, while the Son's throne as God is eternal, it equally belongs to him 'as man' 'as a result of his passion, victory and resurrection' and, because, as the risen Lord, he rules over an everlasting kingdom in which everlasting life is bestowed.[24] Equally, Psalm 110.1 (Vulgate) where God states: 'Sit at my right hand and I will make your enemies a footstool for you', refers not simply to the Son as God who eternally resides with the Father, but also to the incarnate Son especially in so far as he will reign in glory at the end of time.[25] Unlike Jesus, the angels are merely servants of the salvation inaugurated by him.[26]

Because of Christ's superiority to angels, Christians are called to an even greater commitment of faith and perseverance in response to Christ than the commitment and faith required in response to the promises made by the angels in the past (see Heb. 2.1-4). For Aquinas, the reason for this is threefold: first, because of Jesus' divine authority as Creator and as Son of God; secondly, because Christ's words 'are words of eternal life'; and thirdly, 'because of the sweetness of their observance, for they are sweet: "His commands are not heavy" (1 Jn. 5:3); "My yoke is sweet and my burden light" (Mt. 11:30); "This is a yoke which neither we nor our fathers have been able to bear" (Ac. 15:10)'.[27] Here we see an example of how Aquinas employs various scriptural passages that augment the argument contained within Hebrews itself.

While it might appear that man is of no account and vile because of sin, yet 'the cause of the Incarnation is God's care for man (*causa autem incarnationis est memoria Dei de homine*)'.[28] It is the incarnate Son who was 'the son of man' and so made a little less than the angels, in that he would, unlike the angels, take upon himself our suffering and death. Nonetheless, it was precisely because of his becoming less than the angels that he is exalted above the angels.

---

[23] See *In Heb*. 1.4-6 [50–54].

[24] *In Heb*. 1.8-10 [60].

[25] See *In Heb*. 1.13-14 [79–84].

[26] See *In Heb*. 1.13-14 [86–88]. While Aquinas sees the risen incarnate Son as superior to the angels and risen human beings as equal to Angels, I have argued, contra Aquinas and the tradition, that human beings as created in the image and likeness of the Son are superior to the angels by the mere fact that they are human beings. See my article: 'Of Men and Angels', *Nova et Vetera* 3/2 (2005), pp. 369–80.

[27] *In Heb*. 2.1-4 [90].

[28] *In Heb*. 2.5-8 [107].

'Christ won the crown by the struggle of his passion.'[29] While as divine the Son was eternally perfect, yet as incarnate he was made perfect through his suffering (see Heb. 2.10), because 'he had to be made perfect by the merit of the passion: "Ought not Christ to have suffered these things and so to enter into his glory" (Lk. 24:26)'.[30] In so perfecting himself through the cross he was able to bring many sons to glory.[31] Now Christ is crowned with the glory of his risen body and also with the brightness that 'comes from the confession of all people: "Every tongue should confess that the Lord Jesus Christ is in the glory of God the Father" (Phil. 2:11)'.[32] Notice again, that, for Aquinas, it is the incarnate risen Son who is crowned with splendour and glory that exceeds the splendour and glory of the angels.[33] Moreover, it is those who are members of his Church through faith who recognize and proclaim his supreme glory and primacy.

Now the reason that Christ is not ashamed to call us his brothers is that, for Aquinas, 'he that sanctifies and we who are sanctified have one origin, namely, of the Father'.[34] However, if Christ and all of humankind are brethren, then it is appropriate that we not only come to participate in his divine nature through grace and so be like him, but that he share in our human nature and so be like us – 'because the children share in flesh and blood, he himself likewise partook of the same nature'.[35] For Aquinas this assuming of the same nature was not in the abstract, but 'in an individual, and from the seed of Abraham'.[36] Thus Christ 'assumed a nature without sin, but with the possibility of suffering, because he assumed a flesh similar to the sinner: "In the likeness of sinful flesh" (Rom. 8:3)'.[37] In the days of his flesh the Son of God 'wore flesh similar to the sinner, but not sinful (*idest in quibus gerebat carnem similem peccatrici, non peccatricem*)'.[38] For Aquinas this truth has soteriological signifi-

---

[29] *In Heb.* 2.5-8 [113].

[30] *In Heb.* 2.9-13 [128].

[31] See *In Heb.* 2.9-13 [125–133].

[32] *In Heb.* 2.5-8 [112].

[33] While we will examine how Christ became one with those whom he saved, Aquinas, commenting on Hebrews' employment of Isa. 8.17: 'In him I hope', makes a very important distinction. Aquinas notes that many have previously held that Christ did not have faith or hope but only charity. However 'I answer that hope is one thing and trust another: for hope is the expectation of future happiness; and this was not in Christ, because he was happy from the instant of his conception. But trust is the expectation of help, and in regard to this there was hope in Christ, inasmuch as he awaited help from the Father during his passion' [134].

[34] *In Heb.* 2.9-13 [130].

[35] *In Heb.* 2.14-18 [137].

[36] *In Heb.* 2.14-18 [148].

[37] *In Heb.* 2.14-18 [138]. See also 139–41 and 9.23-28 [478].

[38] *In Heb.* 5.1-7 [254].

cance. Following Anselm's argument that sinful man was under a debt, yet, precisely because of his sinfulness was unable to make good that debt, therefore 'it was necessary that the one who satisfied be man and God, who alone has the power over the whole of the human race. By the death of God and man, therefore, he destroyed him [the devil] who had the empire of death.'[39] Thus Christ was like unto his brethren 'in all things, I say, in which they are brethren, not in guilt but in punishment (*non in culpa, sed in poena*). Therefore, it behooved him to have a nature that could suffer.'[40]

Moreover, it is precisely because the Son took upon himself our sin-scarred humanity that he could be tempted as we are and so become the compassionate high priest. In this, 'he [Paul] shows its utility. As if to say: I do not speak of Christ as God, but as man. Therefore, in that, i.e., in that nature which he assumed, in order to experience in himself that our cause is his own... Or, another way: He became merciful and faithful, because in suffering and being tempted he has kinship to mercy.'[41] Now, while temptations could not arise within Christ himself since he did not possess concupiscence, yet, for Aquinas, because he was a member of Adam's race, he could be tempted from without by earthly prosperity, vainglory and adversity. In this way he was tempted like us 'for if he had existed without temptations he would not have experienced them, and then he could not have compassion. But if he had sinned, he would not have been able to help us, but would need help.'[42]

Now Christ is not only superior to the angels but also to Moses in that he was faithful to God not merely as a servant within God's

---

[39] *In Heb.* 2.14-18 [143].

[40] *In Heb.* 2.14-18 [150]. In his *ST* Aquinas would develop this understanding in that he clearly recognizes that the humanity the Son assumes is not some generic humanity but precisely a humanity taken from the fallen race of Adam. First, because it would seem to belong to justice that he who sinned should make amends; and hence that from the nature which he had corrupted should be assumed that whereby satisfaction was to be made for the whole nature. Secondly, it pertains to man's greater dignity that the conqueror of the devil should spring from the stock conquered by the devil. Thirdly, because God's power is thereby made more manifest since, from a corrupt and weakened nature, he assumed that which was raised to such might and glory (*ST*, III, 4. 6). Christ ought to be separated from sinners as regards sin, which he came to overthrow, and not as regards nature which he came to save, and in which 'it behooved him in all things to be made like to his brethren, as the Apostle says (Heb. 2.17). And in this is his innocence the more wonderful, seeing that though assumed from a mass tainted by sin, his nature was endowed with such purity (*ST*, III, 4, 6, ad 1). See also *ScG*, IV, 30, 28. For a more comprehensive discussion of this issue in Aquinas, see T. Weinandy, *In the Likeness of Sinful Flesh: An Essay on the Humanity of Christ* (Edinburgh: T&T Clark, 1993), pp. 47–53. It should be noted that Aquinas quotes the Letter to the Hebrews at least 208 times in his *ST*.

[41] *In Heb.* 2.14-18 [154].

[42] *In Heb.* 4.14-16 [237].

house as was Moses, but as a Son who was the actual builder of
God's house. The Son as man was faithful to God in that (1) 'by not
attributing to himself what he had, but to the Father'; (2) 'he sought
the Father's glory and not his own'; (3) and 'he obeyed the Father
perfectly'.[43] What Aquinas has done here is define the authentic
nature of sonship. A son always acknowledges, in gratitude, his
dependence upon his father for his existence. He equally, therefore,
seeks the glory of the one upon whom he is dependent, and finally
this gratitude and solicitousness is expressed in his perfect, loyal
filial obedience.

Christ's sonship is witnessed in the fact that he is the builder of
God's house. Thus what is also supremely important for Aquinas is
that Christ's supremacy resides in the fact that he has brought into
being the Church – God's house in which all the faithful dwell. As
the Father created the world out of nothing through his Son, so
now, through that same Son, 'God created that house, namely, the
Church, from nothing, namely from the state of sin to the state of
grace'.[44] It is the members of the Church who assume the filial
attributes of Christ for they become children of the Father through
the transforming work of the Holy Spirit.

Jesus, the Great High Priest

The Letter to the Hebrews, having established that Christ, as the
glorious incarnate Son, is superior to the angels and to Moses, now
turns its attention to his being the Great High Priest who is superior
to Aaron and his priestly descendants because of the pre-eminence
of his sacrifice and the everlasting covenant that it establishes. For
Aquinas the importance of Christ's priesthood lies in its 'end and
utility', that is, its usefulness lies in the fact that human beings are
now able to obtain eternal life.[45] Aquinas notes that it was the Son
of God as man, and not as God, who was appointed High Priest by
his Father.[46]

We perceive how important the humanity of Christ is for Aquinas
in his comments on the phrase that, 'although he was a Son, he

---

[43] *In Heb.* 3.1-6 [159].

[44] *In Heb.* 3.1-6 [164]. See also 159–69.

[45] *In Heb.* 5.1-7 [242]. See also 239–41. It is interesting that in respect of our own
present day concerns over defining the nature of the priesthood and its proper
ministry, Aquinas states: 'Therefore, just as the things which pertain to the worship of
God transcend temporal things, so the pontifical dignity exceeds all other dignities.
Therefore, high priests should not entangle themselves with secular business and
neglect the things that pertain to God: "No man being a soldier to Christ entangles
himself with secular businesses" (2 Tim. 2:4)' [243].

[46] See *In Heb.* 5.1-7 [252–57]. See also *ST*, III, 22, 3, ad 1.

learned obedience from what he suffered' (Heb. 5.8). While the Son, as God, was omniscient, and for Aquinas, from the moment of his conception he, as man, possessed the beatific vision, yet 'there is a knowledge gained by experience'.[47] Now this learning of obedience was through suffering, and what the incarnate Son learned through his obediential suffering was compassion for his fellow human brothers and sisters who were enslaved by sin and death, a compassion that he did not literally possess as God prior to the Incarnation, since God is impassible, but which he now literally possessed in a human manner.[48]

> Christ accepted our weakness voluntarily; consequently, he (Paul) says that 'he learned obedience', i.e., how difficult it is to obey, because he obeyed in the most difficult matters, even to the death of the cross (Phil. 2:8). This shows how difficult the good of obedience is, because those who have not experienced obedience and have not learned it in difficult matters, believe that obedience is very easy. But in order to know what obedience is, one must learn to obey in difficult matters, and one who has not learned to subject himself by obeying does not know how to rule others well. Therefore, although Christ knew by simple recognition what obedience is, he nevertheless learned obedience from the things he suffered, i.e., from difficult things, by suffering and dying: 'By the obedience of one many shall be made just' (Rom. 5:19).[49]

What is significant here is not merely that Aquinas recognizes the importance of Christ's human obedience for our salvation, but that he could not truly 'learn' how to rule as our King and Lord, and so hold us to obedience, if he did not himself first 'learn' how to obey. This is exactly, for Aquinas, what Hebrews continues to point out: 'and being made perfect he became the source of eternal salvation to all who obey him' (Heb. 5.9). Christ was made perfect through his obedience, and being 'altogether perfect, he could perfect others. For it is the nature of a perfect thing to be able to engender its like',[50] and this engendering likeness is accomplished through his engendering in human beings the filial obedience of faith.

---

[47] In Heb. 5.8-14 [259].

[48] I am not comfortable with Aquinas' and the tradition's attribution of the beatific vision to the earthly Jesus. See my 'Jesus' Filial Vision of the Father', *Pro Ecclesia* 13/2 (2004), pp. 189–201. For Aquinas, God as God is not literally compassionate in the sense that he suffers emotionally as do human beings. Nonetheless, Aquinas does argue that God is supremely compassionate in that he alleviates the causes of suffering – sin, evil and death – and he does this primarily through the sending of his Son. See T. Weinandy, *Does God Suffer?* (Edinburgh: T & T Clark, 2000), chs 6–8.

[49] In Heb. 5.8-14 [259].

[50] In Heb. 5.8-14 [260].

The heart of Aquinas' commentary on Hebrews 7–10 is to demonstrate, in accordance with the Letter itself, that Christ's priesthood and its salvific effects fulfil and so are superior to the Old Testament priesthood and its effects. The hermeneutical key to this interpretation, again in keeping with the Letter, is one of prefigurement and fulfilment. Thus both the priests of the Old Testament and Melchizedek's priesthood prefigure Christ's priesthood in different manners. Christ, too, like the priests of the Old Testament will offer a sacrifice, but unlike them, and like Melchizedek, his priesthood is forever.[51] Because the sacrifices of the Old Testament were corruptible and thus imperfect, the priests were multiplied.

> This was a sign that the priesthood was corruptible, because incorruptible things are not multiplied in the same species. But the priest who is Christ is immortal, for he remains forever as the eternal Word of the Father, from whose eternity redounds an eternity to his body, because 'Christ rising from the dead, dies now no more' (Rom. 6:9). Therefore, because he continues forever, he holds his priesthood permanently. Therefore, Christ alone is the true priest, but others are his ministers: 'Let a man so account of us as the ministers of Christ' (1 Cor. 4:1).[52]

The superiority of Christ's priesthood, as we will shortly see, resides in the perfect nature of his sacrificial death on the cross. Moreover, it is the perfect nature of Christ's sacrifice that will merit his resurrection as the glorious eternal High Priest.

Now for Aquinas, the Old Testament Law according to the Letter to the Hebrews sets forth four qualities of a priest which Christ fulfils perfectly and so surpasses and fulfils what has gone before. The first is that the priest must be holy. 'But Christ had this perfectly. For holiness implies purity consecrated to God: "Therefore, also the Holy which shall be born of you shall be called the Son of God" (Lk. 1:3); "That which is conceived in her is of the Holy Spirit" (Mt. 1:20); "The saint of saints will be anointed" (Dan. 9:34).' The second is that the priest should be innocent, which is purity to one's neighbour. 'But Christ was completely innocent, being one who did not sin.' The third is that the priest should be unstained with regard to himself. 'Of Christ it is said in a figure: "It shall be a lamb without blemish".' Fourthly, the priest must be separated from sinners. While Christ ate with sinners, yet he lived a

---

[51] In his *ST* Aquinas states that the sacrifice of Melchizedek better foreshadowed the participatory nature of Christ's sacrifice as well as its effects in that it consisted of bread and wine and so prefigured 'ecclesiastical unity, which is established by our taking part in the sacrifice of Christ' (III, 22, 6, ad 2).

[52] *In Heb.* 7.20-28 [368]. Aquinas argues in a similar manner in his *ST*, III, 22, 5.

perfectly holy life, 'and to such a degree he was separated that he was made higher than the heavens, i.e., exalted above the heavens'.[53] This exultation was again as man, for this 'is more in keeping with the Apostle's intention, because he is speaking about the high priesthood of Christ, who is a high priest as man. So he is seated in that way, because the assumed humanity has a certain association to the godhead.'[54]

We now recognize why Christ's priesthood is superior and it first of all pertains to a threefold relationship that, in turn, effects his exaltation. First, it pertains to his relationship to the Father as the all holy Son. Secondly, it pertains to his relationship with his fellow human beings in that being 'innocent' he has never been found guilty of sin, that is, he has never sinned against anyone, but instead, in his innocence, has consistently loved everyone. Thirdly it is in relationship to himself, in that he is himself holy and without blemish within his own being. This threefold holiness in relationship to God, others and himself has separated Christ from everyone else even though he associated himself with sinners, and therefore his priesthood has merited for him an everlasting superiority that exceeds all others. Moreover, Christ not only merited his own risen glory, but as head of the Church he also merited humankind's risen glory.[55]

Moreover, it is as man that Christ is 'a minister of the holies' and of the 'true tent/tabernacle' (Heb. 8.1-2), 'for the humanity of Christ is an organ of the divinity (*humanitas enim Christi est sicut organum divinitatis*). Therefore, he is the minister of the holies, because he administers the sacraments of grace in the present life and of glory in the future.'[56] Priests are mediators of holiness because they are ministers of the all holy God. Jesus is the supreme High Priest because he is the supreme mediator of holiness in that he is both the all holy Son of God and through his humanity he is the supreme dispenser of grace through the sacraments.[57]

Now while every priest is appointed to offer gifts and sacrifices (see Heb. 8.3), so Christ too must offer something and what he offered was himself.

[53] *In Heb*. 7.20-28 [375].
[54] *In Heb*. 8.1-5 [381].
[55] See *In Heb*. 13.17-25 [768].
[56] *In Heb*. 8.1-5 [382].
[57] In his *ST* Aquinas will equally argue that Christ is the supreme High Priest because he bestows upon those who believe his very divine nature (see 2 Pet. 1.4) and reconciles humankind to God (see III, 22, 1). This is ultimately due to the fact that Christ becomes the head of his body: 'Christ, as being the head of all, has the perfection of all graces. Wherefore, [he is] ... the fount of all grace' (III, 22, 1, ad 3).

But it was a clean oblation, because his flesh had no stain of sin ...
Furthermore, it was suitable, because it was fitting that man should
satisfy for man: 'He offered himself unspotted unto God' (Heb. 9:14). It
was also fit to be immolated, because his flesh was mortal: 'God sending
his own Son, in the likeness of sinful flesh and for sin' (Rom. 8:3). Also it
was the same as the one to whom it was offered: 'I and the Father are
one' (Jn. 10:30). And it unites to God those for whom it is offered: 'That
they may one, as thou, Father, in me, and I in thee, that they also may be
one in us' (Jn. 17:21).[58]

Here Aquinas brings together many of the points he has made
previously within his *Commentary*. Christ's sacrifice was holy
because he offered his own holy life. It was right for him to do so
because he was of the same race of Adam as were all. He offered
himself to the Father, but equally, as man, he offered himself to
himself because he himself is God. Lastly, the causal effect of such a
supreme sacrifice is that it forms an everlasting and unbreakable
communion with God for those for whom it was offered.

While Christ fulfiled in himself all that had gone before him – the
Old Testament priesthood and its sacrifices – yet Aquinas does not
want to disparage their earthly and material importance. The
'sacraments of the Old Law' while inferior 'naturally tend to a
likeness of superior things (*quia naturalites inferiora tendunt in
similitudinem superiorum*). For the Lord wished to lead us by
sensible things to intelligible and spiritual things.'[59] The New
Testament then 'completes and perfects the Old' because through
the new Christ mediates a better covenant by which 'we are made
partakers of the divine nature'.[60]

Aquinas states on a number of occasions that the difference
between the Old and New Testaments is that between 'fear' and
'love'.[61] The reason for this is that within the Old Testament sin with
its condemnation of death continued to reign and in so doing
engendered fear. However, following upon the prophecy of
Jeremiah 31, the new covenant not only brought an interior

---

[58] *In Heb.* 8.1-5 [384]. Aquinas, in the *ST*, argues that as priest Christ must offer a
sacrifice first for the remission of sin, secondly for human beings that they might be
preserved in grace by adhering to God and thirdly so that human beings be fully
united to God. These three ends are accomplished through Christ, the priest, offering
himself, the victim. 'Now these effects were conferred on us by the humanity of
Christ. For in the first place our sins were blotted out ... Secondly, through him we
received the grace of salvation, according to Heb. 5:9 ... Thirdly, through him we
have acquired the perfection of glory, according to Heb. 10:9 ... Therefore, Christ, as
man, was not only priest, but also a perfect victim' (III, 22, 2).
[59] *In Heb.* 8.1-5 [389].
[60] *In Heb.* 8.6-10b [396 and 392].
[61] See for example *In Heb.* 8.6-10b [401]; 10.1-18 [480]; 12.18-24 [696 and 703].

knowledge of the law, but, through the Holy Spirit, 'inclines the will to act as well'.[62] Thus, while 'both the Old and New Testaments were instituted in order that by them the soul might come to God', and, although both are bodily, yet only the New 'contains grace and is holy, and in it divine power works salvation under cover of visible things. This is not so in the Old Testament, because it contained no grace in itself: "How turn you again to the weak and needy elements?" (Gal. 4:9).'[63] The point that Aquinas is making is that the purpose of the Old Testament was to prepare people for the new covenant in Christ, and thus whatever grace that pertains to it is not in itself, but only insofar as is related to and finds its fulfilment in the new salvific covenant made in Christ.

Aquinas again, in accordance with Hebrews, recognizes the Old Testament tabernacle/tent as a prefigurement. However, while the tabernacle of the first covenant prefigures the new, 'in another way, by the first tabernacle the present Church [is prefigured], and by the second, heavenly glory. Therefore, inasmuch as it signifies the Old Testament, it is a figure of a figure; but inasmuch as it signifies the present Church, which in turn signifies future glory, it is a figure of the truth in regard to each.'[64] For Aquinas too, 'the holies' signified the Old Testament and the 'the holy of holies' signified the New Testament, for through it one was able to enter into heaven itself.[65] However, as Hebrews professes, it was Christ who first entered into the heavenly holy of holies and with his own blood by which he won for all humankind an eternal redemption. Here Aquinas stresses the efficacy of Christ's blood. First, Christ's blood cleanses us of sin, and, secondly, the reason that it has such power is because Christ offered his life's blood 'by the Holy Spirit, through whose movement and instinct, namely, by the love of God and neighbour he did this' and thirdly, because Christ himself was 'without blemish'.[66] Thus for Aquinas, Christ's sacrificial offering of his life's blood was no mere mechanical event. What made Christ's sacrifice efficacious was that, through the Spirit of love, he offered his all-holy life to the Father out of obediential love for the Father, and he

---

[62] *In Heb.* 8.6-10b [404].

[63] *In Heb.* 9.1-5 [414 and 415].

[64] *In Heb.* 9.1-5 [418].

[65] Aquinas makes a similar point towards the end of the commentary. 'Therefore, the doctrine of the Old Testament is the doctrine of Christ speaking on earth for two reasons: because there under the figure of earthly things he spoke of heavenly things; furthermore, he promised earthly things there. But the doctrine of the New Testament is that of Christ speaking from heaven, because we turn earthly things into signs of heavenly things by a mystical interpretation. Likewise, heavenly things are promised in it' (*In Heb.* 12.25-29 [717]).

[66] *In Heb.* 9.11-14 [444].

did so out of love for all who were to be cleansed of sin.[67] Love is the foundation of this new covenant in Christ's blood.[68] Equally then, those who believe in Christ are cleansed of dead works, 'which take God from the soul, whose life consists in union of charity'.[69] By being cleansed of sin with its condemnation to death, the Christian casts off fear and is empowered to live in love and so serve the living God. 'Therefore, he that would serve God worthily, should be living, as he is (*Quod ergo vult Deo digne servire, debet esse vivens et ipse*).'[70]

Now while Christ offered a single sacrifice once for all, yet within the sacrifice of the Mass 'we do not offer something different from what Christ offered for us, his blood; hence, it is not a distinct oblation, but a commemoration of that sacrifice which Christ offered'.[71] By one offering then Christ has perfected for all times those who are sanctified because 'Christ's sacrifice, since he is God and man, has power to sanctify forever ... For by him we are sanctified and united to God: "By whom we have access to God" (Rom. 5:12).'[72]

Now the old covenant was confirmed when Moses, taking the blood of goats and calves and mixing it with water, sprinkled the book of the covenant and the people using scarlet wool and hyssop. Jesus fulfils this prefigurement:

> For that blood was a figure of Christ's blood, by whom the New Testament was confirmed ... This is the blood of a goat because of its likeness to sinful flesh [Christ's humanity], and of a calf because of courage [Christ's courage]. But it is mixed with water, because baptism derives its efficacy from the blood of Christ. It is sprinkled with hyssop, which cleanses the breast, by which faith is signified: 'By faith purifying their hearts' (Acts 15:9); and with purple wool, which is red to signify charity ... because the people are cleansed by faith and the love of Christ. The book of the Law is sprinkled, because the passion of Christ fulfilled the Law: 'It is consummated' (Jn. 19:30); 'I have not come to destroy the law, but to fulfill it' (Mt. 5:17).[73]

---

[67] Aquinas emphasizes the importance of Christ's obedience when he comments on Hebrews quoting Psalm 40.6-8 (Vulgate). The Father fitted his Son with a body for the purpose of his passion. 'To what end? To do your will O God' (*In Heb.* 10.1-18 [492]).

[68] 'Christ obtained a result from his passion, not as by virtue of the sacrifice, which is offered by way of satisfaction, but by the very devotion with which out of charity he humbly endured the passion' (*ST*, III, 22, 4, ad 2).

[69] *In Heb.* 9.11-14 [446].

[70] *In Heb.* 9.11-14 [446].

[71] *In Heb.* 10.1-18 [482].

[72] *In Heb.* 10.1-18 [499].

[73] *In Heb.* 9.15-22 [457].

Aquinas creatively links the blood of Christ with the efficacy of faith and baptism, for both are justifying responses to the sacrificial death of Christ, but the efficacy of such responses, by which one is cleansed of sin and made holy, resides solely within that efficacious sacrificial, and so salvific, death. Faith, then, is the unqualified response to Christ's supremacy – the fulfilment and perfection of the old covenant through the offering of his own blood as the new and eternal covenant. Commenting on Hebrews' use of Habakkuk that 'the just man lives by faith', Aquinas states:

> Not only is justice by faith, but the one justified lives by faith (*Nec solum per fidem justitia, sed etiam per fidem justificatus vivit*). For just as the body lives by the soul, so the soul of God. Hence, just as the body lives by that through which the soul is first united to the body, so by that through which God is first united to the soul, the soul lives. But this is faith, because it is the first thing in the spiritual life ... But faith not formed by charity is dead; therefore, it does not give life to the soul without charity.[74]

Here in his *Commentary on Hebrews* Aquinas combines both the teaching of Romans and James. Yes, one is justified by faith, but if one is so justified, one must live out that faith in love. The reason is, and here Aquinas is most insightful, that faith unites us to God and in so being united to the living God of love demands that one, like God, performs the living good deeds of love. However, this is Aquinas' preliminary discussion of faith which he will now address more fully when examining Hebrews 11.

Faith and the Church

Obviously Aquinas believes that Scripture is inspired and that Paul is the inspired author of the Letter to the Hebrews. Yet surprisingly, as he initiates his commentary on Paul's famous definition in Hebrews 1.1, he writes: 'He [Paul] gives a definition of faith which is complete but obscure (*complete sed obscure*).'[75] Aquinas is probably correct in his assessment, and what he will now do is make clear this complete, though obscure, inspired definition of faith.

For Aquinas, in order to define virtues properly, as with all habits, one must define its matter, that is, the area with which it deals, and its end, that is, what good it is intended to achieve. Faith

[74] *In Heb.* 10.32-39 [548].
[75] *In Heb.* 11.1 [552]. Here Aquinas, probably without fully realizing it, is acknowledging that while the author of the Letter to the Hebrews is inspired, yet he is a *human* author and therefore what is said, while true, may not necessarily be the best way to say it.

is a theological virtue in that it has to do with our immediate relationship to God and thus 'its object and end are the same, God'.[76] Following Augustine, the act of faith 'is to believe, because it is an act of the intellect narrowed to one thing by the command of the will. Hence, to believe is to cogitate with assent ... Therefore, the object of faith and of the will must coincide.' Now, the intellect is ordered to the truth and the will is ordered to the good for it is in truth and in goodness that authentic happiness is obtained. Thus, both the intellect and the will seek God who is the fullness of truth and goodness and thus in him alone is found complete happiness. The act of faith thus takes place in this manner. The intellect lays hold of the truth of God and recognizes that such truth is good. However, it is the will, which desires the good, that moves the intellect to lay hold of that good. Thus the will commands the intellect to give intellectual assent to the truth of God. The act of faith, then, is the laying hold of the supreme truth and ultimate goodness, which is God himself.[77]

However, here on earth this fullness of the reality of God is not seen but hoped for. 'The end, therefore, of faith on earth is the attainment of the thing hoped for, namely, of eternal happiness.'[78] This act of faith does not possess the certainty that arises out of natural knowledge (the seeing and perceiving of things), nor is it doubt, as in holding a dubious opinion. Faith 'fixes on one side with certainty and firm adherence by a voluntary choice'. Faith holds what it believes to be absolutely certain. This choice 'rests on God's authority, and by it the intellect is fixed, so that it clings firmly to the things of faith and assents to them with the greatest certainty. Therefore, to believe is to know with assent.' Faith, therefore, is 'a sure and certain apprehension of things it does not see'.[79] While one does not know the truths of faith by natural knowledge and thus with natural certainty, yet one does hold the truths of faith with absolute certainty because of the authority of God who cannot deceive and who is the author of all truth and goodness. Aquinas *humbly* concludes:

Now, if someone were to reduce those words [Paul's definition of faith] to their correct form, he could say that faith is a habit of the mind by which eternal life is begun in us and makes the intellect assent to things that it

[76] *In Heb.* 11.1 [552]. See also *ST*, II–II, 1, 1.

[77] See *In Heb.* 1.1 [554]. Aquinas states in his *ST* that 'the intellect of the believer is determined to one object, not by the reason, but by the will, wherefore assent is taken here for an act of the intellect as determined to one object by the will' (II–II, 2, 1, ad 3).

[78] *In Heb.* 11.1 [553]. See also *ST*, II–II, 1, 4.

[79] *In Heb.* 1.1 [558]. See also *ST*, II–II, 2, 1.

does not see (*fides est habitus mentis, qua inchoatur vita aeterna in nobis, faciens intellectum assentiri non apparenibus*). Therefore, it is obvious that the Apostle has defined faith completely, but not clearly.[80]

While faith in the Christian mysteries allows one to begin to perceive and experience the truth and goodness of God, yet complete happiness 'consists in the vision of God' which will only be achieved in heaven.[81] Moreover, while the act of faith is an act of an individual person, it is equally an ecclesial act, for the person, through faith, becomes a member of the body of Christ, the Church. Thus, in union with the whole earthly Church, individual believers come to perceive and are in communion with the heavenly realities they hope for. This again finds it completion in heaven. 'In heavenly glory there are two things which will particularly gladden the just, namely, the enjoyment of the godhead and companionship with the saints. For no good is joyfully possessed without companions.'[82] As the Trinity of persons are only able to enjoy their godhead in communion with one another so the blessed in heaven are only able to enjoy that Trinitarian communion in communion with one another. True happiness, for Aquinas, always consists in the joy, founded upon truth and goodness, shared in communion with others, whether those others be the communion of the divine persons or the communion of the saints.

Conclusion

What we have found within Aquinas' *Commentary on the Letter to the Hebrews* is a sustained argument, in keeping with the Letter itself, for the supremacy of Christ. This supremacy resides in who he is as the Son of God incarnate and what he has done through his passion and death. These salvific actions have merited for him a place above all the angels, the prophets and the priests. Moreover, it is precisely because of his supremacy that all are called to faith in him. It is through faith that one is united to Jesus and so comes to participate in the life of the Church, and thus equally comes to share in what Jesus himself has merited – eternal life with the Father in the heavenly temple.

While we have obviously not touched upon everything that Aquinas treats in his *Commentary*, yet we have examined the major

---

[80] *In Heb.* 1.1 [558].
[81] *In Heb.* 1.1 [556].
[82] *In Heb.* 12.18-24 [706].

themes.[83] In so doing we have hopefully demonstrated the insight and creativity of Aquinas as well as his love for Christ and his work of redemption. Aquinas, as does the Letter itself, ultimately wishes that our response would be one of deeper faith, for it is faith which recognizes that Jesus is indeed the supreme and only Lord and Saviour – 'the Perfector of our faith' (Heb. 12.2).[84]

[83] Merely to note that Aquinas did have a sense of humour, commenting on that Paul had written 'briefly' (Heb. 13.22), Aquinas states: 'Short talks are most welcome; because if they are good, they will be heard eagerly. If they are bad, they are a little boring' (*In Heb.* 13.17-25 [772]).

[84] It is surprising that the Franciscan tradition, which accentuates the primacy of Christ, does not employ the Letter to the Hebrews to authorize its theological endeavour. The most probable reason is that Jesus' primacy within Hebrews is too closely tied to his death on the cross, and the Franciscan tradition misguidedly wants to disengage his primacy from the cross. For a further discussion of this issue, see T. Weinandy, *In the Likeness of Sinful Flesh*, pp. 135–48 and 'The Cosmic Christ', *The Cord* 51/1 (2001), pp. 27–38.

SELECT BIBLIOGRAPHY

Books

Aillet, Marc, *Lire la Bible avec s. Thomas: Le passage de la* littera *à la* res *dans la Somme théologique* (Fribourg: Éditions universitaires, 1993).

Baglow, Christopher T., 'Modus et Forma': *A New Approach to the Exegesis of Saint Thomas Aquinas with an Application to the* Lectura super Epistolam ad Ephesios (Rome: Editrice Pontificio Istituto Biblico, 2002).

Berger, David, *Thomas von Aquin und die Liturgie* (Cologne: Editiones thomisticae, 2000).

Bonino, S.-T., *St Thomas au XXe siècle*, Actes du colloque du centenaire de la 'Revue thomiste' (Paris: Éditions Saint-Paul, 1994).

Boyle, L., *The Setting of the* Summa Theologiae *of St. Thomas* (Etienne Gilson Lecture; Toronto: Pontifical Institute of Mediaeval Studies, 1982).

Carruthers, M., *The Book of Memory* (New York: Cambridge University Press, 1990).

Chardonnens, Denis, *L'Homme sous le regard de la providence: Providence de Dieu et condition humaine selon l'Exposition littérale sur le livre de Job de Thomas d'Aquin* (Paris: Librairie Philosophique J. Vrin, 1997).

Chenu, M.-D., *Toward Understanding Saint Thomas* (Chicago: Regnery, 1964).

Childs, B.S., *The Struggle to Understand Isaiah as Christian Scripture* (Grand Rapids, MI: Eerdmans, 2004).

Congar, Yves, *Thomas d'Aquin: Sa vision de théologie et de l'église* (London: Variorum Reprints, 1984).

Dauphinais, Michael and Matthew Levering, (eds.), *Reading John with St. Thomas Aquinas* (Washington, DC: Catholic University of America Press, 2005).

Dondaine, A., *Secrétaires de saint Thomas* (Rome: S. Tommaso, 1956).

Emery, Gilles, *Trinity in Aquinas* (Ypsilanti, MI: Sapientia Press, 2003).

Emory, Kent, Jr and Joseph Wawrykow (eds.), *Christ Among the Medieval Dominicans: Representations of Christ in the Texts and Images of the Order of Preachers* (Notre Dame: University of Notre Dame Press, 1998).

Evans, G.R., (ed.), *The Medieval Theologians: An Introduction to Theology in the Medieval Period* (Oxford: Blackwell, 2001).

Foster, Kenelm (ed.), *The Life of St Thomas Aquinas: Biographical Documents* (London and Baltimore: Longmans, 1959).

Garrigou-Lagrange, R., *De Deo uno: Commentarium in Primam Partem S. Thomae* (Turin and Rome: Marietti, 1950).

Hall, Pamela M., *Narrative and the Natural Law: An Interpretation of Thomistic Ethics* (Notre Dame: University of Notre Dame Press, 1995).

Johnson, Luke Timothy, and William S. Kurz, *The Future of Catholic Biblical*

Scholarship: A Constructive Conversation (Grand Rapids, MI: Eerdmans, 2002).

Jordan, M.D., *The Alleged Aristotelianism of Thomas Aquinas* (Toronto: Pontifical Institute of Mediaeval Studies, 1992).

Journet, Charles, *Entretiens sur la grâce* (Paris, Desclée, 1957).

Kerr, Fergus, *After Thomas* (Oxford: Blackwell, 2002).

Kerr, Fergus, (ed.), *Contemplating Aquinas: On the Varieties of Interpretation* (London: SCM Press, 2003).

Le Guillou, M.J., *Christ and Church: A Theology of the Mystery* (New York: Desclée, 1966).

Leget, Carlo, *Living with God: Thomas Aquinas on the Relation between Life on Earth and 'Life' after Death* (Leuven: Peeters, 1997).

Levering, Matthew, *Christ's Fulfillment of Torah and Temple* (Notre Dame: University of Notre Dame Press, 2002).

—*Scripture and Metaphysics: Aquinas and the Renewal of Trinitarian Theology* (Oxford: Blackwell, 2004).

Lubac, Henri de, *Exégèse Médiévale: Les quatre sens de l'Écriture*, Theologie 41 42, 59 (Paris: Aubier, 1959–64). ET: *Medieval Exegesis*, vol. 1, *The Four Senses of Scripture* (Grand Rapids, MI/Edinburgh: Eerdmans/T&T Clark, 1998) vol. 2 (Grand Rapids, MI/Edinburgh: Eerdmans/T&T Clark, 2000).

—*The Sources of Revelation* (New York: Herder, 1968).

McInerny, Ralph (trans), *Thomas Aquinas: Selected Writings* (London: Penguin, 1998).

Maillard, Pierre-Yves, *La vision de Dieu chez Thomas d'Aquin: Une lecture de l' In Ioannem à la lumière de ses sources augustiniennes* (Paris: Vrin, 2001).

Maritain, Jacques, *St Thomas and the Problem of Evil* (Milwaukee: Marquette University Press, 1942).

Marshall, Bruce, *Christology in Conflict: The Identity of a Saviour in Karl Barth and Karl Rahner* (Oxford: Blackwell, 1987).

Minnis, A.J., *Medieval Theory of Authorship* (2nd edn; Philadelphia: University of Pennsylvania Press, 1988).

Narcisse, Gilbert, *Les raisons de Dieu: Argument de convenance et esthétique théologique selon saint Thomas d'Aquin* (Fribourg: Éditions universitaires, 1997).

Nichols, Aidan, *Discovering Aquinas: An Introduction to his Life, Work and Influence* (London: Darton, Longman & Todd, 2002).

Persson, Per Erik, Sacra Doctrina: *Reason and Revelation in Aquinas* (Oxford: Blackwell, 1970).

Pinto de Oliveira, Carlos-Josaphat (ed.), Ordo Sapientiae et Amoris: *Image et Message de Saint Thomas d'Aquin* (Fribourg: Éditions Universitaires, 1993).

Rogers, Eugene F., Jr, *Thomas Aquinas and Karl Barth: Sacred Doctrine and the Natural Knowledge of God* (Notre Dame: University of Notre Dame Press, 1995).

Rouse, M.A, and R.H. Rouse, *Authentic Witnesses: Approaches to Medieval Texts and Manuscripts* (Notre Dame: University of Notre Dame Press, 1991), chaps. 6–7.

Ryan, Thomas F., *Thomas Aquinas as Reader of the Psalms* (Notre Dame: University of Notre Dame Press, 2000).

Schreiner, Susan, *Where Shall Wisdom be Found? Calvin's Exegesis of Job from Medieval and Modern Perspectives* (Chicago and London: University of Chicago Press, 1994).

Smalley, Beryl, *The Study of the Bible in the Middle Ages* (3rd edn; Oxford: Basil Blackwell, 1964).

—*The Gospels in the Schools c.1000–c.1280* (London: Hambledon, 1985).

Somme, Luc-Thomas, *Fils adoptifs de Dieu par Jésus Christ: La filiation divine par adoption dans la théologie de saint Thomas d'Aquin* (Paris: Vrin, 1997).

Spicq, P.C., *Esquisse d'une histoire de l'exégèse latine au moyen age* (Paris: J. Vrin, 1944).

teVelde, Rudi, *Participation and Substantiality in Thomas Aquinas* (Leiden: Brill, 1995).

Torrell, Jean-Pierre, *St. Thomas Aquinas*, vol. 1, *The Person and his Work*, vol. 2, *Spiritual Master* (Washington, DC: Catholic University of America Press, 1996, 2003).

Tugwell, Simon (ed. and trans.), *Albert and Thomas: Selected Writings* (New York: Paulist Press, 1988).

—(ed.), *Early Dominicans: Selected Writings* (New York: Paulist, 1982).

Valkenberg, Wilhelmus, *Words of the Living God: Place and Function of Holy Scripture in the Theology of St. Thomas Aquinas*, Publications of the Thomas Instituut te Utrecht New Series, vol. 6 (Peeters: Leuven, 2000).

van Geest, Paul, H. Goris and C. Leget (eds.), *Aquinas as Authority* (Louvain: Peeters, 2002).

Wawrykow, J., *The Westminster Handbook to Thomas Aquinas* (Louisville: Westminster John Knox Press, 2005).

Weinandy, Thomas G., *In the Likeness of Sinful Flesh: An Essay on the Humanity of Christ* (Edinburgh: T&T Clark, 1993).

—*Does God Suffer?* (Edinburgh: T & T Clark, 2000).

Weinandy, Thomas G., Daniel A. Keating, John P. Yocum, (eds.), *Aquinas on Doctrine: A Critical Introduction* (London: T & T Clark/Continuum, 2004).

Weisheipl, J.A., *Friar Thomas D'Aquino: His Life, Thought and Works* (Washington, DC: Catholic University of America Press, 1974).

Williams, A.N., *The Ground of Union: Deification in Thomas Aquinas and Gregory Palamas* (Oxford: Oxford University Press, 1999).

Wright, John, *The Order of the Universe in the Theology of St. Thomas Aquinas*, Analecta Gregoriana, 39 (Rome: Gregorian University Press, 1957).

Articles

Arges, Michael, 'New Evidence Concerning the Date of Thomas Aquinas' *Lectura* on Matthew', *Medieval Studies* 49 (1987), pp. 517–23.

Antoniotti, Louise-Marie, 'La volonté antécédente et conséquente selon saint Jean Damascène et saint Thomas d'Aquin', *Revue thomiste* 65 (1965), pp. 52–77.

Bataillon, Louis-Jacques, 'La Diffusione Manoscritta e Stampata dei Commenti Biblici de San Tommaso d'Aquino', *Angelicum* 71 (1994), pp. 579–90.

Bonino, Serge-Thomas, 'The Role of the Apostles in the Communication of Revelation according to the *Lectura super Ioannem* of St. Thomas Aquinas', in Michael Dauphinais and Matthew Levering (eds.), *Reading John with St. Thomas Aquinas* (Washington, DC: The Catholic University of America Press, 2005), pp. 318–46.

Bouthillier, Denise, 'Le Christ en son mystère dans les *collationes* du *super Isaiam* de saint Thomas d'Aquin', in *Ordo Sapientiae et Amoris: Image et Message de Saint Thomas d'Aquin. Hommage au Professeur Jean-Pierre Torrell OP à l'occasion de son 65e anniversaire* (ed. Carlos-Josaphat Pinto de Oliveira (Fribourg: Éditions universitaires, 1993), pp. 37–64.

—'*Splendor gloriae Patris*: Deux collations du *Super Isaiam*', in *Christ among the Medieval Dominicans* eds. K. Emery, Jr and J. Wawrykow (Notre Dame: University of Notre Dame Press, 1998), pp. 139–56.

Boyle, John F., 'Authorial Intention and the *Divisio textus*', in Michael Dauphinais and Matthew Levering (eds.), *Reading John with St. Thomas Aquinas* (Washington, DC: The Catholic University of America Press, 2005), pp. 3–8.

Burrell, David B., 'Act of Creation with Its Theological Consequences', in Thomas G. Weinandy, Daniel Keating, and John Yocum (eds.), *Aquinas on Doctrine: A Critical Introduction* (London: T & T Clark/Continuum, 2004), pp. 27–44.

Cessario, Romanus, 'Aquinas on Christian Salvation', in Thomas G. Weinandy, Daniel Keating, and John Yocum (eds.), *Aquinas on Doctrine: A Critical Introduction* (London: T & T Clark/Continuum, 2004), pp. 117–37.

Dahan, Gilbert, 'Introduction', in Thomas Aquinas, *Commentaire de la première épitre aux Corinthiens* (trans. Jean-Éric Stroobant de Saint-Éloy; Paris: Les Éditions du Cerf, 2002), pp. i–xxxvii.

Dondaine, A., 'Introduction', in Thomas Aquinas, *Expositio super Iob ad litteram: Opera Omnia* ed. Leonine; (vol. 25; Rome: Cura et Studio Fratrum Praedicatorum, 1965).

Dupleix, André, 'Saint Thomas maître spirituel', in S.-T. Bonino (ed.), *St Thomas au XXe siècle*, Actes du colloque du centenaire de la 'Revue thomiste' (Paris: Éditions Saint-Paul, 1994), pp. 452–464.

Elders, Leo J., 'Aquinas on Holy Scripture as the Medium of Divine Revelation', in Leo J. Elders (ed.), *La doctrine de la révélation divine de saint Thomas d'Aquin* (Vatican City: Libreria Editrice Vaticana, 1990), pp. 132–52.

Ellul, Joseph, 'Thomas Aquinas and Muslim–Christian Dialogue: An Appraisal of *De rationibus fidei*', *Angelicum*, 80 (2003), pp. 177–200.

Emery, Gilles, 'Biblical Exegesis and the Speculative Doctrine of the Trinity in St. Thomas Aquinas' Commentary on St. John', in Michael Dauphinais and Matthew Levering (eds.), *Reading John with St. Thomas Aquinas* (Washington, DC: The Catholic University of America Press, 2005), pp. 23–61.

Eschmann, I.T., 'The Quotations of Aristotle's *Politics* in St. Thomas' *Lectura super Matthaeum*', *Medieval Studies* 18 (1956), pp. 232–40.

Gils, P.-M., 'Les *Collationes* marginales dans l'autographe du commentaire de S. Thomas sur Isaie', *Revue des Sciences Philosophiques et Théologiques* 42 (1958), pp. 253–64.

Guindon, R., 'L'*Expositio in Isaiam* est-elle une oeuvre de Thomas d'Aquin "bachelier biblique"?' *Recherches de Théologie Ancienne et Médiévale*, 21 (1954), pp. 312–21.

Hankey, W.J., 'Aquinas, Pseudo-Denys, Proclus and Isaiah VI.6', *Archives d'histoire doctrinale et littéraire du moyen âge*, 64 (1997), pp. 59–93.

Glorieux, P., 'Essai sur les commentaires scripturaires de saint Thomas et leur chronologie', *Recherches de théologie ancienne et médiévale*, 17 (1950), pp. 237–66.

Gondreau, Paul, 'Anti-Docetism in Aquinas' *Super Ioannem*: St. Thomas as Defender of the Full Humanity of Christ', in Michael Dauphinais and Matthew Levering (eds.), *Reading John with St. Thomas Aquinas* (Washington, DC: The Catholic University of America Press, 2005), pp. 254–76.

Guindon, Roger, 'La *Lectura super Matthaeum incompleta* de saint Thomas', *Revue de l'Université d'Ottawa* 25 (1955), pp. 213–19.

Humbrecht, Thierry-Dominique, 'L'eucharistie, "représentation" du sacrifice du Christ, selon saint Thomas', *Revue Thomiste*, 98 (1998), pp. 355–86.

Jackson, Timothy, 'Must Job Live Forever? A Reply to Aquinas on Providence', *The Thomist*, 62 (1998), pp. 1–39.

Jordan, Mark D., 'The Competition of Authoritative Languages and Aquinas's Theological Rhetoric', *Medieval Philosophy and Theology*, 4 (1994), pp. 71–90.

Keating, Daniel A., 'Justification, Sanctification and Divinization in Thomas Aquinas', in Thomas G. Weinandy, Daniel Keating, and John Yocum (eds.), *Aquinas on Doctrine: A Critical Introduction* (London: T & T Clark/ Continuum, 2004), pp. 139–58.

Lamb, M.L., 'Introduction', in *Commentary on St Paul's Epistle to the Ephesians by St Thomas Aquinas* (Albany, NY: Magi, 1966), pp. 1–36.

Leget, Carlo, 'The Concept of "Life" in the *Commentary on St. John*', in Michael Dauphinais and Matthew Levering (eds.), *Reading John with St. Thomas Aquinas* (Washington, DC: The Catholic University of America Press, 2005), pp. 153–72.

Levering, Matthew, 'The Pontifical Biblical Commission and Aquinas' Exegesis', *Pro Ecclesia*, 13 (2004), pp. 25–38.

—'Does the Paschal Mystery Reveal the Trinity?', in Michael Dauphinais and Matthew Levering (eds.), *Reading John with St. Thomas Aquinas* (Washington, DC: The Catholic University of America Press, 2005), pp. 78–91.

Manzanedo, M.F., 'La antropologia filosófica en el comentario tomista al libro de Job', *Angelicum*, 62 (1985), pp. 419–71.

—'La antropologia teológia en el comentario tomista al libro de Job', *Angelicum* 64 (1987), pp. 301–31.

Marshall, Bruce D., 'What Does the Spirit Have to Do?', in Michael Dauphinais and

Matthew Levering (eds.), *Reading John with St. Thomas Aquinas* (Washington, DC: The Catholic University of America Press, 2005), pp. 62–77.

McGuckin, Terence, 'Saint Thomas Aquinas and Theological Exegesis of Sacred Scripture', *New Blackfriars*, 74 (1993), pp. 197–213.

McKim, Donald K., 'Aquinas, Thomas', *Historical Handbook of Major Biblical Interpreters* (Downer's Grove, IL: InterVarsity Press, 1998), pp. 86–87.

Morard, Martin, 'Les expressions '*corpus mysticum*' et '*persona mystica*' dans l'oeuvre de saint Thomas d'Aquin', *Revue Thomiste*, 95 (1995), pp. 653–64.

Oliveira, Carlos-Josaphat Pinto de, 'Ordo rationis, ordo amoris: La notion d'ordre au centre de l'univers éthique de S. Thomas', in C.-J. Pinto de Oliveira (ed.), *Ordo sapientiae et amoris*, (Fribourg: Éditions universitaires, 1993), pp. 285–302.

Pinckaers, Servais, 'The Use of Scripture and the Renewal of Moral Theology: The *Catechism* and *Veritatis Splendor*', *The Thomist*, 59 (1995), pp. 1–20.

Prügl, T., 'Thomas Aquinas as Interpreter of Scripture', in R. Van Nieuwenhove and J. Wawrykow (eds.), *The Theology of Thomas Aquinas* (Notre Dame: University of Notre Dame Press, 2005), pp. 386–415.

Renard, J.P., 'La Lectura super Matthaeum V, 20–28 de Thomas d'Aquin (Edition d'après le ms. Bâle, Univ. Bibl. B.V. 12)', *Recherches de théologie ancienne et médiévale*, 50 (1983), pp. 145–90.

Ross, Margherita Maria, 'La "divisio textus" nei commenti scritturistici di S. Tommaso d'Aquino: Un procedimento solo esegetico?', *Angelicum*, 71 (1994), pp. 537–48.

Saward, John, 'The Priest as Icon of Christ: A Thomist Concept', *The Priest*, 50 (1994), pp. 37–48.

Schenk, Richard, '*Omnis Christi Actio Nostra Est Instructio*: The Deeds and Sayings of Jesus as Revelation in the View of Thomas Aquinas', in Leo J. Elders (ed.), *La doctrine de la révélation divine de saint Thomas d'Aquin* (Vatican City: Libreria Editrice Vaticana, 1990), pp. 104–31.

Sherwin, Michael, 'Christ the Teacher in St. Thomas's *Commentary on the Gospel of John*', in Michael Dauphinais and Matthew Levering (eds.), *Reading John with St. Thomas Aquinas* (Washington, DC: The Catholic University of America Press, 2005), pp. 173–93.

Shooner, H.-V., in 'La *Lectura in Matthaeum* de S. Thomas (Deux fragments inédits et la *Reportatio* de Pierre d'Andria)', *Angelicum*, 33 (1956), pp. 121–42.

Smith, J.C., 'Christ as "Pastor," "*Ostium*" et "*Agnes*" in St. Thomas Aquinas', *Angelicum*, 56 (1979), pp. 93–118.

Smith, Janet E., 'Come and See', in Michael Dauphinais and Matthew Levering (eds.), *Reading John with St. Thomas Aquinas* (Washington, DC: The Catholic University of America Press, 2005), pp. 194–211.

Sommers, Mary C., '*Manifestatio*: The Historical Presencing of Being in Aquinas' *Expositio super Iob*', in *Hermeneutics and the Tradition*, Proceedings of the American Catholic Philosophical Association 62 (1988), pp. 147–56.

Stump, Eleonore, 'Biblical Commentary and Philosophy', in N. Kretzmann and Eleonore Stump (eds.), *The Cambridge Companion to Aquinas* (Cambridge: Cambridge University Press, 1993), pp. 252–68.

—'Aquinas on the Sufferings of Job', in *Reasoned Faith* (Ithaca and London: Cornell University Press, 1993), pp. 328–57.

—'Aquinas' Account of Freedom: Intellect and Will', *The Monist* 80 (1997), pp. 576–97.

Synan, Edward A., 'St Thomas Aquinas and the Profession of Arms', *Medieval Studies*, 50 (1988), pp. 404–37.

Torrell, Jean-Pierre, and Denise Bouthillier, 'Quand saint Thomas méditait sur le prophète Isaie', *Revue Thomiste*, 90 (1990), pp. 5–47. Reprinted in Jean-Pierre Torrell, *Recherches Thomasiennes* (Paris: J. Vrin, 2000), pp. 242–81.

Valkenberg, Wilhelmus, 'Aquinas and Christ's Resurrection: The Influence of the *lectura super Ioan.* 20–21 on the *Summa Theologiae*', in Michael Dauphinais and Matthew Levering (eds.), *Reading John with St. Thomas Aquinas* (Washington, DC: The Catholic University of America Press, forthcoming).

Viviano, Benedict T., 'The Kingdom of God in Albert the Great and Aquinas', *The Thomist* 44 (1980), pp. 502–22.

Vosté, I.M., 'S. Thomas Aquinas epistularum S. Pauli interpres', *Angelicum*, 20 (1943), pp. 255–276.

Weinandy, Thomas G., 'Jesus' Filial Vision of the Father', *Pro Ecclesia*, 13/2 (2004), pp. 189–201.

—'The Cosmic Christ', *The Cord*, 51/1 (2001), pp. 27–38.

—'God *IS* Man: The Marvel of the Incarnation', in Thomas G. Weinandy, Daniel Keating, and John Yocum (eds.), *Aquinas on Doctrine: A Critical Introduction* (London: T & T Clark/Continuum, 2004), pp. 67–89.

—'Of Men and Angels', *Nova et Vetera*, forthcoming.

Weisheipl, J.A., 'Saint Thomas Aquinas. Opera Omnia XXVIII. *Expositio super Isaiam ad litteram*', *The Thomist*, 43 (1979), pp. 331–37.

Yaffe, Martin D., 'Providence in Medieval Aristotelianism: Moses Maimonides and Thomas Aquinas on the Book of Job', *Hebrew Studies*, 20–21 (1979–80), pp. 62–74.

—'Interpretive Essay', in Thomas Aquinas, *The Literal Exposition on Job: A Scriptural Commentary Concerning Providence* (Atlanta, GA: Scholars Press, 1989), pp. 1–65.

Yocum, John P., 'Sacraments in Aquinas', in Thomas G. Weinandy, Daniel Keating, and John Yocum (eds.), *Aquinas on Doctrine: A Critical Introduction* (London: T & T Clark/Continuum, 2004), pp. 159–81.

INDICES

INDEX OF SUBJECTS

INDEX OF NAMES